LITERATURE, RELIGION, AND POSTSECULAR STUDIES
Lori Branch, Series Editor

The Writer of a Book, is not he a Preacher preaching not to this parish or that,
on this day or that, but to all men in all times and places?

—Thomas Carlyle

Vox audita perit, littera scripta manet.

—Roman proverb

PREACHING

AND THE

RISE OF THE AMERICAN NOVEL

Dawn Coleman

The Ohio State University Press
Columbus

Library of Congress Cataloging-in-Publication Data

Coleman, Dawn (Dawn Davina), 1973–
  Preaching and the rise of the American novel / Dawn Coleman.
    p. cm. — (Literature, religion, and postsecular studies)
  Includes bibliographical references and index.
  ISBN 978-0-8142-1205-9 (cloth : alk. paper) — ISBN 0-8142-1205-0 (cloth : alk. paper) — ISBN 978-0-8142-9307-2 (cd-rom)
  1. American fiction—19th century—History and criticism. 2. Preaching—United States—History. 3. Preaching in literature. I. Title.
  PS166.C65 2013
  810.9'382—dc23
                    2012018926

Cover design by Mary Ann Smith
Type set in Adobe Minion Pro
Printed by Thomson-Shore, Inc.

♾ The paper used in this publication meets the minimum requirements of the American National Standard for Information Sciences—Permanence of Paper for Printed Library Materials. ANSI Z39.48–1992.

9   8   7   6   5   4   3   2   1

CONTENTS

✢

ACKNOWLEDGMENTS

꙳

I WISH first to thank those who materially supported me in the writing of this book: the American Academy of Arts and Sciences, for a year-long fellowship in 2009–2010 that allowed me to finish my research and writing in residence in Cambridge, Massachusetts, while enjoying the ideal balance of freedom and collegiality; the University of Tennessee, for co-funding my year of leave at the Academy and, through the Hodges Better English Fund and Professional Development Awards, granting needed research leaves, summer funding, and travel reimbursements; and the American Antiquarian Society, where I held a one-month fellowship in 2006 and have happily visited many times since to avail myself of the rich collections and incomparably helpful staff. I am also deeply grateful to those organizations and individuals that supported me during my dissertation years at Stanford, including the Mrs. Giles Whiting Foundation, the Mellon Foundation, the Northern California Association of Phi Beta Kappa, and Thomas and Frances Geballe, whose generosity funded a crucial year of writing and intellectual exchange at the Stanford Humanities Center.

No less important were the many individuals who immeasurably improved this book through their brilliant conversation and astute feedback. I remember with affection and appreciation Jay Fliegelman, whose radiant intellect and unstinting encouragement were a guiding light during my time at Stanford, and whose savvy counsel I have missed since his untimely passing in 2007. Those who knew Jay will recognize how much this book owes to his insights into performance, religion, American literature, and authorship. Equally crucial to the book's formation were Franco Moretti, who provided incisive feedback on the form and structure of my ideas and a superb education in the novel through his founding of Stanford's Center for the Study of the Novel, and Rob Polhemus, a perceptive reader of literature and wise mentor who urged me to enrich my scholarship by reflecting on its autobiographical dimensions. I am also indebted to many other Stanford friends and colleagues with whom I discussed ideas and shared portions of the book at an early stage, including Stanford Humanities Center Director John Bender and the SHC Fellows of 2001–2002; the participants in the American Cultures Workshop, especially Gavin Jones, Joel Burges, and Patty Roylance; and members of the Nineteenth-Century Dissertation Group, including Monique Morgan, Robin Valenza, Christy McBride, Jessica Straley, and Crisi Benford. I am especially grateful to Crisi for countless stimulating conversations about narrative structure and for her patience in letting me talk through my readings of nineteenth-century novels. And for crucial support during those treacherous years at the start of the journey, heartfelt thanks to the fellow members of my dissertation-writing trio, Molly Schwartzburg and Hilary Edwards. Our caffeine-fueled conversations about literature and writing at the Prolific Oven are among my most cherished memories of graduate school.

Since coming to the University of Tennessee in 2005, I have had the good fortune to find a wonderfully generous reader and mentor in Mary Papke; inspiring interlocutors in my fellow Americanists, especially Martin Griffin, Amy Elias, Tom Haddox, and Mark Hulsether; and, in John Zomchick, Chuck Maland, and Stan Garner, truly supportive and encouraging department heads who advocated for me and this book at critical junctures.

I have also benefitted greatly from responses to my work from colleagues more far-flung, most of all David Hall, whom it was my privilege to have as a professor and mentor many years ago at Harvard Divinity School and who graciously read and responded to a draft of this book. For timely, useful comments on various portions of the manuscript I am grateful to Sara Georgini, Ezra Greenspan, Wyn Kelley, Bob Levine, Dan McKanan, Geoff Sanborn, Pat Spacks, Cindy Weinstein, and my fellow Visiting Scholars at the Academy, Dan Amsterdam, Debbie Becher, Angus Burgin, Crystal Feimster, Andy Jewett, Jason Petrulis, and Jamie Pietruska. Many thanks, too, to the generous audiences with whom I shared sections of the manuscript over the years, including the members of the Harvard Divinity School North American Religion Colloquium and the fellows of the American Antiquarian Society, as well as attentive colleagues at American Literature Association conferences, the International Conference on Narrative, the NEXUS Interdisciplinary Conference on Religion and Nation, the Stanford Humanities Conference on Knowledge and Belief, the Douglass-Melville conference, and the inaugural conference of C19: The Society of Nineteenth-Century Americanists.

I wish also to thank the many librarians and staff members who helped me locate and gather needed archival resources. These essential collaborators have included Paul Erickson, Marie Lamoureux, Jaclyn Penny, and Elizabeth Pope at the American Antiquarian Society; Frances O'Donnell at the Andover-Harvard Theological Library; Jim Green at the Library Company of Philadelphia; Irene Axelrod at the Phillips Library in Salem, Massachusetts; Mary Munill in the Interlibrary Loan Office at Stanford; and, at the University of Tennessee, Kathleen Bailey of InterLibrary Services and Humanities Librarian Chris Caldwell.

Sincere thanks are also due to my editor, Sandy Crooms, whose longstanding faith in this book has been an inspiration, and to Eugene O'Connor and the production staff for making my role in transforming pixels into print a surprisingly painless one. I am also grateful to the press's two anonymous readers, whose thoughtful comments improved the book immeasurably.

A version of Chapter 7 originally appeared in *American Literature* in June 2008 and a portion of Chapter 4 as an essay in the *Nathaniel Hawthorne Review* in Spring 2011. I thank the publishers for permission to reprint.

By convention I have saved my most personal debts for last, which seems fitting since I could never do them justice anyway. I am grateful to my mother for sharing her love of reading and debate and for her unwavering confidence in me, and to my father, my first and most dedicated writing coach, for providing the detailed feedback on my youthful essays that instilled a passion for well-developed ideas and trained my eyes and ears in the rhythms of readable prose. As a child I often heard from him the sage advice, "There's no such thing as good writing, only good rewriting," counsel that echoed in my head in after-years and buoyed my efforts in the long dissertation-to-book process. A warm thank you, too, to Mayumi Negishi, who wrote an essay on *Othello* many years ago that startled me with its lyricism and sparked a friendship that has been a steadfast delight and support. Above all, I am immensely grateful to my sons Xander and Neil for bringing me joy that seeps into all hours of the day, and to my husband Ken for providing decades of sustaining happiness and all the treks to Massachusetts, weekend work time, patient listening, and parenting help I needed to bring this book to completion.

G ROWING UP in Orange County, California, in the 1980s, I attended the churches of two superstar preachers. The first, in elementary and middle school, was Robert H. Schuller's Crystal Cathedral in Garden Grove, a "walk-in, drive-in church" known around the world through the weekly television broadcast *The Hour of Power*. Schuller had begun the Garden Grove Community Church in the Orange Drive-in Theater in 1955, rounding up locals with the slogan, "Worship as you are . . . in the family car." Twenty-five years later, the church had grown exponentially and built one of the most striking buildings in America, a giant edifice with walls and roof composed of 10,900 panes of reflective glass—what architect Philip Johnson called a "star of glass" and others said could be mistaken for a "jazzy corporate headquarters."[1] The new structure retained the drive-in option, allowing congregants to listen to the sermon from their cars in front of the church. My parents would drop me off at Sunday school, then drive over and park the van in front of the Crystal Cathedral's ninety-foot-tall glass doors. There they tuned their radio to an AM station, watched the glass doors glide open as the choir sang and fountains sprayed, and settled in for the service, centered on Schuller's inspirational preaching. Odd as this form of churchgoing may seem, it made sense to my ex-bohemian parents. They went to church for the sermon, and why not listen while sipping coffee and relaxing in their own space? No need to get dressed up, make small talk with strangers, mumble along with hymns, or sit and stand on cue. With Schuller you could settle into anonymity and enjoy the sermon from the comfort of your car.

In middle school I started attending the drive-in church myself, and I still have a mental echo of Schuller's hopeful, comforting voice, telling stories about people of faith who had climbed the Alps, risen from poverty to build worldwide business empires, or survived brain trauma to become famous scientists. A student of Norman Vincent Peale, who had authored *The Power of Positive Thinking* and founded *Guideposts* magazine, Schuller excelled in sermons about people who, through resilience and prayer, had achieved greatness against the odds. Although the church was affiliated with the Reformed Church of America, a Calvinist denomination that traces its roots to the Dutch settlers in New York (and that claimed Herman Melville as a childhood attender), I don't remember a word about total depravity or unconditional election. The Bible was a touchstone and a guide, but engaging in scriptural exegesis was a low priority compared with encouraging listeners to trust God and live out their dreams. If Schuller tended to cast Christianity as an individualistic pursuit (and so implicitly endorse the area's political conservatism), he also spoke to the needs of Orange Countians in the second half of the twentieth century, many of whom were transplants eager to succeed in the promised land. The restrained, well-scripted Sunday morning services were no camp-meeting revival, but he was, in a sense, the latest incarnation of the American frontier preacher.[2]

When we moved from central to southern Orange County in 1987, my parents were determined to find a new church with an equally talented preacher. They lighted on one with none of the glamour of Schuller's empire. Here there was no television broadcast, no drive-in, no fountains, no celebrity guests, no building even—just a Baptist-trained pastor in a Hawaiian shirt preaching in a high school gym, where the congregation sat on folding chairs and wooden bleachers. These sermons were more evangelical and exegetical than Schuller's—here one kept the Bible open and scribbled the sermon's main points on the program outline—but just as upbeat and practical. The preacher had the same gift of making God seem real, present, active, and concerned, and of making one's relationship to this God seem like a can't-miss investment of time and energy. His obscurity was short-lived. Each week, there were more chairs, more crowded bleachers, louder singing and clapping along with the brass-heavy praise band. My parents had found Rick Warren and Saddleback Church, a pastor and church whose fortunes would skyrocket over the next two decades. Having long outgrown a high school gym, the church today boasts six campuses across southern California, an active membership of over 20,000, a roster of occasional attenders (those who show up at least four times a year) of 82,000, a panoply of demographic-specific ministries and missions, and a leadership program that has trained more than 200,000 church leaders from around the world in Saddleback's strategies for growth. Warren's *The Purpose-Driven Life* has sold more than 30 million copies, and in 2009 he became the new face of contemporary evangelicalism when he delivered the invocation at President Barack Obama's inauguration.[3] The church's astronomical growth is no doubt due to a multitude of factors, from organizational savvy to an entrepreneurial willingness to experiment with new technologies and formats, but it's hard not to believe, from having sat each week in the folding chairs, that the mainspring of the whole enterprise is clear, accessible, relevant preaching.

Although I no longer share Schuller's or Warren's theological beliefs, I am grateful to have heard moving, inspirational sermons week after week, year after year, in my youth. Sunday mornings were a time of mental rejuvenation, as I looked forward to the worship service and above all to the spiritual exercise of sermon-listening as a time to recenter myself, when I could connect the swarming details of my overscheduled life to a vision of God's peace and love. Contemplating the challenges of the week ahead, I expected to hear God speak to me through some mysterious combination of the preached word and an answering sense of conviction within. The sermon cast the big-picture issues of my life—career goals, relationships, habits of mind and spirit, global and local responsibilities—in the light of what seemed eternal truth. I left with renewed energy and purpose, and years later, reading Émile Durkheim, would feel the aptness of his pronouncement that "the worshipper who has communicated with his god is [. . .] a man who is *capable* of more. He feels more strength in himself, either to cope with the difficulties of existence or to defeat them."[4] Listening to sermons in the southern California suburbs, I felt that strength.

That experience of regular sermon-listening has also given me a sense of connection to the long-standing and vibrant tradition of American preaching. From John Winthrop's sermon on the decks of the *Arbella* declaring the Puritan community a "city on a hill" to Jeremiah Wright's "God damn America!", preaching has played a vital role in our collective life. It has thrived in the Protestant churches of an astonishing variety of denominations, and it has radiated out of the church to shape the country's poems, songs, political oratory, fiction, films, and other cultural expressions in ways we have barely begun to recognize.

This book recovers a crucial moment in the neglected history of the intimate yet often contentious relationship between Protestant preaching and other cultural forms. In the decades before the Civil War, especially in the years around 1850, two trajectories intersected in American life: a boom in preaching, seen in the rapidly increasing number of preachers and church members, and the slow rise of the novel, or its gradual, halting ascent to moral legitimacy and aesthetic autonomy. I make the case that, with fiction during this period still widely disparaged despite its popularity, novelists sought to assert the moral and religious authority of their work through an intense engagement with preaching. While resisting preaching through mockery, irony, and satire, they also envied it, identified with it, and appropriated it as a distinctive and authoritative mode of addressing audiences. They performed, in effect, an elaborate wrestling match with preachers, drawing off their energy while throwing them to the ground. This struggle defined the work of a wide spectrum of novelists, cutting across our usual distinctions between didactic and literary fiction, high and low art, men and women writers.

Despite its cultural importance, the preaching of America between 1820 and the Civil War has long stood in a historical blind spot. Calling attention to the scant scholarship on early modern sermons, Lori Anne Ferrell and Peter McCullough have pointed out that this genre has been overlooked despite the retrieval since the late 1970s of any number of other "erstwhile canonical stepchildren."[5] This situation is even truer for the nineteenth century than for earlier periods. There is no monograph for nineteenth-century American preaching comparable in scope to Harry Stout's *The New England Soul: Preaching and Religious Culture in Colonial New England* or Emory Elliot's *Power and the Pulpit in Puritan New England.*[6] Most books on the subject have focused on individual preachers, such as William Ellery Channing, Ralph Waldo Emerson, Theodore Parker, Charles Grandison Finney, and Henry Ward Beecher, and even surveys and extended analyses tend to follow a biographical organization.[7] My book, with its partial treatment of preaching, cannot fill the gaps left by decades of scholarly dismissal. The project of describing nineteenth-century American sermons—analyzing, for instance, their theological schemata, rhetorical structures, characteristic biblical texts, reception, and functions within local and national communities—would far exceed any one book, especially if one attended adequately to denominational, regional, linguistic, racial, ethnic, and gender differences.

This scholarly neglect of nineteenth-century American preaching reflects the implicit secularism of the humanities and the related disinclination to study religion or religious genres. Despite a putative "religious turn," resistance to foregrounding religion, especially a mainstream white Protestantism associated with multiple forms of oppression and hegemony, can run deep among scholars of literature and culture. In English studies this resistance is to some extent endemic to the discipline. As Michael Kaufmann has explained, the profession of English has long predicated itself on a secularization narrative that abets a rigid distinction between the secular and the religious with respect to its objects of study: based on the assumption that *we* are secular, we proceed as if our proper objects of study are, too.[8] One can also locate the resistance to studying religion in factors specific to the late twentieth century. Jenny Franchot, for instance, in a still-relevant critique from nearly two decades ago, attributed literary scholars' disinclination to study religion in favor of the safer paradigms of gender, race, and class (less so the last) to a conflation of various forms of religion with the Christian right, as well as to the general academic perception of religion as naïve. She charged that it is "as if religious voices, like certain kinds of shame, have become unmentionable."[9] Taking a wider lens, Susan Mizruchi has attributed the sparse work on religion among historians and literary scholars writing from the late 1960s through the 1980s not only to the political ascendancy of the Christian right, but also to such diverse forces as the rise of the field of social history, the decline of mainline Protestantism, poststructuralist skepticism of universals, and an association of religion with cultural conservatism.[10] Church historians and seminary professors have not filled in the blanks left by other academics. As theologian Martin Stringer notes, histories of Christian worship are often written by and for church members and share the faults of other histories in emphasizing text over practice.[11] I would add that the theological premises of such work often make it difficult to integrate with non-confessional perspectives.

Above and beyond these institutional and disciplinary patterns, though not wholly separate from them, the sermon's neglect might be traced to the perception that the genre is dull (the association of the sermon with its figurative meaning of "a long or tedious discourse or harangue"), the paucity of reliable editions, and sheer ephemerality.[12] So many sermons preached in nineteenth-century America were delivered from notes long since burned or trashed or were never written out at all, let alone printed and circulated. Although rare book libraries and historical societies warehouse reams of printed and manuscript sermons, often the ones we might most wish to read—say, those an author may have heard while penning a novel—never made it into a book or archive. Those that do survive, whether entombed in dusty volumes in storage stacks or in sheaves of miscellaneous papers in acid-free boxes, can seem as "unreadable" today as Theodore Parker declared the sermons of the seventeenth and eighteenth centuries were to his own age.[13] One confronts not only their dated theologies but also the inevitable absences surrounding them: the missing rhetorical context of original delivery, including the preacher's *ethos*, vocal intonations and emphases, communicative gestures, strategic silences, and the unspoken knowledge of the community's life at that particular moment. Like all speech of previous centuries, preaching resists historical inquiry.[14]

Despite its recalcitrance, nineteenth-century American preaching deserves a more prominent role in cultural memory. One might begin by recalling how Alexis de Tocqueville marveled at the country's religiosity after his 1831 tour, declaring that here "the sovereign authority is religious" and that America was "still the place in the world where the Christian religion has preserved most genuine power over souls." Remarking on the importance of Sunday sermons, he explained that every seventh day, work and commerce ceased, and "each citizen, surrounded by his children," repaired to church: "there strange discourses are held for him that seem hardly made for his ears. He is informed of the innumerable evils caused by pride and covetousness. He is told of the necessity of regulating his desires, of the delicate enjoyments attached to virtue alone, and of the true happiness that accompanies it."[15] Tocqueville lauded how this communal ritual checked Americans' characteristic utilitarianism and commercialism. Democracy itself, he maintained, depended on this ubiquitous Christianity, as religion taught citizens the morality that underwrote social stability.

Tocqueville's observations capture a historical moment when religion was on the rise and the sermon along with it. From 1776 to 1860, church membership grew from an estimated 17 percent of Americans to 37 percent, figures that do not include the many who attended a church without joining, which in some cases was double the number of members.[16] Much of this growth was among the Methodists and Baptists, who privileged the call to preach over formal theological training.[17] Due in part to their ascendancy, the number of preachers per capita tripled in the first seventy years of the new republic, from eighteen hundred in 1775 to forty thousand in 1845, representing a growth from one preacher for every 1500 people to one for every 500.[18] As Nathan Hatch has argued, this explosion of preaching, much of it by unlettered ministers, reflected and spurred the democratization of Christianity. While the proliferation of preachers was linked to the Second Great Awakening and the rising fortunes of evangelical Christianity, preaching mattered across denominations. Indeed, the most popular preaching enticed listeners to traverse denominational lines. Such "pulpit princes" included Charles Grandison Finney, whose name became "synonymous with the final stage of the Second Great Awakening" in the 1830s and 1840s; Theodore Parker, the learned Transcendentalist visionary and abolitionist who, preaching in the Melodeon Theater in Boston in the 1850s, drew

nse, and caused them to understand the reading."[24] During the post-
period, religious discourses more akin to modern preaching emerged,
bis began to expostulate on the *haftarah,* or reading from the Prophets,
generate *midrashim,* or scriptural commentary.

the time of Jesus, synagogue services regularly included scriptural
retation after the reading, a practice that intensified after the destruc-
f the Second Temple by the Romans in 70 C.E. Though Church Fathers
as Origen (185–254), John Chrysostom (349–407), and, above all,
stine (354–430) shaped the Christian sermon early on, it developed as
in the High Middle Ages, a period known for its preaching friars, its
less *homilia* (books of sermons), *exempla* (books of sermon illustra-
, and *artes praedicandi* (books on the art of preaching), as well as its
ng of indulgences for sermon-listening. But for nineteenth-century
ican Protestants, the decisive historical figure was Martin Luther, who
tionized Christian worship by maintaining that it should culminate
preaching of the word. To facilitate this practice, he translated the
into German so that congregants could comprehend the day's scrip-
reading, which the priest would then explain in his sermon, and wrote
luential Postil, or book of sermons to accompany the lessons for each
y of the year. [25] Nineteenth-century Protestants looked back on Refor-
n preachers such as Luther, John Calvin, and John Knox as standard
rs and pointed proudly to many post-Reformation pulpit luminaries
ll, including George Herbert, Richard Baxter, François Fénelon, and
Blair. None, though, loomed as large in the cultural imagination as
nan Edwards or the two transatlantic celebrity religious orators of the
enth century, George Whitefield and John Wesley. Such illustrious
ears meant that the nineteenth-century preacher, however humble and
ered, stood before believers as the representative of an esteemed sacred
ion.

espite this distinguished lineage, ministers could not take their author-
granted. Antebellum America, especially in the Northeast, was a fluid,
trializing, increasingly pluralistic society awash in information and
eting voices. Disestablishment had changed the rules of the game, and
ninisters, like other men in Jacksonian America, had to make their
n the world through self-promotion, skill development, professional
ctions, and geographic mobility. Surveying the ministry during this
d, Ann Douglas has argued that Northeastern ministers suffered from
-eroding status" and that liberals in particular experienced a discom-
feminization as they distanced themselves from a masculine, theologi-
igorous Calvinism and aligned themselves with a feminine sphere of

three thousand attenders weekly, or nearly 2 perce
and Henry Ward Beecher, who in the 1850s was
to a standing-room-only crowd of three thousan
Brooklyn.[19]

Understanding the period's preaching begins v
superstars to the economic realities underwriting
fact that post-disestablishment ministers were mo
delivering sermons that would attract congregants a
less of whether ministers acknowledged their finan
ically they did not), preaching was central to their
S. C. Abbott, pastor of the First Congregational Cl
for antebellum Protestantism when he declared, "
pel is the pre-eminent duty of the christian mini
whether one was preaching at a camp meeting, in a
in a New England meeting-house, or under the vau
cathedrals that were the pride of mid-nineteenth-
A settled minister preached twice every Sunday,
noon service, for anywhere from twenty minutes to
denomination and local custom. He began with a
used his sermon to explain the relevance of this v
discuss the sermon form more fully in Chapter C
also deliver a Sunday evening lecture on a topic
the church's missionary work. The demand for cl
excessive in our more visual age but was of a piec
public speaking of all sorts, from political stum
arguments to lyceum lectures.[23]

More than just another species of oratory, the
preeminent voice of moral and religious authori
ity in large part from the Christian belief that o
under a divine imperative to communicate God's
tals, as well as from the venerability of preaching
ern culture. Christian preaching can be traced t
the Hebrew Bible: the proclamations of the proph
embedded in descriptions of Hebrew and Israelite
of Mosaic law to a penitent Jewish people after the
lowing the Babylonian exile in the fifth century B.C
reports that on this last occasion, which some Cl
the inaugural moment of preaching, Ezra stood
along with select Levites, addressed fifty thousan
day for a week. He "read in the book of the law o

the
exili
as ra
and

inte
tion
such
Aug
an a
cou
tion
gran
Am
revo
in tl
Bibl
tura
an ir
Sun
mat
bear
as w
Hug
Jona
eigh
fore
unle
trad

ity fo
indu
com
now
way
con
peri
a "fa
fitin
cally

private persuasion and moral influence.[26] Yet as Karin Gedge has countered, this line of thought overstates the feminization of religion as well as the cultural alliance between ministers and women in nineteenth-century America.[27] It ignores, she notes, the fact that ministers continued to be granted a great deal of authority and that this deference was essential to Americans' national identity: "the inordinate respect accorded clergy and the church was a function of the democratic ethos," since Americans, like Tocqueville, believed that democracy depended on citizens' internalization of moral and religious values.[28] To further qualify Douglas's influential argument, one can note that while the liberal ministers at the center of her study do seem to have been more concerned about their professional status than their theologically conservative counterparts were, liberals made up a small fraction of U.S. church members in 1850 and, as Ann Braude points out in critiquing Douglas's generalizations, cannot be taken as representative of American culture.[29] Douglas also distorts the cultural role of these liberal ministers by measuring them by their printed texts; she writes that, like women, they had a "shared preoccupation with the lighter productions of the press; they wrote poetry, fiction, memoirs, sermons, and magazine pieces of every kind."[30] Besides the fact that sermons were not "lighter productions" and that many ministers also published theological treatises, textbooks, histories, and other "weighty" tomes, this view of their cultural output ignores the fact that while some ministers were writers, *all* had the distinctive and profession-defining privilege of commanding the pulpit. Without question Protestant ministers faced new challenges after disestablishment—economic, political, intellectual, social, and theological—but they should not be seen as peculiarly disadvantaged compared with other men trying to succeed in a democratic, capitalistic society. Politicians could be voted out of office; businessmen and farmers could fail. Ministers now had to compete in the marketplace like everyone else, but they had the advantage of occupying a role with enduring and substantial symbolic value.

My approach to preaching in this book has been inspired by the study of lived religion, a field of inquiry that looks beyond the official theologies and institutional histories of religious movements to analyze the practices that shape people's actual religious lives. Indebted to the *Annales* school of sociological investigation, with its ethnographic interest in creating thick descriptions of everyday life, scholars of lived religion try to understand how people appropriate and transform religious traditions. The study of lived religion challenges dichotomies that have long defined religious studies, such as sacred/secular, official/popular, clergy/laity, and high/low, seeking instead to understand religion as working through a social context in which power relations are never as stable as they seem.[31] Approaching these binaries with similar skepticism, religious studies scholar Catherine Bell has critiqued theories of ritual that would frame it as a form of social control, maintaining instead that ritual is a "negotiated appropriation of the dominant values embedded in the symbolic schemes."[32] She shows that clergy and laity work together to construct religious ideas and values and that even when people agree with the ideas codified in a ritual, their appropriation of these ideas is defined by negotiation, complicity, qualification, and struggle.[33] Elaborating on the noncoercive elements of religious practice, Frankfurt school philosopher Edmund Arens has combined Bell's insights into ritual with Jürgen Habermas's theories of communicative action to propose that religion is "at its core a constitutive communicative praxis" that is "genuinely intersubjective and agreement-oriented." That is, the defining feature of religion, and what makes it a communicative praxis rather than an oppressive power structure, is that people within a religious community do not treat one another "strategically" or as means to an end but instead encounter one another "solidaristically" and with an understanding of shared conviction.[34] This perspective has important implications for the study of antebellum Protestant preaching. To see churchgoers as engaged in a negotiated appropriation of the sermon, or preaching as intersubjective praxis, suggests how a democratic people could desire to hear what might otherwise seem an authoritarian discourse.

To consider sermons under the rubric of lived religion is also to regard them not primarily as a literary or even textual form but as a mode of embodied performance. The sermon's original life-world was the church service, in which a single earnest voice addressed an attentive congregation, and regarding the sermon as an event rather than a text gives insight into its appeal. Walt Whitman captured the excitement preaching could produce in his description of listening to the energetic Father Edward Taylor, the long-time pastor of the Seaman's Bethel in Boston who served as a source for Father Mapple in *Moby-Dick*: "the rhetoric and art, the mere words . . . seem'd altogether to disappear, and the *live feeling* advanced upon you and seiz'd you with a power before unknown. Everybody felt this marvelous and awful influence."[35] Taylor was notorious for his tangled logic and theological inconsistencies, but an age enamored of the evangelical idea that true religion was rooted in strong emotion often judged a preacher more by his ability to display and rouse religious feeling than by his theological precision. Though aware that such pulpit performances often lie just beyond our historical ken, I focus in this book as much on preaching as a cultural practice as on the content of specific sermons. If this approach occasionally sacrifices a certain measure of theological analysis, it honors how the orally delivered sermon held a special value for many nineteenth-century Americans. As the twentieth-century theologian and theorist of orality Walter Ong has articulated this value, the spoken word manifests people to one another as "conscious interiors," "forms human beings into close-knit groups," and is central to religious ceremonies because its "interiorizing force [. . .] relates in a special way to the sacral, to the ultimate concerns of existence."[36] One need not concur with Ong's mythologizing of orality to recognize that such beliefs have often elevated speech over writing, both within and outside of religious communities. Pondering the peculiar mystique of orality, Alessandro Portelli notes that even among modern, literate peoples, orality remains "the imagined location of what Lévi-Strauss called 'authenticity,' and others call 'presence.'"[37]

It is worth emphasizing that in focusing on the sermon as a performance freighted with assumptions of authenticity and presence, I do not wish to construct a false dichotomy, pitting the orality of the sermon against the textuality of the novel. Five centuries after the invention of movable type, nineteenth-century culture was permeated with the printed word, which meant that the more complex linguistic structures characteristic of writing, including subordinate clauses, the passive voice, and nominalizations, shaped speech across classes. Yet even in such print-dominated cultures, subtle differences separate the oral and written registers of language. Spoken language tends to use shorter words, fewer adjectives, a more limited and less Latinate vocabulary, coordinate rather than subordinate syntactical constructions, and, in general, less logical complexity.[38] Nineteenth-century sermons were hybrid formations that straddled the spoken and written, with the degree of orality determined by idiosyncrasies of personal style and erudition, as well as by whether the preacher spoke from a manuscript, notes, or the heady inspiration of the moment. Never fully oral, the nineteenth-century sermon was nonetheless first and foremost a performance involving voice, body, text, and audience. For many antebellum Americans, much as for the Puritans described by Perry Miller, the difference between hearing and reading a sermon "would have been the difference others would have found between reading *King Lear* and seeing it played by Richard Burbage. The vital heat, so essential to the kindling of affections, all but evaporated when the sermon was set up in type."[39]

Chapter One draws on a wealth of ministerial writing, including sermons, lectures, homiletic handbooks, and newspaper articles, to trace how a range of relatively elite Northeastern ministers imagined and performed the authority of preaching between approximately 1820 and 1855. A recurrent theme of this chapter is that antebellum ministers sought to compensate for their lack of political power with rhetorical strategies that would win them a more nebulous but, they maintained, no less potent moral and religious authority. While no apologist for these men, I have tried to approach them without undue cynicism and with a sense of compassion for their professional struggles. I do not, then, belabor their sexism, racism, ethnocentrism, or at times vexing air of entitlement. I do, though, want to acknowledge upfront that these ministers often wrote and spoke from assumptions of civic and national belonging and gender and racial superiority and that they often seem oblivious that their positions of privilege are anything other than a well-earned blessing. Also, it should go without saying that given the vastness of American religion, I can make no claim to be comprehensive in my treatment of preaching. I have chosen to give ministers in white, mainstream Northeastern denominations, such as Congregationalists, Presbyterians, Episcopalians, and Unitarians, a weight out of proportion to their numbers compared with the Methodists and Baptists, yet justified, I believe, by their greater cultural capital and, on the whole, more direct relationship to the American novelists discussed in later chapters.[40] Similarly, the decision not to examine the preaching styles of Catholics, African Americans, Native Americans, women, Jews, and the many European ethnic subgroups with distinctive preaching traditions (e.g., German Moravians or Swedish Lutherans) is by no means intended as a judgment that these groups are less worthy of interest or less vital to our knowledge of American culture. The current dearth of antebellum sermon studies means that much remains to be done across the board.[41] Of course, limning the commonalities in attitudes toward preaching even among relatively privileged white Northeasterners is not without its problems. I have had to risk generalization, and some readers may balk at my minimizing of denominational and theological differences. The distinction I make most frequently is between theological liberals and conservatives, whose attitudes toward clerical authority diverged in important respects. I use "liberal" to refer most often to Unitarians and "conservative" to cover a broad swath of religious affiliations adhering to traditional Trinitarian theology—most often orthodox Congregationalists, Presbyterians, Episcopalians, and Lutherans, but also at times Methodists and Baptists.[42] This wide-angle lens reveals how, despite the theological, political, ethnic, and geographical diversity of antebellum religion, we can discern shared attitudes and rhetorical strategies that made preaching a coherent and authoritative practice. We see, for instance, how conservative ministers continued to present themselves as fathers rather than friends; how preachers increasingly imagined ideal pulpit performance as the heartfelt—and emotionally risky—expression of personal truth; how the growing desire to see the preacher perform his subjectivity spurred the shift from manuscript to extemporaneous preaching; and how listeners were exhorted to receive sermons with humility, though not always with unquestioning submission.

One can glean a sense of antebellum ministers' massive claims for the cultural importance of preaching by glancing into *The Power of the Pulpit* (1848) by Gardiner Spring, the popular pastor of Brick Presbyterian Church in New York City. A manifesto on the pulpit's importance to America, Spring's volume invited readers to imagine the Pandora's box that would be opened if the nation's pulpits were to close for a quarter of a century:

> More practical evil would flow from such a destitution than from all other causes put together. Law would vanish with religion. No corrupt propensity would be kept under restraint; there would be no corrective, and no limit but selfishness to the depravity of the human heart. The virtuous would be driven to despair, and the vicious to the darkness and crimes of paganism. It would be a Pagan land, dark and dreary as though the Sun of righteousness had never risen upon it. Owls would dwell there, and satyrs dance there; and around such a dreadful cavern of iniquity, the dragons of the pit would linger and dwell as in their habitation. And the curse of God would be upon it, as it was upon Sodom; and he would extirpate the inhabitants of it as he did the nations of Canaan. His judgments would go forth against it, and as though seven thunders uttered their voices, it would be said in heaven, WOE, WOE, WOE TO THE LAND THAT IS NOT THE LAND OF SABBATHS, AND CHURCHES, AND MINISTERS![43]

This hypothetical jeremiad warned that if America abandoned sermon-listening, it would face no less than apocalypse: a chaos of lawlessness, corruption, depravity, despair, and crime. While unusually vivid, Spring's rhetoric is representative of the zeal with which antebellum ministers affirmed their work as indispensable to public morality and national identity.

Chapter Two examines antebellum conduct books to show how dominant cultural discourses in the mid-nineteenth century continued to disparage novels and often all fiction. Although our usual literary historical narratives downplay ongoing cultural resistance to novels and emphasize their growing popularity, recognizing and understanding this resistance clarifies antebellum novelists' uphill battle for moral authority. Written by ministers and educators positioning themselves as cultural guardians and guides to the young, conduct books reflect not the narrowly religious perspectives many have assumed but a widespread cultural conservatism that perpetuated eighteenth-century censures rooted in a fundamental distrust of the imagination. More often than one might expect, fiction was condemned wholesale, with no recognition that religious fiction was flourishing and only occasional and grudging exceptions made for Sir Walter Scott or plainly didactic writers. In the 1850s, a handful of conduct book authors ventured to defend fiction, but such voices were guarded and few. That is, rather than enjoying a straightforward cultural ascent in the first half of the nineteenth century, the novel experienced both a surge in popularity *and* a strong countercurrent of resistance from those who felt responsible for the country's moral well-being.

Chapters Three through Seven focus on six ambitious novels, all published in the decade around 1850: George Lippard's *The Quaker City; Or, The Monks of Monk Hall* (1845) and *Memoirs of a Preacher, A Revelation of the Church and Home* (1849); Nathaniel Hawthorne's *The Scarlet Letter* (1850); Herman Melville's *Moby-Dick* (1851); Harriet Beecher Stowe's *Uncle Tom's Cabin* (1852); and William Wells Brown's *Clotel; or, The President's Daughter* (1853). While drawing on authors' short stories, letters, newspaper columns, and essays to explicate the rivalry between fiction-writers and preachers, I focus on these longer fictions, or novels, because it was in these works that writers most fully claimed the authority of the preacher and made their boldest assertions for the novel's significance. Those finicky about terms might wonder whether these books are "novels" at all. Lippard's qualify perhaps most readily, though even they have their quirks, as the original publication of *The Quaker City* as ten booklets and of *Memoirs of a Preacher* as a running feature in Lippard's weekly newspaper complicates current notions of a novel as a bound book. *The Scarlet Letter* is so short as to be more novella than novel and has the additional complication of bearing the subtitle "A Romance," a term Hawthorne took care to distinguish from "novel" in the preface to *The House of the Seven Gables*.[44] *Moby-Dick* has an especially odd status, being both "the great American novel" par excellence and, as original reviewers recognized, a strange brew—as one put it, "a singular medley of naval observation, magazine article writing, satiric reflection on the conventionalisms of civilized life, and rhapsody run mad."[45] Scholars have also puzzled over how to categorize it, quarreling with the "novel" label and christening it a "romance-anatomy" or "mixed-form narrative."[46] Even *Uncle Tom's Cabin* struggles in the novel's net. Stowe preferred to call it a story, a narrative, scenes, or a series of sketches, and declared in the preface to the Tauchnitz edition of 1852, "[W]ould that this book were indeed a fiction, and not a close wrought mosaic of facts!"[47] *Clotel*, credited as the first African American novel, is prosy and loose-jointed, with barely connected storylines and didactic digressions; it is also, as I will discuss, a patchwork document comprising a startling number of plagiarized passages. Hardly a book in the lot conforms to the highly crafted ideal of a *Pride and Prejudice* or *David Copperfield,* and the authors' own reluctance to use the term "novel" underscores the stigma that clung to the genre—the one literary genre that, across countries and centuries, "feels the need to deny itself."[48]

My focus on a cluster of novels written around 1850 is not wholly a matter of personal predilection. It is true that some version of the patterns of resistance and appropriation I trace in these novels can be found throughout American fiction. The perennial strength of ministers, coupled with the moral and cultural ambitions of individual authors ill-disposed to bend the knee to religious authorities, has meant that novels have had a complex relationship with preaching throughout American literary history—from the preachy narrator of Susanna Rowson's *Charlotte Temple,* to Sinclair Lewis's infamous Elmer Gantry, to Baby Suggs's joyous sermon in Toni Morrison's *Beloved.* But I would like to suggest that the novels written in the mid-nineteenth century had a peculiarly intense relationship to preaching. Start reading virtually any novel written at this time, and you will hit a sermon or something that sounds like one. I have already pointed to two reasons for this heightened engagement with the sermon: the cultural dominance of preaching in the period and novelists' desire to vindicate fiction against its still-powerful critics. Another factor was the new literary ambition of fiction writers. In America the 1840s and 1850s saw what Jonathan Arac has called the rise of "literary narrative," or self-conscious, self-reflexive fiction that, borrowing the values of German Romanticism, rejected the didactic, conventional, and economically profitable.[49] Working in this mode, authors such as Hawthorne and Melville found analogies between their market-defiant art and the cultural stance of the period's ministers, who also claimed to declare unpopular truths regardless of their reception. Even those writers not often considered literary—for instance, Lippard, Stowe, and Brown—saw their work as morally independent, capable of offering moral visions at odds with those of church authorities and society's majorities. We might locate the beginnings of a cultural acceptance of the novel's divergence from conventional morality in the period's book reviews. As Nina Baym has shown, it was around 1850 that reviewers started to set aside moral yardsticks in evaluating authors and to foreground their aesthetic qualities—a fact that has often been read as a sign that American culture as a whole had granted the novel moral legitimacy, but that may say more about the dynamics of the publishing world, an issue I address in Chapter Two.[50] Yet another major factor driving the novel's intensified engagement with the sermon at mid-century was authorial frustration with the clergy's leadership on the major reform issues of the day, especially slavery. For Stowe, Brown, and to a lesser extent,

Melville, the widespread failure of ministers to oppose slavery or even the Fugitive Slave Law of 1850 discredited them as moral authorities and freed fiction writers to step into a position of moral leadership.[51] A minister who abetted slavery had no rights which an author was bound to respect. For Lippard, the problems of the urban poor were paramount, and his fiction attacked those ministers whom he saw as more interested in preserving their own status than in protecting and defending workers, tenants, orphans, and other victims of the emergent industrial-capitalist order.

To be sure, the novels discussed in this book are only a handful of those, even of the mid-nineteenth-century, that set themselves against preaching. One also finds significant and often antagonistic representations of preaching in such diverse fictions as Catherine Williams's *Fall River,* Henry Wadsworth Longfellow's *Kavanagh,* Susan Warner's *The Wide, Wide World,* and Sylvester Judd's *Margaret,* not to mention other novels by the writers already under discussion, such as Melville's *Pierre* or Stowe's *Dred.*[52] Although I explore in depth a limited selection of now-canonical novelists, I also wish to gesture beyond my chosen novels to the prevalence of the sermon in nineteenth-century American fiction and to suggest that it constitutes something of a national hallmark, one that works to distinguish between American and English novels of the nineteenth century. Instead of thinking about the difference between English and American novels as one of realism versus romance, *à la* Richard Chase, we might consider the difference as one between an English realism defined by its rejection of universals, as Ian Watt had it, and an American realism that grappled with the universalizing impulses of the sermon.[53] Certainly there are major Victorian novels with powerful scenes of preaching. One thinks, for instance, of George Eliot's *Adam Bede* or *Romola,* or Anthony Trollope's *Barchester Towers,* but there are a great many more Victorian novels—including those by Charlotte Brontë, Charles Dickens, Elizabeth Gaskell, and William Thackeray, to name a few—in which sermons, when they appear at all, are sidelights, revealing character or circumstance but offering little commentary on moral issues or on authorship, as they so often do in nineteenth-century American novels. Nor do English novelists seem as interested in experimenting with narratorial preaching voices, notwithstanding Dickens's sentimental effusions or Thackeray's didactic asides. Decorum may have played a role. Noting the relative scarcity of sermons in nineteenth-century British novels, Raymond Chapman has observed that although sermons held a prominent place in the Victorian book market, "a realistic sermon would have seemed out of place in even the more didactic type of novel, and a parody would have been distasteful to the majority."[54] The sense that novels and sermons inhabited parallel realms would seem to reflect the more secure cultural footing of the novel in England by the mid-nineteenth century, which gave English novelists a less urgent need than American ones to claim cultural and moral autonomy by setting themselves against preachers. Other probable factors behind the English separation of novels and sermons were the cultural dominance of Anglicanism, in which a short sermon was one element of a more liturgical worship service, and the state-subsidized parish system, which granted Anglican priests a financial stability that removed some of the pressure to deliver sermons capable of generating pew rents and tithes.[55] Though Dissenters, whose services foregrounded the sermon and who worshipped without state support, thrived, their lesser social prestige made them a less significant rival for ambitious English novelists. America, by contrast, had a long, robust history of sermon-centered worship across classes; all manner of Protestants, from tony Boston Congregationalists to hardscrabble frontier Methodists, attended worship services in which preaching figured prominently. While all such distinctions between national literatures must be provisional given the archive of non-canonical novels, the cultural conditions in mid-nineteenth century America seem to have produced an especially charged relationship between novels and sermons in which preaching was both a rival and a resource.

This book foregrounds two of the most salient ways mid-nineteenth-century American novelists sought to usurp the preacher's role while expounding their own moral and religious ideas: representations of preachers and a form of speech I call "sermonic voice," which borrows the characteristic stylistic features of preaching. These lines of inquiry attempt to capture how preaching, distinct from other oratorical forms and theological discourses, shaped the novel.[56] By paying special attention to how novelists engaged with preaching as a dominant cultural practice, I hope to offer a corrective to scholarship on antebellum American religion and literature that has privileged the notion that in analyzing the interface of these two cultural systems, we should understand religion in terms of its texts or ideas—as the Bible and its commentaries; or as doctrines like Arminianism, Calvinism, providentialism, or millennialism; or as an ideological nexus subordinate to other political or social issues.[57] While I have learned a great deal from such work, the combined effect of these approaches is to ignore the affective, embodied dimension and defining social experiences of religion, along with how those experiences shaped imaginative literature.[58] Protestantism's own tendency to define itself in creedal terms—to insist upon belief as the basis of religious life—goes far to explain this proclivity among literary scholars, as does the accessibility of text and doctrine compared with the difficulty of knowing the lived experience of religion. Despite the challenges of reconstructing absent scenes of religious practice, recovering the contours of these experiences is crucial for comprehending how literature responded to religion.[59] My focus on represented preachers and sermonic voice is an attempt to trace these contours, to provide a heuristic that does not pretend to exhaust the sermon's influence on the novel. The competition with preachers animated countless other elements of the period's novels as well, from their explication of "texts" (an embroidered A, a whale), akin to the preacher's analysis of scripture; to their moral exemplars (virtuous maidens, martyrs to slavery), akin to how preachers invoked biblical characters; to their penchant for narrative structures of redemption, one of the sermon's fundamental tropes.[60]

Preachers take the spotlight in some of the most memorable passages in American literature. In the chapters that follow, I explore the significance of Arthur Dimmesdale's Election Sermon in *The Scarlet Letter* and Father Mapple's Jonah sermon in *Moby-Dick,* as well as lesser-known interludes such as the Popular Preacher's crowd-enrapturing sermon at the beginning of *Memoirs of a Preacher.* These figurations of preachers, which often rewrite and critique actual ministers, are surprisingly intricate. Novels often mock these reimagined preachers, indicting them for claiming moral authority while seducing parishioners, pilfering cash, promulgating intolerance, ignoring social injustices, and blustering self-righteously, but the representations are seldom wholly negative. They often include an elaborate, appreciative ekphrasis of pulpit performance that encodes an uncanny doubling of author and preacher, with novelistic text and authorial biography converging to suggest that an author has set up preaching a sermon and publishing a novel as parallel cultural activities. Through such scenes, novelists critiqued the clergy while refracting their own ambitions for attaining moral authority and their anxieties about addressing a mass audience with potentially unwelcome truths.

My other recurrent focus is sermonic voice, a term I use for novelistic speech that mimics the sound of the sermon.[61] Sermonic voice, which might be spoken by either the narrator or a character, crystallizes the sermon's paradigmatic stylistic and tonal features: syntactic structures characteristic of oratory, such as parallelism, anaphora, antithesis, and repetition; biblical and theological diction; and an attitude of certainty about religious or moral propositions. It must also allow its hearers the possibility of hope or redemption in some form; an eloquent, biblically resonant malediction is no sermon. As the aestheticized voice of the preacher, sermonic voice is more urgent and concentrated than lines taken at random from a sermon. It seems to jump out from the surrounding text and claim authority. When nineteenth-century sermons include language that sounds like novelistic sermonic voice, it is typically in the peroration, when the preacher intensified his rhetoric to drive a point home.

Sermonic voice is recognizable yet versatile. In nineteenth-century novels, it appears in countless theological varieties and in response to myriad philosophical, moral, and social problems—the suffering of the poor, the silence of God, the complexities of the human heart, the outrage of slavery, and more. It occurs, too, with various levels of intensity, from calm assurance to passionate exhortation. In fact, sermonic voice is often *not* hortatory. Nineteenth-century novelists followed the lead of the period's preachers, who were cautioned against exhorting their hearers. Richard Whately's influential *Elements of Rhetoric* advised ministers not to tell their hearers directly what to do since people then rebelled and were "more apt to apply these Exhortations to their *neighbours* than to themselves."[62] Similarly, sermonic voice in nineteenth-century novels seldom sounds the note of a jeremiad, or call for national repentance.[63] "Sermonic" is thus intended as a more precise term than the old standby "prophetic," as well as one with greater relevance in antebellum society. Preachers abounded; living, breathing prophets were rare, more often associated with charismatic religions such as the Shakers and Latter-day Saints than with mainstream Protestantism. Whether sermonic voice sounds prophetic, inspirational, hortatory, consolatory, instructive, or monitory, it conveys emotional intensity. It is thus distinct from the aphorism or maxim, rhetorical forms that present themselves as speakerless pronouncements of universal truths.

The moments I identify as sermonic are precisely the "preachy" ones that many readers today love to hate. This collective aversion to preachiness means that these moments have fallen into a critical black hole, habitually overlooked despite their ubiquity in nineteenth-century fiction.[64] Critiquing the neglect of didactic genres that anteceded the novel, as well as how we tend to "apologize for, dismiss, or downright ignore" novelistic didacticism, J. Paul Hunter describes the scorn of many modern readers: "Why should we care about, readers now may well wonder, the origins of moralistic, lapel-gripping techniques that we temperamentally resist and wish did not exist?" Yet didacticism, he rightly maintains, is central to the novel's origins, and perceiving the past with any fairness means recognizing that readers "actually seem to have enjoyed" being told what to do.[65] I take as a working premise that many readers of the eighteenth and nineteenth century, and perhaps even of the twentieth and twenty-first, have found didacticism desirable and valuable. Each of the major novelists I discuss, whether or not we would label them "didactic," incorporates sermonic voice in some way, from the narrator of *The Quaker City* relating that an "old book" holds that a rapist will be punished with "an eternity of wo; wo without limit, despair without hope; the torture of the never-dying worm, and the unquenchable flame, forever and forever"; to Ishmael expostulating, "Be sure of this, O young ambition, all mortal greatness is but disease"; to the narrator of *Clotel* beseeching readers to "proclaim the Year of Jubilee."[66] Sermonic moments such as these are seldom straightforward and often bear unexpected relationships to the novels in which they appear. Reading them well means being alert to their potential ironies, to how they are balanced against other voices in the same novel, and to how they fit, or don't, with views an author has stated elsewhere. To condense radically a number of points developed in subsequent chapters: Lippard does not simply moralize; he heightens plot points with imaginative and lurid religious visions, then sermonizes on these visions as if they were sacred scripture. Hawthorne avoids preaching, but the narrator's single sermonic exclamation in *The Scarlet Letter* is one of the most significant lines in the book. Melville, stretching the limits of his long-developing democratic sermonic voice, uses Ishmael to preach sermons that outfit classical ideas in Christian garb. In *Uncle Tom's Cabin,* the narrator's sermons shift from sentimental to visionary, and from feminine to masculine, while some of the novel's best preaching is saved for the "lowly." In *Clotel,* Brown was in constant motion, folding the religious discourse he found in others' pamphlets, sermons, and lectures into a novel that negotiates two very different modes of preaching: in his "Little Eva"-type character, the evangelicalism he thought his white audience in the United States most wanted to hear as part of an abolitionist argument; in his narrator, a liberal faith that mirrored the religious values of the British Unitarians among whom he wrote the novel.

Throughout, I have kept in mind the fact that in all of these novels, even the most didactic, sermonizing is necessarily provisional, shot through with an "as if" by the nature of the fictive context. Seeming to claim finality, a sermon in a novel can be only, as Robert Frost wrote of poetry, a "momentary stay against confusion."[67] Even as the novel offers up its sermonic moments as islands of stasis, it inevitably engulfs those moments, denying the sanctity of the sermon as a genre. Explaining the scandal of Salman Rushdie's *Satanic Verses,* Walter Siti describes a similar process: "What is intolerable is the idea that the literary text is more powerful than the sacred text, that it can encapsulate the sacred text and turn it into narrative material, thereby inserting it into the mobile flow of the passions—and subjugating it to the novelistic law of and-and rather than to the either-or that guarantees the sacred text its fixity and authority."[68] Though not a sacred text in name, the sermon, too, claimed an authority that the novel could not respect.

In challenging ministerial authority, American novelists advanced a form of social and cultural change recognizable today as secularization, a process we should understand as defined not by the rejection of religion, but by the fragmentation of religious beliefs and discourses and their redeployment within new, nonecclesiastical institutions and media. As sociologist Danièle Hervieu-Leger explains, secularization in this sense is "not the process of the eradication of religion in a massively rationalized society, but the recomposition of the religious within a broader redistribution of beliefs in a society in which no institution can lay claim to a monopoly of meaning."[69] With this dispersal and reconstitution of religion, "religious" and "secular" institutions and practices come to share moral authority.[70] One can also see the secularization at work in nineteenth-century American culture as the functional differentiation of societal subsystems, in which, as sociologist Karel Dobbelaere writes, religion becomes one subsystem among many and "the religious authorities of institutionalized religion [lose] control over the other subsystems like polity, economy, family, education, law, etc."[71] That "etc." can be read to include literature, as long as one adds that literature in the nineteenth century was not merely differentiating itself from religion but also trying to claim its power in numerous ways, including enchanting the world, defining self and reality, and shaping character and behavior. Integral to the secularizing process of differentiation is autonomization, in which subsystems claim self-determination by "reject[ing] religiously prescribed rules."[72] For American literature, the first religious rule to break was that of deference to the clergy; after that, authors challenged religious norms on everything from sexual mores to slavery to the nature of subjectivity. The idea that American literature gained autonomy through subsystem differentiation resonates with Pierre Bourdieu's claims regarding the changing field of art in France, where "[e]specially since the middle of the nineteenth century, the principle of change in art has come from within art itself."[73] Although Bourdieu is most concerned to show the divergence of literary value and economic success, his description of those writers who gained the esteem of their peers as achieving "consecration" speaks to the reconstitution of religious values. Like their French counterparts, American literary writers were declaring their independence from the marketplace and religion while aspiring to special status and authority.[74]

To be clear, in saying that novelists participated in secularization, I do not wish to invoke a sweeping secularization thesis in which the novelistic reworking of sermons indexes an ineluctable, teleological process of disenchantment inherent to modernity. This overly broad notion of secularization has long been under attack for its analytical imprecision (its conflation, for instance, of individual, social, political, and legal patterns) and spotty applicability outside of Western Europe, and it has always imperfectly explained the social and cultural situation of the United States, where religious institutions and individual belief remain strong.[75] The American case, as José Casanova cautions, disrupts the "stadial historical consciousness that views unbelief as the quasi-natural developmental result of a kind of secular coming of age and of adult maturation."[76] Recent work on secularization in the social sciences has stressed its cultural contingency and reversibility and taken pains to distinguish it from secularism as a worldview or political project.[77] There is a greater awareness than ever that religion does not fall away to reveal a secular substrate and that in the modern world the secular and religious are fluid, interpenetrating, mutually constitutive, and culturally determined categories.[78] Keeping these insights in mind, we can see the nineteenth-century American novel as not only participating in the autonomization associated with secularization but also, in some cases, claiming as part of that freedom the power to articulate perspectives that are secular in ways imaginable only as a dialectical response to a particular Protestant milieu.[79]

Thus each novel dances with the sermon in its own way—always in dynamic, productive tension yet never using quite the same steps. What *Preaching and the Rise of the American Novel* tries to do is to reconstruct cultural expectations surrounding antebellum sermons and novels, then elucidate how novelists worked with and against preaching to claim a moral authority equivalent to that of the clergy. Although I do not expect or even wish to kindle in readers the enthusiasm for sermons I myself once felt, I hope that considering preaching from the inside, with respect for those who felt charged to speak from the pulpit and for those who listened with eager ears, will illuminate how even the most skeptical and rebellious authors could find in sermons a powerful precedent and analogue for their own cultural ambitions.

CHAPTER 1

⁓⁂⁓

Creating Authority
in the Pulpit

I N CHAPTER 8 of *Moby-Dick*, Ishmael sits in the Whaleman's Chapel and eyes the bow-front pulpit with the jutting fiddlehead scrollwork. How full of meaning, he thinks: "For the pulpit is ever this earth's foremost part; all the rest comes in its rear; the pulpit leads the world. [. . .] Yes, the world's a ship on its passage out, and not a voyage complete, and the pulpit is its prow."[1]

The pulpit is the world's prow? One hardly expects this pious declaration from a melancholy ex-schoolmaster on his way to sea. Such rhetoric belonged to the clergy, as when Ralph Waldo Emerson told the Harvard Divinity School seniors preparing for the ministry, "The office is the first in the world," or when New York Presbyterian Gardiner Spring wrote in *The Power of the Pulpit* (1848) that the pulpit "has power above the field of battle, above the Forum, above the Senate-house."[2] Antebellum sermons resounded with the idea that the Protestant ministry was the most exalted calling known to humanity—that it was the "highest office God allows to man," that this "sacred office" was the "chief instrument of glorifying God," and that there was "no higher honor to which man may aspire on earth."[3] Orville Dewey, a leading Unitarian and a minister with a strong connection to Melville's family, described the elation that came from addressing the assembled masses:

> [W]ho that stands, though as the humblest teacher, amidst the crowded throng, of the young and the old, the strong and the weak, the joyous and the sorrowful, can help trembling and exulting at the same time, at the

greatness of his sublime vocation? Who can help feeling that the place
whereon he stands is holy ground; that the spot to which a thousand eyes
are directed for consolation, for guidance, and holy impulse, is a spot where
one of the noblest actions of life is to be performed, where the noblest work
is to be done, for time and for eternity.[4]

Here Dewey claimed not only a supreme moral significance for the preacher,
who did the world's "noblest work," but also cultural preeminence, as the
preacher drew together hundreds of diverse individuals in a collective spiritual experience.[5]

Melville likely intended Ishmael's mimicry of this rhetoric to be ironic,
at least in some measure. It is consonant with the naïveté Ishmael displays
in many of the shore chapters, like his ridiculous efforts to avoid sharing a
bed with a cannibal or his expostulations against Queequeg's "Ramadan."
Pertinent to the irony is Melville's implicit jab at the political uselessness of
the clergy. When most Northern ministers responded equivocally to the passage of the Fugitive Slave Law in 1850, opponents of slavery were indignant
that the self-proclaimed guardians of American morality had so little to say
against racial injustice. To say in 1851 that the pulpit led the world was to
many a bitter joke. Yet *Moby-Dick* is always teetering between sobriety and
jest, and Ishmael's proclamation is more than, as Lawrance Thompson put it,
a "sarcastic sneer."[6] In announcing the sermon's authority, however naïvely,
Ishmael establishes the standard of moral and cultural leadership to which
Moby-Dick aspires. Like so many other antebellum novelists, Melville wanted
fiction to stand in the same high place as the sermon, and fiction writers, to
enjoy moral and professional equality with preachers, the supposed "leaders
of the world."

This chapter traces how antebellum preachers created the moral authority that novelists envied. Certainly ministers could not take their authority
for granted. The disestablishment of religion, which began with the Revolution and was completed by 1833, meant that ministers faced new pressures
to prove their worth to congregations. No longer quasi-magisterial figures
allied with the civic order and attached to a community for life, they now
belonged to a private profession accountable to a changeable and demand-
ing clientele.[7] With congregations paying pastors directly, church members
were more inclined to delay inviting licentiates to take on full pastorates,
to dismiss ministers who displeased them (or some faction of the congregation), and to keep salaries as low as possible.[8] Ministers typically served
many different communities over their lifetimes, a result either of being
forced out or of climbing the career ladder to better positions. They also

occupied an ambiguous position within the public sphere. Many state constitutions prohibited them from filling political office, and after Republicans protested the Federalist clergy's preaching against Thomas Jefferson in the election of 1800, preachers tended to keep partisan politics out of their sermons—at least until the late 1840s, when the political issues at the center of national life, slavery above all, increasingly overlapped with the pulpit's moral purview.[9]

Faced with these new conditions of professional mobility and political marginality, ministers had to take responsibility for producing their own moral and cultural authority. Bald assertion of the nobility and sacredness of their work furthered this end, as did more tangible efforts. New seminary curricula focused on subjects that "enhanced the minister's expertise and professional credentials," such as classical languages, theology, and sacred rhetoric.[10] Once employed, many ministers abided by new rules of pastoral decorum, such as gravity and social aloofness, that safeguarded their dignity; the newly professionalized minister was "the spiritual friend of all and the social friend of none."[11] Ministers also increasingly defined themselves as members of a national profession, a process facilitated by growing networks of reform societies and benevolent associations that gave them opportunities to exercise influence beyond their local congregations. But nothing mattered more than how one preached. Delivering the morning and afternoon Sunday sermons was a minister's paramount duty, his most visible public act, and the most obvious arena in which he competed with his fellow clergy for tithe-paying, pew-renting church members.[12] As Andover Theological Seminary President Ebenezer Porter declared in his influential textbook, *Lectures on Homiletics and Preaching* (1834), "If a minister would maintain the respect of his hearers, it is a maxim which I have no fear of repeating too often, 'whatever else he does or neglects to do, he must *preach well.*'"[13]

What did it mean for a minister to "preach well"? The question is vast. A Kentucky Methodist hollering about damnation at a camp meeting looked and sounded very different from a New York Unitarian reminding parishioners of their familial and civic duties in a neoclassical church, or from a Pennsylvania Lutheran following communion with a homily in a country chapel, or from a Baptist slave exhorting his peers on a Virginia plantation. Below I trace several of the defining norms and ideals of antebellum preaching, focusing on educated ministers in the elite, predominately white denominations of the Northeast, as it was these ministers who enjoyed the greatest cultural prestige in antebellum America and with whom the novelists discussed in later chapters primarily competed for moral and cultural authority. Distinguishing as necessary between theological conservatives and liberals, I explore how ministers reflected on their practice. Although I give significant attention to the liberals because of their outsize influence on antebellum American literary culture, it is worth remembering that conservative theology had far greater purchase on the culture as a whole.[14] I discuss first how ministers symbolically constructed their relationship to their congregations, then how they created authority through the rhetoric and performance of preaching.

A father, friend, or foe?

Ministers laid the groundwork for their preaching by schooling church-goers in the nature of ministerial authority. Karin Gedge has described the relationship between ministers and their congregations as undergoing a decisive shift in the antebellum period from paternal to fraternal: "no longer a stern gatekeeper and lawgiver, [the minister] must now serve as a confidant, loving friend, and a counselor." While this generalization has a good deal of truth, theologically conservative ministers were reluctant to abandon a paternal notion of ministerial authority. They were also much more likely than liberals to adopt an authoritarian stance and to claim a divine commission for their work. An ordination sermon by David D. Field, minister of the Congregational Church in Stockbridge from 1819 to 1837, reveals certain foundational assumptions about ministerial authority that persisted throughout the antebellum period. Field admonished the congregation that the minister was "over you in the Lord" (1 Thes. 5:12)—a position that entailed numerous solemn responsibilities, from administering ordinances to censuring church members to preaching the "whole system of faith," which meant not shirking disagreeable doctrines like eternal damnation. Although the minister was supposed to exercise his office with appropriate humility, the bottom line was that he was a representative of Christ whom the congregation was obliged to hold in high esteem. The minister's proper relationship to his people, Field wrote, "is paternal, or rather it is pastoral; a government in which, by instruction, kindness and example, the flock of God are to be led on to peace, safety and glory."[15] Both of Field's primary figurations of authority— the "paternal" and the "pastoral"—encoded the idea that the laity needed the minister's superior wisdom. Spiritually, the minister was first among equals.

As a democratic ethos reshaped the clerical profession, conservatives increasingly balanced their call for hearers to respect the minister's authority with an emphasis on the minister's weighty obligations to his hearers. New York Episcopalian Samuel Seabury engaged in this high-wire act when preaching on the relationship of the clergy and laity in 1844. Making the case for ministerial authority, he stressed that as ministers of Christ, the clergy represented Christ, just as a government's ministers represented the government. The Christian minister's primary obligation was thus to Christ, not to the people—or, put plainly, a minister was not bound to seek to please the congregation that paid his salary. At the same time, though, Seabury held up as an example Paul, who made himself "a servant to all" that he might gain some, an especially challenging example to ministers since, as Seabury acknowledged, the Greek *doulos* meant not simply servant but "*slave.*" Without mentioning Southern slavery, Seabury clarified that ministers, following the example of Paul and Christ, should gladly serve their people through any humble labor necessary.[16]

But such gestures of humility were seldom the minister's last word. Seabury's peroration returned to the main task at hand—exhorting listeners to grant their ministers all due authority:

> And I warn you, brethren, against being led astray by the clamors that are raised about priestly authority and tradition, and the specious claims that are set up for liberty of thought and unlimited private judgment; and I ask you to consider seriously whether the real end of all this clamor be not to oppose the just authority of Christ's ministers; to unsettle your creeds, to disparage your standard of faith; to undermine the Christian laws and safeguards of sound public opinion; to erect private fancy in the place of collective wisdom, and in short to deprive you of the liberty of law only to enslave you to the bondage of anarchy.[17]

To question the minister's "just authority" was to risk one's faith, to abandon the guidance of collective wisdom, and to enter the "bondage of anarchy." Such rhetoric made the real "slave" of this address not the minister, but the too-independent-minded listener who undermined law and order by failing to respect the minister's superior moral and religious judgment. Like Spring in *The Power of the Pulpit,* Seabury drew a bright line connecting ministerial authority and social order.

A corollary of the conservatives' emphasis on ministerial authority was the idea that humanity's stubborn sinfulness and innate resistance to saving truth required ministers to approach their hearers as antagonists. Indeed, a rhetoric of violence pervaded descriptions of preaching centered on the traditional drama of Christian redemption. Finney described the preacher's mission with characteristic force: "Ministers should never rest satisfied until they have ANNIHILATED every excuse of sinners."[18] Drawing more explicitly on biblical images of warfare, Porter primed his students for their first pastorates by urging them to use their sermons as weapons: true pulpit eloquence "makes even the stripling warrior, 'valiant in fight'; and enables him to cut off the head of Goliath, with the sword wrested from his own hand."[19] Similarly, Amherst College president and Presbyterian minister Heman Humphrey told young men entering the ministry that they needed a stock of sermons written beforehand, as "A soldier should have a good supply of cartridges, or at least should learn how to make them with facility, before he approaches the enemy's lines."[20] Philadelphia Reformed Dutch minister George Bethune summoned much the same militaristic language in warning young pastors against announcing the heads of their sermons: "What would we think of a general, who should advise his adversary of his plan of attack? Yet the hearts of those we address are naturally at enmity with the truth."[21] Even Henry Ward Beecher, who famously championed a God of love, told ministers in his *Yale Lectures on Preaching* that their job was to assimilate Christian truth to their own lives and "with that, strike! with that, flash! with that, burn men!"[22]

To a certain extent, violent metaphors came with the territory in conservative preaching; Puritan preachers had sought to convey spiritual power in this way, too, in particular the idea that the "sword of the Spirit" could take the form of a sermon.[23] Yet the frequency of such language among antebellum ministers may also have reflected the new professional realities. The harsh truth was that post-disestablishment ministers had a newly adversarial relationship with their congregations. A congregation dissatisfied with its minister felt within its rights dismissing him and calling a new one, and a minister who wanted to keep his job had to proceed cautiously and not get too comfortable. Those who managed to secure a pastorate had to preach consistently satisfactory sermons while negotiating relentless demands for pastoral care—prayers and comfort at sickbeds and deathbeds, the officiating of funerals and marriages, personal counseling and afternoon visits. Again and again the pastoral literature warned ministers to safeguard their morning hours for sermon preparation and not to ruin their health through overwork. As Humphrey wrote to his son, and by extension to all young ministers, a congregation would never deliberately endanger a minister's health but would make such persistent demands that the harmful effects would be "as injurious as if an enemy had done it."[24]

Despite facing the same professional pressures, liberals were much less eager than conservatives to portray ministers as battling their congregations, and they seldom figured the sermon as a valiant storming of obdurate hearts. Instead, they tended to frame the relationship between a minister and his congregation in egalitarian or familial terms. We might take as a touchstone for this issue the series "On the Mutual Relations, Duties, and Interests of Minister and People," which ran in the Unitarian *Christian Register and Boston Observer* from August through November 1841. The series made several points with which conservatives would have agreed, such as that the relationship between a minister and his people was not to be regarded as a financial arrangement and that the people should not value their minister for the prestige he lent their village or for the value his pastorate added to their real estate. But the series diverged from conservative sensibilities in its emphasis on the minister's lack of authority: "The relation between a Minister and his People is one of *equality*. There is neither dominion nor servitude on either side." More pointedly, the minister had "no authority nor command"; the relation between him and his congregation was "one of brethren."[25] Or as Salem Unitarian John Brazer (whom Hawthorne praised in his youthful "Spectator") had clarified the decade before, the minister is a "helper and friend indeed, but [. . .] is and can be nothing more."[26] Unitarians preferred to see ministers as gifted spokesmen for a common faith, not as men chosen by God to save sinners.

Yet a lingering sense that a congregation was bound to follow its minister's guidance often undercut the liberal rhetoric of brotherhood. Boston Unitarian Henry Ware, Jr., for instance, wrote that a minister should speak with his congregation as "a friend with a friend, or a parent with his children"—an uneasy juxtaposition of egalitarian and hierarchical models of relationship. Moreover, when the pastor rose to speak, he was to remember both that he was "in the midst of acquaintances and friends," and that although a few individuals in the congregation might resist his message, his hearers on the whole trusted him and had "put themselves in his power."[27] The ideal minister thus bore something of a paradoxical relationship to his congregation—both brotherly father and authoritative friend. Some liberals suggested that the minister should play different roles to different parishioners depending on their age. The same *Christian Register* article that maintained that the minister's relationship to his people was one of "brethren" also said that the minister should treat those more aged with respect, those his own age as brothers and sisters, and those younger than himself as children. The congregation was to reciprocate this family feeling:

Children should fly to the arms of a faithful minister as to a father indeed, who is ready to aid them in all that is most conducive to their true happiness. Youth should unbosom themselves to him, with something of the freedom they would to a real brother; and the heart of age should grow

warmer at the presence of one, who stands in so sacred and endeared relation.[28]

This familial model made the minister's authority dependent not on due deference or on the public's acquiescence to a divinely ordered state of affairs
but on generationally defined sympathies. The result was that while the minister was clearly imagined as a moral guide to the young, his relationship to
his generational peers and elders was less well defined. For a neighbor to
regard the minister as a brother, or for the heart of the aged person to "grow
warmer" in his presence, did not require attaching any special importance
to his teaching. In emphasizing fellow-feeling, the egalitarian and familial
models of pastoral leadership weakened the minister's authority.[29]

Sermonic discourse

Among the educated, predominately white congregations of the Northeast,
the early nineteenth century saw a decisive shift in the conception of good
preaching, from a scholastic emphasis on explicating the Bible and expounding correct doctrine to a new focus on the sermon as a practical discourse
that moved hearers to right belief and action. A sermon was to be, the influential Edinburgh rhetorician Hugh Blair wrote, a "persuasive oration."[30] Or
as Finney asserted, "To preach doctrines in an abstract way, and not in reference to practice, is absurd."[31] Antebellum preachers had, in a sense, rediscov-
ered first principles, as Augustine's foundational treatise on preaching, the
fourth book of *On Christian Doctrine* (426), had insisted that the preacher's
ultimate goal in delighting, moving, and instructing hearers was to convince
them to take action.[32] The nineteenth-century move toward practical preaching arose from several converging and interconnected historical currents,
including the evangelicalism that had entered American life with the Great
Awakening in the 1730s and blossomed with the second Great Awakening in
the early nineteenth century; the Romantic emphasis on feeling as the linchpin of true religion; and the pervasive influence of Scottish Common Sense
philosophy, which maintained the accessibility of truth.[33]

The shift in preaching from teaching doctrine to motivating personal
change brought with it a looser, more essayistic sermon style. Ministers no
longer depended on the backbone of *exordium, narratio, partitio, refutatio,
epilogus*—the five-part, Ciceronian structure of many Protestant sermons in
the sixteenth and seventeenth centuries. Gone, too, was the dependable sermon form of the Puritans—text, doctrine, proofs (or reasons), and uses (or

applications), often further subdivided into "heads" that served as a guide to logic and memory for both minister and hearers.[34] Antebellum preachers still began sermons with a text, or verse from the canonical scriptures, but spent much less time than their forebears explaining its significance within a theological system or correlating it with other passages in the Bible. Instead, the sermon now focused on the text's moral and spiritual relevance, as the "application" gained new prominence and, in some cases, took over the whole. Heads were optional. Emerson celebrated this newly free-form style when he called preaching "the speech of man to men,—essentially the most flexible of all organs, of all forms."[35] Speaking in the early 1870s, Henry Ward Beecher could do no more than vaguely suggest that new structures might be emerging to replace the old ones. Old-fashioned, methodical textual explication was only one way to preach: "A descriptive sermon, a poetical sermon, and a sermon of sentiment, have, severally, their own genius of form."[36] But he did not describe what this "genius of form" might look like; apparently it was to come from individual inspiration and effort, not a new set of rules.

However loosely organized a sermon, its rhetoric was one of complete conviction, eschewing gestures of compromise, speculation, or ambiguity in favor of divine truths and moral certitude. It was, as Hortense Spillers has written of African American preaching, "the discourse of primary certainty that banishes all doubt to the realm of the inconsequential."[37] Whether an antebellum minister preached a judgmental Father or a loving Son, whether he dealt in syllogisms or anecdotes, he spoke from the pulpit with the authority of a seemingly unshakable faith.

This tone of conviction reached its climax in the peroration. There the minister had to drive home his point so that it touched his hearers' hearts. As Porter exhorted his students, "[Y]ou *must awaken feeling,* especially in the close of your discourse, or you come utterly short of the great end of preaching."[38] To win this emotional response, a minister had to control his voice, raising it gradually in pitch and volume throughout the sermon. Starting with too much emotion was fatal. Porter warned, "The discourse that begins in ecstasy, to be consistent with itself, must end in phrenzy."[39] A respectable minister typically wanted to achieve not frenzy but something closer to the crescendo of a musical performance: "Be sure that the final sentence leaves every soul vibrating like a swept harp."[40]

Another constitutive feature of antebellum sermons—and perhaps, too, the sermons of most times and places—was their reliance upon redemption narratives. Liberal or conservative, rational or evangelical, preachers wrote listeners into stories in which divine grace and, often, human effort repaired and redeemed human sins and shortcomings.[41] Sermons might castigate, exhort, command, or rebuke, but their ultimate word to listeners was never one of condemnation. They offered, that is, what Edmund Arens has identified as a core element of communicative-religious praxis: "the dimension of promise," or the guarantee of a "relieving and reconciling liberation from political, social, physical and psychic bondage and mortality's grip."[42] Few if any sermons held out *all* these forms of liberation, but intimations of redemption defined the genre.

For theological conservatives, narratives of individual redemption typically centered on Jesus' death as the atonement for human sin, or what ministers called "preaching the cross of Christ."[43] Effective preaching created in listeners a profound sense of dissatisfaction with their sinful condition (an earlier age had called it "sermon-sickness"), moved them to repent of their sins, inspired them to have faith that Christ's sacrifice provided for their salvation, and brought them to submit themselves to the rule of a just and merciful God. Evangelicals elaborated on this paradigm by emphasizing the necessity of a dramatic, emotional "new birth" conversion experience that marked the beginning of one's Christian identity. The pervasiveness of evangelicalism meant that even the orthodox, who supposedly believed that God had predetermined who would be saved, regularly connected individual redemption with repentance and reform.[44] Whether or not conservative sermons focused on a conversion experience, they promoted, in effect, a version of the ancient redemptive structure that appears throughout the Hebrew Bible. Erich Auerbach has described this pattern as one of "humiliation and elevation," in which a transcendent, majestic God lifts up those who have been dishonored and defeated.[45] For antebellum theological conservatives, an individual's humiliation lay both in the inescapable reality of human sin and in the sufferings and trials of existence itself, while the promised elevation meant spiritual renewal now and a glorious bodily resurrection at the Last Judgment.

Liberal preaching also offered its hearers a redemption narrative, though typically a less dramatic one. Often described by contemporary critics and later generations as dry and overly rationalistic, liberal preaching is better understood as pietistic, intent on transforming and purifying the inner life.[46] As Boston Unitarian Francis Parkman put it in a seeming oxymoron, "Rational Christianity addresses itself to the heart."[47] For liberals, achieving a purified inner life depended not on a single, decisive moment of repentance and self-abnegation but on progressive religious illumination and the continual pursuit of Christian character. Unitarian George Putnam refuted the notion of a once-and-for-all conversion experience: "The true religious life of the soul is a series of changes—new and repeated accessions of religious light; the vision enlarged, the aim raised, the spirit renewed from time to time."[48] Liberals also emphasized that salvation lay not in *believing* that Jesus had died for one's sins, but in *doing* as Jesus had taught. As Worcester Unitarian Aaron Bancroft reminded his congregation, in a sermon that began with the text, "Work out your own salvation with fear and trembling [. . .]" (Phil. 2:12–13), Jesus had "left traces of his footsteps, that you might follow him to the gate of heaven."[49] Liberal preaching sought to inculcate the piety that would sustain and guide the faithful on this heavenly pilgrimage.

Although liberal preaching rejected the "new birth" model in favor of cultivating ongoing spiritual improvement, it resembled conservative preaching in its attempts to prompt individual contrition. Rather than reminding listeners of how they were inherently flawed or had transgressed God's laws, it sought to arouse their consciences. Daniel Walker Howe has traced the importance of conscience for Unitarians, who regarded it as the highest of the human faculties, the one that could not be "indulged excessively." Unitarians often centered preaching around this idea, reminding the most wayward listeners that they had an innate moral sense, "quickening" the consciences of others so that they could see the fine points of moral behavior, and showing all how they could fulfill their daily moral obligations.[50] An article in the *Christian Register* rebuked those who shunned the challenging, conscience-awakening sermons that might prompt real "*regeneration*": a deep reformation not of action alone, "but also and above all [of] the habits of thought and feeling, the sentiments, the principles, the motives of conduct." The preacher's task was to prompt transformations of character—to cause hearers "to perceive, and feel, and confess to themselves, that they are not what they ought to be and might be." In effect, the article called for preaching to create a distinctively liberal experience of humiliation—a sense of dissatisfaction with oneself that faintly echoed the agonizing evangelical experience of "conviction of sin." After creating this kinder, gentler conviction, preaching was to show listeners how to sanctify themselves through prayer and self-discipline.[51] Focused on this process of sanctification as a form of redemption in and of itself, liberals had much less to say than conservatives about rewards in the afterlife.[52]

Ideals of pulpit performance

Regardless of message, the antebellum sermon derived a great deal of its authority from the performance of the preacher—how he used his eyes, hands, body, and voice to carry his hearers through the hour. Ministers played their living presence as a trump card against the books, newspapers, journals, and other printed materials that competed for a congregation's attention, declaring, "The press cannot be a substitute for the pulpit; no institution can supersede the necessity of preaching," and "Nature demands the presence, the sympathy, the eye, the voice, the action, the expressive countenance of the living teacher."[53] Ministers, especially conservatives, called attention to the uniqueness and value inherent in preaching by bemoaning the chasm between the sermon as document and the sermon as event.[54] Spring, for example, dedicated a chapter in *The Power of the Pulpit* to extolling the superiority of the "living teacher" over the printed page, stressing that the preacher's "vividness of voice and gesture often tells even more than his words" and that the preacher's "warm heart and glowing lips" appealed far more powerfully to reason, to conscience, and to the passions than did print on paper. He described his sense of dissatisfaction in being able only to read eighteenth-century sermons:

> When you *read* the discourses of Whitfield [*sic*], you can scarcely be persuaded that he was the prince of preachers; and that the author of those printed pages was the man who collected 20,000 hearers on the open field at Leeds; who fascinated all ranks of society; who held Hume in profound admiration; and who brought the infidel Chesterfield to his feet, with outstretched arms, to rescue the wanderer from the fold of God [. . .]. You read his sermons, but the *preacher* is not there. That glance of his piercing eye that hushed thousands to silence in the open field, is not there. That voice, at a single intonation of which a whole audience has been known to burst into tears, is not there. That instant communication between the living speaker and his hearers, which creates so powerful a sympathy, is not there.[55]

More than simply a paean to Whitefield or to the power of the performed sermon, Spring captured how preaching could draw its appeal from its status as communal event, when a listener joined "all ranks" in hearing and responding to the preacher's voice.[56]

In praising the living preacher so highly, ministers betrayed their anxiety about the ephemerality of their work. When, for instance, Congregationalist minister and Andover theology professor Edwards Park claimed, "[I]f the sermons preached in our land during a single year were all printed, they would fill a hundred and twenty million octavo pages," he seemed to be straining to make the nation's preaching a visible, tangible good.[57] Calvin

Stowe, a professor of sacred literature at Andover and the husband of Harriet Beecher Stowe, lamented the sermon's ephemerality in unusually pointed terms. Looking over the sermons of the late Congregationalist minister Moses Stuart, Stowe mourned their inability to represent the man at his best. They lacked the "kindling enthusiasm" that marked his spoken sermons, while abounding in the traces of orality that weigh down a book: "the digressions, the repetitions, the egotisms, the general want of compactness, which give vivacity to a lecture, rather deaden the impression of a book." All too accurately he predicted that Stuart's printed sermons would not outlive the man himself.[58]

Although much about preaching is inevitably lost to us, ministerial writings reveal many of the qualities considered essential to good preaching. Rule one was sincerity, or the idea that preaching should reflect the minister's piety. It was axiomatic that one could deliver convincing, inspiring sermons only if one believed one's own message deeply. Good preaching welled forth from personal religious experience, especially prayer. Sermons found their source in, as conservatives put it, "lifting up [one's] heart to God," "constant communion with God," and "living continually in the light of the burning throne."[59] Or as Humphrey misquoted Luther, *Bene orasse est bene precasse*— to have prayed well is to have preached well.[60] An 1833 pamphlet, originally printed as an article in the *Quarterly Christian Spectator*, elaborated on this idea by listing the fourteen pious sentiments all preachers needed, from a "peculiar sensibility to the honor of God, and a desire for His glory, so strong as to amount to a RULING PASSION," to a sense of personal responsibility for converting sinners.[61] Regardless of denomination, ministers were supposed to feel their theological principles wholeheartedly.

But what if it came time to preach and a minister did not feel especially pious? The idea seems to have been virtually unspeakable in the antebellum period, but in a question-and-answer session following one of Henry Ward Beecher's lectures on preaching in the early 1870s, one man asked this question. At first Beecher dished out the standard homiletic wisdom: that any minister who could not work up enthusiasm for the gospel should find another line of work. He then conceded that sometimes his own father would preach louder when his heart flagged, reporting (with, one suspects, a certain oedipal glee) that Lyman had once told him, albeit in self-rebuke, "I always holloa when I have n't anything to say!" Henry Ward told the questioner that just as you should give to charity in order to feel more charitable, so you should "act as though you had the feeling, even if you had not, for its effect in carrying your audience whither you wish to carry them."[62] If you don't feel it, fake it.

Piety, or the appearance thereof, was considered a *sine qua non* for good preaching but was by itself insufficient. The minister was also expected to draw upon more personal interests and feelings—something closer to the gritty, half-conscious selfhood we call authenticity. Addressing the Pastoral Association of Massachusetts, Presbyterian minister and Williams College president Edward Griffin advised against choosing subjects simply because they seemed popular or striking: "Consult your own joys or trials or necessities to know what to say and in what order. Copy your own heart and views. These are the most interesting sermons. Here heart answers to heart."[63] This was the Romantic sensibility in full flower: to engage hearers, a minister must reveal some intimate aspect of himself—his "heart and views." Similarly, Henry Ware, Jr. counseled that a minister should "choose topics on which his own mind is kindling with a feeling which he is earnest to communicate," and that "the most efficient speaker is he who throws his own soul into his eloquence."[64] Arguing for an even deeper personal investment in preaching, Dewey admonished, "*Self-study is the secret of preaching.*" He elaborated, "From the toiling brain and the beating heart, from the springs of original meditation, and from the fountain of tears, must every sermon be drawn."[65] Or as one old salt who went to hear Father Taylor opined, "'What I likes along o'preachin' [is] when a man is a-preachin' at me I want him to take somert hot out of his heart and shove it into mine,—that's what I calls preachin'.'"[66] Across denominations, the sermon was idealized as a personal, autobiographical utterance.

The desire for preaching that seemed to display the minister's private feeling helped drive the rise of extemporaneous preaching, perhaps the most important development in Protestant preaching in the first half of the nineteenth century. Traditionally, the denominations that insisted upon an educated ministry, such as Congregationalists, Episcopalians, and Presbyterians, produced ministers who wrote sermons during the week and read them from the pulpit on Sundays. To compose a sermon with care was to respect the sacred office and one's hearers, as well as to enlighten the congregation with one's erudition. But as the evangelical denominations that flourished during the Second Great Awakening increasingly drew in listeners with ministers who spoke not from a manuscript but "from the heart," even preachers in the more staid denominations began to set aside their written discourses in favor of outlines, notes, and mental rehearsals.[67]

One of the most influential calls to extemporaneity in nineteenth-century America was Henry Ware, Jr.'s *Hints on Extemporaneous Preaching* (1824), a slim volume widely cited by both liberals and conservatives.[68] Well before Emerson critiqued Unitarianism as "corpse-cold" in 1846, Ware decried the "constrained, cold, formal, scholastic mode of address" common in New England churches, the "cold reading" of sermons, and the "coolly" written discourse. What was needed instead was warmth: the "free, flowing, animated utterance" that pours forth from the heart "warm with love" and the spirit that is "warm and stirring" with joy, peace, faith, and hope.[69] A minister could achieve this warmth through a new method of sermon preparation. He was to choose a topic that mattered to him, study it, meditate on it, turn it over in the back of his mind during conversation, finish preparing by taking an hour to pull his thoughts together (though such efficiency took practice, Ware warned), and, once in the pulpit, speak with such single-minded focus that he forgot himself and was propelled forward by the current of his thought. Such extemporaneity produced a unique sympathy between a minister and his hearers—"a direct passage from heart to heart"—and a more kinetic, mesmerizing performance than manuscript reading:

> There is more natural warmth in the declamation, more earnestness in the address, greater animation in the manner, more of the lighting up of the soul in the countenance and whole mien, more freedom and meaning in the gesture; the eye speaks, and the fingers speak, and when the orator is so excited as to forget every thing but the matter on which his mind and feelings are acting, the whole body is affected, and helps to propagate his emotions to the hearer.[70]

Ware's breathless periodic sentences mimic the energy of the extemporaneous preacher in action, whose passionate delivery of his sermon transmits the religious affections directly to his hearers. Content here matters less than the sheer spectacle of the exemplary man of faith in the pulpit—the excited preacher's lit soul, free gesture, speaking eyes and fingers.

Not every minister was eager to try this experiment, and Ware deftly parried the objections of those reluctant to stand before their congregations unshielded by a manuscript. To those who protested that extemporaneous preaching promoted inaccuracies, he extolled the incomparable value of impassioned expression. To those who said it led to vague declamation, he distinguished between an extemporaneous sermon and an unpremeditated one and maintained the necessity of writing periodically to sharpen one's mental discipline. To demurrals that not everyone was suited to extemporaneous preaching, he urged practice and more practice. His title page quoted Quinctilian: "*Maximus vero studiorum fructus est, et velut præmium quoddam amplissimum longi laboris, ex tempore dicendi facultas,*" or, "To speak well extemporaneously is truly the fruit of great study and ample labor." To those who complained that extemporaneity disallowed close reasoning, he argued that since few of a minister's hearers were "thinkers or readers," they should not be addressed with rigorous argumentation they were disinclined or unable to follow. Even educated hearers, he said, would sleep through a scholarly discourse presented from the pulpit since they could find better material of that sort in books. Moreover, extemporaneity could actually improve the sermon's intellectual quality, as the situation of facing an audience from the pulpit forced a minister to think more clearly and creatively than he could in his study. As the preacher tried to impress his point upon his audience, apt illustrations and metaphors would flash upon his mind. Citing the French homiletician François Fénelon, Ware wrote that a speaker carried along with his discourse experienced "new views of a subject, new illustrations, and unthought of figures and arguments" that probably never would have occurred to him in his study.[71]

One of the most fascinating aspects of *Hints* is how Ware made his case by acknowledging—and stoking—ministers' fear of public humiliation. Allusions to this fear constitute a subtle, recurrent motif of *Hints*. Every preacher put himself and his authority on the line when he rose to address an audience, and a manuscript at least ensured the smooth flow of speech. If it risked putting hearers to sleep, it was a reliable hedge against pulpit catastrophe. Ware granted that preaching was an intimidating rhetorical situation, in which "the solemn stillness and fixed gaze of a waiting multitude, serve rather to appal [*sic*] and abash the solitary speaker." He assured readers that many ministers succeeded in preaching extemporaneously only after long struggle and "mortifying failures." He sketched, too, in Gothic detail, the horrifying prospect of that experience a later generation would call stage-fright: "the distress which attends the loss of self-possession, which distorts every feature with agony, and distils in sweat from his forehead"—or, yet more vividly, "that incubus, which sits on every faculty of the soul, and palsies every power, and fastens down the helpless sufferer to the very evil from which he strives to flee."[72] A Methodist might war against Satan in the pulpit; for Ware, the real demon a minister battled was his paralyzing fear of his audience. The only solution lay within, in single-minded concentration on one's message.

Ware then turned the tables by warning ministers that they risked public humiliation if they did *not* preach extemporaneously. There might be occasions, he said, when "the want of this power may expose him to mortification." Funerals, baptisms, Sunday mornings when public events demanded a last-minute topical sermon—all called for an ability to preach on short notice. Developing facility in extemporaneous preaching was worthwhile if it allowed one to avoid even once the "mortification of being silent when he ought to speak, is expected to speak, and would do good by speaking." He further warned of the embarrassment that came from writing a sermon and yet, despite time-consuming preparation, still making a poor showing in the pulpit. A preacher armed only with notes might on occasion limp through a sermon with "discomfort and chagrin," but many manuscript preachers gave similarly disappointing performances with the "additional mortification of having spent a larger time" preparing them.[73] Ware's obsessive recurrence to ministerial "mortification"—that embarrassment so intense it feels like death itself—indexes the anxiety that haunted the preacher's seemingly routine performance of authority.

Over time, nineteenth-century homiletic literature increasingly endorsed extemporaneity, as churchgoers typically preferred to hear ministers speak than read.[74] One of the most prominent advocates of extemporaneity after Ware was revivalist Charles Finney, who cautioned that the "evil" of preaching from manuscript lay in how it fastened the minister's eyes to the page, preventing him from gauging his audience's response. By watching his hearers for signs of comprehension, a preacher could repeat his point through additional examples and explanations "until even the children understand it perfectly." Like Ware, Finney stressed that the key to successful extemporaneous preaching lay in feeling one's message deeply and that, however initially daunting, addressing a congregation without a manuscript was a skill that could be acquired through training and practice. Unlike some of his peers, he saw no need for preachers to write sermons for the sake of training their minds. Writing, he claimed, was mere "mechanical labor" that impeded actual reasoning, and a written sermon was a schoolboy exercise with nothing to recommend it. Only extemporaneous preaching could capture the crucial affective dimension of Christian teaching: "We can never have the *full meaning* of the gospel, till we throw away our notes."[75] The minister who, shackled by a manuscript, could not communicate that the gospel *felt* like good news had failed in his mission.

Few ministers rowed against the tide by opposing extemporaneous preaching. Humphrey offered one of the more sustained defenses of manuscript sermons, arguing that it instructed listeners, rather than simply moving them, and insisting that the preaching style that worked best in Arkansas or Missouri was not necessarily the one best suited for New England or New York, or what would work best in Arkansas or Missouri fifty years hence. Better-educated audiences deserved more closely reasoned sermons.[76] Such objections may have held some truth, but they also masked anxiety about how extemporaneous preaching might corrode the ministerial profession. "Not one minister in fifty," Humphrey said, "becomes so able a theologian as

if he had accustomed himself to preach, part of the time at least, from manuscript." Losing theological rigor, which even supporters of extemporaneity
agreed came with abandoning sermon-writing, meant losing the intellectu-
ality and erudition that had long been a cornerstone of ministerial identity
and status. Another minister with a good word for manuscript preaching was
Henry Ripley, Professor of Sacred Rhetoric and Pastoral Duties at Newton
Theological Institution, whose influential textbook, *Sacred Rhetoric,* maintained that ministers should gain proficiency in both manuscript and extemporaneous preaching, as writing would make a minister more precise and
thoughtful; extemporaneity, more familiar and direct.[77] Ideally the minister
who preferred a manuscript would know his text well enough that he would
be able to extemporize once the discourse was underway.

The shift toward extemporaneity also troubled ministers who worried
that the practice would encourage them and their colleagues to work less and
thus be less professionally respectable. Whereas those who favored extemporaneity pointed to the time this method freed for study, Humphrey objected
that *"every man is as lazy as he can be,"* and that ministers who did not write
their sermons were bound to procrastinate in their sermon preparation.
Similar anxieties surface in *Hints in Preaching without Reading,* a Presbyterian pamphlet that followed up on the General Assembly's 1841 resolution
that ministers should no longer read sermons from the pulpit. Extemporaneity did not mean that ministers should *"indulge themselves in loose extemporaneous harangues, nor serve God with that which cost them naught* [. . .] for
our church in every age has insisted upon a careful, even *laborious* preparation." Committed to a vocation of "constant and unremitted labor," ministers were to spend just as long preparing their Sunday sermons even as they
shifted from reading manuscripts to preaching from notes.[78]

Whether a minister extemporized, read, or mingled the two modes, he
had to perform his message with body and voice. One of the most comprehensive guides to sermon delivery was William Russell's *Pulpit Elocution*
(1846). This volume stressed that the preacher should move freely and naturally, with the "whole bodily frame" expressing his thoughts and feelings.
Certain core principles should guide his movements, including *force,* since
nothing was more contemptible in the pulpit than weakness; *freedom,* or ease
and self-possession; and *adaptation,* or a congruence between the meaning
of one's words and the gestures and movements accompanying their delivery.
More specifically, the preacher should stand up straight and well-balanced,
ideally with his feet at a forty-five degree angle to each other, one slightly
in front of the other, and gesture with "free and flowing movements." He
was not to slouch, stoop, stand with feet flat on the floor, bend both knees,

keep his arms at his sides, thump with his fist, hold his hand like a knife, motion too often with his left hand, or place his hand too often on his heart when not referencing his personal feeling (Dimmesdale, take note). Regional and national peculiarities were also frowned upon as reflecting local "habit" rather than the *"perfect truth"* of nature: the French and Italians were too gestural and grimacing; the English, either too rigid or too inclined to make hammering motions; Southerners, too "oratorical"; New Englanders, too stiff and angular; and Westerners, simply "grotesque." Having studied and internalized the correct gestures and rhythms, the minister was to be, above all, unselfconscious. He was to retrain himself in private, then forget himself in the pulpit.[79]

Perhaps reluctant to draw attention to the similarities between preaching and secular oratory or, worse yet, acting, ministers seldom dwelled on such rules of gesture and movement in their sermons and textbooks. Advice to young preachers often mentioned the minister's body only to deride thinking about it as sheer egotism. Humphrey scorned the young minister whom one might see "carefully adjusting his cravat and every lock of hair," and Porter scowled that the minister's "exhibition of himself, in any form, is so inconsistent with the sacred delicacy and elevation of his work, that it rarely fails to excite disgust."[80] Ministers who deigned to allude to the preacher's body often did so rather abstractly. Sermons and textbooks praised ministerial "energy" or reminded young preachers to make eye contact.

Ministers had more to say about how one should sound in the pulpit. Listeners continued to value the combination of gravity and warmth known as *unction,* a metaphor for a holy anointing with oil that meant "deep spiritual feeling."[81] The preacher who spoke with unction projected a sense that he was *"earnest* and *affectionate"*—that he took his calling seriously and cared for his people.[82] Such was the recommended baseline tone, to be embellished at rhetorical climaxes and in the peroration with bursts of animation or heightened pathos. Preachers could strike the wrong note in many ways. One commonly criticized mode of speech was a "pulpit tone," or a solemn, soporific, or gloomy monotone—what Russell identified as a "hollow, sepulchral, morbid voice."[83] Also discouraged was yelling or any "displeasing *loudness or violence of voice,"* which could make the preacher sound like a "common crier."[84] Nor were preachers to grow angry or overly contentious as they spoke. Porter decreed that the principle of delicacy "absolutely forbids an angry, austere, or querulous manner of address," and that though such luminaries as Jonathan Edwards and George Whitefield invoked terror and the threat of divine wrath, they never did so with the "unfeeling severity of denunciation" observable in the nineteenth-century pulpit.[85] Even Finney distanced himself from a too-vitriolic style by declaring that if a minister had to preach on divisive doctrinal points, "let him BY ALL MEANS avoid a controversial *spirit and manner* of doing it."[86] Unitarians objected not only to an openly contentious style, but also to one that was merely "too confident, too dogmatical, too oracular," as such speech was perceived to betray a lack of respect for the congregation.[87] Although some preachers used a confrontational style to their advantage—Theodore Parker, for instance—mainstream preachers generally avoided sounding polemical.

Also widely frowned upon was trying to get a laugh in the pulpit. In *The Philosophy of Rhetoric* (1776), a landmark rhetoric textbook reprinted forty times in the nineteenth century and available in the United States through the 1840s, Scottish clergyman and rhetorician George Campbell cautioned that although ridicule might be an acceptable rhetorical tactic for legislators and lawyers, it was "utterly incompatible" with the seriousness of the ministerial office. Anything in a sermon that might provoke levity, jesting, or laughter amounted to "an unpardonable offence against both piety and decorum."[88] Following suit, Porter held that a "preposterous levity" degraded both the minister and his office, and Bethune explicitly denounced sarcasm, puns, quips, caricatures, "ludicrous acting of a story," and "*jocoseness* of any kind."[89] At stake was not simply ministerial dignity but also the hearers' personal piety: "Let once the boisterous laugh ring round a place of worship, and its echoes will disturb the meditations of the pious for many a long day."[90] Liberals, too, frowned on laughter in church. Unitarian F. W. P. Greenwood harrumphed, "It is unpleasant to see levity in a teacher of religion, even though he be young."[91] In the mainstream churches of the Northeast, the sermon remained a solemn event.

How to listen to sermons

"He that hath ears to hear, let him hear," Jesus concludes parables in the gospels.[92] Such succinct and enigmatic counsel was no rule for antebellum ministers eager to guide the reception of their own words. Rather, they sought to maintain the authority of the pulpit by offering pointed instruction in *how* to listen to sermons.

Above all, hearers were to take the sermon to heart. On this point and many others, conservatives followed the principles George Whitefield had laid out in "Directions How to Hear Sermons." There he had told Christians that they should listen to sermons not out of curiosity or a desire to have one's "ears entertained," but because they had a sincere longing to understand "sacred truths."[93] Representative of mid-nineteenth-century conservatives, Humphrey denounced the public's seemingly insatiable desire for sermons as a "morbid craving for excitement" and complained, "This is a bustling and *hearing,* rather than a *thinking* age. To hear, hear, hear, seems to be the all important concern, in the estimation of one half the Christians in the land. Multitudes would be glad to hear three or four discourses, every Sabbath in the year, and as many more on the intervening days of the week."[94] Humphrey argued that one should not preach three times on Sunday, no matter what the people thought they wanted. If the people heard and dwelled on the morning and afternoon sermons, it would be enough.

One bad habit ministers tried to prevent was that of applying the sermon's message to one's friend, spouse, or neighbor rather than to oneself. Whitefield had warned that when preachers were discussing a sin or urging a duty, listeners were not to search for the mote in their neighbor's eye or cry, "this was designed against such and such a one," but should rather "turn their thoughts inwardly, and say, Lord, is it I?"[95] Recycling these injunctions, a New England Tract Society reprint of British Baptist minister Robert Hall's sermon "On Hearing the Word of God" read: *"Hear the word with constant self-application.* Hear not for *others,* but for *yourselves."*[96] Finney expressed the same idea more vividly: "Beware, and *not give away all the preaching* to others. If you do not take your portion, you will starve, and become like spiritual skeletons." Alluding to Jesus' apothegm that "man shall not live by bread alone, but by every word of God," Finney told listeners they could not mentally pass along their portion of the preached word without suffering themselves.[97]

Ministers also warned listeners against apathy, which could hurt the quality of the sermon by discouraging the preacher. Nantucket Congregationalist John S. C. Abbott, Hawthorne's and Longfellow's classmate at Bowdoin, told his congregation to pay attention during the sermon, because if "lethargic fumes" filled the church, the minister "must inhale the drowsy influence." Ministers could hardly be expected to preach fervently if everyone was falling asleep.[98] A *Christian Register* writer told those who complained about their minister's "coldness" that they had to take responsibility for the problem: "As the minister is to act upon the people, so the People are to act upon the Minister [. . .]. The fire will not burn on one side, if cold water be thrown on it from the other."[99] Here the threat of a "cold" Unitarianism came not from overly intellectual sermons or ministers clinging nervously to their manuscripts, but from torpid listeners. Whatever authority a minister commanded, the people exercised power, too, in their visible engagement or inattention.

Although conservatives and liberals agreed that listeners should follow up on the sermon by meditating on its application to their lives, conservatives were more intent on protecting the preacher from post-sermon criticism. The Hall tract, for instance, told Christians that if the sermon contained substantive instruction, the listener should "overlook imperfections" of form and delivery. Hall also dissuaded listeners from meeting afterward to discuss the sermon, urging them rather to treat the message as a "treasure" they were anxious to guard.[100] The 1831 tract "On Hearing the Word" ended with a stanza from George Herbert's *The Temple:*

> Judge not the preacher; for he is thy judge.
> If thou mislike him, thou conceiv'st him not.
> God calleth preaching, folly. Do not grudge
> To pick out treasures from an earthen pot.
>   The worst speak something good. If *all* want sense,
> GOD takes a text, and preacheth patience.[101]

Even mediocre sermons contained a core of divine truth that listeners were obliged to discover, and those worse than mediocre were to be heard respectfully nonetheless. To listen critically was to treat the sermon as if it were a profane entertainment. Urging listeners to be receptive rather than evaluative, Porter explained that a critic "comes from the Sanctuary, like worldly people from a tea party or the theatre. His conversation shows that his mind has been occupied by a literary or vagrant curiosity." A sermon did no more for such superficially minded listeners than provide them with "religious small talk," which, far from edifying them, led them "to profane the Sabbath, offend God, and harden their own hearts."[102] Treating the sermon as a performance to be critiqued missed the point entirely. One nineteenth-century satirist catalogued the thirty-eight complaints a congregation had made about its minister's preaching. The preacher's sermons were too long, and too short; too loud, and too quiet; too personal, and too abstract; too focused on election, and too much on practical duties; too opposed to slavery, and not opposed enough.[103] The point: the minister could not please everyone.

Liberals were less adamant that listeners approach the sermon reverentially. Some sounded a good deal like the conservatives, as when Unitarian Samuel Osgood wrote that churchgoers should use the sermon as a "means of self-examination and worship" and not profane the sanctuary by turning it into "a theatre of flippant criticism."[104] Others, though, objected to stifling critical reflection on the sermon and framed preaching and listening as a more collaborative and democratic experience. The same *Christian Register* writer who critiqued preachers who were "too confident, too dogmatical, too oracular" maintained that not only did hearers have a "right [. . .] to form their own judgment in respect to the doctrines delivered from the pulpit as religious truth," they had the "duty" to exercise "an independent but candid judgment." Lay people should think for themselves, neither rejecting doctrines without consideration nor swallowing them whole. If a minister had a duty to preach what he, after careful consideration, believed to be the truth, so too had listeners an obligation "to give him a candid hearing, to weigh his arguments, and allow them all the influence on their hearts and lives, to which they are entitled. It is not, however, their duty to take his word, or his arguments for more than they are worth." Hearers were to try to follow the reasoning laid out in the sermon, check it against the Bible, and speak with the minister in more detail if a line of thought still seemed unconvincing.[105] Articulating the implicitly dialogical nature of the sermon in more poetic terms, Henry Bellows, pastor of the Unitarian Church of the Divine Unity in Manhattan, where the Melvilles rented a pew in 1850, said, "Truth, especially moral truth, is, of its very essence, oracular. It issues from its shrine, to find the argument that upholds it in the hearts of its hearers."[106] That is, the sermon was to be a catalyst to a hearer's own meditations. Or as Emerson put it in addressing the Harvard seniors, "Truly speaking, it is not instruction, but provocation, that I can receive from another soul."[107] Though far more skeptical of straightforward moral instruction than his erstwhile Unitarian colleagues, Emerson spoke for the liberal sense that the preacher had a responsibility to set in motion the listener's own moral reflection.

Liberal or conservative, sermons set the standard for morally and religiously authoritative discourse in antebellum America. Lacking political power, ministers claimed individual morality and religious truth as their rightful domain. As Unitarian George Burnap declared, ministerial "influence, withdrawn from secular channels, [is] only the more powerful for being confined to spiritual concerns"; ministers in the pulpit now spoke "with an authority which is conceded to no other mortal."[108] No other mode of public speech made larger claims for its own importance or insisted that hearers heed it more carefully. Yet if moral authority seemed the ministers' to lose, it was also now a privilege to be earned, since in a democratic society under religious voluntarism, preachers had to turn their theological convictions and biblical learning into compelling, pew-filling performances. This destabilization of moral authority opened up the field to other contenders, including those most unlikely of upstarts, the novelists.

CHAPTER 2

The Slow Rise of the Novel
in America

I N T H E "Reading" chapter of *Walden* (1854), Thoreau heaps contempt on novels and those who read them. Scorning the silliness of fictive love stories, he mocks "the nine thousandth tale about Zebulon and Sephronia," parodies an advertisement for a novel ("The Skip of the Tip-Toe-Hop, a Romance of the Middle Ages"), and ridicules the absorption of novel-readers: "All this they read with saucer eyes, and erect and primitive curiosity." The result of novel-reading is physical and mental dissolution: "dulness [*sic*] of sight, a stagnation of the vital circulations, and a general deliquium and sloughing off of all the intellectual faculties." Novels are mental junk food, "gingerbread" far less nourishing and more popular than the "pure wheat or rye-and-Indian" of the *Iliad* in Greek.[1]

Far from idiosyncratic and curmudgeonly, such grumblings were representative of the sentiments of many educated Americans before the Civil War who, in books telling their fellow citizens how to live, exhorted readers to shun novels for more edifying fare. This chapter surveys the evidence of more than twenty conduct books published in the United States between 1828 and 1857 to demonstrate that resistance to the novel remained strong throughout the first half of the nineteenth century, contrary to what one might expect given the emphasis in our literary historical narratives on the novel's growing popularity and cultural acceptance during this period. What is remarkable about the advice on novel-reading in these books is not the invective brandished against novels—the vivid denunciations of the genre will be familiar enough to students of eighteenth- and early nineteenth-century America—but the sheer persistence and pervasiveness of anti-novel condemnation across writers of various backgrounds addressing different audiences. Just as surprisingly, many conduct book authors frowned upon not only "novels" but fiction altogether, while those who directed their attention to novels typically treated them as a class, without discriminating among them according to national origin, literary mode, religious perspective, or didactic intent. One might imagine that the educators and moralists who penned conduct books would regard, say, a cheap reprint of a torrid French romance limning the travails of amorous aristocrats with greater disapproval than an American-authored tale about a New England miss choosing the path of true virtue, but in fact they seldom paused long enough to acknowledge a difference. Instead, they invoked centuries-old anti-fiction rhetoric with a consistency that reveals how deeply rooted anti-novel ideology was in nineteenth-century American culture. With this resistance in mind, we can perceive more clearly the challenge nineteenth-century American novelists faced—how they made their bids for moral authority from within a culture that was only grudgingly beginning to grant fiction respectability.

This chapter is thus intended as something of a reminder, an attempt to resurrect and reinforce the half-forgotten story of nineteenth-century Americans' distrust of the novel. Terence Martin has shown that between 1800 and 1820, the influence of Scottish Common Sense philosophy on an already moralistic culture led to strong prohibitions against fiction. Accepting the metaphysical assumptions of thinkers like Dugald Stewart, Thomas Reid, and Hugh Blair, Americans distinguished between the worlds of "actuality" and "possibility," associating the former with knowledge, maturity, and life in the world and the latter with imagination, childhood, and irrelevance. In this schema, fiction, as a product of the imagination, lacked positive value for adults. At worst, it was a threat to morals; at best, if indulged in moderation, a harmless diversion.[2] Building on Martin's work, Michael Davitt Bell has pointed to the continuing prevalence of Common Sense philosophy in college curricula to make a point that is essentially the one this chapter underscores and elaborates: that for the first half of the nineteenth century, "conventional opinion" condemned fiction as "deeply dangerous, psychologically threatening, and even socially subversive" and that Charles Brockden Brown, Washington Irving, Edgar Allan Poe, Hawthorne, and Melville wrote in an environment hostile to the romance, a "climate in which the fictionality of fiction was accentuated and condemned."[3] Corroborating this observation, Ronald Zboray has explained how a "popular positivism" and concern for "self-culture" in the period steered readers, especially those in

the working class, away from fiction and toward facts and "useful knowledge": "Everywhere in America a person who wished to read fiction had to
overcome significant institutional, religious, and cultural discouragements
to it."[4] Yet scholars since Bell and Zboray who have called attention to antebellum anti-fiction discourse have tended to cast it as peculiarly Protestant,
without acknowledging that it was culturally representative or noting its circulation among non-religious writers as well. Such is the case with David
Paul Nord, who describes the anti-novel polemic of the American Tract
Society; Candy Gunther Brown, who explains how mid-nineteenth-century
evangelicals continued to question whether even religious novels were moral;
and Paul Gutjahr, who traces the contentious relationship of Protestants to
fiction from the mid-nineteenth century forward to show that many Protestants disapproved of novels until the last quarter of the twentieth century.[5]
Considering both religious and secular perspectives, Barbara Hochman has
demonstrated in her examination of attitudes toward fiction in the United
States between 1870 and 1920 that "[u]ntil well into the twentieth century
fiction-reading was an extremely popular but still contested social practice."
She cites to good purpose Roger Chartier's wry observation that "the novel,
like the bourgeoisie, always seems to be rising."[6]

Despite the scholarship showing that hostility toward novels persisted
throughout the nineteenth century, awareness of antebellum anti-novel discourse has been imperfectly integrated into our literary histories, with many
continuing to reinforce the idea that the middle of the century witnessed
the "The Triumph of the Novel," per the second chapter of Nina Baym's
influential *Novels, Readers, and Reviewers: Responses to Fiction in Antebellum America.*[7] Invocation of this rather too-celebratory idea tends to find
its justification in three major trends of the antebellum period: the growing
acceptance of novels and praise for their virtues in periodical reviews, which
Baym details; the novel's burgeoning popularity; and the rise of religious fiction. Although each indicator provides a useful picture of the novel's fortunes
at mid-century, each also has significant limitations, revealing the necessity
of charting the novel's status through a diversity of measures.

One of the most influential arguments for the novel's mid-century victory
comes from Baym's "Triumph of the Novel" chapter. Analyzing hundreds of
book reviews published between 1840 and 1860 in major periodicals, Baym
shows that reviewers increasingly spoke favorably of the novel as a genre during this period and that by 1850, the sophisticated vocabulary available for
reviewing novels signaled that "the novel had entered the world of intellectual discourse."[8] Baym's study also demonstrates that by mid-century reviewers had stopped criticizing the novel as inherently corrupt and that only

one of the twenty-one magazines surveyed, the Methodist *Ladies' Repository,* regularly denigrated the genre as such. Working from a similar archive, James Machor has argued that distrust of novels "gave way in the antebellum era to a public recognition—manifested and conducted most volubly in the periodical press—that Americans were devoting increasing amounts of time to fiction reading."[9] Machor's framing of the reviewers' shift in attitude as one from "distrust" to a "recognition" of readers' habits points, as he discusses, to the reviews' continuing moralism; though no longer condemning fiction, reviewers still read for a story's overall moral effect.[10] Although Machor may well be correct in his larger point that reviewers were a significant influence on middle-class conventions of reading fiction (though Ronald and Mary Zborays' work on reader response to fiction has challenged this claim), we should be skeptical of the idea that periodicals were the only important public commentators on the novel, or that "they formed an interpretive community whose assumptions constituted *the* public forum for the reading and writing of fiction in early-nineteenth-century America" (my emphasis).[11] Periodicals may have offered the most specific guidance in *how* to read fiction, but they were not the only significant public voices commenting on fiction or shaping attitudes toward it. We should not forget that magazine essays represented not a neutral public discourse but the viewpoint of an industry with an economic stake in respecting fiction. Many periodicals used fiction or reviews of fiction to fill their pages, and a few belonged to publishing houses that also brought novels to market.[12] As G. Harrison Orians pointed out years ago, the chance to gain readers by running fiction gave reviewers and editors an incentive to proclaim its virtues or at least not denigrate it, resulting in "considerable liberalism in the magazines and news-sheets" when it came to reviewing fiction.[13] Also worth remembering are the social and professional networks that created reciprocal relationships among editors and reviewers across the publishing industry. If reviewers formed an "interpretive community" whose work functioned as a "corporate and communal" endorsement of fiction, these shared values were perhaps due less to a general shift in cultural attitudes than to the strength of these industry-specific networks and the desire to procure favor and avoid giving offense within them.[14] As Lara Cohen discusses, an endemic "puffing" system, in which favorable reviews could be bought for complimentary copies, favorable reviews in exchange, or outright cash unsettles the idealized notion—first promulgated by the antebellum publishing industry itself—that the period's literary criticism exemplified a noncommercial, democratic public sphere. Widespread puffery demonstrates "that the proliferation of print did not guarantee the democratization of print culture"; canny operators, including authors who went so far as to adopt a third-person stance to review their own books, could and did achieve great influence behind the scenes.[15] In short, for all the value that periodical reviews have in suggesting an evolving public discourse around the novel, they should not be read as a metonym for the culture as a whole.

An equally common measure of the novel's ascendancy at mid-century is its popularity: novel publication and novel-reading were both surging. John Austin has shown that the number of fiction titles that were either bestsellers or, in Frank Luther Mott's term, "better sellers," skyrocketed between 1820 and 1850. He also demonstrates that fiction grew longer in this period, with novel-length works edging out short- and medium-length stories.[16] That is, the period saw a concurrent rise in fiction's popularity relative to other genres and in the length of that fiction, with works increasingly looking like those longer, more involved fictions we today call novels, whether they were titled tales, legends, romances, or novels. Further quantitative evidence comes from the charge records of the New York Society Library from the years around 1850; analyzing these records, Ronald Zboray has shown that between 1847 and 1849, novels accounted for only 21 percent of the total books charged, but that for the years between 1854 and 1856, this figure rose to 45 percent.[17] The Zborays have also documented the explosion during the antebellum period of American fiction, as opposed to European reprints, reporting that the two decades between 1837 and 1857 saw "at least 2,305 new American-authored fiction titles in book form."[18]

It is thus undeniable that Americans were reading more fiction in this period, but we should not conflate popularity with cultural authority or assume that because many more people were reading novels that these books also enjoyed cultural respectability or were widely esteemed as having moral value. Evidence from the diaries of antebellum readers suggests that it was not unusual to enjoy novels yet feel ambivalent about doing so, just as someone today might indulge in a television program or video game as a guilty pleasure. Indeed, as Mary Kelley has suggested, the prohibitions against fiction may have increased its allure.[19] The Zborays relate how one woman writing in 1833 lamented staying up late to read Maria Edgeworth's *Belinda*: "'[W]ith exceeding foolishness again read Belinda, a thing that does me no possible good,'" and how a New Haven schoolteacher journaling in 1849 described locking herself in her room to finish Fredrika Bremer's *The Neighbors*—"'and long I read, and leaf after leaf I turned [. . .] till I was almost spellbound'"—only to berate herself the next morning for her binge: "'I'll never read again till I learn to control myself.'"[20] Similarly remorseful was a young woman in North Carolina who, as Kelley reports, wrote in her diary,

"'I have again for the first time in three or four years (I believe) been guilty of reading a *Novel*.'" Kelley remarks that the woman's expressions of regret "read almost as conventions, as acknowledgments made with little or no conviction" and reflect "less the power of proscription than the nearly irresistible appeal of the novel."[21] But too hastily declaring the novel—and the autonomous female reader—the winner of this conflict distorts the antebellum reading experience by minimizing the internalized censure that coexisted with pleasure. Indeed, the fact that the young woman had not succumbed to novel-reading in three or four years suggests that the novel's appeal was less irresistible than we might like to think, and the desire to respect cultural prohibitions stronger.

Finally, growing cultural acceptance of fiction in this period is often inferred from the proliferation of religious fiction—Unitarian novels like Catharine Sedgwick's *A New-England Tale* (1822), Calvinist ones like Sara Ann Evans's *Resignation* (1825), and evangelical blockbusters like Susan Warner's *The Wide, Wide World* (1850) and Maria Cummins's *The Lamplighter* (1854).[22] The publication and popularity of such novels point to changing cultural attitudes but do not translate into a general sanction for reading fiction. Discussing the continued Protestant resistance to fiction at mid-century, Gutjahr notes not only the influence of Common Sense philosophy but also the beliefs that fiction "inflamed the imagination and thus the passions" and that it leeched time from Bible-reading and devotional practice. Brown shows that some evangelicals objected to Christian novels because they led to more dangerous fictions and consumed "time, money, and energy that should have been invested in an urgent struggle against the forces of evil."[23] And Nord adds that antebellum Protestants objected to fiction "precisely because it was false," which one might read as an internalization of Common Sense philosophy or as the legacy of the Puritan distrust of the imagination, or both.[24] As I discuss below, few conduct books of this period even mentioned the existence of religious novels.

Our drive to create a unified literary historical narrative for the novel should not deafen us to the conflicting discourses that surrounded it at mid-century. If, as Hochman has shown, the novel's rise was "uneven" at the end of the century, hampered by continuing suspicions about the genre's value, it was even more so fifty years earlier. In mid-nineteenth-century conduct books we find a much less liberal perspective on novel-reading than the periodical reviews Baym discusses, yet one no less essential for our understanding of the novel's cultural position.[25] An ancestor of that now-popular genre "self-help," conduct books were written to provide young men and women with moral and practical guidance on subjects related to assum-

ing the responsibilities of adulthood, such as managing one's time, living a
faithful Christian life, staying healthy, cultivating appropriate friendships,
adjusting to the duties of marriage, and choosing one's reading material
wisely. Distinct from etiquette books, conduct books served "an almost
anthropological function by codifying society's idealized expectations
in regard to proper behavior in life, as opposed to behavior in society."[26]
They are a particularly valuable source for understanding the novel's cultural position in that they provide insight into middle-class values.[27] That
the period's conduct book authors were, as the historian Isabel Lehuu has
written, generally "white, middle-class, educated New Englanders, affiliated with various Protestant denominations and often supporters of Whig
doctrine," might seem to limit their representativeness, but these identity
markers also indicate the extent to which they wrote from a socially and
economically dominant position invested with the power to define cultural respectability.[28] Of diverse professional identities, these authors were
reformers, journalists, educators, physicians, women writers, and clergymen.[29] The ministry was the best represented profession among conduct
book authors, but we should not take this fact to mean that their views
were narrowly religious and thus marginal to a public discourse assumed
to be secular. The ministers hailed from a variety of faiths—not only from
Methodism, often associated with a world-renouncing piety, but also from
Congregationalism, Presbyterianism, Episcopalianism, and Unitarianism.
Though theologically conservative clergy tended to be more critical of novels than liberals, even liberals treated them with skepticism. Further, these
ministers' views can be assumed to have some continuity with those of the
public, given the cultural dominance of Protestantism before the Civil War
and the fact that religious voluntarism gave ministers a good reason not to
stray too far from the cultural biases of their parishioners. Regardless of
professional affiliation, conduct book authors were at least as representative of middle-class values as the periodical editors and reviewers whom
Machor calls "avatars of the dominant culture" and exemplars of middle-
class reading practices.[30] That both of these roles, periodical reviewer and
conduct book author, assumed a stance of cultural guardianship reveals a
tension within the middle class between conservative and liberal perspectives on novel-reading. The liberal position would eventually win out, but
the conservative one was neither vestigial nor marginal.

   It is worth observing that conduct book writers had a vested interest in
discouraging novel-reading, just as periodical reviewers did in encouraging
it. The very act of writing a conduct book might be said to prejudice one
against novels insofar as novels were potential rivals in the attempt to shape
behavior and values. Though conduct book authors did not condescend to

acknowledge this rivalry, they could hardly help realizing the new cultural role of a great deal of antebellum fiction, which was, as Richard Brodhead has argued, to enact a form of parental guidance—to be "another monitory intimate, another agent of discipline through love."[31] Clerical authors of conduct books may have felt an even stronger sense of competition with novels, fearing that Americans would turn to moral and uplifting stories rather than to their ministers for spiritual guidance. They may also have perceived the form itself as an agent of secularism, since, as William Warner has written, novels furthered the desanctification of books through their disposability, ephemerality, anonymity, and commodification.[32] This desanctification devalued not only the Bible but also religious literature such as devotional manuals and printed sermons. Ministers may also have resented the novel as a competitor for Americans' precious Sunday leisure hours. One can read this rivalry at work in Methodist minister Daniel Smith's alarmist anti-fiction rhetoric in *Lectures to Young Men* (1852). Warning readers about the spiritual perils of staying at home with a novel on Sunday afternoon, when one was supposed to be at church for the second service, Smith related an anecdote—a dialogue-heavy, suspense-driven one, naturally—in which a young man accompanies his friends to church one Sunday and, though he starts listening with no particular interest in spiritual things, takes a growing interest in the sermon. He feels as never before an "immediate duty to turn to God." But then, fatally, he remembers the novel he has not finished reading. Looking back on this moment, the young man wails:

> What came between me and my God? Am I not giving the history of many, when I say it was the fascinations of a novel? I had been reading one the previous day, and had left it with an earnest desire to know the close. I had indulged myself in novel-reading until it had become a passion—until almost everything else was forgotten for its pleasures. And now, as the sermon closed, the thought of that story rose before me. Shall I read it? was the mental question. I knew that, if on my return home I turned to its pages, every religious impression would be obliterated; and during all the closing prayer, during all my walk home, the struggle was going on—and the novel conquered. The voice of the Spirit was silenced.[33]

Here the desire to resolve narrative suspense is an all-consuming lust at odds with spiritual concerns. Not far beneath the surface lies the conflict between the novel and the minister—one the minister loses when the young man's urge to keep reading drowns out the altar call.

Another point worth clarifying about antebellum conduct books is that they discouraged young *men* as well as women from reading novels.[34] To be sure, cautions about the perils of novel-reading were more often directed toward women, who were presumed to have more leisure time for reading fiction and less inclination for more serious works, such as the oft-recommended biographies, histories, essays, and travels. But young men were not given a pass when it came to pleasure reading. Conduct book authors admonished young men to abjure reading fiction or, at the very least, to keep this addiction-producing tendency in check. Such warnings reflect the fact that both men and women were avid novel readers, as suggested by the subscription lists of such fiction-intensive periodicals as the *Southern Literary Messenger* or by the New York Society Library records, which show that between 1854 and 1856, novels constituted 46 percent of the books men charged and 44 percent of the books women charged.[35] The anti-novel rhetoric that conduct books directed at men reinforced their emphasis on the cultural model of masculinity Sarah Newton has called the Christian Achiever ideal. This ideal encompassed both the Franklinian values necessary for success in the new capitalistic system—self-discipline, ambition, energy, industriousness, and an unceasing sense of purpose—and traditional Christian values like compassion, kindness, and integrity.[36] On occasion, conduct books for men even couched their anti-novel rhetoric in gendered terms. In *The Young Husband* (1840), William Andrus Alcott, a physician, reformer, and one of the leading conduct book writers of the age, exhorted readers, "Let us then— especially those of us who are heads of families, or who are destined to be such—resolve to encourage narrative, biography, travels and voyages, manners and customs, &c., and let alone fiction."[37] In most antebellum conduct books for men, as for women, the life well lived included little to no time for reading novels.

Below I first outline the conduct books' most common objections to novels, distinguishing when necessary between those critiques set forth by most conduct book authors and those specific to the Methodists, fiction's harshest critics. I then analyze a few examples of an emergent pro-novel rhetoric, often guarded and self-contradictory, in which conduct book authors struggled to articulate how the novel might have a unique, genre-specific social value.

The case against novels

The most vivid denunciations of novel-reading incorporated metaphors that had been a staple of anti-novel discourse for centuries. Like Thoreau disparaging novels as "gingerbread," many conduct book authors likened novels to unhealthy food. Unitarian minister George Burnap warned young men in 1840 that as with all "dainties," one should indulge in novels only sparingly. They were "sweetmeats," and anyone who spent day after day reading them would "soon be overtaken with nausea, sickness, and disgust."[38] William Greenleaf Eliot, a Unitarian minister and the founder of Washington University in St. Louis, warned young men that novels could no more fortify the mind than "sweetmeats and confectionery" could strengthen the body. Acceptable as "occasional refreshment," they were "absolutely pernicious" as daily food.[39] Women received similar dietary counsel. Though one might expect the independent-minded women's rights activist, abolitionist, and pioneering journalist Jane Grey Swisshelm to adopt a liberal attitude toward women's reading material, she cautioned young women in *Letters to Country Girls* (1853), a book based on her advice column in her *Pittsburg Saturday Visiter* [*sic*] in the late 1840s and 1850s, that "[r]eading for amusement hours at a stretch, is like eating for half the day together." A reader's mind was not to be a stomach but a factory, "where the raw material is taken in and improved in value."[40] Thomas Clark, Episcopal Bishop of Rhode Island, told young men and women in 1855 that they should not "glut" their immortal minds with "works of fiction," since doing so stimulated a desire for increasingly sensational stories. The habitual reader for amusement became "a gouty epicure, and the dish must be highly seasoned to stimulate his palate."[41] The more one read, the more lurid the stories one craved. Conduct book authors who compared reading to harmful and uncontrollable eating reinforced the idea that readers were "passive and somnolent, indeed [. . .] virtually mindless," as Janice Radway has written with respect to twentieth-century critics' use of metaphors of consumption to denigrate mass culture.[42] The overall effect of such rhetoric was not to advocate a balanced diet of reading that included fiction, but to argue for the superiority of abstinence, since it was ultimately the "food" that was in control, not the eater.

Comparisons of novels to food often sat alongside more sensational language equating them with alcohol and condemning them with temperance rhetoric.[43] John Todd, a Congregationalist minister and outspoken abolitionist, wrote in *The Daughter at School* (1854) that his reply to a young lady who asked how many novels she could read would be that of the physician whose patient asked how much brandy he could drink: "'a little won't hurt you much, but none at all won't hurt you any.'" Where "novels and romances" were concerned, his readers' mantra should be "touch not, taste not, handle not."[44] Similarly, Swisshelm sought to lessen fiction's appeal for young women by telling them that to spend half the day reading a novel was "like eating opium, or drinking brandy; for it is practiced just for excitement, and to kill time."[45] Even Sedgwick, one of the nation's most popular and respected novelists, could write in *Means and Ends; Or, Self-Training* (1839) that reading "*poor novels*" was like trying to live on "bar-room cordials, water-gruel, and rehashed hashes." Further, she warned that the "captivation" of *all* fiction "should put you on your guard, my young friends, and teach you that temperance, if not abstinence, is your duty."[46]

For a few critics, most of whom belonged to theologically conservative religious traditions, comparisons of fiction to sweetmeats, brandy, and opium did not go far enough. These writers summoned the language of poisoning, pica, necrophagia, and pollution to warn the young away from fiction's corrupting influence. Some used this rhetoric incidentally, as when Clark, bemoaning the popularity of "works of mere amusement," fretted that young people were increasingly "fed with nothing but this innutritious and perhaps poisonous aliment."[47] Others were more pointed. Southerner Virginia Cary, for instance, offered a gruesome variation on the theme of novel-reading as gluttony when she compared those who consumed "the garbage of the circulating libraries" to corpse-devouring monsters: "A mind that can take pleasure in the trash of silly novels, which may be raked from the charnel houses of literature, deserves to be compared to the female monster in the Arabian tales, who fed upon dead bodies." A reader should resist the desire for such food as one would resist "the depraved desire to eat chalk and other unnatural food, which betokens a diseased state of the animal system."[48] Such stomach-churning images were continuous with a cultural rhetoric that associated reading novels with mental and spiritual pollution. Todd warned that just as standing outside on a lovely but damp moonlit night could kill you, so the human heart contained fibers that were "destroyed by the subtle poison drawn from novels and romances."[49] More explicit yet was Sarah Barnes's rhetoric in *A Book for the Eldest Daughter* (1849). Besides deploring novel-reading as "a most ruinous, time-wasting, heart-defiling practice," Barnes wrote of novels, "If they shine, it is only as the rotting log, or putrescent carcase, which is phosphorescent because decaying; if brilliant, it is only as the will-o'-the-wisp, which is caused by impure and fetid gases."[50] Comparing reading novels to inhaling graveyard gases may seem over-the-top, but it mirrors many other conduct book denigrations of reading as defilement—as the equivalent of handling "pitch," listening to "filthy conversation," inflicting "stains" on one's character, or wading in an "overflowing ditch."[51]

With a tenacious life of their own, the derogatory metaphors wielded to disparage novels often circulated unaccompanied by argument or justification, as if the harmfulness of novels were a self-evident truth.[52] Those authors who bothered to elaborate on the reasons for avoiding novels tended to focus on the mentally deleterious effects of imaginative writing. Margaret Coxe, principal of a female seminary in Cincinnati and author of *The Young Lady's Companion* (1839), warned young ladies that when the "habit of reading works of fiction is once fixed, the whole mental system becomes enervated; the reflective powers are permitted to remain dormant, while the imagination is unnaturally stimulated"; nothing was a "greater foe to religious or mental excellence."[53] Writing in 1853, Mrs. L. G. Abell, author of numerous nineteenth-century advice books for women, sounded a similar note: "*Novel reading* is another undue stimulus to the brain, and is often a fruitful source of evil to the mind. It weakens the mental faculties if habitually practiced, and wastes those energies of the soul in idle sympathies, that were given us for active use and benevolent effort."[54] The idea that fiction vitiated the intellect appears even in the conduct books of temperance author and literary entrepreneur Timothy Shay Arthur, the second most prolific American author of fiction in book form between 1837 and 1857, with 106 volumes of fiction to his name.[55] Any young lady who indulged a great deal in novel-reading, Arthur wrote, lacked "strength of intellect" and would never become "a woman of true intelligence."[56] He gave young men much the same advice: if novel-readers "do not actually stand still, [they] make but little advance in intellectual improvement."[57]

As part of the worry that novels turned young people's brains to jelly, cultural guardians maintained that reading novels would sap young people's desire and ability to read more instructive works. In volumes addressed to both sexes, Clark held that reading novels made more serious studies seem "dry and disagreeable"; Presbyterian minister Matthew Hale Smith, that knowing "the contents of the last novel, will not improve your minds, or impart to them vigor"; and Todd, that none could "rise up from such reading and go with pleasure to the sober duties of life, or to reading and thoughts that are rational."[58] Some conduct book authors were vexed at the thought of young adults spending their time reading novels as opposed to nonfiction. Affirming that "truth is always better than fiction," Daniel Smith asked, "Why ever spend our time in reading a poor, not to say a bad book, when we may, at the same time, be reading one of the highest order?"[59] Alcott put the argument that novels diverted readers from "better books" more pragmatically: "For—to use language which every New Englander will understand— who wishes to be always collecting cents and dimes, when he might just as well gather dollars?"[60] Novels were an investment unworthy of a young man's time.

One twist on the argument that fiction distracted young people from better reading came from Horace Mann, the pioneering education reformer,

U.S. Representative from Massachusetts from 1848 to 1852, and, through
his marriage to Mary Peabody, Nathaniel Hawthorne's brother-in-law. In a
lecture delivered to young men in Boston in 1849 and printed the next year,
Mann eschewed the typical tactic of urging his listeners to reject novels for
"rational" fare and instead tried to enhance the appeal of science by claiming
that it offered the same emotional rewards as fiction: "One thing is certain.
If men can love fiction, they can love science better. Men love fiction because
they love wonder and excitement; but nothing is more true than that truth is
more wonderful than fiction. No invention of the imagination is so exciting
as the revelations of science." Science would so supplant fiction in rousing
men's wonder, he declared, that future ages would look back on those whose
imaginations were satisfied with the *Arabian Nights* or stories of fairyland
with the pity one felt for "the savage whose highest idea of regal adornment
can be satisfied with beads of glass and jewelry of tin."[61] The metaphor resonated with the Common Sense philosophers' belief that a love of poetry and
art characterized "primitive" societies and anticipated Thoreau's derision of
novel-readers' "primitive curiosity."[62]

Despite the prevalence of the idea that fiction enervated the mind, the
seeming corollary that it inflamed the passions seems to have been rarer.
Methodist minister Daniel Wise was one of the few to invoke this hoary
notion, a variation of Plato's claim in Book X of *The Republic* that good poetry
stirred up irrepressible passions. Addressing young men, Wise described the
perils of fiction with the vividness of a seasoned storyteller. Fiction turned the
soul into a "smouldering fire" so that when the "guilty opportunity" arrived,
"The spark ignites. The soul is in a blaze of passion. The sin is committed.
The deed is done: and guilt binds its fearful burden upon the conscience,
with chains of triple steel." He pointed to Dante's depiction of the adulter-
ers Paolo and Francesca, who met their mutual ruin by reading together of
the love-struck Lancelot. Such scenes, he held, were representative of novel-
reading, and those who balked at the idea that a novel could have ill effects
were infatuated with this type of reading: "you *love* it—passionately love it!"
The charge resonates with Cathy Davidson's observation that early American advice literature imagined that the "engrossed reading of the wrong text
[was] itself a kind of seduction."[63] For evidence of the novel's threat, Wise
appealed to the experience of novel readers everywhere, who knew that such
books "*corrupt the heart, through the imagination.*"[64]

If such claims that novels led the young astray sexually were scarce by the
mid-nineteenth century, a more common argument was that novels—and
indeed, all fiction—created dissatisfaction with the actual world. Moralists
condemned fiction for distorting social and moral realities, or promoting

"false views of life," and for creating overly excitable young people, mainly women, in the process.[65] Arthur wrote that the typical female novel reader ended up disappointed with her life because, failing to find herself surrounded by the same "ideal perfections" she had read about, she received perpetual shocks to her "over-refined sensibilities."[66] Sarah Gould's *A Golden Legacy to Daughters* (1857) echoed the notion that fiction was full of airy illusions leading to overwrought nerves; Gould complained that many works on the market "with romantic titles and fascinating stories" were "full of visionary speculations and sentimentalism, which create nothing more or less than a morbid sensibility."[67] Similarly, Arthur Freeling's *Young Bride's Book* (1849) criticized fiction for inspiring a "contempt for ordinary realities" that led the young wife to neglect her husband, children, and domestic responsibilities as she pursued her unholy passion for reading fiction. Setting his sights on perverted public taste, Clark stressed that fiction could not sell

> unless every thing be made as *intense* as possible; every character, good or bad, must be exaggerated into an angel or a devil; every pathetic scene must be heartrending; every escape from peril, miraculous; every storm, a hurricane; every sunrise, the harbinger of something transcending human experience; and every nightfall, draws the curtain of darkness around transactions, harrowing beyond description.[68]

However seemingly quaint, objections to the period's fiction as lacking verisimilitude prefigured the critiques of postbellum writers who reacted to sentimentalism and sensationalism by writing fiction in a new, self-consciously realist mode.

One of the most serious charges leveled against fiction was that it interfered with the Christian life. Coxe warned her readers that if they were susceptible to fiction's charms and found themselves caught up in "vain dreams of an ideal happiness" that led them to neglect their duties, then, if they wished to follow the Savior, they were "not to indulge in the reading of works of fiction, even sparingly: *total abstinence* from them is essential to restore moral and mental health." But even readers without this weakness were to avoid the injurious example of fiction that emphasized material concerns and rewards. Coxe quoted at length the counsel of Mary Martha Sherwood, the prolific British Evangelical writer for children and young people, who had warned young women against all books that represented "happiness as proceeding from outward circumstances, or depending upon certain external relations of life, such as husbands, wives, children, possessions, honours, beauty, &c."[69] Such blanket censure covered virtually any story with a conventional happy ending. Readers were reminded that they should prefer God's blessing to any worldly reward and that meditation and devotion were far preferable to the spiritual deceptions of fiction. Pitting fiction against piety in *Letters to a Sister* (1850), Alcott held women accountable for the souls they damned while frittering away their time reading novels or other worthless books. He charged that young women who read "Byron or Bulwer" were wasting "that time God had given them for the sole purpose of enabling them to snatch a younger brother, sister or dependent, from eternal woe!" For a young woman to indulge in such frivolous reading was equivalent to "murdering" time and, worse, to "practically murdering one or more of those immortal spirits for whom time was made."[70] Alcott's hyperbole illuminates the daunting demands at the heart of antebellum ideologies of middle-class womanhood, in which women were morally obliged to dedicate those few minutes not already spent meeting others' physical and emotional needs to guarding family members' spiritual well-being. From this perspective, a woman's choice to read fiction constituted a real threat to the immortal destinies of all those who depended on her religious influence and prayerful solicitation for their souls.

In one of the most polemical attacks setting novels against religion, the Methodist minister Wise argued that reading novels prevented one from answering the Holy Spirit's call to conversion. His anti-fiction diatribe climaxed in the story of two young women forced to choose between novels and Christ:

> As, in a certain revival, two persons were awakened who were inveterate novel readers. Their favorite books stood in the way of their conversion. They were willing to be Christians, if their idol could remain undestroyed. This, of course, was impossible, and they saw it. One of them yielded, gave up her novels, and became a joyful convert. The other determined to cleave to her favorite books, whether she obtained religion or not, and was soon freed from serious feelings. She preferred novels to Christ, and Christ forsook her! Nor is she alone. Thousands have made the same choice, and have experienced a similar fate. Reader, will you abandon novels? By all your desire for intellectual and moral improvement, I beg you to forsake them at once, wholly, and forever.

As in Smith's story about the young man who *almost* accepted Christ but who lost his spiritual focus when he returned to his novel on a Sunday afternoon, the love of novels stands between the half-awakened sinner and full conversion. For Wise the main problem was the unsavory characters novels introduced—the "thieves and profligates" whose company sullied the mind: "Can your soul be a bright mirror in which none but pure images are reflected, after such reading?"[71] Like nearly all antebellum conduct book authors, Wise made no mention of novels designed to promote morality and religion, setting forth instead the logic of mutual exclusivity in which one representative soul "preferred novels to Christ, and Christ forsook her!"

Less dogmatically, several conduct book writers conceded that some novels were better than others but maintained that reading the acceptable ones led so quickly to reading the unacceptable ones that it was best to avoid them all. In *The Young Man's Guide* (1833), an exceptionally popular book that ran through twenty-one editions between 1833 and 1858, Alcott wrote that "if fiction is allowable at all, it is only under the guidance of age and experience"—that is, the counsel of a mentor. Those men who had little leisure for reading did best "to abandon novels wholly," for "If they begin to read them, it is difficult to tell to what an excess they may go; if they never read one in their whole lives, they will sustain no great loss."[72] Or as Smith described fiction's addictive power: "if we once fairly enter the field of fiction, we shall not stop with the select few, but be enticed on to peruse the heterogeneous and pernicious many; and considering truth is always better than fiction, why enter this dangerous path at all?"[73] Describing a similarly slippery slope, Wise in *The Young Man's Counsellor* (1851) held that reading a novel did not necessarily damn you (no talk here of Christ forsaking the novel-reader), but it could kill you as you careened from bad novels to worse:

> Yet in one point they do harm; they create a taste for fictitious reading. This taste soon acquires the intensity of a passion. The mind acquires a craving for excitement, and thus the youth, who begins by reveling among the splendid paintings of Sir Walter Scott's pen, or by subjecting himself to the quiet enchantment of Fredrika Bremer's spirit, will speedily seek the works of more impassioned authors. He will hasten from Dickens to James, from James to Bulwer, from Bulwer to Ainsworth, from him to Eugene Sue, and finally he will steep his polluted mind in the abominations of that Moloch among novelists, Paul de Kock. By this time he is ready for destruction. By venturing into the pleasing ripple, he has been tempted to sport in the heaving breakers, until, caught by the resistless under current, he is borne out to sea, and meets a premature death. How much better to have avoided the ripple! Young man, beware of reading your first novel![74]

Wise painted the reader's ultimate corruption as inevitable; eventually one would be rolling in the mud of Charles Paul de Kock, a Parisian novelist known for his humorous depictions of the lower and middle classes. To start reading fiction was to venture down a path that ended in spiritual degradation and death. Although Wise represents an extreme view, he shared with many conduct book authors the assumption that, faced with the bewildering proliferation of novels and the questionable morality of many of them, the safest strategy was to discourage young adults from looking into them altogether.

An emergent tolerance

A few antebellum conduct books offer a glimpse of more liberal attitudes to come. In some, the pat rhetoric of condemnation coexisted alongside a tentative rhetoric of accommodation. Such authors could be strangely divided in their perspective, both vehemently rehearsing traditional critiques of novels and conceding that novels could in certain cases be a healthy recreation or even morally worthwhile. Cary, for instance, both reviled the reading of novels from circulating libraries as monstrous necrophagia and granted that the age had produced moral fiction "eminently calculated to exalt the moral sense and develop the social virtues"—apparently none of which the circulating libraries carried.[75] Playing it safe, she maintained that instructional fiction was most appropriate for children and that mature minds would progress to more substantive works. Clark, too, muddied the waters, first castigating novels as mentally debilitating, morally polluting, and altogether too intense, then hastening to say that he did not, of course, proscribe all fiction. In fact, some popular fiction could do a great deal of good, cultivating "the noblest affections of the heart," teaching "the grandest lessons" of the age, pressing the claims of the poor, and advocating for "every great cause, political, philanthropic, moral, and religious." Indeed these causes "could not gain the public attention so effectually in any other garb."[76] Writing in 1855, Clark implicitly endorsed any number of sentimental and reformist English and American authors who used fiction to advocate for a "great cause": Harriet Beecher Stowe, of course, but also theoretically Lippard, Dickens, Gaskell, and T. S. Arthur. A similar mid-discourse about-face appears in Arthur's own conduct book. After first admonishing young ladies not to overindulge in novel-reading, calling it a "very serious evil" and connecting it to a weakened mind and overdeveloped imagination, he pivoted abruptly to praising Sedgwick, Maria Edgeworth, and other moral writers and to asserting that reading moral fiction is "necessary to a well-balanced mind." He defended fiction as having a discrete role in the literary division of labor, one that complemented the respective benefits of history, philosophy, and poetry. Namely, it taught sympathy for others, with "well-wrought fiction [. . .] giving to man a love for his fellow-man, and inspiring him with a wish to do good." Only fiction, he continued, presented humanity from the inside, showing us that this fellow man "is fashioned in all things as we are; that he has like hopes and fears, joys and sorrows, and like aspirations after the good and the true."[77] Careening down what looks a good deal like the slippery slope other moralists feared, Arthur grew more and more inclusive as he sought to articulate fiction's value—defending first the moral fiction of Sedgwick and company, then any "well-wrought fiction," then simply fiction. What he ended up saying was that fiction's distinctive, detailed representations of character subjectivity had a unique ability to teach readers how to sympathize with others. Since sympathy had been considered the foundation of morality from Adam Smith forward, Arthur effectively claimed that fiction made readers more moral regardless of whether or not it aimed to instruct. He did not, though, reconcile this line of reasoning with his warnings just paragraphs before about the dangers of overindulging in fiction. He did not conclude, for instance, that while fiction offered many moral benefits, it posed a threat if not read in moderation. His comments were not so well digested as that, making for a real discrepancy between his denouncing too much fiction-reading as a "very serious evil" and his defense of fiction's intrinsic moral value. The ragged seams of this discourse suggest that Americans at mid-century were engaged in an incomplete dialectical process in which the established arguments against fiction sat uneasily next to newer arguments in its favor.

A few writers did use counsels of moderation to resolve the tension between fiction's ritually decried perils and the new reality of abundant moral fiction.[78] One grudging concession came from Eliot, who, like Cary, presented fiction-reading as an acquired taste of childhood, blaming "the inordinate love of novel-reading which marks this generation" on the "multiplication of juvenile books of fiction, of which our Sunday schools and day schools are full" and grumbling that no one could teach a moral anymore without "clothing it in a fictitious tale of love and danger."[79] He granted that while not all novels were harmful, their only proper use was to give "rest or recreation to the mind"; they were no substitute for more serious reading. Coxe went so far as to offer a precise prescription for the type and amount of fiction one could read. Provided one were not the sort to become overly excited by fiction and had a healthy mind, morally sound novels might be enjoyed sparingly, "on an average, one or two in the course of a twelve-month."[80] Such abstemiousness presumably reduced the risk that one would become addicted or move so quickly from one author to another that one degraded one's moral sensibilities.

Even when conduct books conceded that not all fiction was dangerous, they tended to gloss over how to discern the good from the bad. Those who addressed this issue typically shifted responsibility to other moral arbiters. Clark, for instance, admonished readers to be guided by "the general verdict of the wise and good" in winnowing the wheat from the chaff.[81] More pointedly, Burnap told readers to manage the tide of new literature by reading reviews, an intriguing solution given that reviews, judging from Baym's research, almost all evinced a more liberal perspective on fiction-reading than Burnap himself.[82] Others recommended seeking more personal guidance. Barnes, for instance, who reluctantly acknowledged that she did "not pretend to say that there are not works of fiction which may be read with profit," told her readers that they could determine what those exceptions were by letting "your older and wiser and more experienced friends judge for you."[83] Representing a more liberal mindset, Sedgwick left the choice up to the young themselves: "In the wide department of fictitious writing, let your consciences restrain and direct your inclination, and rectify your taste."[84] Of course, this counsel to self-discipline raised its own problems, since one might not feel pangs of conscience until well into an offending volume, at which point one was both morally compromised and, if conscience were heeded, compelled to forfeit the satisfaction of finishing the story. And if the practical alternative to a parlor strewn with half-read novels was to seek direction from reviews, mentors, and rumor, then appeals to conscientious restraint were hardly liberating.

Conduct book authors seldom pronounced judgment on specific writers, but the grand exception was Sir Walter Scott, a perpetual touchstone in discussions of fiction's social and moral value. For many, Scott stood in a category by himself, exempt from the usual proscriptions. Cary, for instance, confessed that she had read Scott with "great pleasure by way of recreation" and held that his work was far preferable to other pastimes of youth: "surely one of Scott's best romances, or a sublime piece of poetry, would fill up a leisure hour more profitably than chess, or cards, or riddles, not to mention the senseless games in vogue among the young and thoughtless."[85] Similarly, Burnap, who compared novels to dainties and counseled not wasting money on "novels and other ephemeral frivolities," praised Scott and Edgeworth as an antidote to bodily exhaustion and mental depression just as effective as the natural tonic of green fields and blooming flowers. Scott, he wrote, was "one of the great benefactors of the human race," who mingled "the highest intellectual and moral instruction with the most exquisite pleasure."[86]

Not everyone was so keen on Scott. Todd, who discouraged all fiction-reading, declared that Scott was no exception and cited British abolitionist William Wilberforce's opinion of the Waverley novels: "'I am always sorry that they should have so little moral or religious object. They remind me of a giant spending his strength in cracking nuts.'"[87] Alcott, too, maintained that Scott's fiction was far less valuable than didactic works: "The careful study of a single chapter of Watts's Improvement of the Mind is of more real practical value than the perusal of all that the best and most voluminous novel writers, Walter Scott not excepted, have ever written."[88] Even Sedgwick discouraged readers from letting a love of Scott keep them from more serious reading. She cautioned that though the novels of Scott and Edgeworth were indeed better than the usual "trash" of the circulating libraries, one should not waste time rereading Scott. Readers who found themselves picking up *Ivanhoe* to peruse it a second time, while neglecting books that might teach them something new, should wait to indulge this questionable pleasure until they were "indisposed and listless, or [. . .] condemned to a steamboat."[89]

It is striking how rarely conduct books praised novelists besides Scott or any American novelists at all. In a rare moment of recognition for the "American Scott," Alcott wrote that James Fenimore Cooper's fiction, as well as Washington Irving's, was not as harmless as some believed. Just because one person could read these authors without suffering negative effects did not mean that others would escape unscathed. For one who had read these novels to contend that they had done no harm was to rationalize a bad habit, or as Alcott put it, drawing on temperance rhetoric, "As well might the dram-drinker—now seventy years of age—contend that spirit-drinking is salutary." In short, it was irresponsible to countenance seemingly inoffensive novels such as Cooper's when so many led to "moral turpitude."[90] As for other American novelists, Sedgwick got a nod from T. S. Arthur, but only for her more tract-like works: *The Poor Rich Man and the Rich Poor Man, Live and Let Live,* and *Home.*[91] The other authors named as appropriate reading for young people were all British and Continental women— Edgeworth, Mary Brunton, Amelia Opie, Grace Kennedy, Sophie Cottin, Fredrika Bremer—and even these received only occasional mention. Dickens was disparaged despite his popularity, as in the above-quoted counsels of Matthew Hale Smith and Daniel Wise that set him alongside romancer Edward Bulwer-Lytton. The disinclination to grant moral or cultural value to the most famous novelist writing in English in the mid-nineteenth century reveals the profound disjunction between the moral discourse surrounding novel-reading and Americans' actual reading practices.

After the Civil War, advice literature began to adopt a more tolerant stance toward imaginative writing, though as Hochman has shown, fiction was still regularly censured. One example of growing liberalism can be found in Catharine Beecher and Harriet Beecher Stowe's *The American Woman's Home* (1869), which addressed novel-reading in the course of discussing proper "domestic amusements." Although one might expect this volume to advocate for fiction given Stowe's obvious investment in its moral value, it instead evidences a discourse in transition, one that held that whatever benefits fiction might confer, it also harbored significant threats. After explaining that "confusion and difference of opinion on the subject" had arisen because of the difficulty of differentiating various classes of fiction, the Beechers defended fictitious narrative as "necessary and useful," pointing to the parables and allegories of Scripture as "divine examples." Still, the question of "what kind of fabulous writing must be avoided and what allowed" was not easily answered. Far from endorsing fiction across the board, they recycled the moralistic anti-fiction rhetoric popular before the war: "No works of fiction which tend to throw the allurements of taste and genius around vice and crime should ever be tolerated; and all that tend to give false views of life and duty should also be banished." As for those works written for "mere amusement, presenting scenes and events that are interesting and exciting and have no bad moral influence," the decision about whether or not to read them depended on an individual's temperament: "phlegmatic" natures might benefit from the stimulus, while those who already had "quick and active imaginations" might be injured. Fiction was thus still imagined as a physical substance acting on a passive consumer, but now whether it was healthy or unhealthy, medicinal or poisonous, depended on the individual, not the text itself. Yet readers were not left to make their own determinations as to a novel's possible moral effects; they were to seek counsel from "editors, clergymen, and teachers," who were responsible for reading widely so they could "warn others of danger." Gatekeepers were to undertake this risky mission using the same precautions as those physicians who—here the metaphor of pollution resurfaced—"visit infected districts" while striving to limit their exposure to disease.[92]

What we learn from nineteenth-century conduct books is that 1850 was no magic turning point in American letters, when the novel, like a prodigal son come home, at long last received paternal blessings and a place at the table. Attaining cultural respectability was a much more gradual process, and those adults who saw themselves as responsible for guiding and instructing young people erred on the side of caution. They resisted endorsing a genre that had long been considered morally and intellectually inferior, one associated in the popular imagination with candy, confections, and sweetmeats, or, worse, alcohol, poison, pollution, and death. The pervasiveness of anti-novel ideology suggests that it was not identifiable with a specific religious or professional position, but part of the fabric of middle-class values. Those cultural guardians who distinguished between better fictions and worse did so gingerly, wary of granting the young too much license or of speaking too well of a genre whose seemingly intrinsic pleasures might detract from more useful reading or weaken the intellect. To the extent that we take antebellum conduct books not as the marginal, self-serving discourse of an out-of-touch religious minority but as the expression of mores and values still widely respected, though seldom blindly followed, their disdain for fiction and warnings against novels as a class suggest that antebellum Americans continued to be skeptical about the value of fiction. The conduct books' codification of this skepticism illuminates why Thoreau sneered at novels in his own guide to living and why so many antebellum authors were ambivalent about writing fiction—why, for instance, Hawthorne mocked himself as only a "writer of story-books" and Susan Warner included the counsel "Read no novels" at the end of *The Wide, Wide World.* [93] To author a novel was still a dubious enterprise, which meant that those who did so had to stare down a host of influential naysayers. One of the chief ways novelists held their ground was to claim the sermon as their own. The proper metaphor for a novel, as they would have it, was neither filth nor food nor phantasm but a sublimity-infused, morally relevant sermon. No author claimed this idea more fervently than George Lippard.

CHAPTER 3

The Radical
Protestant Preaching of
George Lippard

G EORGE LIPPARD was one of the most widely read authors in antebellum America, a prolific writer and impassioned labor advocate who
penned an impressive array of novels, short stories, patriotic legends, and
essays between 1841 and his death in 1854 at age thirty-two. *The Quaker City;
or, The Monks of Monk Hall; A Romance of Philadelphia Life, Mystery, and
Crime* (1845) may have been "the best-selling American novel before *Uncle
Tom's Cabin*," and in the late 1840s, when other novelists had difficulty paying their bills, his writing brought in between $3000 and $4000 annually.[1] Yet
he has always skulked on the fringes of the canon, a quirky bit player in the
drama of American literature whose subversive sensationalism makes him
a welcome counterpoint to the canonical genteel writers of the 1840s. What
this two-dimensional portrait leaves out are the religious and moral dimensions of his fiction that came to the fore as he matured.[2]

Literary history has tended to treat Lippard's moralism and religiosity as
a virtual fig leaf for his scandalous content. There is a persistent assumption
that, as Daniel Couégnas writes of Gothic novels in general, "the commercial
laws that gratify the 'inadmissible' dreams of the reader must still pay the
wages of morality and censorship in order to survive."[3] In this vein, Leslie
Fiedler could call the moralizing that follows Arlington's killing of Mary's
seducer in *The Quaker City* "false and forced, Lippard's amends for having
lingered so lasciviously over the details of the rape," and even David Reynolds, who has done more than anyone to give Lippard a place among the

period's writers and to bring to light his religious commitments, has included him with those "dark reformers [who] were inventing moral disguises for notably immoral, sometimes even sacrilegious ponderings."[4]

Against this view of morality as disguise, I read Lippard's religious and moral ideals as an animating force behind his fiction. While his religious values evolved over the course of the 1840s, as he transitioned from the Methodism of his childhood to a more idiosyncratic and radical Protestantism, they consistently included anti-sectarianism and compassion for the poor. By the late 1840s, he was advocating a theologically liberal faith that emphasized the "brotherhood" of all people and the dignity of labor and that found inspiration in the theologically innovative idea that Jesus was a "class-conscious worker," born among the poor and for the poor.[5] This faith called for improving the lives of the laboring poor through such concrete reforms as public education, land redistribution, and fair pay for workers. Grounded in these beliefs, Lippard resented the moral authority of Protestant ministers, whom he saw as largely indifferent to economic inequity, and held that fiction could edify the common people and call the privileged to account more effectively than sermons. "The great object of literature," he declared, "is the social, mental and spiritual elevation of Man," a commitment to didacticism that challenged the aesthetic philosophy of his friend Edgar Allan Poe, who in a December 1848 lecture on "The Poetic Principle" criticized the "heresy of *The Didactic*" and averred that the soul of poetry was not duty, truth, intellect, morality, or conscience but the contemplation of beauty.[6] Lippard countered that literature "merely considered as an ART is a despicable thing" and that "A national literature without a great Idea is plainly a splendid church without a preacher or congregation."[7] American literature, including fiction, was not to be "splendid" for its own sake but the forum for a sermon to the multitude. His keen sense of the antagonism between the ministry and fiction led him to become the period's most outspoken advocate for the idea that novelists should supersede ministers as the country's moral leaders.

Lippard's rivalry with preachers came to a head in the late 1840s in the pages of his newspaper, the *Quaker City* weekly, above all in the serialized novel with which he inaugurated it, *Memoirs of a Preacher, A Revelation of the Church and Home* (1849). But we see the seeds of competition much earlier, in the short fiction of the early 1840s and in *The Quaker City*. This chapter traces the deep roots of his religious ambition and anticlericalism, as seen in several early newspaper columns and stories, and explains the continuity between his religious views and Philadelphia Universalism of the 1840s. It then turns to how Lippard claimed moral authority for fiction by doing battle with ministers real and fictive in *The Quaker City* and *Memoirs of a Preacher*.

From Methodism to fiction

Lippard seemed destined for the Methodist ministry. As a child, he attended first a Mennonite church for a few years, then the local Methodist church where his parents were members.[8] His unofficial religious instruction included listening to the itinerant Methodist preachers who visited the Lippard home tell tales of frontier evangelism and to his aunt describe the German pietists who had settled along Germantown's Wissahickon creek in the seventeenth and eighteenth centuries. Legend imputes early piety: he would supposedly gather his playmates into prayer meetings and conduct his own improvised services with exemplary "religious earnestness and decorum."[9] A series of family tragedies in his youth may have intensified his religious seriousness; between 1830 and 1843, he lost his grandfather, mother, father, and two of his sisters.[10]

Lippard even took a few steps down the path to ordination. He officially joined the Western Methodist Episcopal Church at age fifteen and, soon after, accepted the offer of a local woman to finance his education for the ministry. Encouraged by his pastor and church elders, he reportedly "jumped at the chance" despite the protests of his aunts and sisters.[11] In 1837, he moved to Rhinebeck, New York, to attend a school that would prepare him to study at Middletown College (later Wesleyan University), with the goal of becoming a Methodist minister. The experiment did not last long. Lippard enjoyed his studies, especially the poetry of the Hebrew Bible, but chafed at the discrepancies he saw between Christian ideals and practice. As an adult, Lippard explained that he abandoned the ministry because one day, while he was walking with the Methodist minister with whom he boarded, the minister bought a bag of large, juicy peaches and devoured them without offering his pupil a single one. Lippard brooded over this behavior and decided, "If such are the fruits of piety, I will have none of it."[12] If the too-neat pun signals revisionary autobiography, the anecdote nonetheless reflects his adult belief that the clergy were sensual and selfish.

Whatever Lippard's reasons, leaving school in 1837 was risky, as the country was plunging into one of the worst financial crises in its history. After briefly working as a legal assistant, Lippard abandoned a career in law for a bohemian life on the streets that allowed him to launch himself as a writer. Soon he had penned satirical newspaper columns for *The Spirit of the Times* and a couple of romances—*The Ladye Annabel* (1841) and *Herbert Tracy, or The Legend of the Black Rangers* (1842)—and by January 1843 was writing for the *Citizen Soldier,* a weekly newspaper supporting the state militia. He rose to be its chief editor and writer just six months later, transforming it from a militaristic rag into a family newspaper that included sentimental verse, short religious essays, and fiction.[13]

Lippard's *Citizen Soldier* writing adumbrates many of the religious attitudes that would define his mature work. A predilection for religious satire and sense of literature as a high calling is on display, for instance, in a mock sermon in "The Spermaceti Papers," a column that caricatured the editorial staffs of the *Saturday Evening Post* and *Graham's Magazine* for their delusional literary aspirations.[14] The column lampooned "Spermaceti Sam," based on the portly Samuel Patterson, editor of the *Post* between 1843 and 1845, and "Rumpus Grizzle," or Rufus Griswold, editor of *Graham's* in 1842 and 1843 and a licensed Baptist minister without a regular congregation. One of the most irreverent of Lippard's "Spermaceti" columns mocks Sam's and Grizzle's self-congratulatory excitement as they hatch the idea for America's next great periodical. In it Grizzle lays out the heads for a sermon on "fatness," a metaphor for the worthless writing Lippard saw filling the pages of the *Post* and *Graham's*. Grizzle takes for his text the inapt but verbally convenient "And Jeshuran waxed fat" (Deut. 32:15), then intones, "1st, Fatness considered as Fatness. 2d. Fatness considered as spermaceti. 3d. Fatness considered in relation to pork, especially pork prepared as ham."[15] Another line or two, and the joke warms up to ridiculing "grey ham," or *Graham's*. The sermon's inanity mocks not only the repetitions and tautologies of evangelical preaching but also the American literary establishment's failed pretensions to offer readers substantive literature. To parallel editing and preaching by mocking Griswold for delivering sermons stolen "from Tillotson and Taylor" and for padding his newspaper too heavily with recycled material was to raise the bar on magazine editing, casting it as a sacred vocation.

But Lippard was more than a satirist even in his early twenties. He was also beginning to write his own religious—and wildly sensational—fiction. "Adrian, the Neophyte," for instance, which ran on two front page issues of the *Citizen Soldier* in the summer of 1843 and was soon printed as a thirteen-page pamphlet, represents religious devotion as noble and preaching as the highest imaginable calling.[16] Raised a foundling in a Florentine monastery, Adrian is a pious nineteen-year-old who loves nothing more than to pray at sunset before a cross illuminated by sunbeams and to imagine the sublime spectacle of millions adoring the host. The story's Catholicism is pure medieval romance, with Adrian's prayers "made holy by intense and absorbing feeling" and the monastery described as an idyllic home graced with an abbot's fatherly love and the aesthetic delights of gorgeous organ music and the world's most beautiful paintings. Adrian's creed is simple: in the Abbot's words, "God is thy FATHER—CHRIST the Blessed thy BROTHER—the VIRGIN thy MOTHER." The story turns on Adrian's special calling: since his childhood, the monastery has designated him "One Set-apart," chosen to fulfill the order's rule that once every hundred years, one brother will live continually apart from the rest, except for the single hour each year when he appears and gives a magnificent sermon: "from the pulpit of the Grand Chapel of the Cathedral, he shall speak to the multitude of the wonderful revelations made to his soul in the passing year." It is a striking idealization of the potential power of a single sermon over a mass audience.

Before Adrian can commit himself to this hallowed life, he must pass a test: spend one month amid the temptations of the world—during Carnival, no less. He is assigned to play the harp for a beautiful countess engaged to marry a lord at the end of the month. Like Lippard's own abortive religious calling, the experiment ends poorly. Adrian becomes infatuated with the flirtatious countess, and romantic passion entirely displaces religious devotion. Realizing that he can never have this woman, he despairs and declares himself eternally lost. The climax comes on the fateful day of both the countess's wedding and Adrian's consecration to his calling; the cathedral accommodates the ceremonies simultaneously at, respectively, white and black altars. Immediately after taking a vow of eternal solitude, Adrian looks across the cathedral, sees the bride, and rushes toward her with a dagger. Holding her at knifepoint, he curses her for making him lose his soul. If ever she knows a joy as dear as the thought of God was to him, then may that joy be torn from her! He also places on her the "curse of satiety," so that she may drain all life's pleasures to the dregs yet live on without desire. He flings down the dagger and falls to the floor, dead of a broken heart.

The powerful depiction of religious loss in "Adrian" mirrors Lippard's own rejection of conventional religion and intimates the sense of religious crisis he may have felt in relinquishing his projected ministerial career and, it seems, Methodism. Adrian's fall from grace has a poignancy that transcends its melodrama and resonates with other nineteenth-century crises of faith: "Oh, God—no longer mine—where now is my Religion? My beautiful religion of dreams and shadows? My faith of light? My belief of holy love and hallowed hope? [. . .] Where is now my hope—my heaven—my life? Gone—gone—all gone!" Overwrought as it is, Adrian's cry shares the spiritual despair of Thomas Carlyle's Teufelsdröckh, Hawthorne's Young Goodman Brown, and Thomas Hardy's Jude. Spiritual despair, though, is not the keynote of Lippard, and the story's positive valuations of religious belief and experience prefigure the unorthodox piety of his later fiction. The beatific vision of the worshipping multitude valorizes the idea of a universal, classless religion, central to his thought in the late 1840s. Similarly, the monastery's creed that God is the Father, Jesus the Brother, and the Virgin the Mother looks forward to his later affirmations that God is the father of the human family and Jesus the brother of the poor.[17] Further, the hypothetical scenario of Adrian's glorious annual sermon in the Grand Chapel—a vision never realized—reflects his fascination with preaching as a potential source of religious guidance and human wisdom and his disillusionment with it as likely to fall short of its promise due to human weakness and error.

Lippard's religious earnestness and growing disenchantment with religious oratory are also evident in "Jesus the Democrat," a *Citizen Soldier* story from January 1844.[18] It is set in a beautiful, crowded city church, where a preacher delivers an eloquent sermon from a marble pulpit. As the preacher details with "burning words" Jesus' sympathy for the poor, criminal, sick, and outcast, the church door creaks open and an unkempt, prematurely aged man enters and totters down the aisle. Intent on the sermon, the congregants ignore the stranger and wipe away the not-unwelcome tears that well up as they sympathize with Christ's sufferings. As the stranger collapses on the pulpit steps, a second stranger enters—this one, a handsome, well-dressed "man of the World" who attracts everyone's notice. Oblivious, the preacher proclaims of Jesus: "'look upon him in his tattered robes, his soiled apparel [. . .] and then think of his name—Jesus the friend of the People—*Jesus the Democrat.*'" At this climactic declaration, the dapper stranger morphs into a cloven-hooved, brimstone-scented devil, and the scraggly stranger on the steps rises, rushes toward the minister, and snatches away his Bible. The stranger is, of course, Jesus: his face and garments are transfigured and, bathed in light, he exits through the ceiling, rising "calmly on waves of golden air." The revelation sends the preacher cowering and turns the devil to dust, right after he gloats over the congregation's hypocrisy.[19]

Like "Adrian," this melodramatic fable contains the seeds of several religious ideas that would become central to Lippard's work: that Jesus was himself a poor man who labored for and alongside the poor, that social snobbery is a ubiquitous yet egregious sin, and that even the best sermons do little to move listeners to action. It was a barbed rejoinder to ministers and others who held that the pulpit was supremely capable of inspiring listeners to act whereas fiction aroused feelings that had no outlet. "Jesus the Democrat" made the point that although a preacher in a respectable church might speak beautifully and even truly, and listeners might even weep, his rhetoric was an empty, self-indulgent performance.

Lippard and Philadelphia Universalism

"Jesus the Democrat" captures the fusion of religious and social idealism that would define Lippard's work through the mid- to late 1840s and early 1850s, a period during which he developed a much more liberal, rationalist faith intertwined with a commitment to social justice. His religiosity is generally regarded as shaped by an idiosyncratic blend of traditions: Methodism, of course, but also Hicksite Quakerism, Freemasonry, esotericism, and the German utopian communities that had flourished in Pennsylvania during the previous two centuries.[20] One tradition that, while occasionally mentioned in passing with respect to his work, deserves fuller recognition is the Universalism of antebellum Philadelphia."[21]

Like the Unitarianism that figures far more prominently in literary histories of antebellum America, Universalism was a form of liberal Protestantism that stressed rationalism and piety while rejecting Trinitarian doctrine and the need for an emotional conversion experience. Although the two denominations had much in common doctrinally (and would merge in 1961), they differed markedly in their social profiles. The Unitarians had grown out of the established church in New England and had money, privilege, education, and cultural capital. Universalists had much more populist origins. They traced their roots to the eighteenth-century English emigrant John Murray, a disciple of James Relly, a British evangelical preacher who broke with George Whitefield over the Calvinist doctrine that Christ had died only for the elect. Murray, following Relly, redefined the elect as all of humanity: if Christ died for all, then all would be saved. Dissenters at heart, Universalists argued for the separation of church and state, distrusted church hierarchies, cared little for college or seminary training, and were generally not among the socially and economically privileged. They were also, as the name implies, committed to the doctrine of universal salvation, an idea consonant with the democratic spirit and optimism of the post-Revolutionary period.[22] One of the denomination's most influential theologians was Elhanan Winchester, who in 1781 split from the orthodox Baptists to found the first Universalist Church in Philadelphia, the Society of Universal Baptists, which claimed as an attender physician and Declaration-signer Benjamin Rush. Winchester wrote one of the Universalists' most important treatises, *Dialogues on the Universal Restoration* (1788), which maintained that because infinitude was a property only of God, not of sin or evil, punishment after death would be finite and conclude with the restoration of all things to God. A major theological shift in Universalism came in 1805 with Hosea Ballou's *Treatise on Atonement*. It rejected the Calvinist assumption that God the Father needed to be appeased through the death of Christ, arguing instead that the purpose of the atonement was to demonstrate God's love for humanity. Ballou also held that a loving God had no interest in persecuting his children after death and that "hell" was a metaphor for separation from God in this life. Although Ballou's influence on the denomination was tremendous, not all Universalists wanted to dispense with the idea of hell, and dissension arose between those who held the "Restorationist" position that wrongdoers needed to endure some compensatory pain after death before being restored to God and the "ultra-Universalists" who believed that God confined punishment to earthly existence.

Universalism had a strong presence in Philadelphia from the founding of Winchester's church until about 1845. The first national convention of Universalists met there in 1790, and through the 1840s Universalism was a popular alternative to evangelicalism among the working classes. For the city's white, native-born artisans and mechanics, it was a means of affirming Protestant identity and mutual solidarity while resisting the cultural and political dominance of the orthodox clergy. It was also much more politically radical than evangelicalism. From the 1820s until the Panic of 1837, Universalists and Free Enquirers were the two main radical groups in Philadelphia that challenged capitalism by espousing the labor theory of value.[23] First Universalist Church was, in fact, a seedbed for labor organizing in the 1820s. There minister Abner Kneeland sponsored a discussion society for labor advocates; William Heighton delivered an address that rallied Philadelphia workers to the Mechanics' Union of Trade Associations, "the nation's (and perhaps the world's) first bona fide labor movement" and a springboard to the creation of the Philadelphia Working Men's Party; and Theophilus Fisk pastored before leaving the denomination in the 1830s to become a radical labor leader who advocated for an eight-hour workday when workers were striking for ten, coined the term "white slavery," and wrote such incendiary speeches-turned-tracts as "Capital Against Labor" and "Labor, the Only True Source of Wealth."[24] Although Philadelphia Universalists gained members after the Panic of 1837, they were on the decline by the mid-1840s due to an upsurge in evangelicalism, financial difficulties left over from the depression, and waning radicalism, attributable in part to the influx of Irish immigrants.[25] Nationally, Universalism hit its peak in 1847–1848 and tapered off after 1850.[26]

Although Lippard does not seem to have joined a Universalist church, he had a strong link to the denomination in his friend Charles Chauncey Burr, minister from 1845 to 1847 of the Second Universalist Church, a Restorationist congregation. Burr was a gust of wind on the dying flame of the city's Universalism, a popular speaker whose "large meeting-house was filled, often to overflowing, during his entire term of service" and whose church was billed in 1847 as "one of the largest congregations in the city."[27] At Burr's request, Lippard spoke to a packed house in Second Church following the publication and mass sensation of *The Quaker City*. Burr also officiated at Lippard's unconventional wedding on the banks of the Wissahickon in 1847, wrote a glowing biographical essay on him that was printed as a preface to *Washington and His Generals* (1847), and in 1848 featured him as a contributor to his reformist periodical, *The Nineteenth Century*, which included essays by, among others, Fisk and Horace Greeley, another Universalist. Burr was even expected to write a biography of Lippard after his death, a volume that never materialized.

Beyond the personal and professional connections to Burr and his circle, Lippard advocated religious and social values that overlapped significantly with those of his Universalist and ex-Universalist peers. Given that the denomination was losing power as an institution in Philadelphia and elsewhere in the late 1840s and early 1850s, it is perhaps most productive to think of him as picking up where the Universalists as such were leaving off. Borrowing the language of Raymond Williams, one might say that he drew on structures of feeling and belief constitutive of a residual cultural formation, a labor-oriented Universalism, to advance an emergent form of nonevangelical, anti-ecclesiastical, yet still religiously committed social and political radicalism—one that fed into the renewed radicalism coalescing in Philadelphia in the late 1840s with the arrival of English Chartists in the 1840s and of German refugees starting in 1846.[28] Lippard's residually Universalist form of radicalism was defined by equal measures of love for humanity and righteous anger at social and economic oppression. Doctrinally, Universalists in Philadelphia from the 1820s through the 1840s stressed, as part of the commitment to universal redemption, the loving fatherhood of God and brotherhood of humanity, as well as a Biblicist pietism uninterested in the German higher criticism. They were united, too, by the many religious ideas and practices they opposed: Calvinism, revivals, sectarianism, church hierarchies, clerical greed and indifference to the poor, and often anti-Catholicism, since they regarded Catholics as a fellow religious minority oppressed by an evangelical majority. Socially and politically, they were radicals, opposing capital punishment, the banking system, all forms of authoritarianism, and the exploitation of labor by capital, while celebrating republicanism, egalitarianism, and producerism. These values permeate Lippard's essays and fiction from the mid-1840s forward. One sees the doctrinal overlap between Lippard and his Universalist contemporaries in, for instance, the narrator's affirmation in *The Quaker City* that Jesus died "for all men's sins, and all mankind's salvation"; in Lippard's declaration in an 1848 speech that America is an altar "to the Divine principle of brotherhood among men!"; and in the testimony of Charles Lester, the protagonist of *Memoirs,* that false religions deny *"that principle of Universal Brotherhood which flowed from the life of Christ himself."*[29] Lippard's commitment to the Universalist doctrines of the brotherhood of humanity and the fatherhood of God was most pronounced in the pages of *The White Banner* (1851), the publication intended to be the organ of his secret society, the Brotherhood of the Union, but that appeared only once due to high production costs and limited funds. There he wrote that two Spirits had ever struggled for the mastery of souls: "One is a calm holy spirit, which, with clear eyes, and a loving heart, beholds in God the all-loving Father of an united Human Family—the Spirit of the MASTER, which we will attempt to embody in the word BROTHERHOOD." The other is a Spirit that sees God as Father of only part of humanity and that thrives on sectarianism and results in atheism.[30] The article "Religion" in *The White Banner* offered an even more clearly Universalist intermingling of religious and social visions. Equating religion with familial love and trust in a God who is "the Father of Us All," it was also adamant about what religion was not:

> Note-shaving is not Religion. Marble pillared churches are not religion. The swindling of poor men by learned Bishops in not religion. Robbing your neighbors six days in the week, and going to Church on the Seventh is not Religion. Devoting a life-time to gathering pennies is not Religion. Preaching a creed which teaches John the Presbyterian to hate James the Catholic, is not Religion. Religion is not found in elegant churches, or prettily bound books—much less is it heard from the lips of Smooth-speech, the polite preacher, or Sodom-speech, the wrath-preacher.[31]

This statement of faith participates in the city's Universalist tradition of linking true religion with advocacy for the poor and an opposition to capitalist exploitation, sectarianism, ecclesiasticism (especially the Presbyterian sort), anti-Catholicism, apolitical piety, and hellfire preaching. A few pages later Lippard condemned capital punishment, another social issue central to Universalist reformism, as he lambasted a ministerial contemporary for "blasphem[ing] the name of Christ by making him the prop of the Gallows, and turning his Gospel of Love into a Gospel of the Gibbet and the Hangman."[32] Like the Universalists who figured prominently in campaigns against the death penalty in the 1830s and 1840s on the grounds that it was government-sanctioned vengeance unbefitting the children of a loving God, Lippard regularly condemned capital punishment as malicious and aligned "the gallows" and "the gibbet" with hatred for the poor.[33] In the late 1840s Lippard also came to concur with the Universalists in rejecting the doctrine of eternal punishment, though he seems to have been ambivalent about relinquishing hell altogether. For instance, the 1848 short story "Jesus and the Poor," which ran in both Burr's *Nineteenth Century* and Lippard's *Quaker City* weekly, includes a reworked episode from *The Quaker City,* in which a Mechanic confronts the Bank President whose bank has robbed the poor of their earnings and summons him to "the bar of God" the next morning. After the Mechanic commits suicide and the Bank Director dies of apoplexy the next day, the narrator asks whether the Bank Director has in fact "gone *yonder* to meet his victim." The reply is equivocal: "The Good and Merciful God has flung between our eyes and the Shadow of Eternity an awful veil. Did we believe in the Heathen Creed which preaches an endless Hell, and has a Gibbet for its Gospel, we might follow up to Judgment the Soul of the Bank President." Lippard added this second sentence to the original version of the scene in *The Quaker City,* suggesting his increased discomfort with the idea of hell. But unable to forego the pleasure of imagining justice executed in the afterlife, he kept the description of how the director, brought to the "Bar of Almighty Justice," might "crouch and tremble" before God when confronted with his victims and even added new lines, not included in the novel, about how one might see the train of widows and orphans pouring lead on his soul. Then, backpedaling from this fantasy of judgment, he reiterated the uncertainty of the afterlife and asserted that the mere fact of the bank director's death "preaches a lesson worth all the terrors of a creed-begotten Hell."[34] He renounced hell even more decisively in the late essay *"The Bible." What It Is, and What It Is Not* (1854), which, eschewing visions of divine punishment, affirmed only that all creatures will "progress eternally": "*God is a Father. The entire race of man are his children. He did not create those children to be miserable here or hereafter.*"[35] Still, commentary on hell was rare in his writing, the religious commitments of which centered on the transformation of human society.

The most significant way Universalism seems to have influenced Lippard was in his preoccupation with justice—a major theological issue for Universalists, since affirming that God would save everyone raised the possibility that he did not reward good and punish evil. The theological split within Universalism can thus be seen as variant attempts to balance the moral scales set swinging by the prospect of universal redemption after death, with the Restorationists keeping hell, though one of limited duration, and the ultra-Universalists holding that all sin finds retribution in this world. While Lippard seems to have had Restorationist sympathies, as suggested by his condemnation of those who preach *everlasting* punishment and his imaginative dalliances with the Bar of Almighty Justice, his fiction also suggests an affinity for the ultra-Universalist belief that God punishes sin in this life, a doctrine alive and well in antebellum Philadelphia. Fisk, for instance, preached it in *The Pleasures of Sin* (1827), a feverish sermon that justifies his successor's comment that he drew ample audiences "gathered by sensational topics and held by sensational manner."[36] Indeed, Fisk's sensationalism and popularity raise the possibility that Lippard may have borrowed both content *and* style from Philadelphia's Universalist churches. From the text, "The way of transgressors is hard" (Prov. 13:15), Fisk argued that sin may give pleasure in the short term but leads inevitably to divine punishment in this life:

> There are flowers in the garden of guilty pleasure, but beneath them the speckled serpent hisses! [. . .] There are fountains and pools, but they contain nought but the black waters of despair. There vice may be seated upon a dazzling pavilion, decorated in all the shining apparel of this lower world—but the dagger of death is hid beneath her robe! Words may fall from her lips, but they are false as perjury—her breath is a pestilence—her touch contamination, despair and death![37]

Serpents, fetid water, daggers of death, pestilence—Fisk was as adept with Gothic tropes as any revivalist preacher, or Lippard. To show that God met earthly vice with earthly punishments, Fisk summoned examples from the Hebrew Bible, including the swallowing of Jonah, the destruction of Jerusalem, the desolation of Babylon, and the fire and brimstone rained on Sodom and Gomorrah. God does not put off judgment but "brings every deed unto judgment as soon as committed, and brings upon *every one* that doeth evil, wrath, tribulation, and anguish."[38] In Lippard's own day, Asher Moore, minister of First Church from 1840 to 1848, expounded on the doctrine of this-world retribution at length in *Universalism: The Doctrine of the Bible,* invoking the inhabitants of Sodom and Gomorrah and those destroyed in the Flood as prime examples of those who "suffered a premature and violent death as a punishment for their sins."[39]

Echoing these Universalist preachers, Lippard offset a renunciation of hell with fictive representations of God punishing sin in the here and now. That is, his stories, in which time and again evildoers meet grisly ends, can be read as exempla of divine justice that do the theological work of Universalism by demonstrating how God acts in the world. A bank director's apoplexy or an adulteress's poisoning may seem crudely improbable or sensational, but from a Universalist perspective they are revelatory, illuminating how God executes justice by smiting the wicked before our very eyes.

Competing sermons at Reverend Pyne's church

Though not typically classed with the period's didactic fiction, *The Quaker City* is intensely moralistic. In the introductory "The Origin and Object of this Book," the dying lawyer enjoins the author to write a book that will further a litany of moral and religious ends: "To defend the sanctity of female honor; to show how miserable and corrupt is that Pseudo-Christianity which tramples on every principle ever preached or practiced by the Saviour Jesus; to lay bare vice in high places, and strip gilded crimes of their tinsel."[40] Many scandalized readers, of course, saw no trace of Christian principle in the novel's voyeuristic urban tour of drunkenness, public corruption, seduction, incest, and murder.[41] To them, splattered brains and naked "snowy globes" did not "lay bare vice" but merely flesh, pandering to a depraved public appetite for sex and violence. There is no denying that the novel revels in the sensuality it condemns—that it dwells on the bodies of Dora, Mary, and Mabel, undresses the women whenever it can, lingers over Mary's drug-induced sexual passion, and revels in a slew of gruesome deaths: the Widow Smolby's skull slammed on an andiron, Dora poisoned and shrieking, Job Joneson writhing in apoplexy, Ravoni knifed in the back, Devil-Bug crushed under a rock, Algernon Fitz-Cowles burned to a crisp.

Yet for all its prurience and bloodlust, the novel promotes widely accepted moral values.[42] The main storyline, Byrnewood Arlington's quest to avenge his sister Mary's seduction, upholds feminine "virtue" and middle-class sexual mores. A subplot advocates for the sanctity of female chastity regardless of class, as Arlington regrets his seduction of Annie, a serving girl, and seeks to rescue her from further depredations. The novel's cast of rogues argues for countless other virtues: the drunk Monks, for temperance; the financial deceptions of Fitz-Cowles, for honest business practices; the duplicity of Reverend Pyne, for the clergy's integrity; the adultery of Dora, for marital fidelity, and so on. When the novel pleads sympathy for the likes of Arlington, Bess, and Devil-Bug, the point is to encourage compassion for sinners who were themselves sinned against. And when it inflicts terrible punishments on wrongdoers, the point, as already suggested, is not only to shock or titillate but, more importantly, to reveal the ultimate goodness and justice of God. In terms of moral principle, perhaps the only significant way in which the novel deviated from the contemporary status quo was its privileging of moral justice over human law, as when the narrator condones Arlington's murder of Lorrimer or allows Mabel to enjoy Livingstone's fortune through Devil-Bug's deception.

To emphasize that *The Quaker City* offered readers valuable moral guidance—and that they were unlikely to find a better guide in church—Lippard depicted the novel's only minister, the Reverend F. Altamont T. Pyne, as a full-blown scoundrel. An oily, tippling liar, Pyne uses his parishioners' charitable donations to feed his vices at Monk Hall and, in scenes that could hardly have been more shocking to nineteenth-century readers than to today's, tries to rape the girl he has raised as his daughter.[43] His name is a rich joke. The aristocratic-sounding "Altamont," or "high mountain," mocks his pretensions, while "Pyne" situates him among the lower classes by suggesting his church's "uncomfortable benches of unpainted pine."[44] The pun with "fat pine," or kindling, also alludes to his tendency to "blaze up in his sermons," especially when preaching on hell, and to his fitness for the eternal flames.[45] That F. A. T. Pyne's given name is "Dick Baltzar" may also be a joke about the lust lurking beneath the clerical façade.[46] Pyne both borrows from the stock "reverend rake" figure popular in the period's sensational fiction and alludes more immediately to a major church scandal of 1844, the trial of New York Episcopalian bishop Benjamin T. Onderdonk for inappropriate and unwanted sexual behavior with several women in his church.[47] Yet Lippard in "Key to the Quaker City" (1845) discouraged readers from identifying Pyne too closely with any one minister, maintaining that Pyne personified the clergy's worst vices and that in Philadelphia there were "no less than three Rev. Dr. Pynes."[48]

Chapter 3 of Book 3, set in the dingy upstairs lecture room of Pyne's "Free Believers and True Repenters" church, is a central scene in the novel's moral landscape. Here Lippard both mocked the city's preaching as sheer bigotry and set forth two counter-sermons advocating a compassionate, sentimentalized Christian ethic. Unwilling to fight the preaching of his day with story alone, he wrote as if people needed to hear, or read, *better* sermons.

Pyne's sermon caricatures the ignorance and parochialism of the city's anti-Catholic preaching, but as the novel's only represented sermon, it also comments on the city's preaching more generally, a point highlighted by the diverse congregation composed of "male of female, old and young, high and low, rich and poor." The service centers on the commissioning of three missionaries being sent to Rome to convert the Pope to the "Universal Patent Gospel," or, as Pyne jingoistically calls it, the "American Patent Gospel." Either way, the concept of a "patent gospel" epitomizes the divisiveness and sectarianism of Pyne's preaching. His doctrine is, in his words, "a gospel of fire and brimstone and abuse o' the Pope o' Rome, mingled in equal quantities—about half o' one and half o' tother." He denounces the Pope, Monks, Nuns, all the Sisters of Charity, and the orphans in their care; calls for the firing of all Catholics and a renewal of the Inquisition; and praises John Calvin, whom he lauds for burning Servetus at the stake. The sermon brings together everything Lippard loathed about religious orthodoxy: Calvinism, anti-Catholicism, self-righteousness, narrow-mindedness, and disregard for the poor. Even the sermon's form is offensive; Pyne's exclamations beginning with "Down with" and "Up with" belonged to political sloganeering, not the pulpit. The Free Believer congregation is also held up for ridicule, as they greet the wild tale of the Pope turning a group of tract-wielding American Patent Gospellers into sausages with deafening shouting and foot-stomping and a "perfect hurricane of applause," which sounds "like the voice of some huge monster."[49] In *Memoirs,* Lippard would revisit and revise this cynical commentary on the preaching favored by the common people.

Just as the transfigured Jesus in "Jesus the Democrat" rises as a silent rebuke to the preacher and his congregation, so here a pious individual rises to correct the assembled Christians. As the applause dies down, an old man stands and identifies himself as an American citizen who fought as a boy alongside his father and George Washington during the Revolution. For Lippard, whose patriotism was a form of religious faith, a Revolutionary War veteran embodied heroism and virtue far more reliably than any minister. The Free Believers wait eagerly to hear the veteran endorse their intolerance, but instead he dares to question the project of sending missionaries to Rome. He has had a "passing thought" while "our Reverend Brother was enchaining you all with his eloquence"; Quaker-like, he prefers his own fleeting—and possibly divinely inspired—thoughts to the minister's bombast. The speech that follows claims a moral equivalence to preaching by bearing all the markers of sermonic voice: theological diction, oratorical sentence structures, a tone of conviction about moral and religious truths, and an element of hope or redemption. It also mirrors Lippard's own moral and religious preoccupations, elaborating on an earlier authorial footnote that censured hypocritical public leaders, including ministers, and affirmed that "For the religion of Jesus Christ, our Savior and Intercessor, the author of this work has a fixed love and reverential awe."[50] The veteran explains what this "religion of Jesus Christ" might look like by asking whether the missionaries might not be better employed in Philadelphia: "Are there no holes of vice, to be illumined by the light of God's own gospel? Are there no poor, no sick, no needy?"[51] With rising passion, he calls for the church to send its missionaries into the city.

These "home missionaries" could help the orphans deprived of the $2 mil-
lion left them by Stephen Girard (one of Lippard's hobby-horses), cure the
city's "hideous moral sores," and denounce the city's wine-drinking, slanderous, seducing, mob-inciting ministers by telling them, "as God will tell them
one day, that they are a blot upon the name of Jesus!"[52] On this last point the
veteran glows white-hot: "[T]hese are not the characteristics of God's own
Ministers, but rather the fuel with which the Devil will kindle a hell for their
souls!"[53] Ironically, the speech that starts so humbly and condemns ministers
who make "violent appeals to excited mobs" ends up nearly as overheated as
Pyne's sermon.

The messages, though, are quite different. The veteran's speech is a prime
example of what Edmund Arens has called prophetic preaching: that which
objects in the name of God to the prevailing conditions of "political, social,
economic, and religious injustice." Rather than aiming to build individual
piety or reform behavior, prophetic preaching critiques the morality of social
institutions and practices. Like any preaching, it cannot be wholly negative; it
must share the "promise of a new, just, and benevolent order."[54] Accordingly,
the veteran's preaching condemns ministerial vice and corruption while
exhorting listeners to adopt a compassionate, self-sacrificing ethic focused
on caring for the city's poor and sick. In a novel much more concerned with
exposing vice than mapping reform, the veteran's call for home missionaries
is one of the few specific proposals for ameliorating poverty.

The veteran's rhetorical thrashing of the ministry compensates for the
serious physical punishment the story itself never gives Pyne. Whereas the
seducers Lorrimer and Fitz-Cowles endure "premature and violent death[s]
as a punishment for their sins," as Moore described the workings of God's
justice, the embezzling, hate-mongering would-be rapist Pyne gets a virtual
slap on the hand. He is tickled, threatened with a poker, and pitched down
a stairway, incidents from which he emerges bruised but not broken. When
in the denouement a newspaper reports that he is being brought to trial
for seducing the daughter of a wealthy merchant, the story does not follow
through to a verdict; the minister is left literally unjudged. It may be that Lippard feared that jailing or killing off even a vile clergyman would make an
already scandalous novel seem simply antireligious.

Incensed, the Free Believers and True Repenters toss the veteran into
the street. The reader, however, cannot yet leave the pews. A new preacher
rises in the veteran's place—the narrator, giving Lippard another chance to
condemn Pyne, as well to complement the veteran's call to social action with
an appeal to sentimental piety. As Pyne prays, the narrator launches into
sermonic voice, beginning, "Prayer! Ho, Ho! Was that a fiend's laugh as he

heard the mockery of that prayer ascend in tones of blasphemy to the very throne of God?"[55] The diatribe that follows is a string of scornful rhetorical questions infused with indignation that Pyne is profaning the name of Jesus with his "curses, falsehoods, and impious vulgarities." Then, shifting tone, the narrator tempers condemnation with uplift through rhetorical questions that propose that prayer is the young mother whispering to her first-born, or the father trembling at the bedside of his dying daughter.[56] This sermonic redefinition of prayer argues for a sentimental piety that sanctifies secular emotions, in particular the poignancy of parental love and so, by extension, the parent-child relationships central to the novel—those of Devil-Bug, John Davis, and the Arlingtons with their daughters. Oddly enough, and suggestive of how Lippard's sentimentalism was always sliding into sensationalism, the narrator's sacralization of familial feeling has its material analogue in the twin marble statues of Religion and Love in Dora Livingstone's sumptuous boudoir.

The seductive preaching of Ravoni the Sorcerer

The most compelling preacher in *The Quaker City* is not a Christian minister at all but the enigmatic Ravoni the Sorcerer, an unexpectedly complex figure in a novel rife with moral dichotomies. A beautiful courtier to the kings of pre-Revolutionary France and consummate physician and surgeon, he has discovered the secret of eternal youth and seeks to while away eternity by founding a new religion. Besides being a figurative and perhaps literal seducer of women, he is a spiritual seducer of both sexes, one who allures followers with appealing doctrines and beautiful speech while robbing them of their autonomy. Lippard uses him to underscore the dangers of giving oneself over to powerful preaching of any sort, no matter how persuasive.

That Ravoni cannot be read as satire is evident from the overlap between his "New Faith" and Lippard's own religious values, especially those articulated in "Adonai, the Pilgrim of Eternity" (1849) and other late pieces.[57] Like Lippard, Ravoni condemns the violence done throughout history in the name of God and envisions a future free of war, crime, and the class divide between rich and poor. He also rejects institutional religion, promising that the coming utopia will have no clergy and that families will worship in their homes. His defiant declaration that the new faith will arise "in the name of Man and for the good of Man!" echoes Lippard's own insistence that religion tend to humanity's physical needs. Ravoni goes, though, perhaps a step beyond Lippard's own religious idealism in his Emersonian exaltation of a de-Christianized God immanent in the natural world: "Through all matter, through sun and sky and earth and air, he lives, the soul of the Universe! We are all beams of his light, rays of his sun; as imperishable as his own glory! To us all, he has entrusted powers, awful and sublime."[58] The declaration flirts with parody, but Lippard lends it credibility with an authorial footnote clarifying that the speaker presumably intends a reference to the "doctrine of magnetic influence" that pervades space, linking all humans to one another and to God.

That Ravoni's sermon, unlike Pyne's, is eloquent and plausible signals readers to be wary not simply of religious fanaticism but of all religious oratory, in much the same way that *Moby-Dick* warns against the dangers of succumbing to a powerful, well-spoken visionary. Like Ahab, Ravoni is no workaday preacher but a popular leader of that distinctive sort Max Weber associated with charismatic authority, in which the leader breaks from conventional institutions and systems to declare a new order, inspiring followers to consider him divine.[59] When Ravoni tells his congregants they are beams of God's light, they respond with star-struck fervor, hailing him as a god. His sermon is ineffably powerful; it is vain to try to describe his hand, eye, expression, or voice, which strikes "the mysterious chords of every heart."[60] As with other charismatics, seeming divinity cloaks serious moral flaws. Besides the fact that as a mesmerist he wields an unfair advantage over his listeners, he employs resurrection men to steal dead bodies; drugs Annie so he can "resurrect" her to demonstrate his power to his disciples; attempts, like Pyne, to exploit Mabel for his own purposes; and has abused his role as a physician to collect an entourage of beautiful young women from around the world. For those readers who might not see past Ravoni's dazzle, Lippard has the narrator call him an "eloquent Blasphemer" and includes as a footnote the disclaimer that his speeches are "*not* the opinions of the author, but of the character" and that he does "not hold himself responsible for a single word or line."[61]

With Ravoni, Lippard cautioned readers against falling for dynamic, appealing preaching—the kind that could disarm even the virtuous. Luke Harvey is drawn into Ravoni's circle of disciples against his will and after hearing him is "no more himself," shouting with the others, "We are thine! [. . .] *I* am thine!"[62] Mabel is offered a chance to leave Ravoni but chooses to stay when she meets his magnetic gaze. His ability to master otherwise admirable individuals fleshes out the offhand cynicism of Sylvester Petriken, who muses that if his magazine fails, he might as well become a preacher: "Why not start a Church of my own? When a man's fit for nothin' else, he can always find fools enough to build him a church, and glorify him into a saint—."[63] The talented, energetic Ravoni is all the more dangerous because he reels in not the fools alone but the young and idealistic. Moving beyond the caricature of Pyne, Lippard used Ravoni to put readers on their guard against any preachers exercising impressive oratorical powers.

The preachy narrator of *The Quaker City*

Though critical of how preaching could manipulate its hearers, Lippard did not hesitate to tap its emotive power for fiction by assigning his narrator numerous didactic digressions, many of which exult in God's punitive justice. Many of these digressions stop short, though, of sermonic voice as I have defined the term. While including distinctive stylistic features of the sermon, such as biblical language and oratorical cadences, they do not offer or imply the message of hope or redemption essential to sermonic voice, promising instead only punishment for the wicked. One of the most striking of these near-sermonic moments appears immediately after Mary's seduction. In it Lippard practices a sleight of hand in which he treats his own imagination—his ability to spin legends dramatizing moral ideals—as the basis for religiously authoritative speech. After pointing ominously to the darkness and silence of the Rose Chamber, the narrator relates a purported legend. An "old book of mysticism and superstition" says that far off in the sky hangs an invisible Awful Bell that angels toll when the Unpardonable Sin is committed on earth:

> The peal of the Bell, hung in the azure depths of space, announces to the Guilty one, that he is an outcast from God's mercy for ever, that his Crime can never be pardoned, while the throne of the Eternal endures; that in the hour of Death, his soul will be darkened by the hopeless prospect of an eternity of wo; wo without limit, despair without hope; the torture of the never-dying worm, and the unquenchable flame, forever and forever.[64]

If there is only one unpardonable sin, the narrator continues, it is the "foul wrong" committed that day in the Rose Chamber of Monk-Hall. While the language of the passage is sermonic, the purport is not. Principles are declared with oratorical rhythms, conviction, and biblical diction—the final phrases rework Mark 9:44, "where their worm dieth not, and the fire is not quenched" —but this moment holds no glimmer of hope or redemption. It is a curse, not a sermon. In contrast with Mark 9, in which Jesus says, "If thy hand offend thee cut it off," because it is better to go through life with one hand than to go to hell with two, the novel offers no such hope here that severance of the appropriate member will save one's soul. Indeed, this passage may be as close as Lippard ever came to endorsing the idea of an eternal hell. The threat seems real enough, except that it comes from a mystical, superstitious old book, which might seem to allude to the Bible if the Bible ever mentioned an Awful Bell, and calls rape, rather than "blaspheming the Holy Ghost," the "unforgivable sin."[65] To be sure, Lippard's revision might itself be considered blasphemous in its implication that a woman's body is as sacred as God's spirit. As in the vision of the Bank Director before the Bar of Almighty Justice, the narrator raises the possibility that the wicked will endure everlasting punishment, even while elsewhere disclaiming the doctrine. The passage sounds like immutable malediction yet is in substance a fanciful melodramatic flourish.

Devil-Bug's apocalyptic dream-vision, "The Last Day of the Quaker City," is by far the novel's fullest elaboration of this sort of quasi-sermonizing, in which an imagined scenario is presented as the basis for authoritative-sounding biblical and oratorical language. In setting forth this eschatological vision, Lippard sidestepped the problem of hell by postulating an awesome, supernatural, this-worldly scenario of divine justice—one that invokes, like the Universalist preachers, the story of Sodom and Gomorrah. When the vision opens, Devil-Bug is delighted by the dystopia he beholds. A royal palace sits where Independence Hall used to be; a new nobility lords over the poor; preachers have brought back the gallows. Then the real nightmare begins: the dead rise from their graves, and "Wo unto Sodom" appears in flaming letters across the sky. Hideous scenes unfurl: ten thousand corpse-piloted coffins floating on the river, a war between armies of the dead, corpses marching next to the clergy in the city's grand procession, horror when the living see the dead at their sides, a sky full of red thunderbolts striking down the living, tidal waves of land swallowing the corpses. The Ghost, a Virgilian tour guide to the apocalypse, gets the last, almost-sermonic word. He exhorts Devil-Bug to witness with the angels the destruction of the Doomed City and to shout with them, "Wo, WO UNTO SODOM." Again, damnation is threatened without hope for redemption.

The one truly sermonic moment in the vision comes when the narrator reveals that the destruction of the old world precedes the founding of a new one. The narrator's song of joy celebrates the impending elevation of the poor, when "the God of the Poor would arise in his might, and crush the lordlings under the heel of his power!"[66] Here, for once, the narrator mitigates declarations about how God will punish the wicked with a clear vision of salvation. The song is prophetic on two fronts, both denouncing injustice and promising a benevolent order to come:

Joy to ye all! Your God arises; his arm is uplifted; already the rumbling of his chariot wheels draw near! No more hunger now, no more crying for bread. No more huddling down in squalor, and want, and cold. The avenger comes—Shout ye poor, shout from your factories and work-benches, from your huts and dens of misery—shout!

This passion for the physical redemption of the working poor would define the last decade of Lippard's life, leading him to found the Brotherhood of the Union, whose members vowed to support the principle that "Every human creature hath a right to Life, Liberty, Land and Home; to the means and circumstances of temporal, moral and spiritual development."[67]

The song of joy in Devil-Bug's vision is an unusually upbeat moment of sermonizing for the narrator of *The Quaker City*, typically more intent on announcing that God will judge the rich than that he will save the poor. When, for instance, the banker Joneson suffers a sudden and agonizing death on the floor of Davis the mechanic, a scene Lippard truncated for "Jesus and the Poor," the narrator points to the dead body and intones with the alternately lyrical and emphatic rhythms of a skilled preacher:

He had obeyed the subpoena of the Suicide; he had gone to meet his pale
   Accuser before the Throne of Eternity.
God is just.
This is a truth we often hear preached, but it falls upon our ears with a
   hollow sound.
God is just.
Come hither, all the world, come to the chamber of Want and Suicide, and
   gaze upon this picture of God's Justice.[68]

This dark funeral sermon underscores that Joneson's sudden death represents the workings of divine justice while getting in a dig at ministers. Readers have heard about God's justice from preachers, but the novelist is the one who can *show* "all the world" the greedy banker purple and writhing on the floor. Unlike a preacher, though, the narrator addresses not those who should mend their ways to avoid divine judgment but those who might be tempted to take justice into their own hands. The city contains hundreds of villains like Joneson, but "Let them all pass—God is just." It is a Psalmic sermonic meditation: sooner or later, God will smite our enemies.

Reflecting the narrator's penchant for reveling in the prospect of divine judgment, one of the novel's most insistent and protracted sermonic moments comes when the narrator warns the rich that God will hold them to a higher standard. When Devil-Bug realizes that Mabel is his daughter and begins to remember his love for her mother Ellen, the narrator steps in to defend him and to exhort readers who have enjoyed comfortable circumstances not to hold themselves superior to the Monk Hall doorkeeper. The sermon begins with a long rhetorical question that implicitly takes as its text Jesus's apothegm, "For unto whomsoever much is given, of him shall be much required":

> Oh, tell us, ye who in the hours of infancy, have laid upon a mother's bosom, who have basked in a father's smile, who have had wealth to bring you comfort, luxury, and a home, who have sunned in the light of religion as you grew toward manhood, and been warmed into intellectual life by the blessing of education; Oh, tell us, ye who with all these gifts and mercies, flung around you by the hand of God, have, after all, spurned his laws, and rotted in your very lives, with the foul pollution of libertinism and lust; tell us, who shall find most mercy at the bar of Avenging Justice—you, with your prostituted talents, gathering round your guilty souls, so many witnesses of your utter degradation, or Devil-Bug, the door-keeper of Monk-Hall, in all his monstrous deformity of body and intellect, yet with *one* redeeming memory, gleaming like a star, from the chaos of his sins?[69]

Whereas the sermon after Joneson's death indicts only capitalists who participate in "legalized robbery," this one sets its sights on a much wider audience—those who have enjoyed the advantages of a comfortable upbringing yet have gone on to pursue "libertinism and lust," euphemisms for such urban, male entertainments as drinking, theater-going, and brothel-visiting. The passage evinces a decided class-consciousness in its insinuation that God calibrates moral standards to one's material and spiritual advantages, employing a logic similar to that which Harriet Jacobs would use to dissuade her privileged readers from sneering at her sexual transgressions: "But, O, ye happy women, whose purity has been sheltered from childhood, [. . .] do not judge the poor desolate slave girl too severely!"[70]

The sermon catalyzed by Devil-Bug's surge of feeling for Ellen continues for three more paragraphs, a passage that would be hard to miss in a less sprawling novel. As if in retort to moralists who condemned novels for corrupting the young by creating sympathy for criminals, the narrator declares that people such as Devil-Bug should be pitied because the community failed them by not providing religious instruction: "And in this great city, there are thousands upon thousands hidden in the nooks and dens of vice, who, like Devil-Bug of Monk-Hall, have never heard that there is a Bible, a Savior, or a

God!" It is a nonsectarian critique of the city's ministers for neglecting their religious obligations and a claim for the preacherly abilities of narrator and novel, underscored in the subsequent, oratorical, thrice-repeated cry that the poor have not heard that there is "a Bible, a Savior, or a God!" The sermonic interlude's final and most emphatic point condemns those who disregard the bodily suffering of the poor. Like the outspoken veteran, the narrator castigates the Quaker City and, implicitly, its clergy for sending missionaries abroad without having "one single throb of pity, for the poor, who starve, rot and die, within its very eyesight!"[71] Later in the 1840s Lippard would continue to critique foreign missionary work while also arguing that the poor might avoid starvation by organizing themselves into labor unions and mutual aid societies rather than waiting for others to notice them and feel throbs of pity.

After *The Quaker City* appeared in print, Lippard refuted charges of its immorality with more preaching against the clergy in "Key to the Quaker City: or, The Monks of Monk Hall" (1845), a twelve-page appendix much less well known today than Stowe's longer, freestanding *A Key to Uncle Tom's Cabin* (1853). Lippard's "Key" first pointed to real-life analogues for the story's characters and settings and clarified the backstory involving the two girls born on Christmas Eve in 1824 and 1825. Then, waxing sermonic, Lippard resumed his denunciation of the ministry by asserting that Devil-Bug's dream depicted the end result "of the corruptions of republican principles" and that the city's principal purveyors of corruption were greedy capitalists, office-hungry politicians, and, above all, the "idle and pampered priesthood." Much like Frederick Douglass in the "Appendix" to his *Narrative,* Lippard stressed that he opposed not Christianity itself, but ministers' perversion of the faith. Assuming the role of a rival preacher, he warned that God would judge those hypocritical ministers who were "wont to ride rough-shod over the souls of the poor" and who, after indulging their vices, showed up in church to preach boring or fanatical sermons. Lippard drove home his indictment of ministerial malfeasance by excoriating the Episcopal priests who had authorized the sale of the scandalous transcripts of Onderdonk's trial and cataloguing an arsenal of ministerial sins: ignoring the suffering of the poor, preaching irrelevant or polemical sermons, threatening nonbelievers with eternal damnation, advocating capital punishment, and supporting overseas missions. Lippard closed the "Key" with a lengthy excerpt from a contemporary review that extolled his novel as supremely moral—"There is a deeper and holier moral in this work, than in any American novel of the age"—and that argued that the novel showed "how pure was the religion of the Saviour: how utterly corrupt is the superstition and bigotry of some of his pretended followers."[72] In juxtaposing a condemnation of ministerial vice with a reviewer's praise for *The Quaker City*'s morality and piety, Lippard promoted a logic of supersession, in which righteous novels would assume the ministerial function of providing the public with moral leadership.

The idea that a novel should come before the public as a preacher also informed the 1849 preface to *The Quaker City,* where the sermonic tone is more paternal than prophetic. Here Lippard explained that he had learned about vice in Philadelphia by working in an Attorney-General's office, "the Confessional of our Protestant communities," a metaphor that sought to authorize his writing as an outgrowth of the priestly role he had played in the community.[73] After defending his honesty and purity, he closed the preface with a long, didactic address to the young men and women who might read his book, beseeching them to reject anything in its pages that seemed immoral or impure or that conflicted "with the great idea of Human Brotherhood, promulgated by the Redeemer." The address ended with the rhythmic imperatives and biblical language of a sermon's peroration: "Take the book with all its faults and virtues. Judge it as you yourself would wish to be judged. Do not wrest a line from these pages, for the encouragement of a bad thought or a bad deed."[74] Preacher-like, Lippard assumed the stance of one who held himself responsible for the morality of his audience.

Memoirs of a Preacher

In the latter half of the 1840s, Lippard increasingly represented novelists and ministers as rivals, a tendency on full display in *Memoirs of a Preacher: A Revelation of the Church and Home* (1849), the novel that kicked off his story paper, the *Quaker City* weekly, on December 30, 1848.[75] The very fact that he had taken to producing a weekly paper with the masthead motto, "A Saturday Paper for Universal Circulation," suggests his desire to rival the clergy. *Memoirs* began on the front page, preceded by a Prologue written as an open letter to Pennsylvania Episcopal Bishop Alonzo Potter. This letter may be the most overt instance in antebellum letters of a novelist rebuking a minister and declaring the moral superiority of novels to organized religion. Lippard began with a pose of humility—"I am conscious of the immeasurable distance which separates an humble Author from a Bishop"—but was soon attacking Potter for calling French novels insipid and immoral. Indignant, he asked Potter whether he had actually read Eugène Sue's *Wandering Jew, Mysteries of Paris,* or *Martin the Foundling,* each of which demonstrated distinct moral virtues. Sue, he declared, was a more effective and earnest moral leader than any Bishop: "[H]ave not his Fictions embodied the Truth, in language more forcible and with greater sincerity of heart than ten thousand Diocesan sermons?" Guns blazing, he contrasted the morality of French novels with the immorality of the church, pointing an accusing finger at the publication of Onderdonk's trial proceedings, Trinity Church's ownership of tenement slums and a red-light district in New York City, and the "Borgian luxury" of English bishops who took in $200,000 a year while hundreds of thousands died during the Irish famine. He even exhorted Potter personally: "Think of this, Reverend Sir. Think of it when you are alone. Look it in the face. Slowly, quietly, immerse your soul in the awful importance of the subject." He concluded by declaring that he would write a novel that would not merely stand above the Bishop's censure but also "accomplish much good." As in his "Key," he maintained that he was not against all ministers, only the corrupt ones, and that his novel would depict one of the many humble preachers who as a home missionary "visits the haunts of fever, poverty, and pestilence." Its aim would be not to trash negative examples but to celebrate a worthy, self-denying minister.[76]

As with so many prospectuses, the description did not match the work that unfolded. *Memoirs* depicts in lurid detail two wicked ministers and presents only briefly and ambiguously a compassionate and self-sacrificing one. Even more directly than *The Quaker City*, *Memoirs* argues that novelists must usurp the ministerial role of moral leadership and reveals Lippard's envy of preachers' ability to address audiences without the mediation of print.

Set in Philadelphia in 1843, *Memoirs* is a fast-paced story centered, like *The Quaker City*, on plots of seduction, revenge, and inheritance. The protagonist is Charles Lester, a young man determined to find the scoundrel minister who married his sister then libeled her in the newspapers, driving her to an early grave. This minister is soon revealed to be the "Popular Preacher," also known as Edmund Jervis, whom Lester finds enrapturing thousands at a large Philadelphia church. Immediately after the sermon, Jervis whisks away a poor young woman, Fanny, from the mourners' bench to the mansion of a wealthy capitalist friend. This capitalist, Caleb Goodleigh, has had two past lives—one as a licentious obstetrician (like the priest, the physician poses a threat because he can abuse his private access to women) and one as an importer of slaves from Africa who once sunk an entire ship of human "cargo" at sea to elude the authorities. Deep within Goodleigh's labyrinthine home, Jervis mesmerizes Fanny so she can serve as a clairvoyant for him. He intends to seduce her afterward but, like Pyne with Mabel, never quite gets the chance.

The Popular Preacher has a Catholic analogue in the Converted Monk, the novel's other reprobate cleric. Years before, when the mother of Fanny and her brother Ralph lay dying and half-delirious after childbirth, she called in the Converted Monk, an ex-priest named Lemuel Gardiner, who convinced her to bequeath her fortune, including her children's inheritance, to his church to ensure her salvation. Gardiner is as thorough a rascal as Jervis. Besides exemplifying the duplicity of Catholic priests by never having converted from Catholicism at all, he has seduced the mother's impoverished cousin, driving her to obtain an abortion, and, after the mother's death, laid claim to the dead woman's estate and her two young children, Harry and Ann, soon renamed Fanny and Ralph. The mother's cousin stole the children and raised them as her own but now is dying and about to leave them destitute. Fanny is on the brink of falling prey to one of several seducers prowling about, including Jervis, and Ralph is contemplating a life of crime. For these two, a corrupt priest has been the root of all evil.

True to Lippard's practice of meting out providential endings, justice is eventually served all round. The orphans' inheritance is restored, Fanny and Charles Lester marry, and virtually all the humble but moral characters end up farming their own land in Indiana. The villainous clergymen are both punished. Like Pyne, Jervis gets a relatively mild comeuppance—public humiliation after he proves himself a coward in a fire, and a near-lynching in Indiana after he tries to pull off a sham marriage with Fanny. Gardiner comes in for harsher treatment, suggesting that Lippard was less tolerant of Catholics than his satire of Pyne's anti-papalism might imply. Bent on murder-suicide, Gardiner sets Goodleigh's mansion on fire, locking himself and the capitalist in a tiny, airless iron room in the center of it. After being tortured as the walls heat up, priest and capitalist perish together in the inferno, their charred bodies found clasped together in a death struggle. It is an apt punishment for both. The priest has died because of his ties to moneyed power and his vindictive desire to punish someone, and the capitalist has suffered his own fatal middle passage in cramped and suffocating quarters, dying "the death of a leprous negro in a burning ship."[77]

And what of the promised humble home missionary? He appears early on as the minor character William Marvin, an older, obscure Millerite preacher who wears a plain, threadbare coat and lives alongside and ministers to the poorest of the poor. Because he nursed Lester's brother during a bout of smallpox, Lester entrusts him with the $15,000 that belong to Fanny and Ralph and enjoins him to find the children or, if he has not found them within a year, to donate the money to the charity of his choice. Marvin's protestations of unworthiness vouch for his honesty. But then Marvin disappears for almost the entire novel, displaced as a comforter of the poor by his daughter and a Quaker woman, suggesting that if Lippard saw authors taking over the ministerial function of providing the public with moral guidance, he imagined women filling ministers' traditional role of aiding the poor. Marvin returns at the end only to help run a massive camp meeting convened to await the projected Second Coming—which ends with the disappointment and humiliation of Christ's nonappearance. The Prologue's claims notwithstanding, Lippard could not rein in his hostility toward the clergy. Even the novel's sympathetic minister is deluded and pitiable.

While all the novel's ministers come in for serious critique, the lightning rod for Lippard's anticlericalism is Jervis, who, like Ravoni, is both a seductive public speaker and a literal seducer of women. Lippard avoided identifying him with any one minister by first calling him only the "Popular Preacher," then later revealing that "Jervis" is a pseudonym, but his character would have reminded antebellum readers of at least two ministers notorious for their personal lives, Episcopalian Samuel Farmar Jarvis (1786–1851) and Methodist John Newland Maffitt (1794–1850).[78] Jarvis, a wealthy Episcopalian minister, had been tried for marital cruelty in a much-publicized 1839 case in Connecticut. Although better known as an antiquarian and scholar than as a preacher, Jarvis allegedly had smooth, cosmopolitan manners and a "quite prepossessing" appearance that may have inspired Jervis's urbanity and good looks. In a civil trial, Jarvis's wife Sarah charged her husband with a decade's worth of outrages, including physically abusing her and their children, failing to support her financially, paying improper attention to the German governess, and—much like Jervis, who slanders Lester's sister— circulating about her "most wrongful and injurious reports for the purpose of turning against her the current of public opinion." Jarvis denied everything and accused Sarah of insanity. The state legislature adjudged him not guilty.[79]

Even given the Jervis/Jarvis homonym, Jervis was just as likely to make contemporary readers think of celebrity preacher John Maffitt. Born in Dublin, Maffitt married, had three children, and worked as a tailor (a vocation he would later try to deny) before separating from his wife and emigrating to the United States in 1819. After affiliating with the New York Methodists, he became an acclaimed yet always controversial evangelist. Scandal hit in 1822 when the *New England Galaxy* ran reports of his heavy drinking and inappropriate behavior with young women, charges he denounced as libel. His case came before an ecclesiastical court, where he was charged with "1. Falsehood 2. Infidelity 3. Betraying confidence 4. Ridiculing persons coming to the altar 5. Loose, light, and lascivious conduct." Or to be more precise, Maffitt had supposedly recycled his sermons; professed that he did not believe in the Trinity; gossiped; "laughed in his sleeve" at an older man whom one of his sermons had moved to tears; drank too much; and, worst of all, flirted shamelessly with various women, including the three sisters of one of Maffitt's chief accusers, Alexander Jones, Jr., when Maffitt was staying with the Jones family for a month. The court found Maffitt not guilty, while censuring him for "want of judgment and prudence."[80] Maffitt won the libel case. This trial seems to have inspired several aspects of Jervis, including his questionable sincerity, his smirking at penitent hearers after the sermon, and his predatory behavior with young women in families offering him hospitality. The Maffitt case may also have inspired Lippard to center a novel on a young man determined to defend a sister's honor against a lecherous minister.

At the 1822 trial, Maffitt begged forgiveness and promised to be more "watchful and prudent" in the future, but this was easier said than done.[81] Writing *Memoirs* in 1849, Lippard could draw not only on that early trial, whose accusations and counter-accusations lived on in pamphlet form, but also on Maffitt's long, checkered history of preacherly triumph and private indiscretion. Maffitt had recovered from disgrace to become a nationally acclaimed revivalist in the late 1820s and 1830s, preaching in both rural and urban areas and drawing at times thousands of listeners. His preaching style was short on argument and long on rhetorical flourishes and vivid images, which one contemporary attributed to his "long course of novel-reading." From fiction, supposedly, he crafted a style that dealt heavily in "jewels, stars, rainbows, and all that gaudy, glittering imagery, which constitutes the imaginative orator's peculiar capital and stock in trade."[82] Maffitt's fame, especially in the South and West, was such that he was selected chaplain to Congress in 1841 and, after his death in 1850, included in Presbyterian minister William Buell Sprague's nine-volume compendium, *Annals of the American Pulpit* (1856–1869), designed to honor America's best preachers from 1620 to 1855.[83] Yet his relationships with women were a constant source of trouble. When his wife and three children eventually followed him from Ireland to the United States, they settled in New Orleans, then Galveston, while he continued to travel widely and, some claimed, tried to justify his separation from his wife by circulating slanderous reports about her. At the same time, critics accused him of attending far more to his female than to his male converts. The cloud over his personal life broke in 1847, when, during a period in which his wife died and he was preaching a series of sermons at a crowded church in Brooklyn, he decided to marry one of his auditors, whom he met for the first time at the mourners' bench. She was the sixteen-year-old Frances, or "Fanny," Smith, stepdaughter of Judge John Pierce of

Brooklyn. The age difference alone shocked many, and critics charged that he had preyed on the girl's vanity and seduced her by getting her drunk. The marriage did not last. Maffitt was exasperated with his young wife's lack of piety and fondness for dress and flirting; Fanny chafed under his heavy-handed rule and unflappable belief that he knew what was best for her. After a few months, Fanny was living in a boarding house and Maffitt was back on the road. Rumor had it that Maffitt had gone so far as to arrange for a friend and fellow pastor to seduce her, so that it might be easier to divorce her for infidelity, while Judge Pierce charged that Maffitt—"this *infamous, lying, drunken villain*"—was circulating stories that his daughter had already been pregnant with another man's child when they married. The separation became final when after a brief reconciliation Fanny refused to obey Maffitt and returned home to her mother.[84] She died of typhus not long after. This disastrous marriage damaged Maffitt's reputation, as did further rumors of impropriety in the late 1840s, but he continued to lead revivals throughout the late 1840s. When he died suddenly in 1850, his defenders claimed that the many false accusations against him had literally broken his heart (they cited the coroner's report); his critics alleged suicide or *delirium tremens*.[85]

Maffitt's sordid history was a goldmine for Lippard, and the many points of connection between Maffitt and Jervis render implausible Lippard's claims that the novel indicted no one in particular. In the March 10, 1849 issue of the *Quaker City* weekly, Lippard noted that many readers had written in with guesses as to the "original" of Jervis and that the Western papers were iden-tifying him with Maffitt. Lippard denied it outright: "Once for all, we must state this impression to be altogether erroneous. With Mr. Maffit [*sic*] we have nothing to do, either in the walks of literature, or in the walks of daily life. We do not attack persons."[86] These protests that, in effect, any resem-blance to persons living or dead was entirely coincidental were most likely Lippard's attempt to protect himself from a lawsuit—a smart move, given that in 1822 Maffitt had sued the *New England Galaxy* for libel and won. Despite this disclaimer, there is good reason to think that Lippard wrote more truly when he later claimed that the story "contained too much truth [. . .] to be called a fiction" and was rather "a picture of *real life*."[87] Lippard had known about Maffitt since at least 1843, when as editor of the *Citizen Soldier* he had written a blurb referring to him as a "popular preacher" and seconding the New York papers' critique of him as one who generated excite-ment but exercised little real influence.[88] Jervis follows this model: besides also being a "Popular Preacher," he is so indifferent to his hearers' spiritual development that he leaves the church building soon after preaching, while the most distressed are still standing at the mourners' bench. Further, many of the details surrounding Jervis mirror the descriptions of, and accusations against, Maffitt. Jervis, too, is an eloquent, successful preacher from an indeterminate background who, in good Methodist fashion, vividly paints images of heaven and hell for audiences drawn from all classes of society. He also, like Maffitt, is a master of sexual impropriety who exploits his itinerant status to flirt with women, especially fashionable ones—Maffitt, one "Miss H." in Nashville; Jervis, Sophia Snawlip—and smiles ambiguously as he moves among the penitent, as if he might be laughing at them, or flirting.[89] Finally, he, too, tries to end a new marriage by spreading unsavory rumors about his wife; in both cases, the wife is soon dead. Lippard's naming the object of Jervis's intended seduction "Fanny" is another nod to the knowing reader.

In modeling Jervis on Maffitt, Lippard did more than simply make hay from scandal. He also intervened in the public debate surrounding Maffitt by telling a story that rebutted his defenders, in particular a lengthy pamphlet about his marriage, Moses Elsemore's *An Impartial Account of the Life of the Rev. John N. Maffitt* (1848). The pamphlet, as the title suggests, adopted a tone of neutrality, celebrating Maffitt's eloquence while also crediting the idea that he paid inappropriate attention to his female parishioners and conceding that he was partly to blame for his two unhappy marriages. After weighing the evidence of the minister's defenders and detractors and reprinting letters from Frances Smith, Judge Pierce, and Maffitt himself, Elsemore concluded that the charges against Maffitt must be untrue because such a villain could not have gone unexposed while succeeding so brilliantly as a revivalist. In *Memoirs* Lippard demurred: public success did not preclude a preacher from performing so faultlessly that he duped even close observers. The novel makes this point when Lester, scrutinizing Jervis at the mourners' bench after the sermon to determine whether or not the preacher is also his seducer's sister, finds that he cannot plumb the man's character and that the preacher seems completely sincere: "'It cannot be the same!' he murmured, gazing upon that Face, which was softened in every line by the impulse of deep religious feeling. 'No! I am mistaken!'"[90] And yet Jervis is the seducer Lester seeks. Beyond pointing up clerical hypocrisy, the scene acknowledges that preachers could be complex individuals with deep religious feelings *and* a history of immoral behavior—a nuanced point in a world that wanted to see religious devotion as intimately linked to moral action and ministers as either men of God or atheistic charlatans. Jervis warns readers to be on their guard against all preachers, no matter how religiously fervent.

The description of Jervis's sermon that unfolds over several chapters early in *Memoirs* is surprisingly complex, far more so than the one in Pyne's church. It shows Lippard wrestling with the phenomenon of popular, evan-

gelical preaching—disdaining it, envying it, and meditating on its short-
comings. Jervis, so far identified only as the Popular Preacher, delivers a
spellbinding sermon on the apocalypse to a large, diverse, overflowing congregation at the fictional "St. Simon's," which the narrator insists should not
be identified with any particular Philadelphia church. Young and old, rich
and poor line the galleries, aisles, and windows, filling the church from the
door to the pulpit steps. All strain to hear the preacher's clear, musical voice.
Though not a Millerite, Jervis is exploiting public anxiety about the end of
the world by describing scenes of flames and final judgment, with heaven for
the "Saved" and God's vengeance for the "Lost," a message the novel scorns
as shameless fear-mongering. Those who throng to hear the sermon but cannot enter the church shove and shout, suggesting that any such sermons they
have heard have done them little good. Heat and crowds make the air inside
oppressive and "almost—pestilential," a commentary less on the notorious
difficulty of ventilating large urban churches than on the threatening sermon. Fear is the listeners' dominant mood. Though at times their response
defies description—"Words are vain to describe the effect of these words"—it
is something like a vast, prolonged wailing, "as though a multitude were tossing in the ocean waves, and uttering their last cry ere they sank forever." The
metaphor gives an ominous spin to the rhetoric of the sublime associated
with great preaching: the sermon is like a mighty wave, a force of nature, but
able only to destroy, not uplift.[91] The sermon assumes an even more sinister
dimension when, a few chapters later, Jervis mesmerizes Fanny and another
character, an incident implying that he, like Ravoni, uses his "magnetic" abilities to exercise a seductive power over listeners.

Yet even as the novel holds the sermon up for critique, the chapters in
St. Simon's suggest an envy of popular preaching by balancing satire with an
admiration for the preacher's ability to command his audience. The narrator
lingers on the vast crowd drawn from all classes and on the pulpit's immediate and extensive power: "Every soul hung on the Preacher's voice. When
his accents fell, you were appalled by the awful stillness of the place. When
his voice arose in thunder tones, it was answered by an hundred others." The
people shriek, sob, moan, and shout for joy, and the preacher's words are
"printed on the hearts of thousands." His voice moves even the most resistant
hearers: Lester, having tracked down the preacher only to avenge his sister's
seduction, is swept up in the collective emotion and the images "of a calm
bright world beyond the grave." His heart melts, he sighs deeply, the tears roll
down his cheeks. He shudders without knowing why.[92] The extended sermon
scene highlights the comparative advantages of preachers versus authors.
Preachers address an audience that is real, tangible, seemingly unified, and

able to be immediately and visibly moved. The novelist puts mute words on a page and hopes to find an audience that is necessarily scattered, asynchronous, distractible, and openly critical.

While envying the preacher's power, Lippard was unwilling to cede an inch of moral or theological ground to Jervis or the evangelical ministers he represented. Just as the veteran's and narrator's speeches counter Pyne's preaching, so here two speakers promoting Lippard's own views on Christian faith parry Jervis. The first is that of the ingenuous Fanny, who explains at the mourners' bench that she has barely listened to the sermon because she was so worried about her dying mother (i.e., unbeknownst to her, her mother's cousin). Her inattention makes the point that sermon-listening is less important than caring for the sick and dying or, by extension, any of the city's suffering poor. Fanny answers Jervis's question about whether she goes to church by saying that although she is usually too tired from working all week to attend on Sunday, she has often thought while sitting at home that "with all our wretchedness, we poor people are the very kind of people whom our Saviour came to make happier." And when she has prayed while sewing, she has felt "'a warm feelin' here—here—as if the good Lord had spoken in his own way, even to me.'"[93] Fanny articulates two of Lippard's own religious principles: the radical message, associated with Philadelphia Universalism, that Jesus came primarily to be a comfort to the poor and the more traditional pietistic message, common to his German ancestors and the Methodism of his youth, that personal devotional feeling is the touchstone of true religion. The novel affirms the value of Fanny's testimony when the eavesdropping Lester sheds a tear.

Then Lester, too, steps back and comments on the scene at St. Simon's. More complex and intellectualized than Fanny's naïve piety, Lester's response suggests Lippard's attempt to come to terms with the popularity of religious beliefs and practices he rejected. After Jervis leaves the building, Lester leans against the pulpit railing, dispirited and confused, incredulous that the preacher who has proclaimed the damnation of sinners so mercilessly could be the perjurer and murderer of his sister. He reflects that though some would find "food for mirth and derision" in the hell-fired theology and emotional displays, one cannot call a religion false for these reasons alone, or even because the minister is a hypocrite. He ponders, "Admitting that the Preacher is a sensualist and these manifestations of Religion are extravagant to the last degree, shall I therefore call this Religion a falsehood, the mode of worship an idle play, a hollow mockery? Not so—not so." His meditation ends with the creedal proclamation (cited in part above), "I feel most vividly that *that Form of Religion only is false which teaches one sect to deride another, and with its dogmas buries and confounds that principle of Universal Brotherhood which flowed from the life of Christ himself.*"[94] In naming sectarianism the cardinal sin and Universal Brotherhood the supreme virtue, the novel strikes a delicate balance, both critiquing organized religion and affirming the worth of the common people whose eagerness to hear preaching such as Jervis's would seem to open them up to scorn.

At stake in this negotiation is democracy itself, as criticizing the public's religious judgment calls into question the principle of self-government. If the people cannot be trusted to choose their religious leaders wisely, how can they be trusted to choose their political representatives? Lippard had largely ignored this issue with Pyne, whose church he had ridiculed even though it included "male and female, old and young, high and low, rich and poor." There the spectacle of massed humanity is repulsive: the hearers are "packed together [. . .] like sardines in a tin box."[95] *Memoirs* presents the array of classes and ages assembled to hear the preacher much more sympathetically: "Young and old, rich and poor, the fashionable and the rude laborer, the poor woman who sold vegetables in market, and the rich one who merely squandered her husband's money—all were there, presenting contrasts vivid and innumerable."[96] Lester's creed echoes this more tolerant perspective by affirming that one of the benefits of religion is its ability to foster communal solidarity.

But then, as if impatient with attempting to make peace with popular preaching, Lippard jumps onto the page to defend the novel's superiority to the sermon. It is one of those rare moments when the author rather than the narrator speaks in the middle of the story. After defending the notion that "mere worldlings" such as Lester could have genuine and worthwhile religious ideas, Lippard turned to his main point—that novelists have a religious vocation and might, in fact, do more good than ministers:

> And even the Writer of Novels, who now sends these words to you, from his isolated room, may sometimes feel some impulses born of Eternity stirring within his bosom. Can you believe it? The pen which now writes, may do a braver, better work for Humanity, than the pen which merely writes a Sermon in defence of a mere creed, or turns ink to gall again, by putting down on pure white paper, some horrible Dogma of Theology, stolen from the cells of Heathen barbarity. Will you admit it?
>
> [The Writer of Novels] thinks that the Novel which goes every where, and speaks to all hearts—speaks perchance to fifty thousand people at the same moment—may be made the instrument of that kind of Christianity which has only one word in its vocabulary—Brotherhood.

He thinks—this profane Writer of Novels, mark you—that he, even he, has a work to do in the world, and that his work is to speak the wrongs and the hopes of Humanity in the parables of Fiction.

And sometimes there comes a thought to him, that he is doing a better work by writing Novels, than he would be doing were he to put himself to making Sermons and tinkering Creeds. That the talent which is given him, is not given to be crushed. That when his pen no longer moves, and when the hand that grasps it has gone to dust—when his place in your streets is vacant, and his room no longer witnesses his lonely vigil—that even then the words which he has written may do a good work in some heart yet unborn; and that some humble soul, sitting down by the wayside of the world, may bless his memory—even his, the Writer of Novels.

And thus it is, my respectable scorner of Novel Writers, that the Novel Writer has something good in his heart, and something Divine in the impulse which guides his pen.[97]

Here Lippard elevated both his message and his medium, advocating for a radical, Universalist-inspired version of Christianity against the orthodox preachers' "heathen barbarity" and for the democracy and universality of the novel against the irrelevance and sectarianism of the sermon. Whereas a popular preacher might address thousands in a packed church, a novelist, even one who scribbled in obscurity, could speak to "fifty thousand" at once (more even than gathered to hear the legendary Whitefield) as well as to future generations, who would "bless his memory." Nowhere was Lippard clearer that he wanted to see novelists triumph over ministers in American culture.

Lippard also made this point vividly in an editor's column in the January 27, 1849, issue of the *Quaker City* weekly, the same issue that carried on its first page Chapter 16 of *Memoirs*, which describes the powerful effect of Jervis's preaching on the gathered listeners. The column presented the author as a romantic artist whose work achieved far more than that of more prestigious men, especially ministers. It began by ironically conceding that the novelist's tools—"a quire of writing paper, a bottle of ink, and a steel pen" (worth just thirty-seven cents, he says)—were nothing compared to a golden-hilted sword, a pocket full of bank notes, or a high pulpit decked out with velvet and gold fringe. The author takes up his tools alone in his narrow, dingy room on the city's outskirts, a "hermit in a brick wilderness." His only comfort is a novel he has written, which is no less than "his Soul bound up in a brown paper cover." This novel tells stories of the rich few who oppress the many, of the millions who are cheated, starved, and hanged, and of such consola-

tions as the "divine tenderness of woman." It reaches readers in all thirty
states simultaneously: the mechanic in his New York garret, the traveler in
the cabin of a Mississippi steamboat, the planter in his Virginia mansion,
the forester by his watch-fire in the Maine snows. It soon crosses national
boundaries. An American soldier in Mexico reads it out loud to his com-
rades. "[S]ixty thousand" English people read it. Translated, it travels across
Europe: it is "a Pilgrim over all the Earth, free to wander from the hut to the
Palace, and free to wander forever." The preacher may "say the same things to
a thousand people every Sunday in the year," but the novel preaches a better
message and reaches a far wider audience.[98]

Although Lippard championed novel-writing over preaching, he seems
not to have been able to imagine the novel as morally authoritative without
sermonic discourse. The narrator of *Memoirs* preaches less often than that
of *The Quaker City* but more directly and at greater length. One chapter in
particular carries a great deal of the novel's didactic burden. When young
Ralph climbs to the top of the half-constructed Girard College to elude the
villains he fears are chasing him, the narrator turns to the reader and says,
"Let us place the young outcast once more upon the marble roof, and listen
to a Sermon preached by 'a writer of immoral books.'" Readers are then told
that if they are reading only for the plot, they can skip the next chapter, but
if they "wish to hear a sermon, with Girard College for a pulpit," they should
read on. Lippard's regular invocation of Girard College as a symbol of the
oppression of the poor, especially in the name of religion, would have clued
in many readers to the sermon's probable message. In letting readers choose
whether or not to read a sermon whose purport they can guess, Lippard
sought to defuse potential resentment—and acknowledged that sermons and
novels resisted mixing. The next chapter's title, "A Sermon from the Top of
Girard College, By 'A Writer of Immoral Books,'" continues the polemic of
Lippard's earlier rant from "the Writer of Novels."[99]

The unapologetically digressive Writer's sermon offers a collective vision
that compensates for the story's focus on selfish, corrupt individuals. Like
other reformist novelists of his day—Elizabeth Gaskell in *Mary Barton*
(1845), for instance, or Charlotte Brontë in *Shirley* (1849)—Lippard struggled to adapt the novel to the representational demands of complex, systemic
social and economic problems. When Goodleigh dies, one evildoing capitalist has been punished, but the problem of capitalism remains untouched.
When the virtuous characters are rewarded with land out West, the problems of urban tenancy are evaded. The Writer's sermon, in contrast, foregrounds collectivities and institutions. Its first line, "Doth not a curse rest
upon the Great City?" sets the tone. With variations on this question serving

as a refrain, the sermon first denounces a series of types whose behavior implicitly undermines the integrity of social institutions: the Unjust Judge, who punishes the poor more severely than the rich; the Editor, who corrupts public morals by running ads for abortifacients; and the Lawyer, who argues any case for gold. Then, more radically, the sermon critiques capitalism, echoing ideas that Lippard had advanced in his 1848 address to the Philadelphia convention of the Industrial Congress, a short-lived political organization that advocated land reform and the ten-hour day.[100] The sermon decries "the universal fever for the fruits of labor, without labour's [sic] honest work" and the "eternal combat, between man and man, between weak and strong, and all for the wages of the poor man's toil." It also suggests that a return to the land will help solve the problems of economic inequality. The Writer sets the cursed city against the mountain valley, "where the air of God is free," and invokes the words of Thomas Jefferson, idolized as a truth-speaking "apostle of Humanity," as a virtual scripture: "A GREAT CITY IS THE SORE OF THE BODY POLITIC." Like all sermons, this one holds out hope, ending with a postmillennial vision of the new Jerusalem: "A GOLDEN CITY! Golden with brotherly love, golden with justice higher and deeper than 'old English law,' golden with impulses born of God, and working for the good, not of the greatest number, but of the whole number[!]"[101] Whitmanesque in anticipating future readers, the Writer speculates that if this novel should "wander down the pathway of the next century, and encounter the eyes of 1949, how will the readers of that era, living amidst a redeemed civilization, wonder at the barbarous laws and fiendish theologies of the year 1849?" Here the Writer speaks as a preacher, not a politician, eschewing specifics about how humanity might go about achieving the harmonious new social order. Lippard's address to the Industrial Congress in 1848 had been similarly vague. It maintained that someday every worker would live on his own land and that the nation would be free of capitalists and speculators, but did not delve into strategy: "Even while we may differ with regard to details, and hold various opinions as to the method of Progress, let us never, for an instant, cease to gird to our hearts the holy thought of 'BROTHERHOOD.'"[102]

The Writer's sermon is the novel's most fully articulated rejoinder to the Popular Preacher. It calls for collective salvation in this world rather than individual salvation for a few in the next, and it does so in a style as vivid and exclamatory as that of the era's evangelical preachers. Most strikingly, the Writer takes readers on an aerial tour of the city and, with characteristic Lippardian voyeurism, shows them the city's uncovered housetops. Like a Methodist preacher at a camp meeting, the Writer invokes supernatural beings to intensify his gloomy scenes, inviting readers to picture the "fiends

of darkness" who look on and laugh and the witnessing angels who cry
tears of blood.[103] He then describes scenes of urban misery and corruption
with the melodramatic intensity evangelical preachers typically reserved for
the crucifixion of Jesus and the agonies of the damned. The lonely widow
starves "with her babe lying dead upon her breast," bank directors plan their
"legal robbery of the common people," the "White Slave" toils at her needle,
and a rich man's son propositions an overworked seamstress, who in capit-
ulating will cross "the line which divides Heaven and Hell."[104] The Writer
heaps especial scorn on a priest who, having just finished a powerful sermon against Catholics or perhaps French novels, glides home to his study to
drink wine and write a sermon defending the riches of Trinity Church. The
Writer exhorts the priest to look across eighteen hundred years to the Sea
of Galilee, where "The Christ who has just been preaching to multitudes of
the Poor, is now sitting in their midst, feeding these poor with actual bread!"
Like a Methodist preacher describing the torments of hell and the ecstasies of
heaven, the Writer contrasts the scenes of the city's miseries with the vision
of Jesus feeding the poor and the final promise of the "Golden City."[105]

Perhaps no antebellum author defended the moral value of fiction as
vociferously as Lippard. Yet even as he extolled novelists in his editorial columns and made fiction the centerpiece of the *Quaker City* weekly, he seems
to have grown impatient with stories as a vehicle for his social vision. In a column in the May 12, 1849 issue of the *Quaker City,* which carried that week's
installment of *Memoirs* on the front and back covers, he declared that "the
only rule of literary composition worth minding" was the principle, "Have
something to say, and say it with all your might."[106] He continued to write
fiction, but his work in the late 1840s suggests he felt he could never speak
mightily enough on paper. From his speaking engagement at Burr's church in
1845 until his death in 1852, he lectured throughout the Eastern states building support for the Brotherhood of the Union.[107] He conducted an especially
robust public speaking program in 1848, when he addressed the Industrial
Congress; ran for the office of district commissioner of Philadelphia, which
he did not gain; and campaigned for presidential candidate Zachary Taylor.
He was supposedly a remarkable speaker whose performances matched the
energy of his print persona. He would, as his first biographer has it, begin a
speech in a low monotone charged with "a quiver, a thrill, which shows you
that the speaker feels what he says," then step forward, raise his voice, and let
loose a torrent of words. Fueled by righteous fervor, he gestured freely, "now
raising one arm to heaven; now bringing down both hands at a time, as he
emphatically denounces some giant wrong; now pointing the 'slow finger of

unmoving scorn' at some petty meanness; and now stamping his foot passionately."[108] The novelist had become a preacher in the flesh.

Lippard also pressed beyond print in the last years of his brief life by
founding and running the Brotherhood of the Union, a quasi-religious secret
society dedicated to the unity of men of all classes and creeds who wanted
to work toward the "harmonious" relationship of labor and capital, the equi-
table distribution of land, and the realization of America as the "Palestine
of Redeemed Labor."[109] Inspired by the Odd Fellows and the Masons (to
both of which organizations Lippard belonged), as well as by Rosicrucian-
ism and the Bavarian Order of the Illuminati, the Brotherhood inducted
members and ran meetings according to elaborate rituals designed by Lippard himself.[110] With this organization, he sought to educate and uplift the
laboring men who might not be reached by print or even speeches: "Many
persons, who cannot receive ideas through the means of Books, or oral lessons, may be instructed by means of rites and symbols."[111] As a precursor to
the Knights of Labor and several other labor societies after the Civil War,
the Brotherhood may be Lippard's most significant legacy.[112]

Too often reduced to the sensationalism of *The Quaker City*, Lippard
was a versatile author who in less than a dozen years crafted an extraordinary career as editor, writer, and political activist. Still haunting the borders
of the canon, his fiction merits further attention for how it combines elements often considered incongruous—sensationalism and moral didacticism, sentimentalism and radical politics, working-class consciousness and
Protestant faith. As I have tried to show, his work also throws into relief the
tension between antebellum novelists and ministers, revealing how novelists resented fiction's lowly status and the clergy's complacent assumption
of moral authority. In writing novels that slammed the clergy and preached
politically radical sermons readers were unlikely to hear in church, Lippard
claimed moral authority for fiction while promoting a new gospel centered
on this-world redemption of the poor. The novelists discussed in subsequent
chapters were seldom as vehement in their anticlericalism, but they, too,
often sought to establish fiction's moral authority through the two-pronged
strategy of humiliating clerical characters and presenting moral visions in
sermonic voice. In *The Scarlet Letter* Hawthorne would turn to both of these
devices—though with an un-Lippardian smirk that mocked both the preachers and his own ambitions.[113]

CHAPTER 4

᎗

Secularizing the Sermon in
The Scarlet Letter

A S AN ADULT, Rose Hawthorne related a deliciously symbolic incident from her father's boyhood that her aunt Elizabeth, or "Ebe," had told
her. As a child Ebe had owned a tinted bust of John Wesley, one with flowing, white hair and a countenance that seemed to say, "'My sermon is endless!'" Hawthorne hated this bust even at the tender age of four and, failing to
convince the family to get rid of it, took matters into his own hands. Having
discovered the "hollowness" of this "melancholy" bust—in Rose's story, the
words sound like a protest against Methodism itself—young Nathaniel took
it outside one winter day, filled it with water, and waited for the ice to burst
it, like a pitcher. Wesley held his own; the plaster did not break.[1]

The episode speaks both to Hawthorne's deep-seated resistance to religious authority and to the enduring strength of that authority. Although
Hawthorne's fictive treatment of religious concepts such as sin, confession,
and perfectionism is familiar critical territory, his imaginative engagement
with the preaching of his own day has been overlooked. The most memorable preachers of his fiction—Ilbrahim's mother in "The Gentle Boy," Reverend Hooper in "The Minister's Black Veil," and Dimmesdale—are typically
regarded as commentaries on the religion of the seventeenth century, not the
nineteenth. Yet Hawthorne grew up and wrote in a world full of preachers,
and we cannot understand the value he claimed for his fiction without reading his stories in this context. After examining Hawthorne's early experiences
with sermons, I first discuss how his short stories and sketches reveal his

disenchantment with preaching and his sense that fiction should displace it. I then turn to *The Scarlet Letter* to show how Hawthorne critiqued his contemporaries' adulation of ministers by using Dimmesdale to satirize a famous Salem preacher and how he brought his preacher/author doubling to a head by figuring preaching as a powerful, meaningful mode of speaking that novelists might well envy even as they denied the sermon's claims to totalizing truth and sacred difference.

Despite trying to smash Wesley, Hawthorne in his youth was no religious iconoclast, perhaps because his religious upbringing included latitude for him to develop his own beliefs. Childhood Sundays were spent listening to sermons with his mother and sisters at Salem's Congregationalist First Church, where John Prince served as pastor from 1779 to 1836. An uncontroversial minister better known for his scientific experiments than for his preaching, Prince won Hawthorne's abiding respect. Hawthorne would later recall him in terms that suggest a firsthand knowledge of the ministerial adulation he ascribes to *The Scarlet Letter*'s Puritans; Prince was "the good old, silver-headed clergyman, who seemed to me as much a Saint then on earth as he is now in Heaven."[2] As for theology, Prince's church occupied an ambiguous position during the 1810s, a key decade for the splitting of Unitarian and Trinitarian congregations. As late as 1827 members were required to sign an agreement confessing belief in Christ as savior and committing to strict Sabbath observance.[3] Yet the church was known for its liberal tendencies, and William Ware included a biographical essay on Prince in his two-volume *American Unitarian Biography*.[4] The bustling Manning household exposed Hawthorne to other shades of Protestantism as well: his grandparents worshipped at William Bentley's liberal East Church; his conservative aunts, with the orthodox at the Tabernacle.[5]

"The Spectator," the newspaper Hawthorne created and hand-printed as a teenager, is a surprisingly religious production that, for all its playfulness, captures a youthful piety in line with liberal Congregationalism. The first issue's "Prospectus" explained the paper's high and noble purposes, including reforming morals, instructing and amusing readers, and advancing "the cause of Religion."[6] In support of these goals, Hawthorne filled the paper with short homiletic essays on themes well suited to a liberal pulpit, including hope, benevolence, courage, ambition, idleness, solitude, and the transience of life as reflected in the passing year. He also applauded the sermons of two rather different ministers, reflecting how freely antebellum Americans crossed denominational lines in pursuit of a good sermon: William Staughton, an English Baptist immigrant who led a church and theological seminary in Philadelphia and visited Salem in the summer of 1820, and Henry

Colman, a Unitarian who would serve as the pastor of Salem's Barton Square Church when it split from East Church in 1824. In praising Colman, Hawthorne managed to pat himself on the back as well: "We have never before heard a sermon which so perfectly coincided with our own sentiments."[7]

In college Hawthorne turned away from organized religion. Disdaining the theological conservatism of Bowdoin, he skipped mandatory chapel and dodged the revivals, joked with his mother about falling asleep in services, and griped to Ebe about being forced to hear the school's president William Allen preach a "red hot Calvinist Sermon" on Sundays.[8] Before entering, he had made it clear to his mother that he would not be preparing for the ministry: "Shall you want me to be a Minister, Doctor or Lawyer?" If so, too bad: "A Minister I will not be"—a veritable no! in thunder.[9] A year later, he reiterated that "being a Minister is of course out of the Question" and proposed authorship as the alternative. He facetiously cast it as the abandonment of all piety: "But Authors are always poor Devils, and therefore Satan may take them." Moral dichotomies ripple beneath the surface here: one avows not the ministry, but authorship—not God, but Satan. Choosing authorship meant competing not only with the "scribbling sons of John Bull" he mentions in the same letter, but also with religious authority.[10]

Hawthorne's adult religious views were a mystery even to contemporaries, and his relationship to preaching, private. As a young man he checked out dozens of seventeenth- and eighteenth-century sermons from the Salem Athenaeum, as well as a couple of volumes of contemporary sermons, including one by Colman. But whatever appeal Unitarian sermons had for him was short-lived. In 1842, he grouped them together with the *Christian Examiner,* *Liberal Preacher,* and Unitarian polemics as "all such trash" and wrote that he preferred "the narrow but earnest cushionthumper of puritanical times" to "the cold, lifeless, vaguely liberal clergyman of our own day."[11] Nor did he wish to sit in a pew. He avoided attending church in Salem and Concord and declined Sophia's invitation to hear Father Taylor.[12] His antipathy to churchgoing was so marked that after his death friends and family felt compelled to try to recuperate this aspect of his life. Publisher James T. Fields blustered, "His religion was so deep and broad that he could not bear to be fastened in by a pew-door," and Julian Hawthorne reported that his father was a "tolerably diligent reader of sermons" who preferred those of Laurence Sterne and Jeremy Taylor.[13]

One of Hawthorne's earliest stories captures his sense that the nineteenth-century fiction-writer was both the Protestant preacher's double and his secular replacement. In "Passages from a Relinquished Work" (1834), originally intended as the opening piece of a story collection called "The

Story-Teller" and eventually published in *Mosses from an Old Manse* (1846), a light-hearted young man leaves the home of his stern foster father, a village parson whom irreverent parishioners call Parson Thumpcushion, to be an itinerant storyteller. Having escaped one preacher, the Story Teller meets another, the sober-minded young itinerant Eliakim Abbott. The two break bread, and Abbott proves so bashful and easily discouraged by the trials of the wayfaring life that the Story Teller feels obliged not to leave him. A fairy-tale quality marks the encounter and the pairing, with the preacher all but named as the Story Teller's doppelganger: "We were a singular couple, strikingly contrasted, yet curiously assimilated, each of us remarkable enough by himself, and doubly so in the other's company. Without any formal compact, we kept together, day after day, till our union appeared permanent." Abbott clearly symbolizes traits that the insouciant Story Teller acquired under Thumpcushion but must shed or repress to succeed in his chosen career—above all his anxiety that he should be pursuing a vocation in which he strives to better humanity, not pander to its earthly pleasures.[14] But if Abbott is the Story Teller's repressed conscience, he is also his repressed fear, melancholy, helplessness, and inability to perform in public—in short, the worst of his youth. While Abbott performs miserably in the pulpit and cannot seem to learn from his mistakes, the Story Teller, like Melville's confidence man, uses his skill as a performer and his insight into human nature to succeed among strangers. When the Story Teller fails in his first attempt at spinning stories on the stage, he refunds his disappointed auditors their money and dedicates himself to perfecting his craft. He cultivates "wide observation, varied knowledge, deep thoughts, and sparkling ones; pathos and levity, and a mixture of both, like sunshine in a rain drop; lofty imagination, veiling itself in the garb of common life; and the practised art which alone could render these gifts, and more than these, available," a catalog of virtues applicable to Hawthorne's own fiction, however self-satirically Hawthorne may have intended the parallel.[15] The Story Teller's commitment to his chosen work is transformative, catapulting him from youth to manhood: "ridiculous as the object was, I followed it up with the firmness and energy of a man." He proceeds to enjoy flirtatious encounters and the thrill of high spirits. At the one performance described, the laughter is constant, the improvisation inspired, the applause so vigorous it breaks the benches. He succeeds so well that when, looking back as a self-professed "bitter moralizer," he pontificates about "how much of fame is humbug [. . .] and how small and poor the remnant," he seems to speak only half the truth.[16] The crowd may have been tickled by slapstick, but the Story Teller achieved his aim of entertaining the masses—and gained maturity in the process. If the story expresses Hawthorne's anxiety about pursuing a career with no obvious moral meaning, it also validates the artistry of fiction-writing and the pleasures of success.

"Passages" ends by reinforcing its defense of storytelling against preaching. When the Story Teller receives a letter from Thumpcushion, he is pained and holds the letter unopened, imagining first that his guardian is grim and disapproving, then that he is sorrowful and self-reproaching. And then the Story Teller burns the letter without reading it and continues on his way—an act of rebellion that figures the rejection of ministerial authority as the precondition of storytelling. Yet the tale does not end on quite that note, just as Abbott and Thumpcushion were not the last preachers to walk the pages of Hawthorne's fiction. Unable to escape the past, the Story Teller cannot stop thinking that in burning the letter he has made an "irrevocable choice between good and evil fate," phrasing that leaves ambiguous which one he has chosen.[17] Even if one interprets storytelling (versus, possibly, a return home) as the "evil fate," Hawthorne's Romantic notion that authors were Satanic heroes—self-determining "poor devils"—redeems and glamorizes this "evil." That the Story Teller continues to travel with Abbott, who labors to convince him of the "guilt and madness" of his chosen life, underscores the difficulty fiction has escaping its moralistic past. It is hard not to see the nervous, helpless Abbott as a thorn in the Story Teller's side, an ill-matched fellow-traveler who should say to the Story Teller what the hyperscrupulous minister Babcock finally says to his chance traveling companion Christopher Newman in Henry James's *The American*: "I am very uncomfortable. I ought to have separated from you a month ago."[18] And so Abbott should leave the Story Teller but does not. The story is an argument for fiction's liberation from preaching—and a meditation on the cultural and psychic forces that prevent fiction writers from achieving that liberation.

Hawthorne's struggle with the cultural legacy of preaching and its significance for authorship is nowhere plainer than in "The Old Manse," the preface to *Mosses*. As in "Passages," Hawthorne professed to respect the past while proposing a supersessionist narrative in which fiction supplants preaching in New England's cultural landscape. Living in Emerson's ancestral home, Hawthorne claimed to feel intimidated by the manse's former clerical occupants, especially Emerson's grandfather, who wrote three thousand sermons on the manse's desk; such solemn deeds made him ashamed to have written only "idle stories." But the essay's predominant mood is not veneration but vexation, as he fails to find any wisdom at all in the sermons and other religious writings that filled the attic. The leather-bound folios of the seventeenth century and the tracts of two decades back are alike barren. Further, in telling readers that he entered the manse a "twelvemonth" after the funeral of its last clerical inhabitant, he intimated that the era of the minister was past and the mourning period over. More relevant to the current age, he implied, were his own stories, which drew their inspiration from nature itself and perhaps, too, from another work penned in the manse's study, Emerson's *Nature*. Hawthorne presented himself in his preface as interrupting an idyll of walking, boating, and lounging just long enough to pen the stories and sketches collected in *Mosses*. Thus were nature-loving fiction-writers to supplant gloomy, arid sermonizers. Yet the preface, like "Passages," could not disown the sermon altogether. Hawthorne wrote that in moving to the manse he had hoped to write, if not profound moral treatises or stirring histories, at the very least "a novel, that should evolve some deep lesson."[19] In an era in which many influential adults were loath to recognize reading fiction as a legitimate pastime, the statement makes a bold claim—one that testifies both to Hawthorne's serious goals for fiction and, with that key verb, "evolve," to his heterodox commitment to fiction as a means of developing usable truths.

Rewriting Salem's Unitarian saint

Hawthorne's antagonism toward the clergy culminated in Arthur Dimmesdale. Like Jervis in *Memoirs,* Dimmesdale is a hypocrite and coward, a variant of the "reverend rake" type and an intervention in the public discourse surrounding a specific minister—in this case, the Reverend John Emery Abbot (1793–1819) of Salem's North Church. Dimmesdale was Hawthorne's subversive reimagining of Abbot, a beloved minister whose ordination heralded the dawn of liberalism in Salem and who became an icon of liberal faith after dying at age twenty-six, when Hawthorne was fifteen.[20] In modeling Dimmesdale on this romanticized, much-memorialized minister, Hawthorne critiqued not only the hero-worship surrounding Abbot and, indeed, ministers across denominations, especially the deceased, but also the Unitarian belief in the innate goodness of human nature and attainability of human perfection.[21]

The virtual beatification of Abbot began when William Ellery Channing, who had preached Abbot's ordination sermon in 1815, returned to North Church to deliver the sermon of consolation. Channing's ordination sermon had inspired the ire of the orthodox by proclaiming many of the same ideas that would mark his more famous rallying cry to Unitarianism, the 1819 ordination sermon for Jared Sparks in Baltimore—for instance, that preaching Christ meant preaching his doctrines, not the crucifixion alone, that true religion celebrated the goodness in human nature, and that humanity was "formed for endless progress in intellectual and moral excellence and felicity."[22] The consolation sermon followed up on these themes by planting the seeds of an idea that would flourish in Unitarian circles for several generations: that Abbot's unimpeachable character and exemplary death testified to the liberal tenet that Jesus and humanity shared a fundamentally good human nature—and that Unitarianism could create paragons of piety at least equal to those of orthodoxy.[23] Throughout the nineteenth century, eulogies, prefaces to Abbot's sermons, versions of his biography, and church histories all continued to celebrate Abbot as a hero of liberal faith. Though Abbot's death preceded *The Scarlet Letter* by several decades, Hawthorne knew of the event both firsthand—family letters remark upon it, and he was living in Salem at the time—and through local history. Moreover, several events of the late 1840s had sent gusts of fresh air across the flame on Abbot's shrine. After the death of Abbot's fellow liberal clergyman and friend Henry Ware, Jr., memorialists had scrambled to honor Ware by comparing him to the saintly Abbot. When John Emery's father, Benjamin Abbot, died in 1849, an essay in the *Salem Gazette* on the Phillips and Abbot families closed by praising the son as the family member who had, to the greatest degree, "all the qualities that fit men for angels." He was "so pure in life, so pure in death!"[24] New Englanders also praised Abbot anew in letters written for the Unitarian volume of William Buell Sprague's *Annals of the American Pulpit*. Though Hawthorne would not yet have seen these letters in print, he likely knew of Sprague's project, as Salem contributors in the late 1840s included Emerson, Andrew Peabody, Samuel Gilman, Benjamin Abbot, and Charles Wentworth Upham, successor to Prince at First Church and the driving force behind Hawthorne's expulsion from the Custom House. In the 1850s Hawthorne's sister-in-law Elizabeth Peabody would become one of Sprague's most reliable contributors. In the meantime, Hawthorne may have encountered Abbot's burnished memory through Elizabeth and the rest of Sophia's family. Nathaniel and Elizabeth Peabody had joined North Church in 1816, and their three daughters followed suit: Elizabeth in 1816, Mary in 1823, and Sophia in 1827.[25] Although no record remains of young Sophia's perception of Abbot, Elizabeth recalled him through the rose-colored lenses of adolescent adoration and Unitarian loyalty. In her teens she had looked to him as a spiritual adviser; he had talked theology with her and offered to loan her books from his library.[26] In after years, she praised his "rare personality and angelic ministry," which though brief had left an "indelible impression" on Salem and been a "great experience" for the young people in the congregation. She summed up his legacy by hailing him as "one of the exceptional saints who glorified the rise of the Unitarian sect in New England."[27] Eying the wider implications of a legacy that celebrated unsullied human goodness, Daniel Walker Howe has called him "a culture hero to nineteenth-century sentimentalists."[28]

Much in *The Scarlet Letter* suggests that Dimmesdale is a sly rewriting of Abbot. Most notably, Dimmesdale's parishioners regard their pastor with the same intense veneration with which Abbot's remembered theirs. Where Ware had quoted an Exeter classmate saying of Abbot that "'no one regarded him as capable of doing wrong; we looked on him as a purer being than others around him,'" Dimmesdale's admirers see him "as little less than a heaven-ordained apostle."[29] Where Ware had written that Abbot had "an extraordinary reverence for the sacred office," Dimmesdale is, the narrator confides, "a true priest, a true religionist, with the reverential sentiment largely developed."[30] Where the anonymous "Elegiac Stanzas" penned in Abbot's honor lamented, "Could earth no more thy spirit pure controul?," some members of Dimmesdale's congregation declare that the minister is dying because "the world was not worthy to be any longer trodden by his feet."[31] Like Abbot, Dimmesdale is praised for a moral purity that seems to rival that of ministers far older than he and that gains luster from his impending death. He is honored, too, for his ability to address "the whole human brotherhood in the heart's native language," much as the Boston Unitarian minister Francis Parkman had written that Abbot preached "truths, which all minds comprehend, and all hearts can feel."[32] The rhetoric of peak adulation was also much the same. Parkman had compared Abbot to Enoch, whom God translated to heaven, while "Elegiac Stanzas" pictured angels whisking Abbot's soul to heaven: "But look! his spirit soars—it mounts amain! / Earth disappears—Heaven's portals open spread— / Angels descend that spirit to sustain!"[33] Intimations of supernatural intervention surround Dimmesdale as well. To those who hear his final sermon, "it was as if an angel, in his passage to the skies, had shaken his bright wings over the people for an instant," and after the sermon, he is "apotheosized by worshipping admirers."[34] Of course, Abbot was not the only lavishly eulogized minister in the nineteenth century, and for all the parallels, I do not mean to suggest that his posthumous glorification was the sole inspiration behind the rhetoric surrounding Dimmesdale. A similar rhetoric of ministerial eulogy can be found in funeral sermons, obituaries, and Sprague's *Annals,* suggesting that Dimmesdale was also a critique of the culture's persistent idealization of ministers.[35]

Still, several aspects of Dimmesdale's character suggest that Abbot served as Hawthorne's most immediate clerical inspiration. Dimmesdale would have reminded Hawthorne's contemporaries of Abbot in the combination of his youth and lingering, fatal illness. Abbot's creeping respiratory disease (tuberculosis, one assumes) finds its analogue in the undefined ailment that gnaws away at Dimmesdale, forcing him to stagger through his duties with his hand on his chest. Abbot's memorialists attributed his illness to a "feeble" frame and, echoing a common theme of ministerial eulogy, to his "great devotion to the studies and labors" of his office.[36] Likewise, Dimmesdale's parishioners blame his failing health on "his too earnest devotion to study, his scrupulous fulfillment of parochial duty," and—in an embellishment that highlights Dimmesdale's morbid conscience—"the fasts and vigils of which he made a frequent practice."[37] Like Abbot, who set off for Cuba to repair his health, Dimmesdale hopes to find healing in a sea voyage but does not.

Dimmesdale's personal foibles seem borrowed from Abbot as well, despite the widespread sense that, as Parkman put it, "Malice itself could find nothing against him."[38] The scant imperfections Ware attributed to Abbot also define Dimmesdale: nerves and self-doubt. Ware noted that Abbot's mind was "finely strung," that his "sensibility was acute and delicate," and that his heightened sensibilities, while not always under his control, made his personal attachments strong and his religion zealous. Similarly, Dimmesdale has a "nervous sensibility" kept in check through great effort.[39] No word in *The Scarlet Letter* better captures Dimmesdale's suppressed nervousness than the recurrent "tremulous," used to describe his voice, mouth, lips, breath, touch, and even shadow. Closely related to this constant nervous shaking is his self-doubt. While humility was a standard-issue clerical virtue, Abbot seems to have felt his deficiencies keenly: "At times [. . .] his diffidence and self-distrust oppressed him with the idea, that he should disappoint the wishes of his friends, and become a useless being." Abbot had marveled that the responsibilities of pastoral office were "committed to '*earthen vessels*'—who themselves are ignorant and wandering, surrounded with temptations, darkened by error, and polluted with sin."[40] Dimmesdale, too, feels the burden of his sinfulness and fears he will disappoint those who have believed in him. Thus he claims that if he dies it will be because he is unworthy of his office, and thus he tells himself that he stays for the Election Sermon so that the townspeople can say that he leaves "'no public duty unperformed, nor ill performed!'"[41]

But what of Dimmesdale's most obvious sin? Here Hawthorne seems to have used poetic license. No sexual scandal shadowed Abbot, and his parishioners, unlike Dimmesdale's, did not engage in any postmortem character recuperation. Yet Hawthorne had an eye for moral ambiguity, and the documents and lore surrounding Abbot would have provided fodder both for Dimmesdale's corporealization of guilt and for the sexual indiscretions themselves. That is, Abbot, too, had a burning chest—both literally, because of his lung ailment, and, metaphorically, as a sign of his supposed piety. As "Elegiac Stanzas" had it, "The good, ah, how for them thy bosom burn'd" and, when he spoke of Jesus, "How thrill'd that voice, how glow'd that sacred breast!"[42] Hawthorne literalized these metaphors, attributing the minister's fiery chest not to piety but to conscious sin. In making Dimmesdale's burning chest a sign of sin and guilt, Hawthorne hinted at dark secrets cloaked behind Abbot's reputed personal reserve. Ware reported that Abbot did not enjoy talking about himself and that he "knew that religion did not consist in being forward to tell the secrets of the soul."[43] Although no sexual transgression besmirched Abbot's memory, he does seem to have been a favorite of young women—unsurprisingly, given that he led North Church in his early twenties. For Hawthorne, Elizabeth Peabody would have been the readiest example of a young woman who had admired Abbot. Other sources, too, hint at his human appeal. Though not published until 1853, the memoir of Henry Ware's wife Mary suggests that at least a few young women of his acquaintance may have been, like the young woman Dimmesdale passes on his return from the forest, enshrining his image in their hearts so that it imparted "to religion the warmth of love, and to love a religious purity."[44] Born in 1798, Mary was in her late teens and early twenties during Abbot's ministry, and her biographer reported that both she and a friend found in Abbot "a Christian helper when they most needed Christian counsel and encouragement." A week after Abbot's death, Mary sent this friend, who witnessed the young minister's passing while staying with the Abbots in Exeter, a long letter of spiritual consolation that represented the death as an overwhelming personal loss. She professed her "almost entire inability" to write about it yet anguished over it at length. She praised his pure and blessed spirit, mourned the "loved and cherished" earthly form, and affirmed that his memory yet "awakens every emotion of affection which he excited while on earth." She assured her friend that the purification of souls after death meant that those who had died were connected to the living "more closely than earthly ties could bind us."[45] It seems no great leap for Hawthorne to have played out the potential consequences of the sexual tension surrounding this young Salem minister and his female parishioners.

Hawthorne may also have drawn inspiration for the contours of Dimmesdale's character from Abbot's published writings. Aside from the fact that there seems to be little difference between Dimmesdale's Puritanism and Abbot's Unitarianism—both focus on morality and piety with little reference to metaphysical doctrines or biblical authority—two of Abbot's printed sermons are particularly suggestive.[46] "Religious Sincerity" warns readers against hypocrisy and secret sin, and the more theologically distinctive "Knowledge of One Another in a Future State" affirms that social bonds survive the grave—that "friends who have been dear to us on earth, will, *if we and they are worthy,* be again restored to our knowledge and affection" (my italics). Abbot held that only the virtuous, those persons "whose friendship religion has hallowed," would meet in the afterlife—stern philosophy that Dimmesdale echoes in his warning to Hester not to expect a heavenly reunion.[47] Hawthorne may also have taken a cue from the only title Abbot published during his lifetime, *A Catechism of the New Testament,* a twenty-page pamphlet of religious questions for children.[48] Hawthorne treaded lightly in translating this aspect of Abbot's ministry to Dimmesdale's story; one assumes that then as now, the representation of a sexually aberrant minister interacting with children was apt to discomfit readers. The novel allays these anxieties by reassuring readers that children will naturally avoid such sinful men; as Dimmesdale tells Hester, "'I have long shrunk from children, because they often show a distrust,—a backwardness to be familiar with me.'"[49] Pearl is the all-too-significant exception. It is intriguing that instead of avoiding this delicate subject altogether, Hawthorne worked with the idea of catechism to hint at the difficulties raised when a sinful minister is responsible for the moral instruction of the young. There is Bellingham's order that either Dimmesdale or Wilson must catechize Pearl if she is to remain with Hester (after she does not answer correctly Wilson's "who made thee?") and Dimmesdale's temptation after leaving the forest to pervert his catechetical role by teaching a group of young children "some very wicked words."[50] But Dimmesdale is not shown quizzing Pearl on Puritan theology and resists the desire to pollute young ears. The avoidance of such scenes helps preserve whatever sympathy readers might have for him.

My aim in tracing the many parallels between Abbot and the young, attractive, dying, and idealized minister of *The Scarlet Letter* is to show that Hawthorne resisted not merely the hagiographic treatment of ministers common to this period but also, closer to home, the mythology that had grown up around one of the pulpit lights of early nineteenth-century Salem. Hawthorne's revision of Abbot's story in Dimmesdale challenged the Unitarian faith in the possibility of moral purity and in the peculiar moral benefits of Unitarianism, offering in place of these liberal dogmas the unsettling idea that all hearts, even those that seem purest, have something of "the worst" in them that needs to be acknowledged. Like the alchemist that Aylmer in "The Birthmark" aspires to be, Hawthorne in *The Scarlet Letter* transmuted ordinary raw materials into something far different and more valuable. From the obituaries, sentimental verses, hagiographic memoirs, and gossip surrounding a now-forgotten nineteenth-century minister came the memorable figure of Arthur Dimmesdale. Or perhaps it is more fitting to say that Hawthorne reversed the alchemic process, dissolving Abbot's golden reputation into the base realities of professional ambition, pride, sin, shame, and a community's wishful thinking.

The Election Sermon

It is a credit to Hawthorne's art that readers can pity the "miserable priest" at all.[51] If Dimmesdale does not come off as quite the villain that Jervis does, it is only because he is partially redeemed by the poignancy of his internal conflict, evident in his dialogues with Hester and with Chillingworth, in his solitary brooding, and, most dramatically, in his sermons. Dimmesdale's single most powerful act of preaching is the Election Sermon, worth scrutinizing for how it reconceptualized preaching while projecting Hawthorne's authorial anxieties and ambitions.

One way to defamiliarize this climactic scene is to recognize it as a distinctively Hawthornean embellishment to a storyline borrowed in large part from an older novel of ministerial adultery, *Adam Blair* (1822) by Scotsman John Gibson Lockhart. Hawthorne's debt to *Adam Blair* is tremendous.[52] In *Adam Blair,* the title character is a young, upright, much-beloved Calvinist clergyman thrown together in the same house for several months with Charlotte, his dead wife's cousin. Full-spirited, dark-haired, and unhappily married, Charlotte becomes a mother-figure to Adam's beautiful little girl and Adam's conversational companion on countryside rambles. The two drift into platonic yet smoldering intimacy. Soon Charlotte's estranged husband gets wind of the town gossip around the pair's unusual living arrangement and banishes his wife to a deserted castle in the Highlands. Adam, beside himself with longing and despair, pursues Charlotte to the castle, and after a few glasses of wine, a stormy night, a tale of marital woe, and four rows of close-set asterisks, the minister awakens as that rarest of novelistic types, a fallen man.

Illness strikes. Wan and visibly aged after enduring the fever that carries off Charlotte, Adam refrains from public confession just long enough to travel to Glasgow, where a meeting of presbyters is debating the rumors surrounding him. As an older clergyman avows Blair's innocence before the assembly, Blair enters and addresses his fellow clergymen: "The unhappy

Blair, laying his hand upon his breast, answered quickly and clearly, 'Call me no more your brother—I am a fallen man.—I am guilty'"[53] His peers are incredulous, but, shaken and contrite, he reasserts his guilt, announces his intention to become a peasant as his father was before him, and beseeches their prayers. The scene closes with a tableau of repentance: the gathered elders on their knees and Adam weeping with his forehead in the dust. Humbled, penitent, almost broken, he exiles himself to a desolate cottage with his daughter, where he lives and works the land for ten long years, until his former parishioners insist that he resume his pastoral role.

Both *Adam Blair* and *The Scarlet Letter* are stories in which a young Calvinist minister commits adultery with a beautiful young woman and endures a subsequent public humiliation. Both have a little girl to triangulate the relationship and a jealous husband to haunt it. Both have a midnight scene midway through the story in which the minister screams but wakes no one. Both have a lonely cottage where one of the sexual transgressors labors for years before achieving reintegration into the community. And both claim to be historical fictions, Lockhart's in earnest, as *Adam Blair* draws upon the transgressions of the Scottish divine George Adam (1722–1759). Yet for all the similarities of the two novels, they take very different directions at the end, especially in the final scenes of ministerial self-revelation. In *Adam Blair,* there is no glorious exit, "triumphant ignominy," or elevation of any sort. Sin means only sorrow, silence, one's head in the dust. Dimmesdale's confession, in contrast, is famously equivocal, its sincerity marred by the grandiose, Pauline claim that he is "the one sinner of the world!" and that evasive grammatical shift from first- to third-person.[54] And in *The Scarlet Letter,* we have not one climactic speech, but two.

To the speech of confession Hawthorne added the Election Sermon, when Dimmesdale preaches with unsurpassed eloquence and reaches the apex of his professional achievement and popular acclaim. The listeners are entranced and afterward jubilant: "Never, from the soil of New England, had gone up such a shout! Never, on New England soil, had stood the man so honored by his mortal brethren as the preacher!"[55] It is an inspired narrative addition. It magnifies the tragedy by widening the distance between the heights to which Dimmesdale rises and the depths to which he falls, and it prolongs the suspense before the lovers' fate is disclosed. Like Hester, the reader must wait out this uninterruptible discourse.

The sermon's content matters less than one might expect. Readers learn only that the subject "it appeared, had been the relations between the Deity and the communities of mankind, with a special reference to the New England which they were here planting in the wilderness," and that Dimmesdale, unlike the prophets of old, issues no warnings of doom for disobedience. Instead he promises a "high and glorious destiny for the newly gathered people of the Lord."[56] Although this topic was common enough for a Puritan election sermon, there is little distinctively Puritan about the discourse: no introductory text, no biblical proof texts, no mention of Christ, no jeremiadic warnings that declension will bring destruction, no topical references to colonial politics. In fact, Hawthorne may have taken his inspiration for Dimmesdale's discourse not from a Puritan sermon, but from another election sermon he checked out of the Salem Athenaeum, Ezra Stiles's *The United States Elevated to Glory and Honour,* delivered in 1783. Stiles took as his text Deuteronomy 26:19, in which God announces the election of Israel. After tracing God's dealings with the Israelites, Stiles explained that he meant such remarks "only as introductory to a discourse upon the political welfare of God's American Israel; and as allusively prophetick of the future prosperity and splendour of the United States."[57] In assigning Dimmesdale this theme, Hawthorne may have intended not only a limited measure of historical accuracy but also, as some readers have maintained, a critique of the mid-nineteenth-century rhetoric of Manifest Destiny. Henry Nash Smith, for one, went so far as to call Dimmesdale's sermon a "ranting political oration."[58] Perhaps, yet it is also true that crediting Providence for the creation and growth of the United States was the white noise of nineteenth-century political discourse, a pervasive trope that circulated independently of specific national policies. Hawthorne may not have approved, but the topic itself does not damn Dimmesdale or make the sermon a satire.

More important than the sermon's content is how listeners perceive and respond to Dimmesdale's voice. They attend not as ministers instructed, with soul-searching and humility, but as nineteenth-century audiences actually listened, with a readiness to experience the sermon through conceptions of the sublime.[59] Filtering a sermon through this aesthetic paradigm secularizes it by stopping short of claims that it is divinely inspired while still exalting it as a peak experience, individually transporting and communally unifying. A host of rhetorical markers code the Election Sermon as sublime. Dimmesdale's voice has the grand dimensions Burke considered a hallmark of the sublime in nature: it is "high and commanding," gushes "irrepressibly upward," rises "through progressive gradations of sweetness and power," and bears its listeners "aloft," all while being haunted by a "deep," "low" pain. It is also described with the sublime's familiar watery tropes, being likened to the "swelling waves of the sea" and to a natural force that "gushes," "overfills," and "bursts" through the church walls.[60] Further, the sermon seems boundlessness, just as Kant held that one experiences the sublime through those objects that are apprehended but not comprehended—that are "formless" yet whose "totality is also present to thought."[61] This apparent limitlessness is essential to the Election Sermon's power. Listeners are entranced by indiscernible words, the sound seems to "envelop [Hester] with an atmosphere of awe and solemn grandeur," and Dimmesdale's voice contains an insistent note of anguish whose source listeners cannot pinpoint. The sermon is a pervasive, powerful force that defies rational understanding. Rather, Hester listens to the rise and fall of Dimmesdale's voice, which yields "a meaning for her, entirely apart from [the sermon's] indistinguishable words."[62] The response of other listeners, too, suggests that the sermon contains an ineffable teaching. Spilling onto the street afterward, they try to share their experiences, telling "one another of what each knew better than he could tell or hear."[63] To Hester and to the rest of the community, Dimmesdale has conveyed some important meaning—though not one that they can put into words or that the narrator explains.

The narrator takes pains to prevent readers from interpreting these meanings as divine, or as reflecting Dimmesdale's insight into the Puritan God. Like those who described eminent ministers in Sprague's *Annals*, the narrator remains hypothetical about the idea that preaching accesses a supernatural realm.[64] While the community credits Dimmesdale as the conduit of unrivalled inspiration, the narrator explains, in knowing equivocations, that this inspiration "could be seen, as it were" in his extemporaneous departures from the written sermon, and that toward the close of the sermon, "a spirit as of prophecy had come upon him."[65] These qualifications distance the enchanted worldview of the Puritans from Hawthorne's own perspective, which can commit only to the "secondary sublime" that always stops short of affirming a connection between the human and the divine.[66]

What the Election Sermon suggests is that great sermons derive their power not from God's grace but from a minister's private, unspeakable experience and, above all, from his pain.[67] On one level, Dimmesdale's pulpit *cri de coeur* dramatizes the counsel to ministers to write sermons after consulting their own "joys or trials or necessities" and to draw their sermons "[f]rom the toiling brain and the beating heart" and "from the fountain of tears."[68] Yet this scene also challenges axioms about good preaching by implying that the most eloquent sermons are fueled by a pain with ambiguous, complex origins. The narrator has already explained that Dimmesdale owes his popularity to his sorrows: "His intellectual gifts, his moral perceptions, his power of experiencing and communicating emotion, were kept in a state of preternatural activity by the prick and anguish of his daily life."[69] Is this "prick and anguish" godly remorse for misdeeds, sexual frustration, or both? The Election Sermon puts this enigmatic pain on center stage: listeners hear in Dimmesdale's voice "an essential character of plaintiveness," a "loud or low expression of anguish," "the whisper, or the shriek [. . .] of suffering human-ity," a "deep strain of pathos," "a certain deep, sad undertone of pathos," and that persistent "cry of pain."[70] The source of this pain is a mystery. It may be "guilt or sorrow," regret at not having escaped with Hester sooner, or, as some listeners infer, "the natural regret of one soon to pass away."[71] Indeed, this last interpretation would have made sense to nineteenth-century readers given how thoroughly the Election Sermon scene conforms to the rhetoric sur-rounding ministerial farewell sermons. These sermons, like Dimmesdale's, were described as spectacular addresses to a beloved congregation, power-fully delivered despite bodily suffering that portended death.[72] The underly-ing idea was that pain made preaching great: for Dimmesdale, "It was this profound and continual undertone that gave the clergyman his most appro-priate power."[73] The remarkable word here is "appropriate." To imply that Dimmesdale's pain is his most fitting, right, and morally acceptable source of power—more so than, say, his religious faith or the grace of God—is to argue that preaching is the human expression of a tortured self, no more sacred than any other Romantic artistic production.[74]

With Dimmesdale, Hawthorne challenged the assumption that ministers needed to be pious and pure of heart in order to preach well. In *The Power of Preaching*, Spring had called this idea a self-evident truth and described the difficulties that a minister who harbored "secret sin" would have lead-ing his congregation. With a "bosom [. . .] agitated by the thought that he is a suspected man," he would tremble, be troubled, and lose "his relish for his sacred employment."[75] *The Scarlet Letter* describes Dimmesdale's mental perplexity in nearly identical terms, while making the opposite point about the effect of hidden sin on ministerial performance: paradoxically, it quick-ens the means of grace. So much is suggested when the narrator explains that though the older ministers of the colony are more scholarly and pious, only Dimmesdale has "Heaven's last and rarest attestation of their office, the Tongue of Flame." In fact, it is the other ministers' superior piety that pre-vents them from expressing themselves in familiar language: "Their voices came down, afar and indistinctly, from the upper heights where they habitu-ally dwelt."[76] Dimmesdale's sin and sorrow keep him grounded, so to speak. He can connect with his listeners because he is as fallen as they are. Read as counsel to young ministers, *The Scarlet Letter* dangles a Faustian bargain. Would you preach like an angel and enjoy communion with your congregation? Then sin and persist in sin. As long as you feel remorse, guilt, shame, and frustration, you will shine. At least one reviewer of the novel was troubled by this implied link between a minister's "experience in sin" and pulpit efficacy.[77]

The idea that a preacher could derive strength from sin rather than piety stayed with Hawthorne. Reflecting in *Our Old Home: A Series of English Sketches* (1863) on his time as consul in Liverpool, he told the story of a cosmopolitan Doctor of Divinity who sailed in from America, his congregation having sent him to Europe to repair his health. The minister stopped by the consulate for his mail and, charming Hawthorne with his intelligent, lively conversation, arranged to dine with him that night. But the minister neither showed up nor sent his regrets. Days passed, and Hawthorne figured he must have left for the Continent. A week later, a shabby, unshaven figure in a military coat showed up in Hawthorne's office. Behold the minister! A week of dissipation had left him virtually unrecognizable. When Hawthorne started lecturing him—indulging, Hawthorne himself confessed, in "such a fulmination as the clergy have heretofore arrogated the exclusive right of inflicting"—the minister's overwrought contrition made it horrifyingly evident that he was suffering from *delirium tremens*. Hawthorne called the degrading loss of self-control he saw then "the deepest tragedy I ever witnessed" and resolved to deal sympathetically with sinners henceforth. As for the minister, the indiscretion would most likely result in new pulpit power: his congregation "very probably, were thereafter conscious of an increased unction in his soul-stirring eloquence, without suspecting the awful depths into which their pastor had dived in quest of it." The unction came because only in sinning so egregiously could the minister understand his own "latent evil." Without this catastrophic episode, he might have gone his whole life through without being "let into the miserable secret what manner of man he was."[78]

That Hawthorne did not fault the minister for returning to his congregation and, presumably, not confessing his sins abroad—what happens in Liverpool, stays in Liverpool—should prompt us to ask how harshly *The Scarlet Letter* would have us judge Dimmesdale for postponing the dread day of confession. Hester's plea that Dimmesdale now lives a holy life and that his penitence is "sealed and witnessed by good works" speaks a truth as surely as her "What we did had a consecration of its own."[79] From a Puritan perspective, both statements are outrageous, willful rejections of God's law. But to nineteenth-century religious liberals, and perhaps to Hawthorne as well, they are plausible moral arguments because they affirm the value of human relationships over religious rules.

An authorial fantasy

As one of the most vivid representations in Hawthorne's fiction of a writer addressing an audience, the Election Sermon is a window onto Hawthorne's own anxieties and ambitions about publishing. To be sure, the novel's other major characters reflect concerns about authorship as well: Hester, thinking dark thoughts as she sews in solitude; Chillingworth, coldly probing the minister's heart; Pearl, giving voice to "a multitude of imaginary personages, old and young."[80] But in Dimmesdale, and more specifically in his final scene of preaching, we return to the dominant motif of "Passages," the twinning of preacher and author.

If it seems arbitrary to focus on the Election Sermon scene apart from the rest of Dimmesdale's character, the circumstances of the book's composition provide some warrant. When Hawthorne sent Fields the manuscript in January 1850, he explained that the novel's last three chapters had yet to be written—presumably "The Procession" (containing the bulk of the Election Sermon description), "The Revelation of the Scarlet Letter," and "Conclusion." Hawthorne attributed his tardiness with the last three chapters to family illness and other, unnamed interruptions. The break in Hawthorne's compositional process may help explain the shift in tone between accounts of the Election Sermon's writing and delivery, as well as why the minister who marches through the crowd on Election Day is a different man from the one who left Hester in the forest. Moreover, the fact that most of the book was already in Boston—and that Hawthorne now faced the publication of his potentially scandalous novel not as a distant prospect but as a present reality—may help explain why he dwelled on the speaker–audience dynamic in the Election Sermon.

Indeed, in January 1850 Hawthorne needed the financial rewards of success more than ever. Out of work for the previous six months and with a wife and two children to support, Hawthorne was so strapped for cash that his friend George Hillard secretly organized a collection on his behalf. Hawthorne received a letter from Hillard, along with a check for $500, just five days after sending the incomplete manuscript to Fields. Thanking his friend for the gift, Hawthorne confessed that Hillard's letter had brought tears to his eyes and vehemently maintained his belief that people were largely responsible for their own success or lack thereof and that his financial struggles made him ashamed. A week before the book was released, Hawthorne began a letter to Fields with the fervent wish that his fortune would take a turn: "I pray Heaven the book may be a quarter part as successful as your prophecy."[81] He then denied that such good luck could be his.

Read against these personal trials and fierce longings, the scene of the Election Sermon reads as a fantasy of authorial success—a vision of mass acclaim capable of compensating for past suffering and shame. Years later, Hawthorne admitted in his notebooks that when he read the novel's ending to Sophia, he could barely control his emotion: his voice "swelled and heaved, as if I were tossed up and down on an ocean as it subsides after a storm."[82] It may be that one reason Hawthorne's voice shook as he read the Election Sermon scene was that these passages epitomized and dramatized his anxieties about letting loose the novel before him. Dimmesdale's ability to communicate his pain yet not its source echoes the attitude toward authorship in the Custom-House preface, where Hawthorne writes that standing in a "true relation" with one's audience requires both addressing the reader as a "kind and apprehensive, though not the closest friend" and keeping "the inmost Me behind its veil."[83] As Michael Gilmore has noted, Hawthorne both yearned for "a human connection with his readers" and resented a culture that demanded that authors sacrifice a measure of privacy in coming before the public.[84] What the Election Sermon suggests is that Hawthorne hoped to achieve this veiled yet powerful connection not simply with individual readers, imagined as friends, but with that same "wide world" in which the indecorous writer sought "to find out the divided segment of [his] own nature, and complete his circle of existence by bringing him into communion with it."[85]

In fact, Hawthorne wrote about this very act of coming into communion with the public just three days after the publication of *The Scarlet Letter* and the same day that *The Salem Gazette* published one of the first reviews of the novel. The review was as hyperbolic as any author could wish: "Nothing in the whole range of modern literature seems to us more absolutely perfect in its way than this exquisite creation."[86] Seemingly buoyed by praise, Hawthorne told L. W. Mansfield, a poet for whom he had been acting as a paid critic for several months, that when one addressed the world at large, one in effect spoke only to "cognate minds," to those "invisible friends" scattered throughout the world who, though one never met them, understood one better than one's actual friends and family:

> My theory is, that there is less indelicacy in speaking out your highest, deepest, tenderest emotions to the world at large, than to almost any individual. You may be mistaken in the individual; but you cannot be mistaken in thinking that, somewhere among your fellow-creatures, there is a heart that will receive yours into itself. And those who do not receive it, cannot, in fact, hear it; so that your delicacy is not infringed upon.

Whereas the Custom-House preface had frowned on authors who failed to protect their privacy, this letter suggested that one *should* speak one's most intimate feelings to the great wide world because one's meaning, however private, reached only those who understood it, and anyone who understood would sympathize. The extravagant optimism here makes one suspect that Hawthorne knew his luck had turned. In a letter to Fields written that January as he was finishing the manuscript, Hawthorne had described audiences in much less generous terms. There he had talked about printing *The Scarlet Letter* alongside half a dozen other, shorter stories "so that, failing to kill the public outright with my biggest and heaviest lump of lead, I might have other chances with the smaller bits, individually and in the aggregate."[87] Now, with success rounding the bend, he could look on the public not as quarry but as potential sympathizers. We cannot hope, of course, to know the precise nature of Hawthorne's own, secret "highest, deepest, tenderest emotions," alluded to in Dimmesdale's nameless pain. What matters is that by describing authorship in terms that parallel Dimmesdale's experience, Hawthorne implicitly critiqued the conventional wisdom that would have novelists be "genial."[88] Indeed, reviewing the novel for *Graham's*, Edwin Percy Whipple faulted it for a "lack of sufficient geniality," complaining that "A portion of the pain of the author's own heart is communicated to the reader."[89]

With the Election Sermon, Hawthorne seems to have entertained a vision of *The Scarlet Letter*'s own reception. The novel insinuates that most readers will not be able to formulate adequate interpretations of the story—and that these imperfect readings are just fine. The chaotic, rapturous, critical "babble" anticipates conflicting readings of the novel with equanimity, as does the narrator's description of the competing interpretations of what was on Dimmesdale's chest and why. A more tantalizing image of audience response is the collective effervescence following the sermon. As the minister and magistrates leave the church, the murmurs of the crowd coalesce into a mighty shout unprecedented in New England. Following Burke's idea that the "shouting of the multitude" was a form of excessive sound that stimulated a sublime passion, *The Scarlet Letter* compares the crowd's shout with other sounds traditionally considered sublime. It is "more impressive [. . .] than the organ-tones of the blast, or the thunder, or the roar of the sea." It is the "mighty swell of many voices, blended into one great voice by the universal impulse which makes likewise one vast heart out of the many."[90] The scene suggests that Hawthorne harbored a desire to move beyond being merely an "artist of the beautiful" and to claim for his fiction that other, grander, more masculine half of the Burkean dichotomy.[91] It proposes that a novel could produce an aesthetic effect associated with supposedly more serious works and genres such as the Bible, epic poetry, opera, and the sermon. The crowd's sublime response helps frame authorship in noncommercial terms, complementing how Hester allegorizes authorship as artisanal labor.[92] Though it may seem strange for an author to aim for a goal as nebulous as "sublimity," this concept is precisely the one to which some of Hawthorne's most sympathetic readers gravitated. Melville meditated, "It may be that to common eyes, the sublimity of Hawthorne seems lost in his sweetness," and Anthony Trollope wrote that in reading Hawthorne, one could experience "something of the sublimity of the transcendent."[93]

An ethical sermonic voice

Hawthorne's ambiguity makes it impossible to read the figuration of fiction-writing through preaching as an argument that the novel has a unifying moral to convey, but the conclusion does contain one powerful instance of sermonic voice. After tracing the community's interpretations of the origin of the scarlet letter on Dimmesdale's chest, the narrator steps up to the pulpit. First, he gestures to his authorizing text, the (fictive) papers of Surveyor Pue, presenting them in terms that call to mind contemporary descriptions of the New Testament: "[t]he authority which we have chiefly followed, drawn up from the verbal testimony of individuals, some of whom had known Hester Prynne, while others had heard the tale from contemporary witnesses."[94] Besides subtly working to de-authorize the Bible by implying that it, too, may be a work of the imagination, the allusion implies a blasphemous comparison between Hester and Jesus. Read in this light, Hester the adulteress becomes Hester the divine martyr and suffering servant—one who returns, no less, to wipe away tears and comfort the broken-hearted.

From this new gospel, the narrator draws his lesson: "Among the many morals which press upon us from the poor minister's miserable experience, we put only this into a sentence:—'Be true! Be true! Be true! Show freely to the world, if not your worst, yet some trait whereby the worst may be inferred.'"[95] The passionate exhortation, the oratorical repetition, the moralistic rhetoric of "the world" and "your worst"—all add up to sermonic voice. Seeking to soften the force of this sentence, Sacvan Bercovitch contends that since the book is about ambiguity, as evidenced in the various interpretations about the scarlet letter (or its absence) on the minister's breast, this assertion, too, is a limited, partial perspective.[96] Granted, yet it seems that the more salient point is that in a novel full of hypotheticals and indeterminacies, this lone sermonic moment foregrounds how, if we are to arrive at moral principles at all, they must be formulated despite epistemological uncertainty. In a complex world that defies platitudes, one must struggle to draw meaning and morality from the daunting multiplicity of the world and its texts. Ironically, the message that "presses upon" the narrator, as if with supernatural agency, is heterodox. Telling readers to suggest their "worst" to others does not call them to the righteousness that would renounce sin in the first place. Homing in on the scandalous exhortation, one contemporary religious reviewer complained that "sincerity in sin" was no virtue and that a better moral would have been "Be clean—be clean!"[97]

Although immoral in conventional terms, the narrator's sermonic counsel can be seen as profoundly ethical. Challenging the idea that individuals should adhere, or seem to adhere, to strict moral and social codes, it posits a world that accepts individual difference and even deviance. It says that no one is perfect, nor—more radically—should anyone pretend to be. This plea for sincerity supports a major ethical aim of the novel as a genre, which Dorothy Hale describes as "the honoring of Otherness."[98] That is, the narrator's exhortation honors the otherness of individual temperaments, habits, drives, and desires that deviate from moral norms, as well as the otherness within the self that chafes at those norms. Much of Hawthorne's fiction makes a similar point, calling individuals to accept moral imperfections in one another. Young Goodman Brown, for instance, grows to old age miserable and misanthropic because he cannot accept that his neighbors might be less righteous than they seem. "That old woman taught me my catechism!" he cries incredulously upon seeing Goody Cloyse in the forest. The story says, "And so?" What is different about the "Be true!" command is that it focuses not on tolerating others but on tolerating ourselves. The narrator hails us not as judges, but as sinners. The consequence of *not* accepting our moral failings and hinting at those failings to others is that we hold humanity to unattainable ideals and so perpetuate a false, stifling, unjust world—the Puritan community, as Hawthorne imagined it. As Gordon Hutner has explained, only by partial revelation can secrets forge a desirable community, one in which half-guessed secrets inspire self-recognition and sympathy in others.[99]

With this narratorial sermonic moment, Hawthorne further humanizes the act of preaching. Not only does it advocate a non-Christian ethic, it throws open the door to the sausage factory by exposing the messy process of sermon-making—the textual ambiguity and interpretive uncertainty that precede the final, neat sermonic utterance. The story itself is drawn from questionable documents, and the narrator-editor may have diverged from his sources. The story has "many morals" that "press upon" the narrator, language that suggests potentially contradictory morals and disclaims responsibility for any of them. The one moral given defies ready articulation; it must be "put [. . .] into a sentence." And then there are the quotation marks. In scrupulously hedging this one sermonic moment, Hawthorne called attention to sermonic discourse as a conditional, imperfect, human mode of speech. The narrator-preacher weighs texts and ideas, then makes the cloud of ambiguity rain exclamation points. He has formulated a usable truth despite flawed texts and uncertain interpretations. Like the most liberal of liberal preachers, he deliberately undermines his own authority, preaching the sermon but letting the audience know they can do with it what they will. If this conception of humanized, secularized preaching defies the notion that it conveys divine messages, it also indicates a desire to retain the sermon as a rhetorical form. Rather than mocking the sermon or abandoning it altogether, Hawthorne used its paradigmatic features to propose an ethical teaching that made his contemporaries uncomfortable—just as the best sermons were supposed to do.

In *The Scarlet Letter,* Hawthorne captured the rhetorical energy and aesthetic splendor of the sermon while emphasizing that preaching was a fully human endeavor. Against those who would see great preaching as connected to a minister's superior piety, he suggested that the best sermons welled forth from unsanctified fonts of pain and folly. Against those who saw preaching as the translation of a self-authorizing biblical text into a clear moral message, he cast it as a rhetorical gesture resulting from a perplexing encounter with ambiguous, pseudo-authoritative documents. In relativizing preachers' claims to authority, he leveled the playing field for novelists.

The Scarlet Letter thus gave dramatic form to Hawthorne's sense that ministers were unworthy spiritual leaders. "I find that my respect for clerical people, as such, and my faith in the utility of their office, decrease daily," he wrote in his notebooks in 1842. "We certainly do need a new revelation—a new system—for there seems to be no life in the old one."[100] One searches his fiction in vain for this "new system." The usual repositories of antebellum idealism—domesticity, romantic love, communalism, reformism, nature, Transcendentalism—are dissected and scrutinized, not championed. The end of *The Scarlet Letter* toys with the dream of a new system, as Hester promises her sorrowing sisters a "new truth" that will redefine the social order. But this truth is indefinitely deferred, to be revealed in "Heaven's own time."[101] It is no exaggeration to say that Hawthorne's substitute for Protestantism was fiction itself. There he found the revelation of writerly inspiration; there, a new system of motifs, symbols, and subjectivities; there, new life. But rather than letting the sermon die with the old order, he reclaimed it for the new by reinterpreting it as a vehicle of pathos and ethical communication. It was this secularized vision of the sermon that Melville would build on in *Moby-Dick.*

CHAPTER 5

✻

Playing Preacher in
Moby-Dick

UNLIKELY as it sounds, a minister may have sparked Melville's desire to write a book as wild and ambitious as *Moby-Dick*. In 1839, Unitarian Orville Dewey delivered the lecture "On Reading" to the Mechanics' Library Association in New York City.[1] Although Melville probably did not hear this lecture—he was studying engineering in Lansingburgh during the winter and spring of 1839 and sailing on the *St. Lawrence* from June on—he may well have read it later in pamphlet form, especially as he came to know Dewey personally. One of the leading Unitarian ministers in nineteenth-century America, Dewey served as pastor of the Church of the Messiah in New York City until 1848, when he retired to Sheffield, about thirty miles south of Pittsfield. He was also an old friend of Melville's father-in-law, Judge Lemuel Shaw, and the minister who in 1863 baptized the three youngest Melville children.

Some readers today may be incredulous that Melville would take seriously anything Dewey had to say, given how biographer Hershel Parker casts him as Melville's foil, a "seemingly soulless" prig and "cold-hearted, mealy-mouthed pontificator" who inspired the author with smoldering annoyance. Melville, Parker claims, seethed with hidden indignation over Dewey's equivocal response to the Fugitive Slave Law and satirized him with Falsgrave and Plotinus Plinlimmon in *Pierre*.[2] Although there is no denying that Dewey shared the racist attitudes that were nearly reflexive for privileged whites, or that he was reluctant to oppose slavery, his published sermons and lectures suggest a man who was also, as Ann Douglas describes him, "artistic, gentle, and supremely literary."[3] Melville most likely did not agree with his politics, but he may well have read with interest a man whose writing conveys a spirit of open-minded inquiry and disinclination to open radicalism not unlike his own.[4]

Assuming that Melville did not dismiss Dewey's writing out of hand, especially before the Fugitive Slave Law controversy of 1850, we can consider the possibility that "On Reading" planted in Melville a "germinous seed" at least as fruitful as any dropped by Hawthorne.[5] In this lecture Dewey acknowledged, as few ministers were willing to in 1850, that novels could refine the sentiments and even "minister to the truest and deepest wisdom of life." Yet he also, like many conduct book authors, echoed conventional wisdom by asserting that the genre was unable to educate readers or cultivate their "vigor of mind." To tell a story for its own sake was mere "child's entertainment." Not even the novels of Scott were above reproach, as they distorted historical facts and contained too little philosophical analysis. His solution was unusual, even eccentric—not to dismiss novels, but to imagine and describe a new breed of them. First, this new type of novel should include the *dramatis personae* and a précis of the plot upfront. By preempting readers' desire to read for story alone, authors could unspool their fictions with edifying digressions, and the novel "might become a teacher of higher wisdom." A novel in this vein would be a true cultural achievement: "it could pause, and give us reflection, philosophy, moral analysis, maxims of wisdom; passages, like those of Shakespeare, worthy of being committed to memory."[6]

With uncanny accuracy, *Moby-Dick* fulfills Dewey's vision of a new, more intellectual novel in which plot takes a back seat to philosophy. The novel heavily foreshadows the *Pequod*'s fate, practically giving away the plot upfront through Ishmael's premonitions, Mapple's sermon, Elijah's warnings, and, above all, the stories of aggressive sperm whales, including the one that stove the whale-ship *Essex*. Ishmael even says that the purpose of sharing the *Essex*'s story is to show that "the most marvelous event in this book" is "corroborated by plain facts of the present day."[7] One could hardly be clearer about where the story is going. Moreover, precisely as Dewey desired, *Moby-Dick* subordinates suspense-driven narrative to reflection, philosophy, moral analysis, maxims, and Shakespearean speeches. Whether one looks at the characters' soliloquies or the "Cetology" chapters, "Sunset" or "The Blanket," "The Honor and Glory of Whaling" or "The Doubloon," *Moby-Dick* is far less concerned with plot than with the quest for meaning.

The correspondence between Dewey's vision of the worthwhile novel of the future and the distinctive features of *Moby-Dick* may be coincidence. But it seems plausible that Melville came across Dewey's pamphlet sometime in the 1840s, probably after marrying Elizabeth Shaw in 1847, and that the provocative ideas of this prominent family friend made an impression as he transitioned from writing fictionalized autobiographies to novels. We have tended to assume that his desire to write cerebral, philosophical fiction sprang from some combination of native genius and intense, copious reading in the late 1840s, but Dewey's lecture suggests that he may also have wanted to write strange books—those he felt "most moved to write"—because he had been inspired by a minister's thought-provoking plea for a better, smarter novel.[8]

Whether or not Melville was picking up Dewey's gauntlet, he approached the challenge of becoming "a teacher of higher wisdom" more as a problem to explore than as a destiny to fulfill. One of the main ways he confronted this problem in *Moby-Dick* was to experiment with sermonic voice, an aspect of the work largely overlooked despite decades of scholarship on the novel's relationship to religion. Years ago, Nathalia Wright pointed out that the greatest concentration of Biblical allusions and quotations in Melville's work appears in *Moby-Dick* (if we except *Clarel,* whose Holy Land setting swells the number) and that this clustering corresponds with "the most ambitious expressions of Melville's genius."[9] One can say the same for Melville's use of the sermon—that he engaged most intensely and creatively with preaching in *Moby-Dick* because it was there that his artistic and cultural ambitions loomed largest.

This chapter first discusses how Melville in his early work sought to rival preaching with his own democratic sermonic voice, then turns to *Moby-Dick* to examine how he used Ishmael to develop this voice, transforming it through Romantic irony and a morality more often derived from classical philosophy than from Christianity. This playful-serious voice is balanced against the earnest, iconic Mapple, and I trace how the Jonah sermon declares the novel's equivalency to great preaching by staging parallels between preaching and authorship in a seeming homage to and competition with *The Scarlet Letter.* Through such sermonic moments, Melville showcased his writerly talent and argued that an intelligent, wide-ranging novel—one that excelled in "reflection, philosophy, moral analysis, [and] maxims of wisdom"—could offer better insights on the world than actual preaching.

Discovering a democratic sermonic voice

Melville grew up listening to the sermons of Reformed Dutch minister Jacob Brodhead (1782–1855), a native New Yorker who relocated from Philadelphia to Manhattan in his prime to become pastor of the Broome Street

Reformed Protestant Dutch Church, where he served from 1826 to 1837. Melville probably heard Brodhead's preaching from 1826 to 1830, or ages 7 to 11, before Allan Melvill's financial ruin forced the family to leave the city for Albany. Much has been made of this Calvinist element in Melville's upbringing, virtually nothing of Brodhead's skill as a preacher and the effect this experience may have had on Melville's understanding of religious authority.

A tall man of dignified bearing, Brodhead was a popular preacher whose appointment immediately increased attendance and whose name soon became synonymous with the Broome Street church. His preaching drew crowds. For awhile, according to one contemporary, "the church was so thronged that it was impossible to get a pew or sitting without waiting for months."[10] Allan Melvill, who had sought out the preaching of Unitarian wunderkind Joseph Buckminster (1798–1825) before his marriage to Maria Gansevoort, may have attended Brodhead's church for the respectability the affiliation gave him in the eyes of his haberdashery customers, but the widely admired sermons were no doubt also a draw.[11] During Brodhead's tenure, the church flourished with the city growing up alongside it. In the late twenties, when the Melvills attended, the congregation planted trees, put up a fence, paved the walkways with brick, replaced the front wooden steps with a stone portico, built a Sunday School gallery, set up an organ in the gallery, got insured for $10,000, and established a missionary society and an auxiliary to the American Tract Society.[12] The church also forged a personal connection Melville would draw on decades later. His older brother Gansevoort became friends with John Romeyn Brodhead, Jacob Brodhead's son, and when Melville needed help in 1847 securing the English copyright for *Omoo,* he prevailed upon John Brodhead, then the American secretary of legation in London, appealing to the "long-standing acquaintance between our families."[13]

When Melville sat under Brodhead's preaching during his formative years, listening, one imagines, from the newly constructed gallery for Sunday School students, he heard not only and perhaps not even primarily a student of Calvin, but a pulpit prince who exemplified the cultural dominance of Christianity and the clergy. Selected for commemoration in Sprague's *Annals,* contemporaries praised Brodhead's sermons as "well written, natural, and luminous in arrangement," with a delivery marked by a "fine commanding voice, a deep tone of evangelical fervour, and an apparent utter self-obliviousness" that rendered his preaching "powerfully impressive."[14] Others acknowledged his fidelity to the Reformed Dutch church but lauded his ecumenicalism and described his preaching in terms widely used for effective preachers regardless of denomination: "There was a directness, a solemnity, a tenderness in his utterances, evidently springing from a deep conviction of the importance of the truth which he delivered, and a corresponding experience of its power upon his own heart."[15] Many lauded his piety, dignity, ability to rouse pathos, and fine, clear, "sweet" voice that even the partially deaf could understand. When deeply moved while preaching, he wept and brought his hearers to tears as well.[16] If such eulogies were somewhat generic, they also suggest how well Brodhead met the expectations of antebellum audiences.

After Allan Melvill's financial failure and the family's move to Albany, Melville entered the orbit of another powerful minister, John Ludlow, pastor of the First Dutch Reformed Church in Albany. Melville's maternal grandmother was an active parishioner, and after Allan died, Ludlow became a family friend and advisor, visiting the Melvill home almost daily.[17] Ludlow was more bookish than Brodhead—he left Albany in 1853 to become a professor of moral philosophy at the University of Pennsylvania—yet also a well-respected, occasionally masterful preacher. Of his voice, a contemporary wrote, "its tone thundered through the largest edifice, commanding the most distant hearer, and often overpowering those who sat nearer to the pulpit."[18] At his funeral, Sprague praised him for having a "gigantic power both of voice and of logic" and described a time when he had moved his congregation to tears with a single emotion-choked line.[19]

Despite, or perhaps because of, these firsthand experiences with powerful preachers, Melville never seems to have been at ease with ministerial authority. His first book, *Typee* (1846), expressed deep dissatisfaction with ministers as the spiritual guardians of humanity. As if the book were not shocking enough in its depiction of free-and-easy sexual relationships, Melville offended readers in Britain, where the book was first published, by blasting Christian missionaries in the South Seas as selfish hypocrites bringing ruin to an innocent people. His American publishers deemed these condemnations so potentially offensive that nearly all were expurgated. Indeed, the book begins with a minister's metonymic defrocking and symbolic castration. An episode in the first chapter, excised from the American edition, jokes about how the Marquesan natives, having never seen a white woman before, stripped a missionary's wife of her "sacred veil of calico" while trying to discern whether she was human or divine. The offended woman insisted that her husband abandon his missionary enterprise, thus divesting him of clerical and conjugal authority.[20]

Much like Lippard, Melville in *Typee* presented himself as an exposer of ministerial evils—as a righteous preacher denouncing the false preachers. Condemning the enormities committed by Europeans in the South Seas islands, he declared: "These things are seldom proclaimed at home; they happen at the very ends of the earth; they are done in a corner, and there are none to reveal them."[21] None, that is, except himself. Melville's alter-ego Tommo indicts missionaries as the vanguard of the corrupting, unnecessary work of "civilization," with its institutions of property, trade, and toil, and critiques the missionaries' duplicitous, self-glorifying accounts of their impact on Polynesian life. Defending Polynesian society as harmonious, he lambastes the "remorseless cruelty" of whites, pointing to two outrages Melville would later dramatize: the "barbarity" long practiced in England of dismembering a criminal's body and mounting the head on a pike (see *Benito Cereno*), and the "horrors" inflicted by the supposedly enlightened practice of walling up prisoners in the midst of cities (see "Bartleby").[22] In the book's most vehement denunciation of missionary work, and one of the longest passages excised from the British edition, Tommo mourns the Typee as an "Ill-fated people!" destined to ruin because faraway gentlemen in cravats and ladies in silk gowns think it would be a fine idea to minister to the Polynesians' spiritual condition. Even as missionaries "announce the progress of Truth," Christianity brings "disease, vice, and premature death." Tommo spits: "What a subject for an eloquent Bible-meeting orator!"[23] The book's many indictments of missionaries are, in effect, a warm-up for the sermonic speech Melville would develop more fully later; they are the denunciatory half of prophetic sermonizing, condemning injustice but not, in the same breath, showing readers the way to redemption. The only solution was for the missionaries to go home, which Melville knew was not in the cards.

In the four books that appeared between *Typee* and *Moby-Dick*, Melville continued to censure the clergy's alliance with political and social power while experimenting with a more full-fledged sermonic voice—one that was decisively democratic in that it claimed for an ordinary sailor-turned-writer the ability to speak with a moral authority superior to the clergy. One of the clearest examples of Melville's pre-Ishmaelian, reformist sermonic voice comes in *Redburn* (1849). Wandering the docks of Liverpool, Redburn first critiques the city's floating chapels as doing little good, since most sailors often pass by yet never consider entering, then lauds those preachers who, standing on old casks, turn street corners and quays into temporary pulpits. He is impressed that many are robed Anglican priests, high-status clergy who have humbled themselves to reach "a motley crowd of seamen from all quarters of the globe, and women, and lumpers, and dock laborers of all sorts." Claiming always to stop and listen to these sermons, he praises how the preachers hold an audience's attention with plain speech, straightforward precepts, and addresses on "the two great vices to which sailors are most addicted" —a prim elision. Then, as if inspired by these preachers, he breaks out in sermonic voice, implicitly claiming religious authority even for one as lowly as a former sailor: "Is not this as it ought to be? since the true calling of the reverend clergy is like their divine Master's;—not to bring the righteous, but sinners to repentance." He exhorts other clergy to go and do likewise:

> Better to save one sinner from an obvious vice that is destroying him, than to indoctrinate ten thousand saints. And as from every corner, in Catholic towns, the shrines of Holy Mary and the Child Jesus perpetually remind the commonest wayfarer of his heaven; even so should Protestant pulpits be founded in the market-places, and at street corners, where the men of God might be heard by all of His children.[24]

Echoing Tommo in taking ministers to task for their indifference to human suffering, Redburn is more fully sermonic in that he supplements denunciation with proclamation, pointing the way to positive action.[25] But the most interesting feature of Redburn's sermon may be how it invokes supposedly anti-democratic Catholics to shame Protestants for their indifference to the common people: the ubiquity of Catholic statuary in European towns is a rebuke to those who sequester the Protestant symbol of Christian hope— the sermon—behind church walls. The passage can even be read as a call for "men of God" in the broadest sense, not the clergy alone, to take up the preacher's role.

In *White-Jacket* Melville returned to the corruptions that attended the yoking of religious and political power. He wryly describes the ship's chaplain, who, having drunk "at the mystic fountain of Plato," preaches abstruse sermons that the sailors cannot understand and who has nary a word to say about shipboard sins like "drunkenness, fighting, flogging, and oppression." The real problem is not the chaplain as an individual but the unholy union of church and state aboard a warship. Navy chaplains feel little inclination to denounce abuses of power when the officers sit "sword-belted" before them. Sailors are herded to service with shouts of "Go to prayers, d—n you!" without freedom to abstain, regardless of the Constitution's establishment clause. And Christianity's inherent pacifism cannot be preached when the chaplain takes for his pulpit a forty-two-pound gun and is paid a bounty for enemies killed. On these points Melville becomes sermonic, with biblically inflected rhetorical questions and a prophetic tone of righteous indignation. As in *Redburn,* he maintains that effective preaching depends on clerical humility and a fatherly attitude toward one's congregation. The best warship preaching is when a moral captain acts the part of chaplain to his crew; the service in one such case "seemed like family devotions, where the head of the house is foremost in confessing himself before his Maker." Yet perhaps dissatisfied with a vision of preaching insufficiently democratic, Melville added a call to self-reliance: "But our own hearts are our best prayer-rooms, and the chaplains who can most help us are ourselves."[26] Though seemingly laid to rest, the sermon would return in force in *Moby-Dick.*

Sermonic voice in *Moby-Dick*

Moby-Dick announces its likeness to a sermon on virtually the first page: the inaugural biblical text of "Extracts," "And God created great whales" (Gen. 1·21), suggests an idea—the possibility of the whale as a divine agent—that Ishmael will ponder throughout the book. His own sermonizing takes flight in "Loomings," where he guides us about Manhattan on a "dreamy Sabbath afternoon," when the city's ministers would have been preaching the afternoon sermon. Pointing to the idlers gazing seaward, he opens his discourse with rhetorical questions—"What do you see? [. . .] Are the green fields gone? What do they here?"—and concludes his tour with the sententious, "Yes, as every one knows, meditation and water are wedded forever." The motif of Ishmael-as-preacher recurs in subsequent shore chapters when he preaches a "purty long sarmon" objecting to sleeping with a cannibal, harangues Queequeg during his "Ramadan," and defends Queequeg as a member of "the great and everlasting First Congregation of this whole worshipping world," to which Peleg responds that he's "never heard a better sermon [. . .]—why Father Mapple himself couldn't beat it."[27]

But Ishmael is a strange preacher compared with other sermonizers in antebellum fiction. In other novels, as in *Redburn,* sermonic voice typically appears in a few preachy lines—a burst of fervor shooting up through the steady stream of dialogue and narration. Ishmael, in contrast, can preach for one line or for several pages, and his sermons bleed into the surrounding text. Melville's capacious, fluid stylistic repertoire means that Ishmael's sermons often mingle with precepts, meditations, exclamations, invocations, and imitations of Carlyle, himself a borrower of sermonic style. Ishmael riffs and improvises on preaching, ignoring its supposed sacrality. To take the briefest of examples, he follows his meditation on the morbidness of tragic natures with "Be sure of this, O young ambition, all mortal greatness is but disease."[28] Here sermonic voice is evident in the *vanitas* theme, the theological resonance of "mortal greatness," the tone of certainty, and the direct address. But the line is too short and cynical; it straddles sermon and aphorism. Only occasionally does Ishmael launch his truths with the full colors of sermonic voice, yet these moments are some of the most striking and memorable passages in the book—for instance, the final paragraph of "The Lee Shore" ("But as in landlessness alone resides the highest truth [. . .]"); the end of "The Mast-Head" ("Heed it well, ye Pantheists!"); the end of "Brit" ("Consider the subtleness of the sea [. . .]"); the end of "The Blanket" ("Oh, man! admire and model thyself after the whale!" [. . .]"); and the end of "The Try-Works" ("Look not into the fire, O man! [. . .]").[29]

Ishmael's sermons differ from those of other novelistic speakers not only in their resistance to being cordoned off from the surrounding text, but in their defining stylistic mode, that of Romantic irony. As Robert Milder explains, Romantic irony (or philosophical irony, or Socratic irony) characterizes the Ishmaelean attitude toward the universe, self, and literary work. It is the sense that even though human perception and language are inadequate to a chaotic universe, one must nonetheless charge forth to participate in the ongoing creative process of the universe, reveling in fragmentary truths wittily expressed and the "self-generating play of mind upon phantasmagoric reality."[30] Works in this mode, as Anne Mellor explains, are often both "playful and serious"; the artist "simultaneously projects his ego or selfhood as a divine creator and also mocks, criticizes, or rejects his created fictions as limited and false."[31] Milder identifies Ishmael's Romantic irony as a breakthrough for Melville, the rekeying of existential doubt and philosophical despair in a playful register, a result, perhaps, of discussions about Friedrich Schlegel, Romantic irony's leading theorist, with the German-American scholar George J. Adler, or of reading Carlyle or Jean Paul Richter (both of whom had read Schlegel) or writers who had influenced Schlegel, such as Plato, Cervantes, Rabelais, Sterne, and Goethe. Regardless of its sources, the distinctive feature of Ishmaelean Romantic irony, Milder proposes, is its "ontological dread," the idea "that truth is unutterable for its darkness," not only its multiplicity.[32]

Romantic irony marks Ishmael's sermons both in their fascination with the frightening, uncontrollable realities lurking behind everyday appearances (Milder's "ontological dread") and in their meditative, exploratory tone and provisional conclusions. Terror haunts his preaching, as when he exhorts readers not to look too long into the artificial fire, whose "redness makes all things look ghastly," or cautions them against pushing off from the inner island of "peace and joy" into the "horrors of the half known life."[33] Even more consistently, his sermons are exploratory, playfully ruminating over ideas then concluding with heterodox counsel. Reflecting the book's commitment to experience as the basis of knowledge and wisdom—

"a whale-ship was my Yale College and my Harvard"—Ishmael often works toward counterintuitive moral points. His first extended sermon, for example, takes the cenotaphs as the text of a sermon that begins, "O! ye whose dead lie buried beneath the green grass [. . .]," then wends its way through a catalog of cultural contradictions surrounding death, pauses on an aphorism ("But Faith, like a jackal feeds among the tombs"), and at last offers the sermon's perennial consolation of immortality—with the blasphemous twist, "for stave my soul, Jove himself cannot."[34] A similar pattern of dynamic exploration culminating in heterodox morality marks many of the cetology chapters, such as "Brit," "The Line," "The Dart," and "The Blanket." Walter Bezanson has observed that these chapters retain something of the text-doctrine-application format of Puritan sermons, with the text being an aspect of the whale or whaling; the doctrine, a blend of information and meditation; and the application, the chosen topic's relevance to the human condition.[35] Yet these applications are offered only as possible truths. Not only does Ishmael's notorious unreliability mean that his teachings will need to stand or fall on their own merits, but the action of *Moby-Dick* offers little guidance in determining the worth of his wisdom. For instance, although Ishmael praises the flight of the Catskill eagle in "The Try-Works," who even when he dives within the gorge is still higher than the plain, the final chapter has Tashtego nailing the sea-hawk to the mast of the sinking ship, a seeming mockery of lone "eagles" like Ahab. A similar ambiguity impedes appropriation of the sermon at the end of "The Blanket," where Ishmael praises a "strong individual vitality." Queequeg exemplifies this virtue, with his "lofty bearing" that makes him seem like a man "who had never cringed and never had had a creditor," and, in an even stronger verbal echo of "The Blanket," upstanding Starbuck has an "interior vitality [. . .] warranted to do well in all climates."[36] But of what use is Queequeg's self-assurance or Starbuck's vitality to anyone else on the ship? Under the circumstances, an ability to become angry at injustice and rouse oneself to heroic action would seem at least as virtuous as equanimity.

Although Ishmael's sermons never cohere into a systematic worldview, they evidence two of Melville's philosophical preoccupations during the late 1840s and early 1850s, Platonism and stoicism—rival philosophies symbolized in the image of the sperm whale's head hanging on one side of the *Pequod*, the right whale's head on the other. Ishmael takes the sperm whale for a Platonian, who is indifferent to death; the right whale for a Stoic, who faces death with "enormous practical resolution."[37] Melville associated Plato and the Stoics not only with two different, non-Christian ways of meeting death without despair, but also with opposing attitudes toward life. To simplify, Platonians looked beyond matter to ideals such as the soul, while Stoics advocated the cultivation of inner constancy and virtue amidst life's vicissitudes. In the sermonic moments cited above, Platonism appears in the affirmation of shadow as "true substance" in "The Chapel" and in the final declaration of "The Lee Shore," "Up from the spray of thy ocean-perishing—straight up, leaps thy apotheosis!" It is also implicit in the image of the Catskill eagle soaring and becoming "invisible in the sunny spaces," a symbol of idealistic questing and the triumph of aspiration over achievement.[38] Of course, Platonism also comes in for a drubbing at the end of "The Mast-Head," when dreamers slip and regain their identity in horror.

More consistently, Ishmael's sermons draw on stoicism, a predilection established back in "Loomings" when Ishmael assures us that making the transition from schoolmaster to sailor "requires a strong decoction of Seneca and the Stoics to enable you to grin and bear it."[39] Melville had acquired Roger L'Estrange's *Seneca's Morals, By Way of Abstract* by the time he wrote *Mardi,* and in 1854 would give his younger brother Thomas his copy of L'Estrange, inscribing it, "My Dear Tom, This is a round-of-beef where all hands may cut & come again"—as much an endorsement as he would give any philosopher.[40] The exhortation to equanimity at the end of "The Blanket" is classic Senecan teaching, as in, "A good man is happy within himself, and independent upon fortune."[41] So, too, is Ishmael's counsel to Bulkington to front death heroically—"Bear thee grimly, demigod!" (though addressing Bulkington as a "demigod" strikes a more Platonic note).[42] Seneca had praised "the brave man" who could "look Death in the Face, without trouble or surprise," a philosophy he lived out in his own calm acceptance of Nero's death order and endurance of being slowly bled to death.[43] A trace of Seneca appears even in the book's most "Platonic" passage—Ishmael's declaration after contemplating the cenotaphs, "But somehow I grew merry again," which echoes Seneca's "It is no new thing to die, no new thing to mourn, and no new thing to be merry again."[44] In using sermonic form for stoic ideas, Ishmael does something unexpected, as a philosophy committed to emotional equanimity would hardly seem to lend itself to exclamation points or exhortations. Yet in assigning Ishmael stoic sermons, Melville may have found inspiration in Seneca's maxims praising the value of sound advice, such as, "Good counsel is the most needful service that we can do to mankind; and if we give it to *many,* it will be sure to profit *some.*"[45]

In the self-mocking spirit of Romantic irony, Ishmael concedes his probable ineffectiveness as a preacher. He ends "The Blanket" with an exclamation applicable to any of his exhortations: "But how easy and how hopeless to teach these fine things!"[46] His lighthearted pessimism about his sermonizing echoes the preface to *The House of the Seven Gables* (1851), in which Hawthorne proposes a possible moral for his novel, then says that he does not "flatter himself with the slightest hope" that anyone will act on it.[47] With this nonchalant, take-it-or-leave-it attitude toward preaching, Ishmael, like Hawthorne, bears affinity with liberal preachers who held listeners responsible for hearing their own usable truths. As a preacher, Ishmael shares the philosophy of Bellows's declaration that truth finds "the argument that upholds it in the hearts of its hearers."[48] And it is fair to say Bellows's approach to preaching may have had some influence on Melville's own, given that Bellows was pastor of the large and well-to-do Church of the Divine Unity in Manhattan (later called All Souls), where the Melvilles rented a pew in February 1850.[49]

When Ishmael's sermons occur at the ends of chapters, as they often do, they turn the reading process itself into something like a religious ritual. To borrow Richard Cullen Rath's term for textual elements that invite an aural reading, the white space that follows a chapter-ending sermonic passage functions as a "sonic cue" to silence and contemplation.[50] Melville describes one such brief, silent, post-sermon moment in "The Two Temples": "At length the benediction was pronounced over the mass of low-inclining foreheads; hushed silence, intense motionlessness followed for a moment, as if the congregation were one of buried, not of living men; when suddenly, miraculously, like the general raising at the Resurrection, the whole host came to their feet, amid a simultaneous roll."[51] The passage mocks the deathlike torpor sermons supposedly induce but also suggests that preaching might promote personal "resurrection," or regeneration. Translating this ritual moment into the materiality of the printed book, the typographic pauses after Ishmael's sermons create virtual silences that call readers to self-reflection.

Rewriting the seamen's bethel preacher

The stage-like quality of the Whaleman's Chapel establishes a parallel between Mapple and Melville as religious artists. We do not need Ishmael denying that Mapple dabbles in "mere tricks of the stage" to register the scene's artifice—to see that the chapel is a theater; the marble cenotaphs, rope ladder, kitschy painting, and pulpit-prow, a set; the Jonah sermon, a play-within-a-play whose meaning redounds to the novel as a whole. Even the name of the church—Whaleman's Chapel, rather than the usual Seamen's Bethel or Mariners' Church—underscores that we are in a symbolic space

with a dreamlike difference from the actual world. Moreover, Mapple is credited as the inspiration for several of the chapel's unique features. The chapel's
architect has "acted upon the hint of Father Mapple" in giving the pulpit a
side ladder instead of the usual stairs; the painting of the storm-beaten ship is
an idea "borrowed from the chaplain's former sea-farings"; and the paneled,
prow-shaped pulpit reflects "the same sea-taste that had achieved the ladder
and the picture."[52] Mapple's ingenuity anticipates that of Wemmick in Charles
Dickens's *Great Expectations* (1861), who daily retreats from his dreary job as
Jaggers's right-hand man to the house he has transformed into a miniature
castle with moat, canon, turret, and flags.[53] Both the house and the chapel
literalize hoary metaphors—that a man's home is his castle, that the Church
is a ship—but they are also odes to creativity. Wemmick's castle-home and
Mapple's ship-chapel represent the triumph of imagination: the castle-home
over the workaday world, the ship-chapel over rote religiosity. The chapel's
idiosyncrasies are, like *Moby-Dick* itself, concrete arguments for the freedom
to interpret traditional teachings through new media.

Melville also signaled Mapple's author-likeness in his creative transformation of Mapple's supposed original, Father Edward Taylor (1793–1871),
minister of the Seamen's Bethel in Boston from 1830 to 1871. A former sailor,
Taylor was a popular and eloquent preacher with a knack for nautical metaphors. Whitman praised him as the "one essentially perfect orator," he had
ever heard; Emerson, as the "Shakespeare of the sailor and the poor."[54] By the
mid-1830s he was a tourist attraction for Boston visitors, including Charles
Dickens, Harriet Martineau, Fredrika Bremer, Jenny Lind, and possibly in
1849, Melville.[55] In basing Mapple on Taylor, Melville was far less concerned
with painting a portrait of a Boston fixture, as so many others had done,
than with highlighting the similarities between preaching and fiction-writing. Melville retained in Mapple aspects of Taylor that resonated with his
own authorial ideals, such as the authoritative yet common-man demeanor
and the vivid metaphors. "No man ever lived who more constantly talked
in tropes," one of Taylor's contemporaries wrote, and Mapple captures this
spirit at several turns—in comparing Jonah to a "vile burglar," or in the "pan-
ther billow" that leaps over the bulwarks of Jonah's ship.[56] Taylor also had a
focus and self-assurance Melville would have admired: "His spirit is so pos-
sessed with this just idea of the importance of his work," wrote Martineau,
"that praise and even immediate sympathy are not necessary; though the
last is, of course, pleasant to him." She described how Taylor could enthrall
even a small audience: when a miscommunication resulted in only twenty
hearers attending a Christmas Day service, "never did Taylor preach more
splendidly."[57] Although there is no record of Melville reading Martineau,

the situation in Chapter 9 of *Moby-Dick* is similar: Mapple, aloft in his "self-containing stronghold," orates to a small, scattered, unresponsive audience just a few days before Christmas. The image of a preacher who did not fret over his popularity undoubtedly appealed to Melville, who declared to Hawthorne after the publication of *Moby Dick,* "[N]ot one man in five cycles, who is wise, will expect appreciative recognition from his fellows, or any one of them. Appreciation! Recognition! Is Jove appreciated?"[58] Mapple gave form to Melville's fantasy of writing powerfully yet as if he were indifferent to public approval.[59]

Even as Melville borrowed a great deal from Taylor, he changed key details to tighten the parallel between preaching and authorship. Taylor entered the pulpit without manuscript or notes, and his extemporaneous sermons bore all the marks of oral composition: repetition, prolixity, theological inconsistencies, and direct address. He filled his sermons with striking illustrations but "was not given to story-telling."[60] Mapple, in contrast, crafts a tight, coherent, linear narrative whose every word tells; it sounds like a written text. He also has a much more distant relationship with his audience than Taylor did with his. Contemporaries dwelled on the rapport Taylor had with his "Jacks"; Emerson, for instance, praised Taylor for "fusing all the rude hearts of his auditory with the heat of his own love."[61] A remembered sermon fragment captures the visceral connection Taylor reportedly had with his congregation. He is describing a violent tempest:

> [N]ow my friends that our canvass is gone; not a spar left for a jury-mast, and the leak gaining upon us, what shall we do? Hark! Do you not hear the waters rushing in below? Do you not see her settle by the head? Do you not feel her tremble? [. . .] one moment more fellow sailors, and this good ship of ours will sink into the deep; a moment more and we shall be struggling with the eternal waves; but we shall swim and struggle in vain; we must die, if there be no help at hand; and is there none? is there no way of escape? Save yourselves if you can.

At this exhortation, twenty arms in the church were thrown up as if to catch at a rope, and an old man clutched the pew rail as if his life depended on it.[62] Taylor brought the message home by pointing to the lifeboat—Jesus Christ. Just as striking as the theological differences from Mapple, who does not mention Jesus, is the constant effort to engage listeners. Whereas Taylor encouraged his hearers to imagine themselves in the boat, to feel themselves sinking, Mapple conjures the storm as spectacle. The waves spring on Jonah, not the congregation, and the vortex that swallows him poses no danger to

Mapple's listeners. The audience does not stir apart from a brief moment of "quick fear."[63] Such powerful preaching met by minimal response was not necessarily an indictment of the audience or of the preacher. As Edward T. Channing had remarked, "[I]t certainly argues a more spiritual and informed mind to listen silently to grave discourse, and to preach fervently without the slightest sound of favor from the audience."[64] However true to the practice of "spiritual and informed" congregations, the gap between Mapple's passionate performance and his hearers' enigmatic silence embodies Melville's perception of himself as an author least appreciated when performing at his peak.

The originality of Mapple as an artistic creation is even more evident when we recognize how little his sermon resembles other preaching to sailors, despite the scholarly claim that it is a representative folk sermon.[65] Mapple's fast-paced sermon finds little precedent in the predictable language and halting narrative of, for instance, the Jonah sermons printed in *The Sailor's Magazine and Naval Journal,* which pause after every verse or so to spell out theological and moral principles and use little maritime imagery. In fact, a series of articles in *The Sailor's Magazine,* printed just as the movement to establish mariners' churches was gaining momentum, cautioned landlubbing seminary graduates against trying to address sailors in their own lingo, since such language compromised the seriousness of the gospel and threatened to expose the new preachers' ignorance.[66] Mapple's simple message of repentance is also a far cry from the evangelical emphasis on salvation through Christ typically heard in seamen's bethels. An article on "Preaching to Seamen" in the March 1847 *Sailor's Magazine* reminded ministers that their task was to present a plain gospel message and orthodox doctrines, including "the fall and depravity of man, the divinity, atonement, and resurrection of Jesus Christ—regeneration by the holy spirit, [. . .] the eternal happiness of the righteous, and the everlasting punishment of the wicked."[67] Such traditional Christian teachings informed, for instance, Gardiner Spring's *The Bethel Flag: A Series of Short Discourses to Seamen* (1848), which makes virtually no reference to the sea. When sermons to sailors departed from basic doctrines, they often inveighed against the usual vices—drinking, whoring, smoking, swearing, gambling, and Sabbath-breaking. More upbeat sermons reminded sailors they were missionaries to the world, responsible for setting good examples that would lead heathens and savages to Christ. Sailors occupied a unique position in the American religious landscape as both the object of evangelical missions at home and the bearers of "Christian" civilization to distant lands. The rhetoric of those who preached to them is fascinating in its own right, but these men were no Mapples.

Mapple's sublime sermon

While most discussions of Mapple's sermon endeavor to map the seemingly allegorical Jonah story onto the fortunes of the *Pequod,* I concentrate here on the sermon's grandiloquent style, which is both difficult to miss and to make sense of.[68] Many readers seem uncertain whether Melville meant to make fun of it or to revel in it. We can reconcile these two perspectives by recognizing the sermon as written in the mode of the Miltonic sublime. As Bryan Short explains in discussing the final passage of "The Castaway," when Pip goes down to "wondrous depths," the Miltonic sublime reaches back past the psychologized sublime of Kant and Coleridge to eighteenth-century conceptions of the sublime that, reading Milton through Longinus, connected it with destabilized allegory. This Miltonic, allusively allegorical sublime manifests itself in the confluence of certain aesthetic effects that the Romantics rejected as criteria for sublimity—namely, pathos, psychological complexity, vividness, and an ornate style. This mode had particular appeal for Melville because it highlighted the contingency, and sometimes humor, of human attempts to understand God and divine truths.[69]

Like other instances of the Miltonic sublime, Mapple's sermon is built on the fragmentation of allegory. On the surface, Mapple's retelling of the Jonah story might seem to affirm a stable understanding of divine realities, as Mapple announces that the story has lessons for everyone as "sinful men" and for him "as a pilot of the living God."[70] But the sermon itself discards traditional Christian allegorizing about the book of Jonah. Mapple speaks not a word about Jonah's time in the whale and disgorgement prefiguring Christ's descent into hell and resurrection, or about how Jonah's salvation might anticipate the listener's own. Mapple also cuts several biblical references to God. Where the Book of Jonah reads, "But the Lord sent out a great wind into the sea," Mapple's text personifies the sea itself: "But the sea rebels; he will not bear the wicked burden," and "the indignant gale howls louder."[71] When the captain in Mapple's sermon comes to wake Jonah, he shouts only, "What meanest thou, O sleeper! arise!" Gone is the command to "call upon thy God."[72] Nor does Mapple interrupt the narrative to offer theological commentary, unlike actual antebellum preachers, who tended to use biblical stories as racks to hang their theological clothes on. The sermon's single instance of interjected moral commentary is secular, even cynical: "In this world, shipmates, sin that pays its way can travel freely, and without a passport; whereas Virtue, if a pauper, is stopped at all frontiers." Most notably, the closing message of the first strand omits any reassurance of salvation. Mapple simply calls listeners to repent—"Sin not; but if you do, take heed to repent of it like Jonah."[73] As E. M. Forster wrote, "The sermon has nothing to do with Christianity. It asks for endurance or loyalty without hope of reward."[74] Mapple's emphasis on grim endurance foreshadows Ishmael's stoic sermons.

Mapple also departs from Christian allegorizing in the disjunction between the biblical version of Jonah's mission and his interpretation of it. In the Bible, the Lord commands Jonah, "Arise, go to Nineveh, that great city, and cry against it; for their wickedness is come up before me." Mapple paraphrases: "and Jonah did the Almighty's bidding. And what was that, shipmates? To preach the Truth to the face of Falsehood! That was it!"[75] It is as if Mapple seeks with that bright, final exclamation to divert attention from his interpretive shell trick. Taking the divine command to preach against "wickedness" as a mandate to preach truth against falsehood secularizes the pilot-prophet's mission; the new terms are not moral but ontological.

Mapple further exemplifies the Miltonic sublime by placing humanity at the center of concern, fleshing out the bare-bones biblical narrative with pathos verging on melodrama. "Miserable man!" Mapple cries of Jonah, before describing how the prophet prowls and skulks before boarding the ship to Tarshish and trembles under the other sailors' scrutiny. On board, Jonah writhes in self-loathing below deck, then watches the storm in horror: "Terrors upon terrors run shouting through his soul." The sailors who hear Jonah's confession, "become more and more appalled, but still are pitiful."[76] Throughout, Mapple's retelling of the Jonah story derives pathos from the proximity of death, reflecting the Romantic sense of death as "a source of the sublime, an awe-inspiring event that elevated human emotions to peak sensitivity."[77] Mapple reserves, though, the greatest measure of pathos for himself, as the sermon's second strand rolls plaintively through the woes of pilot-prophets who do not speak the truth and jubilantly through the delights of those who do.

The psychological complexity Mapple attributes to the biblical characters further associates the sermon with the Miltonic sublime. Every character has inner conflict. On the run from God, Jonah cannot hide or silence his guilt. When the sailors pause to observe him, "in vain he tries to look all ease and confidence; in vain essays his wretched smile." When he seeks passage on the ship, he speaks to the captain with "hollow voice" and, below deck, suffers agonies of conscience. The sailors, for their part, feel a mingled horror and pity that makes them hesitant to cast Jonah on the sea: "they not unreluctantly lay hold" of him. Even the captain, a cipher in the Bible, ponders and deliberates. He tests Jonah by trebling the fare then, though discerning his guilt, lets him board: "Not a forger any way, he mutters."[78]

Finally, and perhaps most obviously, it is the sermon's vividness and stylistic opulence that mark it as reaching for the Miltonic sublime. A bravura demonstration of *amplificatio,* or expansion of a simple statement, the sermon elaborates on the biblical text with a wealth of interpolated details: Jonah's "slouched hat and guilty eye," the missing key and swinging lamp in the state-room, the whale's "yawning jaws," Jonah's feeling his punishment is just, and so forth.[79] A few passages rise above the rest by combining *diatyposis,* or vivid representation, with other rhetorical features Longinus associated with the sublime. One dizzying artistic display describes Jonah's torments of conscience:

> Like one who after a night of drunken revelry hies to his bed still reeling, but with conscience yet pricking him, as the plungings of the Roman race-horse but so much the more strike his steel tags into him; as one who in that miserable plight still turns and turns in giddy anguish, praying God for annihilation until the fit be passed; and at last amid the whirl of woe he feels, a deep stupor steals over him, as over the man who bleeds to death, for conscience is the wound, and there's naught to staunch it; so, after sore wrestlings in his berth, Jonah's prodigy of ponderous misery drags him drowning down to sleep.[80]

The passage abounds in stylistic markers of the sublime: multiple metaphors, in the comparisons to the Roman race horse and bleeding man nested within the conceit of the remorseful drunk; *hyperbaton,* or the unusual arrangement of words, in the heaped similes and long-delayed subject; present tense for past events ("drags" instead of "dragged"); and periphrasis ("Jonah's prodigy of ponderous misery"). Ornateness is evident in the oxymoronic "giddy anguish" and incessant alliteration (e.g., "revelry" and "reeling"; "strike" and "steel"; "whirl of woe"). Like the end of "The Castaway," this paragraph represents the terrifying drama of approaching God. Pip must almost drown to see God; Jonah feels his own strong, painful connection to the divine when he violates his conscience.

The overarching effect of Mapple's sublimity is to announce that *Moby-Dick* will aim to give readers an experience comparable to that of listening to great preaching.[81] The sermon, in effect, prepares the way for the book's many other sublime elements—Ahab's hunt, Moby Dick, the sea, Ishmael's quest for knowledge, the fellow-feeling of "A Squeeze of the Hand." Yet given the lowly cultural status of fiction, Melville knew that proposing one's novel as the moral and cultural equivalent of a religious experience was quixotic, and the ironies surrounding Mapple suggest that Melville mocked his own desire to communicate forcefully to an enigmatic and often unresponsive reading public. Much about Mapple is bitterly funny. Queequeg wanders away mid-discourse, the congregation regards Mapple fearfully and files out silently after the sermon, and when Ishmael returns to the Spouter-Inn, he does not *reject* Mapple's message but follows only too well the counsel, meant for the "anointed pilot-prophet" alone, to stand forth one's own "inexorable self." Heretically yet cogently he reasons out why he should worship Yojo with Queequeg.[82] Such is the futility, Melville implies, of trying to impress and edify one's audience; one cannot control the message received.

Melville's apparent self-mockery infiltrates the language of Mapple's sermon. Although the sublime is not usually associated with humor, the Miltonic sublime often includes a component of "exaggeration, at times to the point of self-parody."[83] Mapple's soaring rhetoric partakes of this self-parodying exaggeration in the incessant repetition throughout Chapters 8 and 9 of the storm motif, a stock representation of the sublime from Longinus through Burke and beyond.[84] Taken by itself, Mapple's description of the storm that afflicts Jonah might be considered merely a sublime rendition of schematic biblical material, but this storm together with the profusion of storms in and around the sermon becomes parodic. The painting behind the pulpit shows a "terrible storm off a lee coast"; Mapple denounces those who seek "to pour oil onto the waters when God has brewed them into a gale"; sermon-listeners hear the "howling of the shrieking, slanting storm" outside the chapel; and Mapple himself seems storm-wracked, with his heaving chest, tossing arms like "the warring elements at work," "thunders [rolling] away from off his swarthy brow," and "the light leaping from his eye."[85] With this multiplication of storms *ad absurdum,* Melville seems to have lampooned himself for trying too hard.

If the peculiar dynamic at work here—a sublime yet ironized sermon that intimates authorial ambitions qualified by self-deprecation—seems familiar, it may be because Melville was influenced by, and also trying to one-up, Hawthorne's representation of Dimmesdale's Election Sermon. Circumstantial evidence suggests that Melville read *The Scarlet Letter* soon after he met Hawthorne in August 1850, just a few months after the book's initial publication in March 1850 and about five months into the writing of *Moby-Dick.*[86] In Melville's panegyric on Hawthorne's talent, "Hawthorne and His Mosses," written that August, Melville brings up Hawthorne's most recent work only briefly: "I have thus far omitted all mention of his 'Twice Told Tales,' and 'Scarlet Letter.' Both are excellent; but full of such manifold, strange, and diffusive beauties, that time would all but fail me, to point the half of them out."[87] Unlike the detailed, energetic descriptions of the stories in *Mosses,*

Melville's praise for *The Scarlet Letter* is diffuse and evasive. One senses he is fudging—that he has not read it yet or not read it carefully. Still, the actual reading was probably not long in coming, since from the summer of 1850 to the fall of 1851, he lived in Pittsfield, Hawthorne in nearby Lenox, and the two exchanged numerous visits. It is difficult to imagine that during this time Melville did not read Hawthorne's newest, longest, most critically respected work of fiction—and the most acclaimed American literary work that year— or that he dedicated *Moby-Dick* to Hawthorne, "In Token of My Admiration for His Genius," without having read his only novel. Infusing this admiration was, of course, rivalry, and with Mapple's spectacular sermon, Melville demonstrated his ability to create the sublimity Hawthorne had only described.

Mapple's authorial peroration

The conclusion of Mapple's sermon has long been considered a grace note of American letters, with Richard Chase calling it "perhaps the high point of American oratory" and Howard Vincent writing, "Delight is to him who reads Father Mapple's peroration. English prose is nowhere superior."[88] More precisely, we might say that it continues and concentrates the Miltonic sublime that characterizes the sermon as a whole. Pathos surrounds the "pilot-prophet," who is threatened with woes and tantalized with delights, and Mapple's affect magnifies the emotional drama. Pivoting from the woes to the delights, he has "a deep joy in his eyes" and "crie[s] out with a heavenly enthusiasm." Rhetorical devices associated with sublimity intensify the pathos: anaphora (the repetition of "Woe to him" and "Delight is to him"), vivid images ("pluck[ing] sin out from under the robes of Senators and Judges"), and *athroïsmos,* or the accumulation of words and phrases echoing the same idea. The peroration also invokes the language of verticality and elevation that Burke considered essential to the sublime, as in, "and higher the top of that delight, than the bottom of the woe is deep."[89] As elsewhere, one can interpret the excesses of the Miltonic sublime as self-parodic.

Mapple's peroration indexes his authorial ambitions as he worked on *Moby-Dick.* In "Hawthorne and His Mosses," he had written, "[I]f you rightly look for it, you will almost always find that the author himself has somewhere furnished you with his own picture."[90] Mapple's peroration is Melville's self-portrait as post-Impressionist painting—bold, colorful, and slightly caricatured. Or we might see Melville as here acting on the maxim of *White-Jacket* that "the chaplains who can most help us are ourselves." Mapple is Melville helping himself. The core principle of the peroration that the pilot-prophet has an obligation to "tell the Truth" to a hostile world is, as Richard Brodhead has argued, the "prophetic" stance that Melville began to associate with authorship after he met Hawthorne in 1850.[91] But rather than fixating on Melville as "prophetic," we should recognize how he saw actual, living ministers as his main competitors in truth-telling. Writing to Hawthorne while revising *Moby-Dick,* he hinted at their parallel vocation: "Let any clergyman try to preach the Truth from its very stronghold, the pulpit, and they would ride him out of church on his own pulpit bannister [*sic*]."[92] The darkly funny image of a minister being ridden on a rail (tar and feathers optional) suggests that Melville identified with how the public's prejudices gagged and hamstrung preachers, discouraging them from speaking uncomfortable truths. The declaration in the same letter to Hawthorne that "Dollars damn me" implies that authorship is, ideally, something very like a sacred calling.[93]

An excerpt from an antebellum sermon stylistically similar to Mapple's peroration can illuminate how Melville transformed and secularized contemporary preaching in recasting it as authorial self-address. Presbyterian Thomas McAuley (1777–1862), one of the founders and first presidents of Union Theological Seminary in New York, delivered "The Faithful Preacher, and Wages of Unfaithfulness" in 1838 while pastor of the city's Eighth Street Church. Melville may or may not have read McAuley's sermon, but he certainly knew the line from the apostle Paul that McAuley elaborates—"woe is unto me, if I preach not the gospel!":

> So saith this envoy of heaven to a perishing world. "Wo is unto me if I preach not." Wo is unto every minister of Jesus who does not, to the extent of his ability and opportunity, preach the word of reconciliation. Wo is unto every one who measures the amount of necessity laid upon him by blind precaution, or blinder prejudice, and not by the wants of the perishing, the worth of the soul, the will of the Father, the grace of the Sanctifier, and the love of the Saviour. Wo is unto us, my brethren, if we preach not up to the full measure of all our muscular and mental power, excited and invigorated by the energy of the Spirit of him who says, "as your day is so shall your strength be"—"lo! I am with you always, even unto the end of the world."[94]

As this excerpt suggests, Mapple's peroration mimics sermonic form while stripping the preacher's—or pilot-prophet's—mission of its Christian specificity. Mapple, too, uses a string of woes to develop Paul's idea that a preacher labors under unique moral obligations and casts this labor as hearty masculine enterprise—McAuley calling for ministers to use their "muscular and mental power," Mapple proclaiming delight to "him whose strong arms yet support him."[95] Yet Mapple, unlike McAuley or other orthodox preachers, makes no mention of Jesus or the Holy Spirit and does not describe the preacher's goal as saving the souls of the perishing. Rather, he is concerned with preserving the integrity of his own soul, which entails preaching Truth even, if necessary, at the expense of salvation, as well as destroying sin and upholding goodness and an undefined "Gospel duty."[96] Mapple also implies, as McAuley and other preachers typically did not, that the preacher's mission involves challenging civil authorities.

Melville secularized preaching most radically in the sermon's final lines:

> And eternal delight and deliciousness will be his, who coming to lay him down, can say with his final breath—O Father!—chiefly known to me by Thy rod—mortal or immortal, here I die. I have striven to be Thine, more than to be this world's, or mine own. Yet this is nothing; I leave eternity to Thee; for what is man that he should live out the lifetime of his God?[97]

Though seemingly submissive to the divine will, these lines defy Christian teaching. "Mortal or immortal, here I die"? Where is the immortal soul, granted to all? The tone darkens with "I leave eternity to Thee," which may mean that Mapple refrains from presuming upon God's ability to confer an afterlife—or that he scornfully leaves an inscrutable deity to his private perpetuity. The final lines go so far as to hint at God's death. "Mortal or immortal" modifies "Father" as easily as "I," and to "live out" the lifetime of God can mean to outlive him. Indeed, the idea that the true prophet might kill God is hinted at earlier when the sailors suspect Jonah for a parricide. Mapple's implicit rejection of Christian ideas of God at the very moment of seeming communion with him is echoed at the end of "The Castaway," when Ishmael reflects that, like Pip gone overboard, one comes to "the celestial thought" and "feels then, uncompromised, indifferent as his God."[98]

Mapple's veiled pronouncements on authorship are the dark, unspeakable obverse of the book's more open declaration of authorial mission—Ishmael's jubilant paean to the common person at the end of Chapter 26, the second "Knights and Squires" chapter. Instead of suggesting that authors must face a "boisterous mob," as Mapple does, Ishmael declares himself a bard of the common person: "Thou shalt see [abounding dignity] shining in the arm that wields a pick or drives a spike; that democratic dignity which, on all hands, radiates without end from God; Himself!" Instead of hinting that God is punitive and absent, Ishmael celebrates "His omnipresence, our divine equality!" and appeals for divine aid: "bear me out in it, O God!"[99]

His speech echoes Unitarian William Ellery Channing's advice to ministers at the end of "Likeness to God," a landmark liberal sermon in American history and one Melville may have known through his wife Elizabeth's 1848 set of Channing's complete works. Channing exhorted ministers to believe in the greatness of human nature, regardless of appearances. They were to look "beneath the perishing body, beneath the sweat of the laborer, beneath the rags and ignorance of the poor, beneath the vices of the sensual and selfish, and [discern] in the depths of the soul a divine principle, a ray of the Infinite Light, which may yet break forth and 'shine as the sun' in the kingdom of God."[100] Together, Mapple's peroration and Ishmael's reprise of Channing show Melville thinking dialectically about the parallel between authorship and preaching. On the one hand, the author is a solitary, fortressed, somber, truth-telling preacher who defies God and the public alike; on the other, a liberal optimist who, proclaiming the glory of God in humanity, stands for American ideals of democracy and divine order. If Melville found both models compelling, it is nonetheless significant that Mapple's isolato defiance is the masked commentary on authorship and Ishmael's exuberant goodwill, the flamboyant declaration of intent. No need to further alienate a potentially hostile audience.

Mapple and Calvinism

Seeing Mapple as one of Melville's prime representations of authorship means moving beyond the longstanding notion that he is an unsympathetic Calvinist. T. Walter Herbert, one of the foremost explicators of Mapple's supposed Calvinism, emphasizes Mapple's dictum that obeying God means disobeying oneself, an idea he links to the Calvinistic belief in original sin, or the idea that all of humanity is sinful from birth—"In *Adam's* Fall / We Sinned all."[101] However, a belief in the opposition between human will and God's will was not limited to the orthodox. Precisely this point was at issue in Bellows's 1847 sermon, "The Relation of Christianity to Human Nature," which Melville may have read in pamphlet form. Bellows took for his text Romans 7:22–25, in which Paul laments the tension within him between the "law of God" and the "law of sin." Bellows's sermon paints a much more pessimistic picture of human nature than is typically associated with the period's liberal Protestants. A leading light of nineteenth-century Unitarianism, Bellows nonetheless affirmed that in Christianity, "Man is pronounced alien from God"; that there is a "native proclivity to evil in man"; that "hereditary depravity" exists; and that the preacher must address a man "as a sinner, as having a measure of corruption at heart, as having a false bias, as in need of a new birth."[102] Although Bellows differed significantly from Calvinists in that he saw depravity as remediable in this life, his sermon shows how even liberal Protestants—in fact, the Melvilles' own minister—could connect obeying God to disobeying oneself.[103] Melville had sounded a great deal like Bellows when he wrote in "Hawthorne and His Mosses" that "in certain moods, no man can weigh this world, without throwing in something, somehow like Original Sin, to strike the uneven balance." Mapple's sermon occupies this same theologically hazy territory of affirming "something, somehow like Original Sin."[104]

Mapple's alleged "Calvinism" further crumbles when we see that one of the sermon's most significant interpolations to the biblical story is a lengthy description of Jonah's conscience. "Conscience" was associated in this period not with the orthodox, but with liberals, for whom it was a vital concept.[105] In the Bible, Jonah pays his fare, goes down into the ship, and takes a nap.[106] In Mapple's sermon, Jonah lies in his stifling cabin wracked by guilt. Watching the lamp, which hangs straight as the walls and floor tilt and twist, he sees an analogue to his soul: "'Oh! so my conscience hangs in me! he groans, 'straight upward, so it burns; but the chambers of my soul are all in crookedness.'" Mapple then describes how Jonah's conscience tortures him, likening its pricks to the "steel tags" that drive deeper into the flanks of the Roman racehorse the more it plunges, and the stupor that overtakes him to that of a man who bleeds to death, "for conscience is the wound, and there's naught to staunch it."[107] Both the injurer and the injured, conscience registers the violation of moral law. Like the Quakers before them, nineteenth-century liberals saw conscience as a link between humans and God and thus as a moral authority able to trump the claims of traditional theology. Although the imperatives to disobey oneself and to heed one's conscience might seem at odds, liberals reconciled them through a belief in the value of moral education to develop the conscience. Mapple, of course, does not pause in his story-driven sermon to work out this tension.

One might also argue that Mapple is a Calvinist because he asserts that Jonah appreciates God's discipline—that he "feels that his dreadful punishment is just."[108] Herbert correlates this sentiment with Puritan divine Edward Reynolds's notion that sinners should be willing "to justify him [God] that may condemn us, and be witnesses against ourselves."[109] While Mapple echoes this Puritan ideal, Jonah's self-abasement does not point unambiguously to orthodox theology. The idea of interpreting one's afflictions as the will of God and accepting them peacefully has classical roots as well. Seneca voiced such submission to divine decrees, lines Melville underlined in his copy of L'Estrange: "'in all the Difficulties and Crosses of my Life, this is my Consideration; Since it is God's will, I do not only obey, but assent to it; Nor do I comply out of Necessity, but Inclination.'"[110] L'Estrange then asks, "[W]hat can be more pious and self-denying than this passage [. . .]?," didactic commentary echoed in *Moby-Dick* when Mapple lauds Jonah for displaying "true and faithful repentance; not clamorous for pardon, but grateful for punishment."[111] Seneca may not be grateful for his difficulties, but his assent to them is a gesture of humility and pious resignation much like that of Mapple's Jonah. Such parallels speak to the diverse intellectual and religious influences on Melville and the indavisability of typecasting his characters.

A dream deferred

It is impossible to forget that Melville wrote *Moby-Dick* in the shadow of the Fugitive Slave Law and his father-in-law's key role in enforcing it. After months of debate, Congress passed the law on September 18, 1850 as part of the Compromise of 1850 and, to the dismay of many Northerners, Judge Shaw upheld the law when the fugitive slave Thomas Sims came before his Boston court in April 1851. Despite the heightened antislavery passions surrounding this event, *Moby-Dick* does not condemn slavery outright. On this point Mapple is cryptic at best. Although his declaration that a preacher should kill, burn, and destroy all sin and "pluck it out from under the robes of Senators and Judges" certainly seems to allude to defying the Fugitive Slave Law (and more specifically, Shaw), he himself does not do so.[112] Nor does Ishmael pick up the baton. Although he has, as Rowland Sherrill puts it, "taken to heart" Mapple's exhortation to "preach the Truth to the face of Falsehood," he is no abolitionist orator.[113] Of course, one can always decide that the entirety of *Moby-Dick* is a veiled antislavery sermon condemning Calhoun and other proslavery Democrats who had hijacked the ship of state and were hurtling it toward destruction.[114] But why speak in code? It is frustrating that in an 1851 novel filled with preaching, no character condemns slavery outright.

Melville's disinclination to use his art to preach against slavery suggests a certain fatalism about the institution—a sense that abolitionist denunciations and the protests of unhappy African Americans could do little to change the status quo. As Andrew Delbanco has put it, the problem of slavery looked to many in 1850 "as intractable as conflict in the Middle East or AIDS in Africa seems today."[115] Such fatalism haunts the novel's two instances of African American preaching, moments when we might expect Melville to betray an inkling of the cataclysm to come. When Ishmael stumbles into a "negro church" while hunting for an inn in New Bedford, all eyes turn to him, and he sees what seems "the great Black Parliament sitting in Tophet" and a "black Angel of Doom [. . .] beating a book in a pulpit."[116] This lurid rhetoric reflects Ishmael's pre-Queequeg paranoia about non-whites while hinting at retributive justice for white oppressors. There is a tacit logic at work in which the beating of black bodies leads to blacks beating the Bible, which threatens black violence against whites—a threat adumbrated when Ishmael comes under the congregation's collective gaze.[117] But what is the upshot of this experience? Nothing. Ishmael walks on, reflecting only, "Wretched entertainment at the sign of 'The Trap'!" The "trap" refers most literally to the ash-box Ishmael stumbled over on his way in, which, coupled with the church's "smoky light," add up to the offensive joke that this black church is a hellish inversion of a white church.[118] Even if the episode reflects only Ishmael's racism and not Melville's, it delimits the novel's political scope. That is, in pausing early on at the black church, Melville opens up a metaphorical door on antislavery preaching, then shuts it, refusing to take his book in that direction. To do so would be "wretched entertainment" for his readers.

Melville reopens this door a crack with the novel's other moment of African American preaching—Fleece's sermon to the sharks, a scene that conveys an even bleaker perspective on slavery. A pastiche of Saint Anthony of Padua's sermon to the fishes, Fleece's sermon is, on the surface, a joke, played up through his dialect and constant swearing—the "dam noise," "dam bellies," "dam racket," "by Gor!," and so on. But his message is in earnest: "Now, look here, bred'ren, just try wonst to be cibil, a helping yourselves from dat whale. Don't be tearin' de blubber out of your neighbour's mout, I say." It is a plea for decency and compassion, though one soon acknowledged as futile: "No use goin' on [. . .] dey don't hear one word." His irritation with the sharks represents legitimate black anger at white greed and racial injustice, which in 1851 Christian sermons seemed to have done nothing to ameliorate. But like the Angel of Doom's sermon, Fleece's comes to nothing. Missing the cultural subtext, Stubb approves of the discourse ("Well done, old Fleece!" [. . .] "that's Christianity; go on"), and Fleece quits in exasperation. His benediction may be the novel's most misanthropic line: "Cussed fellow-critters! Kick up de damndest row as ever you can; fill your dam' bellies 'till dey bust—and den die."[119] And so his sermon becomes a curse.

Melville is so innovative and accomplished with the sermon form in *Moby-Dick* that it seems ungenerous to belabor the fact that he does not infuse the novel's religious rhetoric with a call to political reform.[120] With Ishmael's philosophical, democratic sermonic voice and Mapple's elaborately rendered, sublime discourse on Jonah, Melville outshone his contemporaries in exploiting the sermon's rhetorical and artistic potential. His skilled reworkings of the sermon demystified preaching and argued for the moral authority of his own fictions, heterodox though they were. The antislavery message would have to wait until *Benito Cereno*—if one reads it as such. In the meantime, Stowe would take, as her premise for authorship, America's need for a mighty antislavery sermon.

CHAPTER 6

The Unsentimental Woman Preacher
of *Uncle Tom's Cabin*

T HAT *UNCLE TOM'S CABIN* is fundamentally a sermon has been
a perennial motif of commentary on the novel. In the *Southern Literary
Messenger* in 1852, George Frederick Holmes wrote:

> Mrs. Stowe, we believe, belongs to this school of Woman's Rights, and on
> this ground she may assert her prerogative to teach us how wicked are we
> ourselves and the Constitution under which we live. But such a claim is
> in direct conflict with the letter of scripture, as we find it recorded in the
> second chapter of the First Epistle to Timothy—"Let the woman learn in
> silence with all subjection." "But I suffer not a woman to teach, nor to usurp
> authority over the man, but to be in silence."[1]

Holmes's review castigated Stowe's unseemly appropriation of male authority
with a biblical passage routinely invoked to deny women the pulpit (1 Tim.
2:11–12), even though Stowe had not physically addressed a congregation,
led public prayer, or aligned herself with the nascent women's rights movement and its call for women's ordination. For Holmes, Stowe was in error not
simply because she had distorted the supposed realities of Southern slavery
but also because, as a woman, she had no right to speak to men as a moral
teacher. Twentieth-century critics echoed the idea that *Uncle Tom's Cabin*
addressed readers with a moral force associated with the pulpit. Referring to

Stowe's childhood in the household of renowned antebellum minister Lyman Beecher, Vernon Parrington wrote that Stowe "could not hope to escape being a preacher [. . .]. She was baptized in creeds and prattled the language of sermons as the vernacular of childhood."[2] Late twentieth-century criticism offered little elaboration on the novel-as-sermon theme, with Ann Douglas pronouncing it a "great revival sermon" and Jane Tompkins declaring that it "provides the most obvious and compelling instance of the jeremiad since the Great Awakening."[3] When it came to the relationship between Stowe's novel and religious rhetoric, the verdict was in, the case closed: *Uncle Tom's Cabin* was a sermon designed to harangue the nation into righteousness. By thus comfortably containing the novel's engagement with religion, we have failed to see how radically this novel reimagines preaching and to understand the political significance of this reimagining.

Both the religious novel par excellence of the American literary canon and the grandmother of American political novels, *Uncle Tom's Cabin* is a crucial site for investigating the intersection of preaching and authorial ambition. In this chapter, I move beyond the obvious generalizations that Stowe's novel is like a sermon or can be simply, tediously preachy in order to take the novel's relationship to preaching as itself an object of analysis. Emphasizing the centrality of preaching to Stowe's authorial self-understanding, I trace how sermonic voice and the representation of ministers articulate the novel's ethical and political goals. More so than perhaps any other author in this study, Stowe believed in the power of preaching—in the ability of this distinctively oratorical, religious voice to effect individual and social transformation.

Focusing on how *Uncle Tom's Cabin* engages with preaching allows for several surprising discoveries and a new sense that however well we think we know this novel, we have only half-read it. Narrowing in on preaching demonstrates, for one, how conflicted Stowe was about claiming the traditionally masculine, culturally authoritative voice at the center of Protestant religious ritual. For as much as she wanted the power and immediacy of the preacher's voice, *Uncle Tom's Cabin* evinces her ambivalence about adopting it, misgivings overlooked in our general failure to attend to the details of Stowe's writing, especially its religious aspects. In fact, the authorial persona that Holmes immediately recognized and dismissed as a "woman preacher" takes form only gradually over the course of the novel. Eager to preach yet uneasy about violating gender norms, Stowe created a narrator whose sermonic interventions move steadily from the culturally feminine to the culturally masculine—from sentimentality to theological vision. Further, this theological vision was one that challenged the boundaries of acceptable religious speech in its grappling with atheistic doubt and in its angry denunciations. Stowe's qualms about her bold appropriation and rewriting of preaching are strikingly revealed in the afterword to the novel as it ran in the *National Era,* a fascinating alternate ending long overlooked in criticism on the novel. Listening for the voice of the preacher also shows how roundly the novel critiques and silences male preachers—proslavery *and* antislavery—and how liberally it puts sermons in the mouths of numerous humble characters, black and white alike. Far from endorsing the efforts of abolitionist clergy or even hoarding sermons for her own narrator, Stowe symbolically transferred the power to preach from the ordained clergy to ordinary people. Stowe's characters speak heartfelt spiritual truths with passionate conviction across the dividing lines of class, gender, and race. Utopian as it may be, the democratic ubiquity of sermonic rhetoric in *Uncle Tom's Cabin* carries liberatory potential that, in its defiance of social, religious, and racial hierarchies, implied new political possibilities.

Becoming an orator

As a daughter of revivalist Lyman Beecher, Stowe knew the excitement of preaching firsthand, and as the sister of seven brothers who entered the ministry, she learned to see it as a virtual family obligation. *Uncle Tom's Cabin* was the logical culmination of Stowe's long apprenticeship to a *de facto* ministerial vocation. From an early age, Stowe had seized opportunities to preach to her peers. Biographer Joan Hedrick explains how Stowe, after experiencing conversion under one of her father's sermons at age thirteen, began writing long notes to the other girls at Hartford Female Seminary, counseling them to seek conversion if they had not yet experienced it and encouraging those already saved to follow Christ's teachings. When Harriet's sister Catharine temporarily left the school under the combined care of the school's teachers, Harriet began to lead classes, faculty meetings, and prayer meetings, emerging in her sister's absence "as the leading voice of the school."[4] She wrote to Catharine: "I found my confidence growing so fast that I actually stood and looked in the eyes of all and 'speechified' nearly half an hour." The next week, she added, "I shall become quite an orator if you do not come home too soon."[5] The fear that Catharine will indeed come home "too soon" suggests Stowe's desire for just such a transformation. A few months later, at age eighteen, she declared to her brother, "You see my dear George that I was made for a preacher—indeed I can scarce keep my letters from turning into sermons. . . . Indeed in a certain sense it is as much my vocation to preach on paper as it is that of my brothers to preach viva voce."[6] Stowe marked her majority by claiming for her writing the same cultural significance and divine imperative as that of her ordained father and brothers.

Actual preaching was, of course, virtually off-limits to respectable white women. The declarations at Seneca Falls and Rochester in 1848 called for churches to allow women the pulpit, but the ordination of women was still anomalous in the elite, white, Northeastern denominations. In fact, the 1830s and 1840s saw a backlash against women preachers even in previously tolerant denominations such as the Freewill Baptists, Methodists, and African Methodists.[7] Female preaching was particularly anathema to Lyman Beecher, who in disputes with Finney vigorously condemned women's right to preach. Critiquing Finney's many supposed abuses of orderly worship, which included allowing women to pray publicly at revivals, Beecher brandished the two well-worn New Testament texts traditionally used to justify exclusive male leadership in the church: 1 Timothy 2:11–12 (the same verse Holmes would cite) and "Let your women keep silence in the churches: for it is not permitted unto them to speak" (1 Cor. 14:34).[8] He argued that even if the Bible showed women praying in public, as in 1 Corinthians 11:3–16, biblical women did so only under the "special guidance of the spirit; a preternatural impulse, which amounted to inspiration." No woman, he said, could address a mixed gathering without an unbecoming loss of "female delicacy." Actresses were the self-evident argument against allowing women to appear on a public stage.[9]

In light of such censure, Stowe's notorious assertion that "God wrote" *Uncle Tom's Cabin* reads as an attempt to disarm paternal disapproval by claiming the "special guidance of the spirit" that her father had relegated to apostolic times.[10] Unlike some of her female contemporaries, Stowe never sought to address an actual congregation, but by the mid-1850s she was challenging the conservatism of those who would deny women the pulpit.[11] A few years after the Congregationalists finally offered a woman, the eloquent abolitionist Antoinette Brown, a pastorate in 1852, Stowe came to the embattled preacher's defense: "Can any one tell us why it should be right and proper for Jenny Lind to *sing* to two thousand people 'I know that my Redeemer liveth' and improper for Antoinette Brown to *say* it?"[12] While staying within the bounds of print, Stowe knew firsthand the difficulties facing a woman who desired to move audiences with the voice of a preacher. *Uncle Tom's Cabin,* her first novel, would dramatize her conflicted relationship with this supremely authoritative form of address.

From sentimentalist to visionary

The narrative voice of *Uncle Tom's Cabin* is remarkably supple. Stowe plays the local colorist when sketching the Kentucky bar and the Quaker settlement, the humorist when describing dilapidated Western log roads, the ethnographer when making racialist generalizations. But the narrator's most distinctive strain is one of passionate intensity, in which the story pauses as the narrator strives to shape the reader's beliefs and values. Many of these fervent narratorial interventions are in sermonic voice, drawing together oratorical form, biblical language, and a tone of conviction. This sermonic voice turns out to be more complex—and less sentimental—than we might expect. It shifts over the course of the novel from sentimental to prophetic, from an acceptably feminine tone to a controversial masculine one—an evolution suggesting that Stowe's confidence, and perhaps her religious and political frustration as well, grew as her story unfolded in the *National Era* from June 5, 1851 to April 1, 1852.

One of the narrator's earliest and most quoted sermonic interjections occurs as Tom gazes upon his sleeping children the night before leaving the Shelby plantation. Characteristic of sermonizing early in the story, this passage calls upon readers to sympathize with suffering, especially that of slaves:

> Sobs, heavy, hoarse and loud, shook the chair, and great tears fell through his fingers on the floor; just such tears, sir, as you dropped into the coffin where lay your first-born son; such tears, woman, as you shed when you heard the cries of your dying babe. For, sir, he was a man,—and you are but another man. And, woman, though dressed in silk and jewels, you are but a woman, and, in life's great straits and mighty griefs, ye feel but one sorrow![13]

The markers of sermonic voice are visible in the passage's parallelism, tone of certainty, and universalizing rhetoric about "life's great straits" and "mighty griefs." While politically progressive in its summoning of sympathy across racial lines (if ethically problematic in its collapsing of difference in that "one sorrow"), this passage stays within the bounds of acceptable discourse for a woman writer. The sermonic language is not yet theological or doctrinal, but rather an emotional plea for fellow feeling. In short, it is sentimental, in the best sense of the word.

As the story grew, Stowe grew bolder as a preacher, with the narratorial interventions taking on an increasingly theological and less sentimental cast. Her greater freedom in preaching may have been due to the enthusiastic response of her original *National Era* readers, who were sending her fan mail and writing appreciative letters to editor Gamaliel Bailey.[14] Assured that she was preaching to the choir, as it were, she engaged more liberally in the language of religious exhortation. For instance, when Mrs. Shelby weeps with Aunt Chloe and Uncle Tom before Haley arrives to transport Tom, the narrator exclaims: "O, ye who visit the distressed, do ye know that everything your money can buy, given with a cold, averted face, is not worth one honest tear shed in real sympathy?"[15] This line in effect rewrites the gospels, borrowing the address and tone of such verses as Matthew 6:30 ("O ye of little faith") and Matthew 16:3 ("O ye hypocrites"), along with Jesus' trademark style of hyperbolic antithesis asserting the worthlessness of material wealth. "[E]verything your money can buy" set against "one honest tear" ensconces sentimentalism in the authoritative syntactic structure of apothegms like "It is easier for a camel to go through the eye of a needle, than for a rich man to enter into the kingdom of God," or "For what is a man profited, if he shall gain the whole world, and lose his own soul?"[16] Harnessing the most morally commanding style available, the narrator has progressed from local appeals for sympathy to pronouncements about its inherent spiritual value, thus crossing the line into the masculine realm of preaching.

Stowe assigns the narrator a male preaching voice even more freely once well into the story. When Haley sells Lucy's baby on the Mississippi and Lucy puts an end to her grief by jumping overboard, the narrator steps in to comfort the reader: "Patience! patience! ye whose hearts swell indignant at wrongs like these. Not one throb of anguish, not one tear of the oppressed, is forgotten by the Man of Sorrows, the Lord of Glory. In his patient, generous bosom he bears the anguish of a world. Bear thou, like him, in patience, and labor in love; for sure as he is God, 'the year of his redeemed *shall* come.'"[17] Baldly sermonic, this passage incorporates repetitive theological diction, the parallelism and anaphora of oratory, and biblical quotation (Isa. 63:4) as it tries to convince readers that a loving God will triumph over evil. Such moments may frustrate readers anxious to get on with the story, but they are less islands of stasis than attempts to situate the novel within the larger narrative of divine redemption implicit in every sermon. As Hortense Spillers has put it, "[T]here is only *one* sermonic conclusion, and that is, the ultimate triumph over defeat and death that the Resurrection promises."[18] By alluding to the Israelite concept of the "year of his redeemed," Stowe suggested that the slaves' redemption would occur not merely at the Resurrection but also in this life. She said, in effect, that though slaves suffered unspeakable horrors now, someday—and the narrator's urgency suggests it might be soon—they would be physically, tangibly redeemed.

What is most striking about the "Patience! patience!" passage is that, as one of the most sermonic moments in an antislavery novel, its primary goal is *not* to exhort readers to identify with the slave or to help bring about an end to slavery. The passage silently assumes the reader's sympathy for the slave, perhaps because Stowe trusted that by this point in the novel, she had adequately trained her readers in such emotional identification. Instead, the sermonic voice takes on the pressing theological problem raised by the everyday tragedies of slavery. How could a loving God allow such suffering? Slavery, like the Holocaust, threatened a crisis of faith for those who sought to empathize with its victims. Stowe explained in the novel's Concluding Remarks that the enactment of the Fugitive Slave Law jolted her into recognizing that she could no longer count on "advancing light and civilization" to defeat slavery, and the rhetoric of the "Patience! patience!" passage fronts this grim realization not with a call for readers to redouble their antislavery efforts but with a strenuous affirmation that God himself will step into the breach.[19] Such rhetoric manifests both Stowe's frustration with this seemingly inextirpable institution and, more surprisingly, an existential anxiety about whether God acts in the world at all.

In fact, the salient feature of the sermonic moments in the last two-thirds of the novel is that they work valiantly to defend God against charges of indifference. Stowe's sermonizing for most of the book, then, reflects not a feminized sentimentality but a masculinized theological vision with an emphasis on God's future action. For example, the night before Emmeline is put on the auction block, the narrator tries to make sense of her mother Susan's situation:

> "But she has no resort but to *pray;* and many such prayers to God have gone up from those same trim, neatly-arranged, respectable slave-prisons,—prayers which God has not forgotten, as a coming day shall show; for it is written, 'Whoso causeth one of these little ones to offend, it were better for him that a mill-stone were hanged about his neck, and that he were drowned in the depths of the sea.'"[20]

Sermonic voice announces itself in the oratorical repetition of "prayers," in the biblical phraseology of "a coming day shall show" and "for it is written," and in the quotation from Matthew 18:6. The passage is dogmatic in its assurance that God has not forgotten the slave and in its threat that God will punish those who cause "little ones to offend"—or to put it without euphemism, girls to be raped. Despite the warning of divine judgment, which the novel has made clear applies to North and South alike, the overall effect of the passage is as much comfort as terror, since a punitive God is at least an active one. As Joshua Bellin has argued, the novel is "activated by a profound theological *despair*," a despair he links to the prospect of "facing a world in which unendurable atrocities must be endured and in which worse atrocities may loom in the future"—in other words, a world in which God does not and will not act.[21] Stowe's battle against this looming despair defines the narrator's sermonizing for most of the novel.

Two more examples can illustrate the point. On one of *La Belle Rivière's* stops, a woman rushes aboard and throws her arms around her chained husband. The narrator soon cuts away: "But what needs tell the story, told too oft,—every day told,—of heart-strings rent and broken,—the weak broken and torn for the profit and convenience of the strong! It needs not to be told;—every day is telling it,—telling it, too, in the ear of One who is not deaf, though he be long silent."[22] This is a strange passage, oratorical in its rhetorical question and in the repetition of "told" and "telling," yet more like a soliloquy than a sermon, as if Stowe addressed not antebellum readers but her own frustration at God's apparent absence. Deprecating the potential efficacy of her own story—"It needs not to be told"—she directed attention to the bitter drama of slavery played out daily before a seemingly apathetic God. Stowe heightened her rhetoric here less to convince her readers to renounce slavery than to guard herself and them against the nightmare of divine indifference.

The defense of God recurs as the narrator meditates on the Mississippi at the beginning of the chapter that introduces Little Eva: "Ah! would that [the waters of the Mississippi] did not also bear along a more fearful freight,—the tears of the oppressed, the sighs of the helpless, the bitter prayers of the poor, ignorant hearts to an unknown God—unknown, unseen and silent, but who will yet 'come out of his place to save all the poor of the earth!'"[23] Stowe here affirms that God will eventually save the suffering slaves but dwells on his inaccessibility: he is "unknown, unseen and silent." The passage betrays an anguish at God's hiddenness that one would sooner expect from Melville than from the daughter of Lyman Beecher. It is as if she poured more of herself than we have realized into the frustrated, angry, religiously skeptical George Harris, and the angst spilled out in narratorial asides that could only partially quell the fear that God would not act or, worse, that there was no God *to* act. In light of the horror and seeming intractability of slavery, the affirmations of divine justice that characterize the narrator's preaching in the latter half of the book should be read not as glib reassurances grounded in unshakable faith, but as a continual effort of the will.

"Concluding Remarks"

Stowe's rhetoric of theological vision crescendos in the "Concluding Remarks," a term itself sermonic—Lyman Beecher often ended his printed discourses with "To Conclude," Finney, his with "Conclusion" or "Remarks." After Stowe, reasserting herself as author, launched a barrage of exhortations calling for readers to renounce slavery (even while telling them it was enough to "*feel right*"), she finally linked her prophecies of divine intervention to her call for political reform in the novel's last few paragraphs.[24] What is distinctive about this ending is its excess—the fact that it sounds even angrier and more threatening than a traditional jeremiad or other antebellum preaching. To be sure, Stowe's closing passage bears numerous resemblances to the American jeremiad as Sacvan Bercovitch defines it. It conflates sacred and secular (the interchangeable hailing of "America," "the Church of Christ," the "nation," and "Christians"), pleads for America's repentance, and wields the familiar trope of America as the new Israel through references to biblical prophecy, most notably, Malachi 3 and 4 and Isaiah 63. But Stowe differed from other American Jeremiahs in asserting not that America had to reform itself because it had a special mission to the world, but that its slavery crisis was a global force threatening apocalypse: "This is an age of the world when nations are trembling and convulsed. A mighty influence is abroad, surging and heaving the world, as with an earthquake. And is America safe? Every nation that carries in its bosom great and unredressed injustice has in it the elements of this last convulsion."[25] As Larry Reynolds points out, these lines allude to the socialist uprisings in Europe at mid-century.[26] She interpreted these upheavals, as well as U.S. slavery, through an apocalyptic framework much more menacing than the comparatively sober postmillennialism of New England Calvinism, which held that Christ would return to Earth *after* the Church brought about a millennial reign of peace and prosperity and that the reformation of the world was a special burden of the Church in America.[27] Against postmillennialism, Stowe warned that the "signs of the times" augured an imminent, universal day of reckoning: "can you forget that prophecy associates, in dread fellowship, the *day of vengeance* with the year of his redeemed?"[28] Although Stowe's final paragraphs revolve around a series of rhetorical questions similar, as Helen Petter Westra notes, to the "deliberately hard-hitting interrogatives found in the application portion of many Calvinist sermons," they outdid the vast majority of such sermons in their apocalypticism and in their attempt to conjure the "theological terror" that James Baldwin took—with perhaps too immediate a sense of these final paragraphs—as the book's primary emotional energy.[29] Such lurid biblical language as "that day shall burn as an oven" is hard to come by in the sermons of orthodox nineteenth-century preachers such as Stowe's father.[30]

One of the most unusual features of Stowe's peroration is that it concludes with a threat, a rhetorical strategy rare in Protestant preaching and one that in this case underscored that the longstanding problem of slavery had reached a crisis point. An antebellum sermon's last sentence or two typically reminded listeners of God's love and mercy, reiterated the path of salvation, invoked God's blessing, or otherwise struck a note of hope. Stowe briefly made this gesture—"A day of grace is yet held out to us"—but then thundered to a close, warning readers that "injustice and cruelty shall bring on nations the wrath of Almighty God!"[31] Nineteenth-century preachers seldom ended an address on such gloomy terms. For instance, Lyman Beecher concluded one of his own quasi-political discourses, an election sermon to the Connecticut legislature, with "Jesus Christ is going on from conquering and to conquer; nor will he turn from His purpose, or cease from His work, until He hath made all things new."[32] Even Puritan jeremiads typically ended more hopefully than *Uncle Tom's Cabin*, as when Increase Mather's sermon "The Day of Trouble Is Near," coupled a threat with the means of avoiding its fulfillment: "And let us remember the words of the Lord Jesus, *Luke 21.36. Watch ye therefore, and pray always, that ye may be counted worthy to escape all these things which shall come to pass.*"[33] Stowe defied with impunity the convention that ministers close sermons by showing listeners the way to God's grace. Confronting a national crisis seemingly impervious to the usual rhetorical appeals, she crafted a hyperbolic sermonic rhetoric designed to shock and frighten the nation into action.

But then, in the novel's final installment in the *National Era*, Stowe retreated from this threatening persona. Her afterword to the paper's readers, which appeared immediately after the Concluding Remarks in the April 1, 1852 issue, betrayed a certain anxiety about the stern rhetoric of the Concluding Remarks' final paragraphs. It was as though she had scrambled down from the pulpit and settled into Rachel Halliday's hearthside rocker:

> The "Author of Uncle Tom's Cabin" must now take leave of a wide circle of friends, whose faces she has never seen, but whose sympathies, coming to her from afar, have stimulated and cheered her in her work.
>
> The thought of the pleasant family circles that she has been meeting in spirit weekly has been a constant refreshment to her, and she cannot leave them without a farewell.
>
> In particular, the dear little children who have followed her story have her warmest love. Dear children, you will one day be men and women; and

she hopes that you will learn from this story always to remember and pity the poor and oppressed, and, when you grow up, show your pity by doing all you can for them. Never, if you can help it, let a colored child be shut out of school, or treated with neglect and contempt, because of his color. Remember the sweet example of Little Eva, and try to feel the same regard for all that she did; and then, when you grow up, we hope that the foolish and unchristian prejudice against people, merely on account of their complexion, will be done away with.

Farewell, dear children, till we meet again.

Separated from the closing jeremiad by only the shortest of printer's lines, this demure, feminized afterword placed the author firmly within the family circle. Retreating from the male authority of judgmental biblical quotation, she aligned herself instead with the feminine authority of maternal affection by offering the "dear little children" who "have her warmest love" the moralism of children's literature: remember and pity the poor and oppressed, do not hold a prejudice against colored children, remember the model child of the story.[34] The final line reinforced her role as a symbolic mother. The effect of this authorial postscript, nearly invisible in the scholarship on *Uncle Tom's Cabin,* is to subvert the preceding jeremiad by transforming it from direct address into a mimesis of direct address, a mere playing with sermonic voice. The wizard behind the curtain turns out to be only a little lady with a pen. Because the final installment of *Uncle Tom's Cabin* in the *National Era* ran twelve days after the book version appeared, it is tempting to speculate that as the novel began to circulate among readers, Stowe sought to distance herself from its fiery rhetoric. Perhaps the most generous reading of Stowe's strange, forgotten dual ending is that she was trying to have it both ways—to claim the masculine authority of preaching *and* the feminine authority of motherhood. If the masculine and feminine modes of speech unsettle one another, they also reveal both as literary performances capable of operating independently of the writer's gender. The dual-gendered ending suggests that on the page, one can speak both as a man and as a woman and so attain a fullness of voice—and, theoretically, authority—unavailable to reformers obliged to address audiences in person.

Disowning the men in black

Far from an afterthought, the frustration with preaching-as-usual visible at the end of the Concluding Remarks defines the novel. Despite Stowe's loyalties to the Beecher clan, the novel mocks, silences, and marginalizes the preachers in its pages.[35] The critique of proslavery preaching is blatant, occurring primarily through two scenes in which a married couple reviews a sermon at home, a situation that reinforces the novel's well-known argument for the moral authority of mothers. In the first scene, Mrs. Shelby rejects her husband's attempt to cite "Mr. B.'s sermon, the other Sunday" as justification for selling Tom and Harry and censures all proslavery preaching: "Ministers can't help the evil, perhaps,—can't cure it, any more than we can,—but defend it!—it always went against my common sense."[36] Her critique deflates *all* preaching on the slavery question—proslavery preaching for defying common sense, antislavery preaching for its apparent futility. Preaching is again tried before a domestic tribunal at the St. Clare home, when Marie paraphrases the "splendid" sermon of "Dr. G—" on the divinely ordained social order: "that some were born to rule and some to serve, and all that, you know." Marie's languid recital of Dr. G—'s racist ideology causes Augustine to fume, and he condemns proslavery religion as being "less scrupulous, less generous, less just, less considerate for man" than his own unredeemed nature. St. Clare's sermonic fervor demolishes the second-hand bromides of Dr. G—, but it is ultimately his mother who deserves credit for his moral reasoning. The scriptural citations of proslavery sermons have no weight with him because, he says, "The Bible was my *mother's* book."[37] As with Mrs. Shelby, the faith of pious mothers carries more moral authority than the sermons of a corrupt clergy.

Stowe's most audacious critique of proslavery preaching was the note in Chapter 12 attributing to Philadelphia clergyman Joel Parker the statement that slavery contained "no evils but such as are inseparable from any other relations in social and domestic life." Alleging that his words had been taken out of context, Parker made his grievances public in the New York *Observer,* and between May and November 1852, he and Stowe sparred in print—he in the proslavery *Observer,* she in the antislavery *Independent.* Hedrick points out that although slavery was the main issue, Parker was also rankled by the "audacity of a *woman* daring to publicly challenge a man and a minister."[38]

When, during this debate, the editor of the New York *Observer* remarked on the "decidedly anti-ministerial" bent of *Uncle Tom's Cabin,* he was likely noticing more than its critique of proslavery preaching.[39] The novel defines itself against preaching as an institution by never showing an antislavery minister in the pulpit or crediting the Northern churches for participating in the abolitionist movement. Only one antislavery minister appears, briefly. As Haley takes Tom south on *La Belle Rivière,* a clergyman tells a group of women discussing slavery that Providence has intended the "African race" to be kept "in a low condition," sententiously citing, "'Cursed be Canaan; a servant of servants shall he be.'" A young man who turns out to be a clergyman interrupts, "'All things whatsoever ye would that men should do unto you, do ye even so unto them.' I suppose . . . *that* is scripture, as much as 'Cursed be Canaan.'" It is significant that this antislavery clergyman achieves authority precisely insofar as he distances himself from his profession. His invocation of the golden rule is devoid of theological embellishment or oratorical style, and in contrast with the proslavery clergyman, who signals his interest in receiving all due respect through his black outfit and grave demeanor, the antislavery clergyman wears no identifying garb and does not mention his clerical status. When the steamboat docks and a woman runs aboard to her chained husband, the young minister rebukes Haley for his trade: "Look at those poor creatures! Here I am, rejoicing in my heart that I am going home to my wife and child; and the same bell which is a signal to carry me onward towards them will part this poor man and his wife forever. Depend upon it, God will bring you into judgment for this."[40] By having the clergyman cite as antislavery evidence his own domestic affections—and, too, with a "thick utterance" that implies strong emotion, even welling tears—Stowe feminized him, effectively subordinating him to her own more masculine, visionary narrator. It is also telling that Stowe limited the clergyman to condemning the slave-trader. Careful herself to show how North and South, slaveholders and non-slaveholders alike were complicit in the system—"But who, sir, makes the trader?"—she kept the clergyman focused on the obvious scoundrel.[41] By thus domesticating and circumscribing the antislavery minister's censure, Stowe nodded to the clergy while reserving to herself the power of a more comprehensive critique.

Democratizing sermonic voice

The flip side of Stowe's reluctance to endorse the clergy was her commitment to the sermonic speech of the laity. Over and above the novel's many scenes of impassioned testimony—most notably those involving Eliza, George Harris, and Augustine St. Clare—a surprising number of characters speak in sermonic voice. The leading lay preachers are, of course, Eva and Tom, both of whom derive their moral authority from an intuitive evangelical spirituality and their confrontations with death. Pained that slaves should suffer and ultimately martyred to her sorrow over slavery, the Little Evangelist comes into her own as a preacher when she is about to die: "Listen to what I say. I want to speak to you about your souls [. . .]."[42] Her salvific message is to the point: her listeners must pray and read the Bible (or have it read to them) so that they can become angels and join her in heaven. As one critic puts it, "The most clearly professional of Victorian preaching heroines is little Eva on her deathbed."[43] But of course Eva is professional only insofar as she has a polished rhetoric of exhortation; the word implies a performativity alien to her strenuously affirmed romantic innocence.

If Tom, the novel's other leading preacher, irritates today's readers, it is in part because he, too, lacks performativity, despite being a grown man. Yet for all Tom's innocence, his preaching is a disruptive force with powerful political implications. On the surface, his piety looks innocuous. "A sort of patriarch in religious matters" among the Shelby slaves, he preaches with a "simple, hearty, sincere style . . . [that] might have edified even better educated persons."[44] Haley even cites Tom's preaching ability as one of his assets as he tries to close the deal with St. Clare. Although Tom never delivers an actual sermon in the novel, he does offer earnest, biblically informed guidance to an astounding array of characters—to Chloe, young George Shelby, Lucy, Prue, St. Clare, Cassy, Sambo and Quimbo, and Legree. His fearless speeches to his masters are arresting for how they claim moral and spiritual authority over whites. Before leaving the Shelby farm, Tom commands young George to obey his parents, especially his mother, and to "'Member yer Creator in the days o' yer youth." At the St. Clares', he pleads for his master's soul with tears and prayers and countless gestures of humility, but he never stops citing Scripture or speaking from a position of spiritual superiority. And at the Red River plantation, he presents Legree with the ultimate sermonic threat. He declares that his own troubles will soon be over but that "if ye don't repent, yours won't *never* end!" Holding the note, Stowe extended this climactic, virtual "Go to hell!" by comparing Tom's outburst to a "strange snatch of heavenly music" and noting the "blank pause" of Legree's mute outrage.[45] Tom's exhortations to his white masters make visible the radical potential of sermonic voice—how it licenses a reversal of power in which spiritual strength triumphs over social conditioning and physical force.

Stowe affirmed a connection between spiritual power and social power by restoring Tom as a religious patriarch among the slaves. "[M]any would gather together to hear from him of Jesus" on Sundays, and Cassy takes to calling him "Father Tom." Like Eva, Tom achieves his greatest rhetorical authority on his deathbed. When Sambo and Quimbo beg him to tell them about Jesus, he "poured forth a few energetic sentences of that wondrous One,—his life, his death, his everlasting presence, and power to save."[46] They weep and beg for mercy. Through such scenes, Stowe suggested the superiority of all heartfelt, untutored sermonic rhetoric over professional sermons.

Stowe bestowed the privilege of sermonic voice not on Tom and Eva alone, but also on a host of non-ordained characters. She thus implicitly argued for a democratic religious empowerment in which ordinary Christians were perpetually ready to preach to one another. Mrs. Shelby illustrates this idea when she challenges her husband's decision to sell Tom and Harry; Mrs. Bird when she tells her Senator husband that "[o]beying God never brings on public evils"; Augustine St. Clare when he denounces slave-holding ideology to Marie and Ophelia, occasionally with biblical flourishes incongruous with his avowed skepticism. Even more radical than these scenes of domestic sermonizing are the examples of preaching across color lines. In counterpoint to Tom's sermons to his masters, the novel presents whites as having a special burden to offer their own religious conviction as an antidote to black despair. Eva performs this function for Topsy, but the duty bears on adults as well. When Mr. Wilson hears George Harris's testimony, he counsels him to trust in the Lord, and when George asks whether there is any God to trust in, Mr. Wilson declares, "There is—there is; clouds and darkness are around about him, but righteousness and judgment are the habitation of his throne. There's a *God*, George,—believe it; trust in Him, and I'm sure He'll help you. Everything will be set right,—if not in this life, in another." Biblical, oratorical speech invests the timid, rather pathetic Mr. Wilson with a "temporary dignity and authority," and George verifies the impromptu sermon's efficacy: "Thank you for saying that, my good friend; I'll *think of that.*" Sermonic speech is again aimed at George's lack of faith at the Quaker settlement, when Simeon describes his own faith in highly metaphorical biblical language then tells George, "Put thy trust in him and, no matter what befalls thee here, he will make all right hereafter." The narrator affirms that had some "easy, self-indulgent exhorter" made this speech, it might have seemed only a "pious and rhetorical flourish"; the fact that Simeon has risked fines and imprisonment makes his rhetoric credible. With Eva preaching to the slaves, Tom preaching to his masters, and Mr. Wilson and Simeon preaching to George, the novel argues for religious exhortation as a two-way street. In moments of crisis, whites and blacks are called to offer each other the gift of an eloquent testimony of faith. Stowe's democratization of sermonic address is a utopian vision in which individuals who share responsibility for one another's moral and religious well-being supplant professional preachers.[47] Sermonic speech, she implied, is most effective not when pronounced by silver-tongued ministers such as her father and famous brother but when gasped out by ordinary people—black or white, high or low—in intense, soul-baring moments.

Stowe's idealization of the inspired, uneducated religious speaker in *Uncle Tom's Cabin* flirts with Methodism, Quakerism, and other forms of laity-empowering Protestantism without committing itself to an open critique of orthodoxy. In taking the Protestant tenet of the "priesthood of all believers" more seriously than most of her coreligionists in the white, theologically conservative Northeastern churches, Stowe advocated an equality of personhood that challenged not simply the institution of slavery, but also, implicitly, the political subjugation of blacks and women. The novel forces a question: why should those who know the truth and who can speak it so well be denied a voice in the public sphere? The fact that neither Stowe nor her narrator directly articulates this question cannot erase the radical political subtext.

Anyone who has taught *Uncle Tom's Cabin* to undergraduates knows how thoroughly they resist its preachiness, despite their fascination with its Christian themes and symbols. Students critique Stowe for telling, not showing, for interrupting the action, for bludgeoning the reader with her evangelical message. Nor have professional critics been much better as they have effectually dismissed the novel's sermonizing as beneath or beyond explication. Looking closely at how Stowe appropriated sermonic voice reveals striking variations in tone and function. Although critics often lump together the novel's various religious elements and align them with its domesticity and sentimentalism under the phrase "religion of the heart," much of Stowe's sermonizing is harsh, desperate, and unsentimental. Yet her afterword in the *National Era* serialization suggested an author frightened by her own daring, so eager to reintroduce herself as a woman and a mother that she risked making the novel's closing jeremiad sound like playacting. Perhaps we see Stowe most at her ease when she is preaching through her characters, claiming the right and duty to speak not for herself alone but for all those who lacked official venues.

Uncle Tom's Cabin reveals the power of a religious novel to overshadow actual preaching. No sermon matched it for worldwide influence: ten thousand copies sold in two weeks and three hundred thousand in the first year in the United States; a staggering 1.5 million copies sold the first year in Britain; and, of course, abridgments, stage adaptations, poems, songs, commemorative plates, translation into dozens of languages, and more.[48] The introduction to the 1852 London edition announced Stowe's triumph over the usual religious fare: "Those who sleep over other religious books, or who snore at church, can pass the midnight hour as they peruse these pages without a nod."[49] Stowe had not only fulfilled her early ambition to "preach on paper" but had outperformed the preachers on their own turf. As Ann Douglas writes, Stowe was "an artist whose achievement was to beat daddy at his own game."[50] The title page of an edition of Lyman Beecher's "Lectures on Intemperance" published in England in the mid-1850s bears witness to her victory.[51] His name as author is followed by the line, "FATHER OF

MRS. BEECHER STOWE"—the patriarch identified through the daughter, the preacher through the novelist.

For as sweet as this father-daughter reversal is, we must liberate Stowe from her status as daughter altogether if we are to understand the cultural significance of her sermonizing in *Uncle Tom's Cabin*. We should see her instead in a broader religious context—alongside, for instance, America's foremost antislavery preacher, Theodore Parker. A religious and political radical who broke from his fellow Unitarians for denying the importance of miracles to religious belief and who sheltered fugitive slaves in his home, Parker preached to thousands each Sunday and lectured to more than fifty thousand people a year on the lyceum circuit.[52] Stowe and Parker were polar opposites theologically, but both stretched the limits of antebellum religious discourse by condemning slavery with unusual vehemence. Parker's sermon "The Chief Sins of the People," delivered a week after the passage of the Fugitive Slave Law, mocked the preachers cowed by slaveholders. He parroted their evasions—"My modesty forbids me to speak. Let us pray!"—and denounced anyone who would return a man to slavery: "[T]o send a man into slavery is worse than to murder him. . . . I cannot comprehend that in any man, not even in a hyena. . . . I can only understand it in a devil!"[53] Read against Parker's righteous indignation, Stowe's efforts to rouse her audience to reject slavery by stirring up their emotions do not seem particularly evangelical or feminine. If *Uncle Tom's Cabin* comes across as overwrought, it may be only because Stowe had found the key to effective antislavery preaching, regardless of theology or gender.

The antislavery preaching of even so charismatic a figure as Parker reveals the impossibility of literally preaching to a nation—and the gap novels could fill. Parker once wrote to a young man that he knew of "no better position than the minister's to move the nation," but his sermon against the Fugitive Slave Law highlights the difficulty of addressing a national audience while standing in Boston.[54] His final paragraphs began, in turn, "O Boston!," "O Massachusetts, noble state!," "America . . . !," yet the sermon never quite transcended its provincial origins. Despite the fact that he followed the tradition of the American jeremiad in recalling America to its historic sense of mission—"Hast thou too forgot thy mission here [. . .]?"—his loyalties were too obviously with New England, which he asserted was "once the soul, although not the body of America."[55] Full of righteous zeal, he lacked all patience with the South and, unlike Stowe, never addressed Southerners directly. Realistically, he could hardly aspire to. Novels had wings as sermons did not. Ministers might imagine they were "moving the nation," but on divisive sectional issues, the need to rally a primary audience—the people who looked up at

them each week—precluded the multiple rhetorics necessary for addressing far-flung audiences. Although *Uncle Tom's Cabin* never entirely sheds
its Northern parochialism either, it could combine the religious passion of a
preacher with a fullness of voice and perspective impossible to achieve in the
pulpit.

Stowe made the most of her constraints. Relegated to preaching in the
pages of fiction, she pushed the rhetorical limits of political sermonizing and
symbolically empowered women and African Americans by having them
preach to white men. If our appreciation of her boldness is hampered by the
novel's inescapable, embarrassing racialism, it is worth remembering that
the novel also inspired and provoked numerous nineteenth-century African
Americans to create their own preachy novels. The next chapter turns to one
of the most immediate and rhetorically savvy of these responses to Stowe.

CHAPTER 7

The Borrowed Robes of
Clotel; or,
The President's Daughter

I N THE FIRST chapter of *Clotel,* the first known novel by an African
American, the eponymous sixteen-year-old daughter of Thomas Jefferson
stands on the block as the auctioneer drives up her price by calling out her
virtues. The first bid is $500, prompting the auctioneer to belittle the crowd's
ignorance of the going rate for such "fancy girls" and to vouch for her "good
moral character." Bids rise to $700. He notes her intelligence. Bids rise to
$800. He promises that she is a "devoted Christian, and perfectly trustwor-
thy." Bids rise to $1200. Finally, he affirms that she is "pure" and chaste, a
"virtuous creature." Her virginity pushes the price to $1500. Sold. In itemizing
a woman's virtues like so many articles in a bill of lading, Brown dramatized
how slavery commodified people, body and soul.[1]

But then the ground shifts under our feet. In summing up the auction
scene, the narrator reports that Clotel's "Christianity [sold] for three hundred; and her chastity and virtue for four hundred dollars more." The math is
off. It was her Christianity (and trustworthiness) that ratcheted up the price
four hundred dollars; her chastity, three. The discrepancy suggests Brown's
ambivalence about how to represent the market value of a slave girl's virginity relative to her piety. His earlier and later versions of this scene reveal
that he was continually revising these two values and their relationship to
one another.[2] Regardless of which virtue cashed in higher, the perpetual juxtaposition of virginity and piety implied that they were linked, while also
paradoxically hinting at future sexual compliance. This tension is especially

evident in *Clotelle: A Tale of the Southern States* (1864), a redacted version geared to Union soldiers, in which the girl's religiosity is mentioned both before and after her sexual purity, a redundancy that makes the second reference to religion—the slave's ability to "make an excellent prayer"—sound strangely suggestive, as if the image of the slave girl on her knees promised sexual favors. "The piety of the Slave is to be a good servant," Brown had told the women of Salem, and for slave women, serving the master could include a great deal.[3]

If the shifting values and freighted rhetoric surrounding piety in *Clotel's* inaugural scene suggests that Brown regarded slave religion with a certain cynicism, it also announces the novel's investment in invoking Christianity in hopes of rousing the sympathies of white readers and converting them to abolitionism. Though typically treated as a secular novel, *Clotel* is infused with religious characters and language.[4] This show of piety seems to be not the result of Brown's own religious fervor, but a canny rhetorical strategy inspired by the unprecedented success of *Uncle Tom's Cabin*.[5]

During 1852 and 1853, Stowe's novel dominated the antislavery conversation in Britain, where Brown had been living since attending the International Peace Congress in Paris in 1849. Nowhere was this more evident than in the pages of the London-based *Anti-Slavery Advocate,* the monthly, eight-page newspaper of the Anglo-American Anti-Slavery Society, an organization Brown had helped found with the British Unitarian reformer and ophthalmic surgeon John Bishop Estlin and a handful of others dedicated to immediate emancipation.[6] One of the paper's primary goals was to stoke the antislavery flames sparked by Stowe's bombshell. References to the novel and its author filled the first issue in October 1852. One article begged readers not to "allow the feelings which the thrilling scenes and fearful developments of 'Uncle Tom's Cabin' have excited in their minds, to pass away without some desire, some effort" to assist the American antislavery cause; another took the London *Times* reviewer to task for caviling at Stowe's representations of slavery; and the last page featured an advertisement promoting antislavery bazaars as a means for readers whose hearts had been touched by the novel to advance the slave's deliverance.[7] From the second issue forward, the paper ran a quotation from the novel in the masthead: "Nothing of tragedy can be spoken, can be conceived, that equals the frightful reality of scenes daily and hourly acting in the United States, beneath the shadow of American law and the shadow of the Cross of Christ." Stowe loomed large in the paper throughout 1852 and 1853, as the paper defended the novel against the criticism of the London *Times* reviewer; tallied the number of copies sold in various editions; described how one publisher employed "400 men, women, and children, constantly occupied in binding the work"; corroborated Stowe's horrific representations of slavery, including relating the story of a "real life" Uncle Tom whipped to death for refusing to renounce his Christian faith; noted the success of the novel in Paris, Italy, Spain, and Germany; reviewed the *Key to Uncle Tom's Cabin*; reported on Stowe's visit to England in 1853; and printed passages from one of Stowe's speeches.[8] That Brown himself found a valuable ally in *Uncle Tom's Cabin* is suggested in the paper's report that he lectured on it to four hundred people at the Athenaeum in Newport, on the Isle of Wight, in February 1853, and in his sending William Lloyd Garrison a letter that May, reprinted in the *Liberator*, in which he declared that the novel had "come down upon the dark abodes of slavery like a morning's sunlight, unfolding to view its enormities in a manner which has fastened all eyes upon the 'peculiar institution,' and awakening sympathy in hearts that never before felt for the slave." The plaudit, an unattributed borrowing from an antislavery festival advertisement, reflects Brown's recognition that Stowe's novel was a game-changer for the antislavery movement.[9]

What Brown learned from Stowe's success that had not been at all clear before the spring of 1852 was that a *novel* could be more effective in creating antislavery feeling than straight-up facts or speeches and, more pointedly, that the novel should be sentimental *and* preachy.[10] Brown took this lesson to heart. *Clotel* abounds in abolitionist sermonic rhetoric, voiced by Peck, Georgiana, Snyder, and the narrator. With antislavery sermonizing, Brown presented readers with the religious arguments against the institution, and with proslavery sermonizing, the role that organized Christianity played in giving it moral sanction. He stressed the latter point in the novel's preface, arguing that if high-status individuals, "especially professed Christians," did not own slaves, slavery would have been abolished long ago and that the mission of the friend of the slave should be to convince "the wise, the prudent, and the pious to withdraw their support" from it.[11] In treating Christians' support of slavery as a prime reason for its continuance, Brown both picked up on a theme Stowe had stressed in her Concluding Remarks, where she had castigated the "Church of Christ," and reiterated the critique of proslavery Christians he had first presented in lecturing for the Western New York Anti-Slavery Society and Garrison's Massachusetts Anti-Slavery Society in the 1840s. Speaking to the Female Anti-Slavery Society of Salem, for instance, he had declared that a slave-trader's joining the church was "only an evidence that when Wickedness, with a purse of gold, knocks at the door of the Church, she seldom, if ever, is refused admission."[12] Shaming churches that supported slavery and celebrating those that opposed it was also a central strategy of the *Anti-Slavery Advocate,* which ran as its first major section, typically on the front page, a "Religious" department that detailed in turn where each of nearly two dozen American denominations and religious organizations, including Presbyterians, Methodists, Quakers, Roman Catholics, and the American Tract Society, stood on the slavery question. In short, Brown and his circle saw winning the support of Christians, individually and collectively, as a moral linchpin in the abolitionist campaign.

Although Brown found it necessary to preach in *Clotel,* he did not feel compelled to write his own sermons. The novel's sermonic rhetoric is a complex tapestry of verbatim excerpts from dozens of nineteenth-century sermons, lectures, pamphlets, periodical essays, and other previously published writing. These silent borrowings, long unrecognized, are mappable today only because of the archives of digitized texts now at our fingertips. The Conclusion acknowledges the novel's debt to the stories of slaves Brown had met as a boatman on Lake Erie, to characters mentioned in abolitionist journals, and to part of a short story by Lydia Maria Child's ("The Quadroons"), but his subsequent "Having thus acknowledged my resources [. . .]" hurries the reader rather too quickly past the issue of his textual borrowing, in particular the fact that the novel includes vast tracts of dialogue and commentary lifted from published writing. If Brown's lack of candor about the extent of his borrowing reinforces the image of him as a "trickster," it also shows his political seriousness in that it allowed him to build on the antislavery sentiment that *Uncle Tom's Cabin* had ignited by ventriloquizing a range of theological and biblical arguments foreign to the abolitionist discourse of his lectures and autobiographies.[13]

Some students of *Clotel* may be dismayed to find that its borrowings go so deep, but the mosaic of sermonic passages in the novel can be read as evidence of Brown's resourcefulness and artistic ingenuity, as well as of his peculiar moment in literary history. Ezra Greenspan explains that Brown worked much like a newspaper editor, drawing from "a common pool of uncopyrighted, unrestricted print information" and recombining these texts into new configurations.[14] The extent of these recombinations and reconfigurations in *Clotel* should prompt us to a fuller awareness of the novel's liminality in the history of African American narrative. The 1850s were, as William L. Andrews writes, a transitional time for black narrative, when, leaving straight autobiographical narratives behind, it "broke most profoundly with discursive conventions and white expectations in an attempt to find new ways of authorizing itself."[15] To borrow in *Clotel* as extensively and silently as Brown did, and to borrow *sermons,* which were supposed to express one's sincerity and conviction, was indeed a break with convention, though one designed less as a gesture of self-authorization than as a pragmatic, efficient strategy for writing an inspiring antislavery novel.

In incorporating proslavery sermonic rhetoric, Brown was, as Robert Levine writes of his relation to sources in general, "highly aggressive [. . .] wresting them from their place in white supremacist culture."[16] The term pastiche is especially apt for these borrowed proslavery passages, given how the novel mocks and otherwise subverts them. However, in using antislavery religious discourse, Brown's approach was much more appreciative and inclusive, reflecting the fact that he opposed white supremacist culture alongside a host of white and black, male and female abolitionists dedicated to ending slavery and promoting racial justice. His sermonic novel orchestrates a vast chorus of fellow laborers that included such eloquent speakers as Garrison, Theodore Dwight Weld, Sarah Grimké, and Robert Purvis. *Clotel* is thus not merely, in Henry Louis Gates's words, "an abolitionist's sermon," but many abolitionists' sermons.[17] In this respect, Brown's novel is continuous with other African Atlantic texts, which, as Heather Russell explains, are often polyvocal, a "*communal, participatory narrative enactment*," with many voices "shar[ing] the stage."[18] As stage manager, Brown assigned his borrowed sermons with care, typically giving Georgiana more theologically conservative rhetoric than that of the narrator. This tendency may suggest his own liberal religious sympathies, but personal expression was not the point. The purpose of *Clotel*'s religious rhetoric was to win Christians for abolitionism by addressing them in their own moral and religious idiom.

Exposing the proslavery preacher

The only ordained minister dramatized in *Clotel* is the Connecticut native John Peck, a "popular preacher" who enjoys "a large congregation with a snug salary" in Natchez, Mississippi.[19] That Peck is a minister is almost gratuitous, as he never preaches a sermon or leads a church service, but his vocation allows him to serve as the novel's representative Southern Christian gentleman—and consummate moral hypocrite. The initial characterizations of Peck are favorable: he makes sure his slaves are "well fed and not overworked"; keeps his overseer in line; and is an amiable host, loving father, and upstanding citizen who gives generously to charity. Only after granting these stereotypical virtues of Southern gentlemen does the novel reveal that he is "nevertheless, a most cruel master."[20] Besides refusing to sell Currer to her daughter Althesa, he drives his field hands until late at night (a statement difficult to reconcile with the earlier claim that he doesn't overwork them), hunts his escaped slaves with vicious dogs, and has shot to death a slave who fought off the dogs with a club. Like Lippard peeling back the layers on Jervis, or Hawthorne on Dimmesdale, Brown demythologized and deauthorized the figure of the pious, respectable clergyman. Going beyond them, he showed how supposed gentlemanliness could go hand-in-hand with a commitment to an unjust, death-dealing social institution.

The tension between Peck's refined persona and objectionable proslavery ideology is most fully articulated in two lengthy speeches drawn verbatim from articles in the *Southern Presbyterian Review* from the late 1840s. Such extensive excerpting of proslavery writers reflected Brown's practice of letting slavery's apologists stand self-condemned through their own words. As he had explained in quoting advertisements from Southern newspapers in his lectures, "I do not present to you the assertion of the North [. . .] or my own assertion; but I bring before you the testimony of the Slaveholders themselves,—and by their own testimony must they stand or fall."[21] Using lines that first appeared in a *Southern Presbyterian Review* book review denouncing the French Revolution, Peck maintains that Adam and Eve had forfeited whatever "natural rights" they had at their creation by disobeying God in the Garden of Eden, which means that "Rights and wrongs are necessarily the creatures of society"—both "artificial and voluntary."[22] By incorporating this politico-theological reasoning into *Clotel*, Brown laid bare the reactionary political philosophy underpinning slavery—a philosophy that rejected the foundational American principle of, in Peck's (and the review's) term, "inalienable rights."[23] Although Peck's tone here is so reasonable as to risk backfiring on *Clotel*'s antislavery project, especially for an audience in Britain, where the French Revolution was viewed with more skepticism than in the United States, Brown apparently wagered that readers would see through the seeming eloquence and rationality and resist the anti-democratic logic.

In a second long, religiously infused proslavery speech, Peck dismisses Carlton's defense of natural rights and declares that he stands with the Bible because it is older than the Declaration of Independence. Yet instead of then arguing for slavery from the Bible, he argues for the necessity of providing slaves with religious instruction—a risky choice on Brown's part, as even antislavery advocates might contend that as long as slavery remained in force, slaves should be taught Christianity. Brown presented this proslavery argument in top form; Peck's speech comes from the notable James Thornwell, one of the South's leading evangelical apologists, a firm believer in social order who advocated a proslavery position stressing the moral and religious obligations of masters to their slaves.[24] Using Thornwell's words, Peck argues that the Bible establishes rights only in connection with duties and that along with the right of slavery comes the duty of giving slaves religious instruction. But the core argument is less biblical than sociological: "our domestic institutions can be maintained against the world, if we but allow Christianity to throw its broad shield over them."[25] That is, if Christianity does not protect slavery, the world will abandon it, a point very similar to the one Brown stressed in his preface to *Clotel,* when he blamed the persistence of slavery on Christians' support for it. By incorporating this revelatory passage from Thornwell, Brown stressed that politics and strategy, not ethics, underlay Southern concern for slaves' religious instruction.

Perhaps to reduce the risk of Peck being read sympathetically, Brown concluded the speech from Thornwell with two lines of his own, both charged with irony for antislavery sympathizers: "Why, is it not better that Christian men should hold slaves than unbelievers? We know how to value the bread of life, and will not keep it from our slaves."[26] To anyone familiar with Brown's *Narrative* or other slave autobiographies, the answer to the first question would have been a resounding "no." As Frederick Douglass had blasted the myth of God-fearing slaveowners, "[O]f all slaveholders with whom I have ever met, religious slaveholders are the worst. I have ever found them the meanest, basest, the most cruel and cowardly, of all others."[27] Brown's own narrative, prefatory to *Clotel,* also highlighted the hypocrisy of proslavery Christians, describing, for instance, how the slave catcher who arrested him and his mother held family prayers with the slaves in custody under his roof. Brown also seems to have counted on readers hearing the irony beneath Peck's assertion that Christian slaveowners would not keep the "bread of life" from their slaves—on their knowing the realities of a grimly enforced religion of servility and, more literally, insufficient food.

Brown satirized proslavery preaching most directly with the missionary preacher Snyder, though here, too, extensive excerpting from a proslavery writer risked undermining the book's antislavery message. The first four-fifths of Snyder's lengthy sermon to the slaves comes from two sermons in Thomas Bacon's *Sermons Addressed to Masters and Servants* (1813), from which Brown lifted and pieced together passages focusing on servitude.[28] The resultant motley sermon exposed how white self-interest dictated the parameters of religious instruction for slaves: Snyder tells the slaves to serve their masters as they themselves would want to be served, to serve diligently and not as "eye-servants," to accept their condition as ordained by God, and to bear "correction" patiently, whether deserved or not. Yet even considering that Brown selected some of the most damning passages from Bacon, including a proslavery sermon was risky, especially given that Snyder takes as his text not an obscure verse from Numbers or Leviticus, but the Golden Rule:

"All things whatsoever ye would that men should do unto you, do ye even so unto them."[29] For abolitionists, using this precept to direct slave behavior was an outrage and the most blatant hypocrisy. But for those uncertain whether Christianity supported slavery, connecting forced servitude to this foundational Christian ethic might have sounded seductively reasonable.[30] It was a gamble to bank on nineteenth-century Protestants seeing the fallacy of Snyder's applying to slaves such familiar ideas as providentially decreed social positions, the spiritual hazards of "riches and power," and God's compensating for unjust punishment on earth with justice in heaven.

To prevent readers from interpreting Snyder's borrowed sermon too generously, Brown undercut it on every side. Most crudely, Snyder lacks the height associated with authority; he is described as "exceedingly low in stature" and called the "low squatty preacher."[31] He also has little respect for his listeners or concern for their spiritual well-being. He rattles up in his one-horse wagon at the last minute and begins preaching without hymn or prayer or affectionate address; Bacon, in contrast, at least opens, "My well-beloved Black Brethren and Sisters."[32] As for the sermon itself, while the bulk comes from Bacon verbatim, Brown added a final section of his own to underscore the absurdity of proslavery Christian teaching (from "Lastly, you should serve your masters faithfully" to "Now let me exhort you once more to be faithful"). There he laid it on thick, as Snyder tells his audience how lucky they are to be slaves, unlike their fathers in Africa, who were "poor ignorant and barbarous creatures," or their owners, who went to great trouble and expense to outfit slave ships and who must endure such vicissitudes of capitalism as bank busts and crop failures: "Oh, my dear black brothers and sisters, you are indeed a fortunate and blessed people."[33] After failing to close the service with a benediction, Snyder transitions to reading a catechism, the first half of which comes, unacknowledged, from the section on "Duties of Servants" in Charles Colcock Jones's *A Catechism of Scripture Doctrine and Practice*."[34] Although catechisms are designed to be a dialogue, Snyder reads both questions and answers. It seems he has taught the slaves nothing—or that they refuse to go along with the charade.

Brown undermined Snyder's sermon most aggressively in the listeners' response to it. Though Snyder's pulpit style is just the sort slaves were believed to like—he speaks with "gesticulations, sonorous voice, and occasionally [brings] his fist down upon the table with the force of a sledge hammer"—the slaves are listless and bored. They lounge under the apple trees sleeping and eating hazelnuts. Afterward they critique the sermon as a performance to impress Carlton and reject its racist message. Aunt Dafney says it best: "I got no notion of dees white fokes, no how [. . .] Dey all de time tellin'

dat de Lord made us for to work for dem, and I don't believe a word of it."[35]
When another adds that the people who wrote the Bible were "great fools" for
putting in it nothing but "servants obey yer masters," Uncle Simon corrects
him, telling him that he heard it read in Maryland and knows there is more
in there than that. The slaves are ignorant, but they are not stupid. Whoever
reviewed *Clotel* for the *Anti-Slavery Advocate*—perhaps Brown himself—
presented this post-sermon parley as a highlight of the book, excerpting it in
its entirety.[36]

After this exercise in missionary preaching, Snyder continues to sermon-
ize at a dinner with Carlton and Huckelby, Peck's overseer, but now to a different tune. Among whites, he drops the proslavery rhetoric that pays his
bills to advocate for labor solidarity and education. Following anecdotes that
center on the ignorance of poor Southern whites, he indicts the South for
not respecting education and industry: "No community can be prosperous,
where honest labour is not hounoured. No society can be rightly constituted, where the intellect is not fed. Whatever institution reflects discredit on
industry, whatever institution forbids the general culture of the understanding, is palpably hostile to individual rights, and to social well-being." These
moralistic declarations come straight from a paper by John Gorham Palfrey,
one of Massachusetts's leading antislavery voices of the late 1840s.[37] Ordained
a Unitarian minister, Palfrey was a Boston luminary who had served as pastor of the Brattle Street Church, editor of the *Christian Examiner* and of the
North American Review, Professor of Sacred Literature at Harvard, member of the Massachusetts General Court, Secretary of the Commonwealth of
Massachusetts, and U.S. Congressman.[38] In assigning Palfrey's words to Snyder, Brown recast the rebuke of a distant Northern magistrate and littérateur
as the common-sense observations of a middle-class Northerner (Snyder
hails from the Mohawk Valley of New York) who has witnessed daily life in
the South. Brown may have believed in the self-incriminating power of proslavery discourse, but he hedged his bets by creating a proslavery preacher
who, off the clock, undermines his own sermons by wielding Northern anti-
slavery arguments.

Antislavery preaching

Where in *Clotel* is the black preacher who talks back to Snyder and Peck? It's
a natural question given the importance of preachers to antebellum African
American culture and to later African American fiction. "The Preacher," as
W. E. B. Du Bois wrote in 1903, "is the most unique personality developed

by the Negro on American soil. A leader, a politician, an orator, a 'boss,' an intriguer, an idealist—all these he is, and ever, too, the centre of a group of men, now twenty, now a thousand in number."[39] Brown, it seems, had little respect for this powerful personality or, indeed, for black folk religion. The only black preacher in sight is Uncle Simon, a dubious figure who wins the admiration of his peers—"'Uncle Simon can beat dat sermon all to pieces'"— but whom the novel accords scant authority. His vocation is barely acknowledged ("Now Uncle Simon was himself a preacher, or at least he thought so"), and he is notably lacking in Christian humility, being "rather pleased than otherwise, when he heard others spoken of in a disparaging manner." Worse, Simon's preaching has taught his fellow Poplar Farm slaves nothing. Ned thinks the Bible contains only "slaves obey yer masters," and the rest dismiss Snyder's sermon only because they know it works to extend Peck's mastery, not because they have any better understanding of Christian faith.[40] On the neighboring plantation of Jones, the slaves supposedly do their own preaching and hold religious meetings whenever they wish, yet here, too, the slaves are ignorant of Christian texts and doctrines. Asked "who made you," a slave replies, "De overseer told us last night who made us, but indeed I forgot the gentmun's name." Another, asked, "Do you serve the Lord?," answers no, he has served only Mr. Jones. A third thinks she knew John the Baptist in Old Kentucky. After letting readers have their laugh with Carlton, the novel uses Georgiana's sorrow to model a more sensitive response: "She did not even smile [. . .] but seemed sore at heart that such ignorance should prevail in their midst."[41] Although these dismissals of slave preaching make Brown seem unappreciative of the creativity and community-building power of black spiritual leadership, they served his abolitionist goals. Whereas Stowe's Tom fed arguments that saints like him proved that slavery must be good for the soul, the evidence of Simon and the unnamed slave preachers on the Jones plantation grant slavery no such redemptive power.[42] Lacking literacy and freedom, the novel says, African Americans will be lamentably ignorant of even the most basic Christian teachings.

The main antislavery preacher in this novel is a white woman: not-so-little Georgiana, Peck's attractive 18-year-old daughter. That Brown made Georgiana an adult, if barely, rather than a child not only opened up obvious marriage-plot possibilities, but also affirmed the right of a woman to preach to men and to play a role of moral leadership in the antislavery moment. Each of Georgiana's three long speeches against slavery (in chapters 6, 10, and 21) is a compilation of texts from contemporary sources, a compositional strategy that allowed Brown to mount detailed arguments from Christian premises he did not typically grant. His lack of concern for theological fine points is evident in the inconsistencies in Georgiana's theology, which, while often theologically conservative, cannot be identified with a particular denomination or religious perspective. Brown's theory seems to have been that if one theological argument failed to persuade a reader to oppose slavery, another might stick.

Georgiana's antislavery teaching in Chapter 6 is arguably the moral center of the novel. In response to her father's pontificating about the un-biblicism of natural rights and the necessity of religious instruction for slaves, she launches into a speech equating the will of God with whatever "produces, secures, or extends human welfare" and holding that everyone has a duty to act accordingly. Since slavery does not further this end, God does not will it, and humanity should not, either. The moral reasoning is thorough, even belabored, less the voice of a young woman fresh from boarding school than that of a clergyman—as indeed it was. Georgiana's speech comes straight from Congregational minister George Allen's *Resistance to Slavery Every Man's Duty*.[43] A grandnephew of Samuel Adams, Allen was the theologically liberal, though not Unitarian, pastor of a church in Shrewsbury, Massachusetts, from 1824 to 1840, who organized his fellow ministers in central Massachusetts to oppose slavery and helped found the Free Soil party in 1848.[44] Brown cut off the original speech just as Allen was getting warmed up—before Georgiana might begin to sound *too* declamatory. After the passage Brown excerpted (ending with the question, "Can that then be right, be well doing—can that obey God's behest, which makes man a slave? which dooms him and all his posterity, in limitless generations, to bondage, to unrequited toil through life?"), the original continues with fifteen more rhetorical questions, pressing ministers to ask themselves whether God could support an institution in which a person was, to paraphrase just a few of the outrages Allen listed, subject to the "will of a despot," unable to hold property, deprived of a country that offered protection, denied a voluntary home, cut off from parents, forced to submit the body, regardless of sex, to the unquestioned will of a master or overseer, and starved physically, mentally, and spiritually.[45] The fiery litany of slavery's injustices is overwhelming as oratory, let alone polite conversation.

Brown affirmed Georgiana's propriety and femininity and bolstered her persuasive power by concluding her first antislavery speech with a borrowed Christian principle whose ethics, strangely enough, would seem to run counter to his own. After citing and glossing a favorite Bible verse of antislavery advocates ("'Thou shalt love thy neighbour as thyself.' This single passage of Scripture should cause us to have respect to the rights of the slave"), Georgiana declares, "True Christian love is of an enlarged, disinterested nature.

It loves all who love the Lord Jesus Christ in sincerity, without regard to colour or condition."[46] These lines come from Thomas Reade's *Christian Retirement: Or Spiritual Exercises of the Heart* (1810), a devotional volume reprinted throughout the first half of the nineteenth century.[47] Brown's one, crucial change was to add the phrase "without regard to colour or condition," thereby politicizing the pietism, a point underscored when Peck rebukes his daughter, "Georgiana, my dear, you are an abolitionist; your talk is fanaticism."[48] But as in so many passages in *Clotel,* Brown has played a risky game in incorporating others' words. The implication that white Christians have a special obligation to love their black brothers and sisters in Christ—that "True Christian love [. . .] loves all who love the Lord Jesus Christ in sincerity"—resonates with Brown's criticism elsewhere of churchgoers who abuse the slaves they worship alongside, but it also suggests that those who do *not* "love the Lord Jesus Christ in sincerity," a category that would exclude, for instance, the plantation slaves kept ignorant of Christian teaching, fall outside the obligations of Christian love.[49] What good does a Christians-first ethic do for those who cannot answer "who made you"? Though one assumes that Brown intended simply to affirm color-blind love as a core Christian principle, Reade's wording reflects a parochialism not otherwise endorsed in the novel.

In Chapter 10, Georgiana resumes preaching to convince Carlton, now a Christian, that Christianity does not support slavery. This sermon strikes a more theologically conservative note than the one in Chapter 6. After beginning with a text, Acts 17:26 ("God has created of one blood all the nations of men, to dwell on all the face of the earth"), she moves to the doctrine: "To claim, hold, and treat a human being as property is a felony against God and man." It is the first line of Chapter 9, "Scripture Argument Against Slavery," in Methodist abolitionist minister La Roy Sunderland's *Anti Slavery Manual* (1837).[50] The next few lines of the sermon veer back and forth between unmarked quotation and lines original to Brown. Brown continues to develop Georgiana's antislavery doctrine with "The Christian religion is opposed to slaveholding in its spirit and its principles; it classes men-stealers among murderers," the words of the late-eighteenth-century abolitionist and Anglican bishop Beilby Porteous, spoken during a debate on slavery in the House of Lords in 1806 and widely quoted by American abolitionists. Perhaps eager to preserve Georgiana's ethos as feminine and even-tempered, Brown truncated Porteous's speech, leaving off the declaration that Christianity classed "men-stealers among murderers of fathers and of mothers, and the most profane criminals upon earth."[51] Instead, he had Georgiana move on to the application, with phrasing that seems to be his own: "and it is the duty of all who wish to meet God in peace, to discharge that duty in spreading these [antislavery] principles. Let us not deceive ourselves into the idea that slavery is right because it is profitable to us." Georgiana then circles back to doctrine, now borrowed from Theodore Dwight Weld's *The Bible Against Slavery* (1838): "Slaveholding is the highest possible violation of the eighth commandment. To take from a man his earnings, is theft; but to take the earner is a compound, lifelong theft."[52] Again, Brown cuts off his source before it grows too vehement for Georgiana—before, that is, Weld's melodramatic description of that lifelong theft as "supreme robbery, that vaults up the climax at a leap—the dread, terrific, giant robbery, that towers among other robberies a solitary horror, monarch of the realm." Georgiana presses instead a renewal of the application, this time with a reference to Christ as Redeemer, a theological move targeting Christian readers: "and we who profess to follow in the footsteps of our Redeemer, should do our utmost to extirpate slavery from the land. For my own part, I shall do all I can."[53] These decisive lines, which appear to be Brown's own, would seem to conclude Georgiana's sermon. Amen, and cue the hymn.

But Brown had more antislavery sermons on tap. Georgiana continues preaching to Carlton for another several hundred words in language that draws largely on *An Address to Free Colored Americans* (1837), an essay prepared by a committee of the Anti-Slavery Convention of American Women in New York City in May 1837 and often attributed to Sarah Grimké, one of the committee's leading members.[54] Grimké might well have come to mind as Brown created a young Southern woman opposed to slavery. Raised in an affluent, slaveowning Charleston home and troubled from childhood by the injustice of slavery, Grimké had as a young woman taken the radical step of becoming a Quaker and relocating to Philadelphia. Her younger sister Angelina moved North as well, and in 1836 they would become the nation's first female abolitionist agents, lecturing for the American Anti-Slavery Society.[55] As an address to free blacks, Grimké's speech is not obviously apropos for Georgiana's attempt to convert Carlton to antislavery, and one suspects that Brown placed it here after first considering it for Georgiana's speechmaking in Chapter 21, when she addresses her newly freed slaves. The language taken from Grimké's address is both plainly sermonic and among the most biblicist and Christocentric in the novel. Georgiana (parroting Grimké) begins by referencing several scriptural passages, most notably Acts 1:8 and Acts 1:14, in which Jesus promises his disciples that the Holy Ghost will come upon them, and they respond by fervently praying "with the women"—a gender inclusiveness that helps justify the preachiness of Grimké's, and Georgiana's, subsequent speech. After the biblical text comes the doctrine to "consider the poor," along with the promise from Ephesians 3:8 that those who do so will be "blessed upon the earth." Georgiana then invokes Matthew 25:40 to narrow in on the antislavery doctrine: "Does not the language, 'Inasmuch as ye did it unto one of the least of these my brethren, ye did it unto me,' belong to all who are rightly engaged in endeavouring to unloose the bondman's fetters?"[56] Finally, there are the anaphoric exhortations of Georgiana's application-heavy peroration, still borrowed from Grimké, through which Brown addressed Christian readers in their own terms:

> Shall we not then do as the apostles did? Shall we not, in view of the two millions of heathen in our very midst, in view of the souls that are going down in an almost unbroken phalanx to utter perdition, continue in prayer and supplication, that God will grant us the supplies of his Spirit to prepare us for that work which he has given us to do? Shall not the wail of the mother as she surrenders her only child to the grasp of the ruthless kidnapper, or the trader in human blood, animate our devotions? Shall not the manifold crimes and horrors of slavery excite more ardent outpourings at the throne of grace to grant repentance to our guilty country, and permit us to aid in preparing the way for the glorious second advent of the Messiah, by preaching deliverance to the captives, and the opening of the prison doors to those who are bound?[57]

This speech allowed Brown to invoke a range of religious arguments for abolition that he did not make elsewhere and that he may not have believed: that the religiously uninstructed slaves were "heathens" on their way to perdition, that prayer should be a central antislavery activity, that God's spirit animated human antislavery effort, and that one should "preach deliverance to the captives" to prepare for Christ's second coming. Even after Carlton leaves, with a tear testifying to the sermon's efficacy rolling down his cheek, the preaching continues as Georgiana explains to her father the incompatibility of Christianity and slavery. Her long, theologically dense monologue pieces together passages from Hartford Congregationalist minister William Weston Patton's sermon *Slavery, the Bible, Infidelity: Pro-slavery Interpretations of the Bible: Productive of Infidelity* (1846) and Grimké's *Address to Free Colored Americans,* with the excerpts from Patton developing the argument that convincing skeptics of Christianity requires Christians to reject slavery as unbiblical and those from Grimké warning that the nation has failed to heed God's demand to proclaim liberty to all.[58] Through these borrowed texts Brown presented sustained theological arguments outside his usual discursive range, which he then reinforced through other characters' responses and the narrator's commentary. After Georgiana speaks, Peck insists on his right to exercise his own judgment but also agrees to say nothing around Carlton about the Bible sanctioning slavery, while the narrator goes a step further and asserts that in speaking Georgiana has "accomplished a noble work" and is her father's "superior and [. . .] teacher."[59]

Georgiana's final sermon appears in Chapter 21, "The Christian's Death," as her slaves gather around her deathbed. Nearly all of this speech comes from William Lloyd Garrison's *An Address, Delivered Before the Free People of Color* (1831), which Garrison wrote based on speeches he had delivered to African American political groups in Northeastern cities in 1831.[60] This speech uses sermonic techniques characteristic of Garrison, including biblical quotation, oratorical sentence patterns, and a tone of moral certainty. Georgiana's speech is a strategic précis of it, one that hits the major points while passing over counsel less urgent for the antislavery cause, such as Garrison's admonition to form societies for moral improvement, or less suited to a young woman, such as the call to join forces politically. In adapting his mentor's address, Brown also sought to minimize the moral burden of newly freed slaves. While he gave Georgiana Garrison's "I dare not predict how far your example may affect the welfare of [. . .] your brethren yet in bondage," he withheld key phrases in the latter half of Garrison's sentence: "but undoubtedly it is in your power, by this example, to break many fetters, or to keep many of your brethren in bondage."[61] The omission drops the implication that free blacks might be to blame for the perpetuation of slavery. Similarly, whereas Garrison warned, "If you are temperate, industrious, peaceable and pious; if you return good for evil, and blessing for cursing; you will show to the world, that the slaves can be emancipated without danger: but if you are turbulent, idle and vicious, you will put arguments in the mouths of tyrants, and cover your friends with confusion and shame," Georgiana says only, "If you are temperate, industrious, peaceable, and pious, you will show to the world that slaves can be emancipated without danger."[62] Gone is the implicit call to turn the other cheek and the warnings that improper behavior will bring shame. Nearly all of the remainder of Georgiana's speech excerpts or paraphrases passages in Garrison's *Address* exhorting the free people of color to live pious lives, educate themselves and their children, and reject the American Colonization Society.[63] Indeed, Garrison's lengthy denunciation of the ACS may have prompted Brown to turn to this address rather than a more recent one, given that George Harris's move to Liberia at the end of *Uncle Tom's Cabin* made critiquing the ACS newly urgent. Brown closed Georgiana's speech on his own words: a direction to heed the abolitionists' workhorse verse, "'Remember those in bonds as bound with them,'" and the pragmatic counsel to hasten North.[64] One can imagine his pleasure in rewriting Little Eva's deathbed scene with Garrison's speech at hand. Not only are the slaves freed, but the dying girl's sermon is as practical as it is high-minded.

The sermonic narrator

The other major antislavery preacher in *Clotel* is the narrator, whose sermons appeal not, like some of Georgiana's, to Jesus Christ, the eschaton, the need to convert the heathen, or even (at least until the Conclusion) the Bible, but rather to moral principles, a benevolent God, and the sacredness of human life. Much of this liberal sermonic rhetoric comes from other sources and cannot, as the words of a fictive narrator, be read as Brown's avowed belief. Yet it may reflect something of his own religious thought in the early 1850s, insofar as it resonates with the Unitarianism of Estlin and the other abolitionists among whom he wrote *Clotel*, as well as with his autobiographies and lectures.[65]

The narrator's liberal preaching begins in Chapter 1, "The Negro Sale." After pointing to mixed-race individuals as the visible evidence of white Southern society's contempt for marriage (black or white) and to the laws and church statutes refusing to legitimate black couplings, the narrator affirms that "it would be doing that degraded class an injustice, not to acknowledge that many of them do regard it as a sacred obligation, and show a willingness to obey the commands of God on this subject." This religious rhetoric, apparently Brown's own, lays the groundwork for the subsequent pious speech, which begins, "Marriage is, indeed, the first and most important institution of human existence—the foundation of all civilisation and culture—the root of church and state."[66] What follows (through "whether by means of instruction, precept, or exhortation") is an excerpt from Unitarian minister Samuel Osgood's translation of German theologian Wilhelm Martin Leberecht de Wette's *Human Life; or Practical Ethics,* quoted by William Bowditch in his *Slavery and the Constitution* at the beginning of Chapter 6, "Indirect Instruction.—No Legal Marriage of Slaves."[67] The remainder of Brown's paragraph, except for the final sentence, follows, often verbatim, Bowditch's application of de Wette's essay to slavery.[68] The theological liberalism of this passage from Bowditch lies in its privileging of marriage, rather than the church or traditional religious practices, as the bearer of moral value and enabler of spiritual elevation. To say that marriage is the only realm in which some feel the "true sentiments of humanity" downplays the Christian community as a cultivator of human virtue and, against notions of original sin, treats humanity as inherently good. Marriage here offers no less than a form of salvation, as husband and wife "become conscious of complete humanity, and every human feeling, and every human virtue."[69] Deprived of these boundless benefits, slaves are morally impaired: "what must be the moral degradation of that people to whom marriage is denied?" Brown drops, though, Bowditch's hyperbolic answer to this question: "Must not the degradation be uncalculated and incalculable? And yet such is the condition of the slaves!"[70] It was one thing to acknowledge the harm done to slaves, another to dehumanize them by calling their degradation incalculable.

Brown returns to this broadly Protestant rhetoric at the end of the first chapter in the prophetic sermonic outburst denouncing Christian hypocrisy. First, in words that appear to be Brown's own, the narrator declares that the sale takes place "in a city thronged with churches, whose tall spires look like so many signals pointing to heaven, and whose ministers preach that slavery is a God-ordained institution!"[71] To extend this critique, Brown inserted passages from Allen too heated for Georgiana yet too good to leave on the cutting room floor. Following Allen nearly verbatim, the narrator thunders:

> What words can tell the inhumanity, the atrocity, and the immorality of that doctrine which, from exalted office, commends such a crime to the favour of enlightened and Christian people? What indignation from all the world is not due to the government and people who put forth all their strength and power to keep in existence such an institution? Nature abhors it; the age repels it; and Christianity needs all her meekness to forgive it.[72]

Though Allen was a Congregationalist, this passage has no identifiably orthodox content, and its call for "indignation from all the world" made it apt for a British audience. Brown also seems to have had British readers in mind when to Allen's declaration that indignation was "due to the government," he added, "and people." The call for popular accountability reflects *Clotel*'s emphasis on convincing Britons to exercise their moral influence on Americans through such measures as severing relationships with slaveholding churches.

The narrator's liberal theology also defines one of the novel's most memorable sermonic moments, the beginning of Chapter 21, which describes the parallel, simultaneous voyages of the Mayflower to Plymouth Rock and the slave-ship to Jamestown, Virginia. This passage comes directly from a speech that Alvan Stewart delivered before the New Jersey State Supreme Court in

1845 as counsel for two African Americans still held as slaves after the Bill of Rights attached to the state's new Constitution, ratified in 1844, prohibited slavery.[73] Engaging in courtroom theatrics, Stewart had just directed everyone to look to the northeast to see what they could behold "on the last day of November, 1620," the phrase with which Brown begins the chapter. The religious rhetoric of these borrowed paragraphs is brief but heightened—for instance, "Hear the voice of prayer to God for his protection, and the glorious music of praise, as it breaks into the wild tempest of the mighty deep, upon the ear of God"—and, as with other preaching by *Clotel*'s narrator, religiously liberal. God is the key figure, not Christ, and the sublimity of music and nature matter more than the content of the hymn or prayer. The Pilgrims are loosely termed "servants of the living God," not English Separatists, and their mission is "to establish religious and political liberty for all," a secularized and wildly inaccurate description of their aims. But theological precision was irrelevant compared with Stewart's, and Brown's, moral point: "These ships are the representation of good and evil in the New World, even to our day."[74] What mattered to Brown was not metaphysics but convincing his readers of slavery's immorality.

Brown's bias toward theological liberalism is also evident in the narrator's sermonic rhetoric concerning Georgiana, much of which reinforces her moral exemplarity and mutes her theological particularity, presumably to make her more broadly appealing. For instance, in a paragraph followed by, "This was [Georgiana's] view of Christianity," the narrator says:

> We learn from Scripture, and it is a little remarkable that it is the only exact definition of religion found in the sacred volume, that "pure religion and undefiled before God, even the Father, is this, to visit the fatherless and widows in their affliction, and to keep oneself unspotted from the world." "Look not every man on his own things, but every man also on the things of others." "Remember them that are in bonds as bound with them." "Whatsoever ye would that others should do to you, do ye so even unto them."[75]

This passage first appeared in an editor's column of the abolitionist newspaper the *New-York Evangelist* in the spring of 1847 and was widely reprinted in the late 1840s, including in Parker Pillsbury's *The Church as It Is: or the Forlorn Hope of Slavery* (1847), from which Brown probably copied it.[76] Although Georgiana has arguably occupied the moral ground staked out in these verses—that true religion lies in caring for others and in resisting slavery—her speeches have also espoused far more divisive theological arguments. By using this moralistic redaction of Christianity to reframe her religiosity, Brown softened the sharp edges that came with assigning her lengthy passages from Grimké. The narrator also liberalizes Georgiana in commenting that "though a devoted member of her father's church, she was not a sectarian," and in summarizing her "philosophy" as the belief that "all men are by nature equal; that they are wisely and justly endowed by the Creator with certain rights, which are irrefragable [. . .]." This last line, along with nearly all the remainder of the paragraph, comes from a eulogy for William Wilberforce delivered by the African American educator Benjamin F. Hughes, erstwhile pastor of the First African Presbyterian Church in Philadelphia, principal of Colored Free School No. 3 in New York City, and a founder of New York's Phoenix Society, dedicated to black educational advancement.[77] Brown returned to this eulogy for the chapter's penultimate paragraph, which follows Hughes closely from "Peace to her ashes!" through the first half of the first sentence of the final paragraph, "In what light would she consider that hypocritical priesthood."[78] In applying these inclusive phrases to Georgiana, Brown repositioned his heroine as a religious liberal while democratizing and degendering the rhetoric of moral heroism.

The eulogy for Georgiana concludes in a secular oratorical mode. Directly after the passage from Hughes, Brown patched in another eulogy, this one given by African American abolitionist Robert Purvis for the Quaker antislavery activist Thomas Shipley, a founding member of the American Anti-Slavery Society and the organization's most prominent Philadelphia member.[79] The narrator now praises Georgiana solely for the happiness she brought by restoring family relationships in granting her slaves freedom. The eulogy closes with a loosely religious invocation of Brown's own: "Oh, that God may give more such persons to take the whip-scarred negro by the hand, and raise him to a level with our common humanity! May the professed lovers of freedom in the new world see that true liberty is freedom for all! and may every American continually hear it sounding in his ear."[80] This reference to God is more rhetorical flourish than theological premise; the emphasis is on an awakened consciousness of the Enlightenment values of "humanity," "freedom," and "liberty."

Alongside the religiously liberal and secular oratory surrounding Georgiana's death, Brown included several sentimental meditations on death that border on the sermonic yet offer little religious consolation. Significantly, the novel neither describes nor marks the precise moment of death, a scene that would have raised questions about Georgiana's perceptions on the threshold of the hereafter. There is no scene in which she, like Little Eva, looks off and exclaims, "O! love,—joy,—peace!"[81] Instead, Brown included a homily on death's inevitability and suddenness (beginning "Death is a leveller") taken from James Montgomery's *Gleanings from Pious Authors* (1846). This discourse on *vanitas* may have suggested to some readers that earthly transience should redirect one to spiritual ideals, but the absence of such a message or any hint of redemption strikes a pagan note. The passage concludes only, "This hour he [man] glows in the blush of health and vigour, but the next he may be counted with the number no more known on earth."[82] The gloomy tone is a far cry from the proclamation in *Uncle Tom's Cabin* that Eva passes "from death unto life!" and that "the bright, eternal doors" close after her.[83] The narrator's lamentations resume in two paragraphs running from "In the midst of the buoyancy of youth, this cherished one had drooped and died" through "yet the thoughts *will* linger sadly and cheerlessly upon the grave," a reflection on grief taken from a sketch first published in the *New England Offering* in 1848.[84] Its sermonic overtones are audible in its oratorical exclamations (e.g., "Oh what chill creeps through the breaking heart"), anaphoric repetitions ("that the eye [. . .]—that the ear [. . .]—that the voice"), and, above all, affirmation that "faith [is] strong enough to penetrate the cloud of gloom which hovers near, and to behold the freed spirit safe, *for ever,* safe in its home of heaven." That last line is all the solace of an afterlife this chapter offers. The excerpt from Hughes, which follows these paragraphs on grief, couches life after death only in the subjunctive: "But if it were that departed spirits are permitted to note the occurrences of this world [. . . .]"[85] No further reassurances are offered, and no pious slave has a vision-like dream of the departed Georgiana, as Tom does of Eva in his darkest hour on the Legree plantation. Instead, the sermons that close the chapter—the eulogies written for Wilberforce and Shipley—suggest that the redemption Brown valued most was the secular one of political liberty.

While the narrator lingers over Georgiana's demise and eulogizes her at length, he sermonizes only briefly upon the death of his title character. Before the taut final sequence of Clotel's life—the men running toward Clotel from both ends of Long Bridge, her wild and anxious looks, the water rolling below, the clasped hands and heavenward glance, the fatal jump—the narrator explains the significance of her desperate act:

> But God by his Providence had otherwise determined. He had determined that an appalling tragedy should be enacted that night, within plain sight of the President's house and the capital of the Union, which should be an evidence wherever it should be known, of the unconquerable love of liberty the heart may inherit; as well as fresh admonition to the slave dealer, of the cruelty and enormity of his crimes.[86]

These two sentences are not quite sermonic as I have been using the term. Though the cadences are oratorical, especially in the second sentence, the theological and biblical diction is sparse. The slave dealer's cruelties are crimes, not sins; the salient fact about Clotel is not her soul, but her "unconquerable love of liberty." And yet the passage functions as a sermon insofar as it assigns her suicide a theological meaning: God ordained it so that it could serve as a symbol of humanity's love of freedom and as a rebuke to slave dealers. We should not underestimate the strangeness of this theological justification. Nowhere else in the novel or in Brown's surviving lectures or autobiographies is slave suffering or death credited to the providence of God. Despite being coupled here with an antislavery message, this theological position has the potential to rationalize any number of slavery-related horrors by casting God as the hidden agent. In spirit it anticipates the language of Lincoln's Second Inaugural, which would posit, in a hypothetical formulation more guarded than that in *Clotel,* that American slavery might be "one of those offenses which, in the providence of God, must needs come, but which, having continued through His appointed time, He now wills to remove."[87] Whereas Lincoln would merely speculate that divine agency had guided the human cruelty of slavery, the narrator presents the idea without qualification: God causes Clotel to die so that she can serve as an example and admonition. This fatalistic theologizing makes sense only when one learns that the entire scene of Clotel's flight and suicide comes wholesale from an 1842 article in the *New-York Evangelist.*[88] As with several other borrowings in *Clotel,* Brown may have gotten more than he bargained for from his source material. Along with the suspense-filled climax and the line about a woman's "unconquerable love of liberty" came the dubious theologizing. That Brown did not excise this assertion suggests his indifference to the theological ramifications of a single line. He may have reasoned that as long as this all-ordaining God hated slavery and loved liberty, what did it matter if his inscrutable system allowed for the death of a single slave? To have God pulling the strings at least dignified his heroine's death.

In the final paragraph of the novel's Conclusion, Brown threw off his borrowed robes and preached without mediation. In a series of anaphoric exhortations, he first called "British Christians" to sympathize with the slave and to refuse fellowship to slaveholding American Christians, then prevailed upon "the whole British nation" to let its voice be heard across the Atlantic begging the descendants of the Pilgrims to "proclaim the Year of Jubilee"— that is, to set their slaves free.[89] The biblical allusions here, in the appeals to the British and in the concluding promise, are thicker than anywhere else in Brown's original prose.[90] Brown was almost certainly mimicking the sermonizing of Stowe's Concluding Remarks, but his rhetoric is markedly more upbeat. Whereas Stowe had ended by threatening readers with the "wrath of Almighty God," Brown gave them the sermon's conventional hope of redemption, declaring that once the Year of Jubilee was proclaimed, "Then shall the 'earth indeed yield her increase, and God, even our own God, shall bless us; and all the ends of the earth shall fear Him.'" If the language of fearing God conjures a glimmer of the holy awe in Stowe's closing threat, Brown at least made explicit the promised blessings. The tonal difference between the two probably speaks both to their theological differences, his greater liberalism not inclining him to represent God as punitive, and to a racially inflected rhetorical strategy. As a black man, he may have worried that playing the role of the scowling prophet would seem to raise the shade of Nat Turner and so make his white audiences nervous.

Although Brown played it safe in his final sermon, one line stands out as an innovation: "let no Christian association be maintained with those who traffic in the blood and bones of those whom God has made of one flesh with yourselves."[91] The surprising phrase here is "made of one flesh with yourselves," which melds two biblical verses: Acts 17:26, in which Paul tells the men of Athens that God "hath made of one blood all nations of men," and Genesis 2:24, which says that a man and his wife will be "one flesh." Whether intentionally or not, Brown called Christians to renounce slavery not merely because blacks and whites were all children of God but also because they were husbands and wives, united in marriages that were, in language Brown borrowed from Child, "sanctioned by heaven, although unrecognised on earth."[92] The final sermonic paragraph thus brings *Clotel* full circle, returning to the point that opened Chapter 1: the incontrovertible fact of mixed-race couplings and the need to bring order out of social and moral chaos by ending slavery.

Every other novelist discussed in this book spent childhood Sundays sitting in the pews of Northeastern churches. Brown endured the first day of the week standing outside a Missouri church with his master's horses, "in the hot, broiling sun, or in the rain, just as it happened."[93] It was not an experience to inculcate a love of the preached word. His later experiences with Christian churches were mixed at best, as ministers in New York and Philadelphia often forbade him to use their sanctuaries for his antislavery lectures.[94] Having seen firsthand so many ministers' hostility and indifference to the antislavery movement, he would write to Garrison in 1853 that he had "long since despaired of anything being done by a clergyman."[95]

But if Brown knew that the clergy could not be trusted to advance the antislavery cause, he also knew—because Stowe's novel had blazoned the fact

across two continents—that sermons wrapped in fiction could have phe-
nomenal power. Armed with this realization, he crafted a novel that embedded preaching in sentimental plots. Georgiana is in this respect emblematic
of Brown's own ambitions in *Clotel*. Just as her "voice of great sweetness" and
"most winning manner" make her preaching persuasive to Carlton, so, too,
did Brown seek with his stereotyped characters and familiar plot devices to
ease the way for the abolitionist sermons at the novel's core.[96]

That the many sermonic passages Brown pieced together have long been
read as seamless wholes suggests how skillfully he joined his borrowed parts,
as well as how much one sermon can sound like another, at least at the distance of a century or so. Read as a greatest hits album of abolitionist speeches
and sermons, *Clotel* is an aesthetically innovative text that is also unusually
representative of the racial, gender, and religious diversity of the abolitionist movement. It is thus a fascinating origin point for the African American
novel and a consummate example of the creativity of nineteenth-century
American novelists eager to capture the moral authority of preaching in the
pages of fiction.

CONCLUSION

❀

The Lingering Rivalry

Exposing the Sermon's Limitations in William Dean Howells's *The Minister's Charge*

T HE SERMON was both the centerpiece of Protestant worship in ante-bellum America and the culture's paradigmatic voice of moral authority. Seeking to avoid the caricature of sermons as tedious and oppressive, I have tried to cast them in a more sympathetic light by showing how ministers worked to make them meaningful, powerful experiences for listeners, and how novelists, resentful and resistant, sought to usurp preacherly authority. The novelists' tango with preaching cannot be reduced to the familiar tropes of subversion and irony. Translating the preacher to the page, they tempered critique with recognition, as both they and post-disestablishment ministers jockeyed for audiences' attention and respect in a crowded public sphere where secular and religious concerns intermingled. Hypocritical and unjust preachers were ever ripe for satire, but novelists also found a tantalizing rhetorical model in the popular or beloved minister addressing a devoted congregation. Novels often register authors' sense of disadvantage: though fiction promised broader distribution through space and time, it also lacked the imagined human presence of embodied performance, the sacred context of religious ritual, and the immediate gratifications of collective audience response. One of the primary ways novelists defied these limitations was through sermonic voice, which, in epitomizing the sermon's rhetorical distinctiveness, carried a special weight for readers accustomed to listening to preaching with respect or even deference. Confronting preachers on their own stylistic ground, novelists challenged Protestant dogma by conveying heterodox and challenging ideas with the sermon's sanctioned moral and religious fervor.

Novelists' usurpation of sermonic voice contributed to a process of secularization in which, as part of the differentiation of social subsystems endemic to modernity, literature developed autonomy from other institutions, religion above all. The years around 1850 represent something of a landmark in this process, as the clergy's faltering responses to social crises, especially poverty and slavery, compromised their moral leadership and as Romanticism fueled the idea that literature—even the lowly novel—could edify the world at least as well as the religious authorities. Novelists writing at this juncture pushed back hard against the entrenched disdain for novels as timewasting and corrupting and, through their canny engagement with preaching, sought an equivalent moral and religious authority for their own cultural productions.

After the Civil War, Protestant preaching remained a major cultural presence. Despite any assumptions we might have that secularism became the new norm as a result of the biblical Higher Criticism, the growth of scientific knowledge, or skepticism born of increasing religious pluralism accelerated by waves of immigration from Southern and Eastern Europe, evidence suggests that postbellum Americans were as religious as ever, at least as measured by their religious belonging and affinity for sermons. Church membership rose from 34 percent of the population in 1850 to 45 percent in 1890, and the latter half of the century saw the heyday of such superstar preachers as Henry Ward Beecher at Plymouth Church in Brooklyn, Phillips Brooks at Trinity Church in Boston, and the peripatetic, transatlantic Dwight L. Moody.[1] Yet the clergy were losing their mystique. Karin Gedge, describing how postbellum newspaper cartoons represented inappropriate relationships between ministers and parishioners as a "farce rather than a mythic tragedy," attributes the nation's new comparative nonchalance toward clerical morality to the chastening effects of a brutal and devastating war that reframed what counted as a threat to the republic.[2] Secularization, or the differentiation and autonomization of subsystems, also relativized the clergy's claims. As professionals in a complex, modernizing world, ministerial foibles—or virtues—had repercussions for local networks but not, it seemed, for the nation as a whole.

Given the decline in ministers' symbolic power, as well as the development and professionalization of the literary field, postbellum novelists were less invested than their predecessors in treating preachers as cultural competitors—less inclined, that is, to figure them as doubles or to mimic the sound of the sermon. Especially in the now-canonical novels of the period, authors tended to ignore preachers, to relegate them to the sidelines, or to treat them as members of a distinct profession, to be described, like anyone, according to the psychologizing, contextualizing procedures of realism. Henry James, for instance, showed little interest in the American preacher unless regarded as a dyspeptic, handwringing nebbish (Babcock in *The American*) or, secularized, as a mesmerizing women's rights speaker (Verena Tarrant in *The Bostonians*). A similar sense that ministers are little more than background noise marks the novels of Edith Wharton: in *The House of Mirth*, for example, the preacher is only a distant, unseen presence separated by a mile of park from Lily Bart, who, unable to reconcile herself to a life of dull propriety, never quite makes it to the service. And in perhaps the most thorough fictive ministerial portrait of the latter half of the nineteenth century, Harold Fredric's *The Damnation of Theron Ware*, the Methodist minister Ware is a case study in provincial small-mindedness and romantic delusion, not a serious rival for the novelist. To be sure, a certain amount of rivalry persisted in postbellum fiction, particularly among writers with a theological or moral point to make—as in Elizabeth Stuart Phelps's critique in *The Gates Ajar* of Mr. Bland's arid sermons on the afterlife, or Mark Twain's parody of a revival in *Adventures of Huckleberry Finn*. The antagonism between preaching and novels may have peaked around 1850, but it enjoyed a respectable afterlife.[3]

One of the most thoughtful sequels to the mid-century novelists' rivalry with preachers is William Dean Howells's *The Minister's Charge* (1886), published the year after Howells's *The Rise of Silas Lapham* and featuring, like the earlier novel, the liberal minister David Sewell. In *The Minister's Charge* Howells followed antebellum authors in dramatizing his authorial preoccupations through a preacher, while parting ways from his predecessors by showing less inclination to satirize or dethrone sermons than to demonstrate how they occupy a cultural function distinct from and lesser than that of novels—one that is less moral and less attuned to the complexity of human nature.

Relatively obscure, *The Minister's Charge* requires a word of summary. In this story, Sewell serves as the reluctant and fretful mentor to a young transplant from the country, Lemuel Barker. The story's precipitating event occurs when Sewell visits the country and insincerely praises Barker's poetry. When the deluded poet writes to Sewell for help finding a publisher, then shows up on his doorstop a few weeks later, a discomfited Sewell discourages him and urges him to return to the country, but before Barker can catch the train home, the well-meaning lie that lured him to Boston becomes the story's original sin. A nigh-farcical chain of disaster besets the hapless rube, who is swindled by confidence men, falsely accused of purse-snatching, thrown in the slammer, humiliated at trial, famished then sickened, and forced to spend a night at a hostel for tramps. Seeing a report of Barker's trial in the paper, a remorseful Sewell tracks down his would-be mentee but is dismayed to find he cannot persuade him to return to the country. Barker insists on making his way in Boston, which he manages to do with significant aid from Sewell. He becomes a man-of-all-work for one of Sewell's friends, a hotel clerk (after dropping Sewell's name), and a reader and companion to one of Sewell's wealthy parishioners. This ambiguous social ascent—always a glorified servant, he never comes close to breaking into a profession—is stymied when he decides that he is morally obliged to become engaged to a working-class girl, Statira, whom he has strung along despite his slackening interest. Resigning himself for her sake to a working-class life, he borrows money from Sewell to become a streetcar conductor. A near-fatal accident on the first day is a *deus ex machina,* succeeding where Sewell could not in sending Barker, after a long convalescence, back to the country and, a coy final chapter implies, eventually separating him for good from his inapt prospective mate. As other readers have explained, the story is a realist check on the Horatio Alger myth of the country boy making good in the city.[4]

But this story is Sewell's no less than Barker's. About a third of the novel is from the minister's perspective, including the first three chapters and the last five, a bookending that encourages readers to identify with his upper-middle-class moralizing.[5] Sewell's main problem in life, it seems, is what to do about Barker. Having once spoken and regretted his false, hope-giving words, he regards Barker's struggles in Boston as trials of conscience, a moral burden reinforced when he sees Barker among the congregants at his weekly sermons and when the young man seeks him out for pastoral counsel. Barker comes to represent for Sewell an interlinked social and moral problem—the seeming intransigence of class difference and the ethical relationship of the higher classes to the lower. Sewell thus partakes of Howells's own moral concerns about social injustice and class inequity during this period. Further, Howells uses the minister's perplexity in the face of Barker—his difficulty communicating with him and his uncertainty about how to help him—to represent the difficulty of escaping one's own class-based prejudices and sympathies, along with the need to try to do precisely that.[6]

As Sewell struggles to make sense of Barker and the lower classes through his professional roles as preacher and counselor, what the novel suggests, strangely enough, is that preaching is more effective than counseling. Although Sewell sees his pastoral interviews as central to his work ("He found it necessary to do his work largely in a personal way, by meeting and talking with people"), it is nearly impossible for him to do this work well.[7] Not only is he no natural—with Barker, for instance, he is, despite his best intentions, alternately rambling and tongue-tied, solicitous and annoyed— but, more importantly, he can never know a situation well enough, or be sure enough which principles to apply to a given situation, to offer guidance that is anything more than a shot in the dark. Thus, when he guesses correctly Barker's romantic problems and gives him the reasonable advice to avoid entangling himself with a woman who will hold him back intellectually and socially, the narrator makes clear afterward that for Barker to follow Sewell's counsel would be a violation of conscience—a denial of "the gleam that lights up every labyrinth where our feet wander and stumble."[8] To Barker this light reveals that turning his back on Statira out of a desire for self-improvement would be a "real cruelty."[9] That Barker's mother has expressed sentiments similar to Sewell's suggests that the error of false guidance is not unique to the ministerial profession but endemic to well-meaning attempts to direct someone else's life where complex moral questions are concerned. As Sewell exclaims in frustration after Barker first shows up in Boston, "Every one of us dwells in an impenetrable solitude! We understand each other a little if our circumstances are similar, but if they are different all our words leave us dumb and unintelligible."[10] More than a confession of Sewell's own short-comings, this declaration sets forth principles central to the realist novel's disruption of romantic notions of sympathetic identification and transparent interpersonal communication.

Whereas *The Minister's Charge* represents pastoral counsel as often leaving individuals more troubled and confused than it found them, an unintended consequence of its presumptions to intimacy, the novel holds up preaching as surprisingly meaningful and effective. Sewell is no superstar, but his liberal sermons on ethics attract a congregation of two or three hundred Bostonians of various classes. The perceptive art student Jessie Carver explains his appeal: "There's something about him—I don't know what—that doesn't leave you feeling how bad you are, but makes you want to be better. He helps you so; and he's so clear. And he shows that he's had all the mean and silly thoughts you have. I don't know—it's as if he were talking for each person alone."[11] Her praise catalogs Sewell's liberal virtues: he inspires moral improvement, avoids obscure theological language, and emphasizes his commonality with his parishioners. Plus, his sermons have the effect of individual address, an idea introduced early in the novel when Sewell's friend Miss Vane says after a sermon, "I never have been all but named in church before [. . .] and I've heard others say the same."[12] Sewell's preaching, then, has the effect of intimate counsel yet is unencumbered with the unreasonable expectations that come with one-on-one pastoral conversations. Sermons can be effective *because* of their impersonality. The moral application is left up to the listener, who may feel hailed but who does not bear the burden of having been personally told what to do.[13]

Much like *The Scarlet Letter, The Minister's Charge* locates the secret spring of successful preaching in ministerial authenticity—not sincerity, or the coincidence of belief and action, but authenticity as the bringing to light of the speaker's inarticulate emotional complexity. Dimmesdale taps this authenticity when he plumbs his shame and pain; Sewell, as he confronts his guilt in misleading Barker and struggles to understand his obligation to him. Like Dimmesdale, Sewell preaches well-received sermons fueled by moral conflict. The first, on "affectionate sincerity," or the necessity of speaking even painful truths, results from the guilt he feels upon receiving Barker's letter requesting help publishing his poems—guilt all the more potent for being hidden, as Sewell has avoided mentioning the letter to his wife. Once Barker starts attending regularly, Sewell gains power from seeing him in the congregation each week. Barker, in effect, gives the minister access to his own otherwise inaccessible depths. When Miss Vane tells Sewell that he seems to look at nobody else during the sermon, he exclaims, "I know it! Since he began to come, I can't keep my eyes off him. I do deliver my sermons at him. I believe I write them at him! He has an eye of terrible and exacting truth. I feel myself on trial before him."[14] In a twist that reflects the liberal devaluation of ministerial authority, the idealized relationship of preacher and listener is reversed, as the minister quails with conviction under the parishioner's gaze. The effect of Barker on Sewell is nearly magical: when the young man's own mind wanders during the sermon, or when he is not in church, Sewell founders. But Sewell's sermons also seem to hit the mark; Barker reportedly regards Sewell "as a channel of truth."[15]

Yet *The Minister's Charge* highlights the limitations of even well-meaning liberal preaching by presenting Sewell's sermons as overly idealistic and individualistic, faults not unique to Sewell but typical of the sermon as a genre, centered as it is on moral abstraction and produced by men "of cloistered lives" whose theories outrun their facts.[16] The novel critiques all of the sermons it describes in detail. After the first, on "affectionate sincerity," Miss Vane shows up at the Sewells' dinner table and, with a twinkle in her eye, exposes the sermon's impracticality by disdaining their spread; she explains that in the spirit of her host's recent sermon she can do no less. Miss Vane's raillery also exposes the sermon's triviality, as she says that she will also stop swearing and stealing her friends' spoons when she hears these other "little sins denounced from the pulpit."[17] Soon the story, too, reveals the limited moral scope of Sewell's preaching. The sermon on the text "The tender mercies of the wicked are cruel" (Prov. 12:10) focuses only on the cruel "tender mercies" of speech, avoiding a more challenging critique of action, especially social action. The novel, in contrast, takes up this issue by implying that the generosity on offer in the baths, beds, and hot meals at the Wayfarer's Lodge might encourage men to loaf and turn to crime. The prime evidence for the latter possibility is the lay-about Williams, a Lodge regular eventually exposed as an unreformed thief. One need not share the novel's skepticism about aiding the poor to see that the story offers a more far-reaching meditation on "The tender mercies of the wicked are cruel."

The moral limitations of Sewell's preaching are even more evident in a subsequent sermon on "effort in the erring" (inspired, once again, by interactions with Barker), on how those who have done harm to another must strive for reparation. Sewell suggests that insofar as a sinner lives in anguish, trying to correct the wrong he has done someone else, sin might be "not wholly an evil."[18] The speciousness of Sewell's moral reasoning becomes clear when the novel's paraphrase of the sermon ends "His text was 'Cease to do evil.'"[19] The verse's brevity and clarity drive home the irony that Sewell has done his convoluted best to deny the significance of evil by shifting the emphasis from *not* doing wrong to comforting his parishioners for sins already committed. This consolatory sermon may be just the sort Carver likes because it "doesn't leave you feeling how bad you are," but in the disjunction between verse and application, and in Sewell's obvious desire to assuage his own guilt, the novel critiques the liberal sermon for a tendency to protect parishioners' self-regard. Like Hawthorne, Howells eschewed Calvinism yet saw the moral downside of the liberal disinclination to reckon with the human capacity for wrongdoing.

As in *The Scarlet Letter, The Minister's Charge* climaxes in a sermon. It is a capstone to Sewell's attempts to translate moral perplexity into usable truth. And it does offer such a truth, or something like. The gist of the sermon, titled "Complicity," is two-fold, though Sewell is too modern a preacher to lay out his points under separate heads. The first is an appeal to human unity: "no one for good or for evil, for sorrow or joy, for sickness or health, stood apart from his fellows, but each was bound to the highest and the lowest by ties that centered in the hand of God. No man, he said, sinned or suffered to himself alone; his error and his pain darkened and afflicted men who never heard of his name."[20] It is a reminder of human connection that mingles the sobriety of John Donne's Meditation 17 ("No Man is an Island") with an Ishmaelian exultation in democratic oneness and George Eliot's sense of sin's far-reaching consequences. The minister's second and more self-serving point is that only those who have the "care of others laid upon them"—say, those like the minister with a "charge"—and who rejoice in their burden will realize the spiritual unity of humanity. Sewell declares that those who care for the "wretched, the foolish, the ignorant" will find them to be "messengers of God."[21] The sermon's closing idea summons the shade of W. E. Channing in glorifying the person who cares for others: "In his responsibility for his weaker brethren he was Godlike, for God was but the impersonation of loving responsibility, of infinite and never-ceasing care for us all."[22] Sewell's discourse is the quintessential nineteenth-century liberal sermon—idealistic, fervent, lyrical, and vaguely socially responsible. Its effect is the late nineteenth-century equivalent of the awed tumult following Dimmesdale's Election Sermon. It is reported in the newspapers, reprinted as a pamphlet, and commented on in newspapers as far away as Chicago, and it strikes "one of those popular moods of intelligent sympathy" when it is misconstrued as a veiled commentary on the telegraphers' strike.[23] Besides marking a high point in Sewell's career, the sermon's reception, fictive as it is, suggests the cultural impact that a sermon could still have in the late nineteenth century.

The point I would like to stress about "Complicity," as the final sermon in both *The Minister's Charge* and in my attempt to trace how American novels positioned themselves with respect to preaching, is that it enacts a delicate negotiation that gives the sermon its due while denying it authority.[24] Sewell's message is not without merit, especially considering Howells's desire for fiction, as Melanie Dawson writes, "to facilitate the type of cross-class sympathy necessary for the nation's very stability."[25] The sermon calls for just these sympathies in its appeals to human unity and its exhortation that listeners should care for their "weaker brethren." Indeed, the mandate to take responsibility for the less fortunate is supported at Barker's own moral decision point, when he realizes that he should offer to marry Statira. To a certain extent, then, the novel allows Sewell's sermon to stand—to provide an answer, for readers eager for such an answer, to the novel's central problem of sympathizing with the lower classes. As Paul Petrie has pointed out, the "charge" of the novel's title refers not only to Barker, as a person entrusted to the minister's care, but also to this final sermon, as the minister's injunction to his parishioners—and through them, one might add, to the novel's readers.[26]

Yet like American novels of a previous generation, *The Minister's Charge* undermines the sermon and asserts the novel's moral superiority. It suggests that even a sermon with a worthwhile ethical point pulls its punches. When Sewell's friend, the newspaper editor Evans, proposes that Sewell preach a sermon on "Complicity," he explains that the idea grows out of his frustration

with "the infernal ease of mind in which men remain concerning their share
in the social evil—," a sentiment Sewell interrupts with "Ah, my dear friend,
you can't expect me to consider *that* in my pulpit!"[27] And, indeed, he does
not. His sermon on this topic says not a word about "social evil" or individual
moral complacency in the face of it. In fact, the title "Complicity" is an odd
fit for Sewell's sermon, which says nothing of shared guilt and would be better titled "Unity" or "Charity." Although Sewell is presented as unconcerned
with fame, his eventual decision to preach a sermon with a tantalizing title
yet skirt its painful or indecorous associations hints at how a preacher, like a
newspaper editor, might aim to "make talk." The moral evasion represented
in Sewell's sermon is perhaps most evident in the text Sewell chooses, which,
again, Howells deploys ironically: "Remember them that are in bonds as
bound with them."[28] A touchstone verse for the antislavery movement, this
text would seem to demand a pointed social application that Sewell does
not provide, an omission implying a parallel between the antebellum ministers who dared not protest slavery and their late-nineteenth-century suc-
cessors who, reluctant to attend their parishioners, avoided preaching on the
problems of urban poverty. This critique of pulpit cowardice adumbrates
Howells's declaration of frustration in "Novel-Writing and Novel-Reading"
(1899): "Let all the hidden things be brought into the sun, and let every day
be the day of judgment. If the sermon cannot any longer serve this end, let
the novel do it."[29] While rejecting obvious didacticism, Howells called upon
the novel to fulfill the sermon's traditional role of exposing sin, or error, and
creating moral conviction.

If the novel implies that Sewell's sermon is not hard-hitting enough, it
also, ironically, undercuts its moral idealism about interpersonal relationships. A final chapter hints at the legitimate pleasure that might come from
escaping the sermon's demands—from being relieved of "loving responsibility" for one's "weaker brethren." When the narrator implies that Barker and
Statira's engagement dissolves and that Barker eventually enjoys a marriage
"which was not only happiness for those it joined, but whatever is worthier
and better in life than happiness," it is a turn of events that undercuts the sermon in at least two ways.[30] One, the vagueness of "whatever is worthier and
better in life than happiness" suggests the fungibility of blessedness. Whereas
the sermon teaches that fulfilling one's duty to others constitutes "a privilege,
a joy, a heavenly rapture," the novel implies that it is of little import whether
Barker and his future wife find fulfillment in caring for the downtrodden or
in some other honorable, undefined way.[31] Two, the patent improbability of
the romantic resolution—that Barker is not obliged to marry Statira because
her devotion has been all along an illusion born of her friend's romantic

notions—is an obvious sop to readers that seems designed to jolt them into recognizing, from their own relief at Barker's escape, that a life of noble self-sacrifice, however idealized in sermons, is an unappealing prospect. The implicit message is that the fine words of a sermon can offer only partial truths—and perhaps not those that lead us to our happiest lives.

In assessing the competition between novelists and preachers for moral authority, one might well ask who won. From the vantage-place of the literature classroom, the novel can easily seem the victor. We assign *Uncle Tom's Cabin* (and credit it for starting the Civil War and ending slavery) and *Moby-Dick,* but not the sermons of Henry Ward Beecher or Henry Bellows; *Clotel,* but not the ministers whose sermons it cannibalizes. Novels have inspired ample scholarship; sermons, little. But when we step outside the academic enclave, the balance of power is harder to discern. Then my years of listening to Schuller and Warren look at least as representative of American cultural life as my years of reading novels. In a recent Pew survey, just over half of respondents self-identified with a religious tradition that can be classified as Protestant, and at least 76 percent of those who attend Protestant churches attended at least a few times a year.[32] All these attenders, we can assume, heard some form of sermon at each service. By way of comparison, a recent National Endowment for the Arts survey shows that only 50.2 percent of adult Americans reported having read a short story, play, poem *or* novel in the previous year.[33] Though more suggestive than revelatory, such quantitative measures of the relative strength of the sermon and the novel must check any sense of the novel's unmitigated triumph. One might also trace the persistent cultural power of preaching and the novel in other, more qualitative ways—in, for instance, the sermonic rhetoric of political oratory, or in the novelistic narrative structures that shape biography and other nonfiction genres. However one attempts to grasp the relative influence of preaching and the novel, it becomes clear that although these two cultural forms continue to borrow from each other, they are now recognized as belonging to distinct cultural realms, each with its own set of rules. The nineteenth-century novelists' expectation that literature might displace religion now seems not merely like wishful thinking, but like a misapprehension of the emerging forms of modern life, in which the processes of cultural fragmentation push religion and literature ever further apart. Despite Whitman's prophecy, "The priest departs, the divine literatus comes," it turns out that priests and literati of all stripes, the latter seldom hailed as divine, have continued to flourish alongside one another.[34]

NOTES

❀

Introduction

1. On the Crystal Cathedral's architecture, see Anne C. Loveland and Otis B. Wheeler, *From Meetinghouse to Megachurch: A Material and Cultural History* (Columbia: University of Missouri Press, 2003), 152–53.

2. Lisa McGirr connects Schuller's ministry with the social conservatism dominant in Orange County from the 1950s through the 1990s. By 1976 the home congregation in Garden Grove, California, had 8000 members; *The Hour of Power* broadcast, 3 million weekly viewers (*Suburban Warriors: The Origins of the New American Right* [Princeton: Princeton University Press, 2001], 105–7, 249–54).

3. Randall Balmer, *Mine Eyes Have Seen the Glory: A Journey into the Evangelical Subculture in America,* 4th ed. (New York: Oxford University Press, 2006), 325–33. Saddleback Community Church website, http://saddleback.com/aboutsaddleback/history/, accessed January 5, 2012.

4. Émile Durkheim, *The Elementary Forms of Religious Life,* ed. Mark S. Cladis, trans. Carol Cosman (Oxford: Oxford University Press, 2001), 311.

5. Lori Anne Ferrell and Peter McCullough, "Revising the Study of the English Sermon," *The English Sermon Revised: Religion, Literature, and History 1600–1750* (Manchester, UK: Manchester University Press, 2000), 2–3.

6. Harry S. Stout, *The New England Soul: Preaching and Religious Culture in Colonial New England* (New York: Oxford University Press, 1986). Emory Elliott, *Power and the Pulpit in Puritan New England* (Princeton: Princeton University Press, 1975).

7. See, for instance, Charles E. Hambrick-Stowe, *Charles G. Finney and the Spirit of American Evangelicalism* (Grand Rapids, MI: William B. Eerdmans, 1996); Dean Grodzins, *American Heretic: Theodore Parker and Transcendentalism* (Chapel Hill: University of North Carolina Press, 2002); Debby Applegate, *The Most Famous Man in America: The Biography of Henry*

Ward Beecher (New York: Doubleday, 2006); and Andrew Delbanco, *William Ellery Channing: An Essay on the Liberal Spirit in America* (Cambridge, MA: Harvard University Press, 1981). On Emerson's sermons, see Wesley T. Mott, *The Strains of Eloquence: Emerson and His Sermons* (University Park: Pennsylvania State University Press, 1989) and Susan Roberson, *Emerson in His Sermons: A Man-Made Self* (Columbia: University of Missouri Press, 1995). More comprehensive yet still biographically oriented discussions of preaching include F. R. Webber, *A History of Preaching in Britain and America, Including the Biographies of Many Princes of the Pulpit and the Men Who Influenced Them,* 3 vols. (Milwaukee: Northwestern, 1957); O. C. Edwards, Jr., *A History of Preaching* (Nashville: Abingdon Press, 2004); and Teresa Toulouse, *The Art of Prophesying: New England Sermons and the Shaping of Belief* (Athens: University of Georgia Press, 1987). For rhetorical and topical approaches to the sermon, see the essays in *A New History of the Sermon: The Nineteenth Century,* ed. Robert H. Ellison (Leiden: Brill, 2010).

8. Michael Kaufmann, "The Religious, the Secular, and Literary Studies: Rethinking the Secularization Narrative in Histories of the Profession," *New Literary History* 38, no. 4 (2007): 607–28.

9. Jenny Franchot, "Invisible Domain: Religion and American Literary Studies," *American Literature* 67, no. 4 (1995): 837.

10. Susan Mizruchi, Introduction, *Religion and Cultural Studies,* ed. Susan L. Mizruchi (Princeton: Princeton University Press, 2001), x. Cf. Kevin Schultz and Paul Harvey, who have explored why historians of modern (post-1865) America have relegated American religious history to a subfield; they point to the persistence of secularization narratives as well as to secularist biases among academics that have safely confined "religious history to a history of the lower classes, or the racialized, or the marginalized" ("Everywhere and Nowhere: Recent Trends in American Religious History and Historiography," *Journal of the American Academy of Religion* 78, no. 1 [2010]: 129–35).

11. Martin Stringer, *A Sociological History of Christian Worship* (Cambridge, UK: Cambridge University Press, 2005), 5.

12. "sermon, n.," OED Online, December 2011, Oxford University Press, accessed February 19, 2012. One of the only reliable editions of nineteenth-century American sermons is Michael Warner's *American Sermons: The Pilgrims to Martin Luther King Jr.* (New York: Library of America, 1999).

13. Theodore Parker, *The Transient and the Permanent in Christianity,* Centenary ed., vol. 4., ed. George Willis Cooke (Boston: American Unitarian Association, 1908), 27.

14. Leigh Eric Schmidt makes this point eloquently: "I can see evangelist George Whitefield's crossed eyes in a portrait; I can still see some of the pulpits from which he preached; I can pore over his sermons; I can read his journals. But I can never lend him my ears or eavesdrop on his prayers" (*Hearing Things: Religion, Illusion, and the American Enlightenment* [Cambridge, MA: Harvard University Press, 2000], 15).

15. Alexis de Tocqueville, *Democracy in America,* trans. and ed. Harvey C. Mansfield and Delba Winthrop (Chicago: University of Chicago Press, 2000), 278, 517.

16. Roger Finke and Rodney Stark, *The Churching of America, 1776–2005: Winners and Losers in Our Religious Economy,* 2nd ed. (New Brunswick: Rutgers University Press, 2005), 22–23. See E. Brooks Holifield on the preponderance of attenders to members (*God's Ambassadors: A History of the Christian Clergy in America* [Grand Rapids, MI: William B. Eerdmans, 2007], 113).

17. In 1850, Congregationalists claimed only 4 percent of total church members in the U.S.; Presbyterians, 11.6 percent; and Episcopalians, 3.5 percent. In the same year, Baptists accounted for 20.5 percent of total church membership; Methodists, 34.2 percent; and Catholics, 13.9 percent (Finke and Stark, 56–57).

18. Nathan O. Hatch, *The Democratization of American Christianity* (New Haven: Yale University Press, 1989), 4.

19. Hambrick-Stowe, xi; Grodzins, ix; Applegate, 4.

20. John S. C. Abbott, *A Sermon on the Reciprocal Duties of Pastor and People* (Boston: Crocker and Brewster, 1841), 4.

21. See Jeanne Halgren Kilde on why the Gothic revival style flourished despite seemingly contradicting Protestants' democratic values and anti-Catholicism. Besides symbolizing aesthetic refinement, Gothic architecture allowed evangelicals to assert Christian unity and reinforced the idea of church as a sacred space distinct from a public sphere made increasingly contentious by debates over slavery. The more democratic amphitheater style associated with, for instance, Charles Grandison Finney's Broadway Tabernacle or Henry Ward Beecher's Plymouth Church in Brooklyn would not become the norm until the 1870s (*When Church Became Theatre: The Transformation of Evangelical Architecture and Worship in Nineteenth-Century America* [New York: Oxford University Press, 2002], 56–83, 112–45).

22. Because my study foregrounds those denominations that considered preaching a male vocation, I use masculine pronouns to refer to Protestant preachers.

23. F. O. Matthiessen remarked that during the antebellum period, "the one branch of literature in which America had a developed tradition was oratory" (*American Renaissance: Art and Expression in the Age of Emerson and Whitman* [1941; New York: Oxford University Press, 1968], xiv). On oratory in the period's literature and culture, see, for instance, James Perrin Warren, *Culture of Eloquence: Oratory and Reform in Antebellum America* (University Park: Pennsylvania State University Press, 1999) and *Oratorical Culture in Nineteenth-Century America: Transformations in the Theory and Practice of Rhetoric*, ed. Gregory Clark and S. Michael Halloran (Carbondale: Southern Illinois University Press, 1993). See also seminal work focused on the early republic: on oratory, Jay Fliegelman, *Declaring Independence: Jefferson, Natural Language, and the Culture of Performance* (Stanford, CA: Stanford University Press, 1993) and Sandra M. Gustafson, *Eloquence Is Power: Oratory and Performance in Early America* (Chapel Hill: University of North Carolina Press, for the Omohundro Institute of Early American History and Culture, 2000); on the tension between literature and voice more broadly construed, Christopher Looby, *Voicing America: Language, Literary Form, and the Origins of the United States* (Chicago: University of Chicago Press, 1996) and Nancy Ruttenburg, *Democratic Voice and the Trial of American Authorship* (Stanford: Stanford University Press, 1998). For a fascinating range of considerations of the interplay of print, orality, and performance in American culture, see Sandra M. Gustafson and Caroline F. Sloat, eds., *Cultural Narratives: Textuality and Performance in American Culture before 1900* (Notre Dame: University of Notre Dame Press, 2010).

24. Nehemiah 8:8.

25. On the history of Christian preaching, see Alistair Stewart-Sykes, *From Prophecy to Preaching: A Search for the Origins of the Christian Homily* (Leiden: Brill, 2000); Ronald E. Osborn, *Folly of God: The Rise of Christian Preaching* (St. Louis, MO: Chalice Press, 1999); Yngve Brilioth, *A Brief History of Preaching,* trans. Karl E. Mattson (Philadelphia: Fortress Press, 1965); and Bernhard Lang, *Sacred Games: A History of Christian Worship* (New Haven: Yale University Press, 1997).

26. Ann Douglas, *The Feminization of American Culture* (New York: Farrar, Strauss, Giroux, Noonday Press, 1998), xi.

27. Karin E. Gedge, *Without Benefit of Clergy: Women and the Pastoral Relationship in Nineteenth-Century American Culture* (New York: Oxford University Press, 2003), 3–6.

28. Ibid., 73.

29. Ann Braude, "Women's History *Is* American Religious History," in *Retelling U.S. Re-*

ligious History, ed. Thomas A. Tweed (Berkeley: University of California Press, 1997), 95. In 1850 Congregationalists accounted for 4 percent of total church membership, and Unitarian Congregationalists were an unidentified percentage of this total (Finke and Stark, 56).

30. Douglas, 8.

31. See David D. Hall, ed., *Lived Religion in America: Toward a History of Practice* (Princeton: Princeton University Press, 1997), especially Hall's introduction (vi–xiii), and other work in this vein such as Charles Hambrick-Stowe, *The Practice of Piety: Puritan Devotional Disciplines in Seventeenth-Century New England* (Chapel Hill: University of North Carolina Press for the Institute for Early American History and Culture, 1982); Colleen McDannell, *Material Christianity: Religion and Popular Culture in America* (New Haven: Yale University Press, 1995); and Laurie F. Maffly-Kipp, Leigh Schmidt, and Mark Valeri, eds., *Practicing Protestants: Histories of Christian Life in America, 1630–1965* (Baltimore: The Johns Hopkins University Press, 2006). Although the editors of *Practicing Protestants* write that one of their goals is to "expand the usual scholarly repertoire beyond preaching and the sacraments" (7), there has been little scholarly work on non-evangelical preaching in nineteenth-century America.

32. Catherine Bell, *Ritual Theory, Ritual Practice* (New York: Oxford University Press, 1992), 182.

33. Ibid., 169–81. On the power of lay people in antebellum America, see, for instance, Hatch, as well as R. Laurence Moore, *Selling God: American Religion in the Marketplace of Culture* (New York: Oxford University Press, 1994) and Jon Butler, *Awash in a Sea of Faith: Christianizing the American People* (Cambridge, MA: Harvard University Press, 1990).

34. Edmund Arens, "Religion as Ritual, Communicative, and Critical Praxis," trans. Chad Kautzer, in *The Frankfurt School on Religion: Key Writings by the Major Thinkers,* ed. Eduardo Mendieta (New York: Routledge, 2005), 386.

35. Walt Whitman, *Prose Works 1892,* ed. Floyd Stovall (New York: New York University Press, 1964), 551.

36. Walter Ong, *Orality and Literacy: The Technologizing of the Word* (London: Routledge, 1982), 74.

37. Alessandro Portelli, *The Text and the Voice: Writing, Speaking, and Democracy in American Literature* (New York: Columbia University Press, 1994), 7.

38. Jack Goody, *The Interface Between the Written and the Oral* (Cambridge, UK: Cambridge University Press, 1987), 263–64.

39. Perry Miller, *The New England Mind: The Seventeenth Century* (Cambridge, MA: Harvard University Press, Belknap Press, 1939), 296.

40. Methodist preaching has received more attention than that of any other antebellum denomination. See, for instance, Frederick V. Mills, Sr., "Methodist Preaching, 1798–1840: Form and Function," *Methodist History* 43, no. 1 (2004): 3–16; Karen B. Westerfield Tucker, *American Methodist Worship* (New York: Oxford University Press, 2001), 36–39, 74–78, 264–65; John H. Wigger, *Taking Heaven by Storm: Methodism and the Rise of Popular Christianity in America* (New York: Oxford University Press, 1998), 25–35, 48–79, 182–85; and Gennifer Benjamin Brooks, "Preaching," in *The Oxford Handbook of Methodist Studies,* ed. William J. Abraham and James E. Kirby (Oxford: Oxford University Press, 2008), 361–75.

41. On women preachers, see Catherine Brekus, *Strangers and Pilgrims: Female Preaching in America, 1740–1845* (Chapel Hill: University of North Carolina Press, 1998). African American preaching is by far the most studied of these various marginalized preaching traditions, even though the relative paucity of extant antebellum sermons by African Americans has made historical inquiry a challenge. Gregory Jackson has noted many of the reasons for the dearth of surviving African American sermons from the eighteenth and nineteenth centuries, including

the loss of African languages, the primacy of oral tradition, "the devastation of the diaspora on African linguistic identity, the regnant place of oral tradition within pan-African culture, the Baptist emphasis on the direct religious experience, and proscriptions against black literacy in the antebellum South" ("America's First Mass Media: Preaching and the Protestant Sermon Tradition" [Malden, MA: Blackwell, 2005], 423). For scholarship on antebellum African American preaching, see, for instance, Eugene D. Genovese, *Roll, Jordan, Roll: The World the Slaves Made* (New York: Vintage-Random House, 1972), 255–79, as well as, more recently, Shane White and Graham White, *The Sounds of Slavery: Discovering African-American History through the Sounds of Songs, Sermons, and Speech* (Boston: Beacon Press, 2005), 120–44; Albert J. Raboteau, *Slave Religion: The 'Invisible Institution' in the Antebellum South,* updated ed. (Oxford: Oxford University Press, 2004), 231–39; Julius H. Bailey, "Masculinizing the Pulpit: The Black Preacher in the Nineteenth-Century AME Church," in *Fathers, Preachers, Rebels, Men: Black Masculinity in U.S. History and Literature, 1820–1945,* ed. Timothy R. Buckner and Peter Caster (Columbus: The Ohio State University Press, 2011), 80–101. Several studies have addressed the preaching of African American women: e.g., Yolanda Pierce, *Hell Without Fires: Slavery, Christianity, and the Antebellum Spiritual Narrative* (Gainesville: University Press of Florida, 2005); Chanta Haywood, *Prophesying Daughters: Black Women Preachers and the Word* (Columbia: University of Missouri Press, 2003); Joycelyn Moody, *Sentimental Confessions: Spiritual Narratives of Nineteenth-Century African American Women* (Athens: University of Georgia Press, 2001); and Richard J. Douglass-Chinn, *Preacher Woman Sings the Blues: The Autobiographies of Nineteenth-Century African American Evangelists* (Columbia: University of Missouri Press, 2001). See also Richard Newman, *Freedom's Prophet: Bishop Richard Allen, the AME Church, and the Black Founding Fathers* (New York: New York University Press, 2008). For studies of African American Protestant preaching suggestive in their applicability to the antebellum period, see Henry H. Mitchell, *Black Preaching* (Philadelphia: J. B. Lippincott, 1970); Bruce Rosenberg, *Can These Bones Live: The Art of the American Folk Preacher,* rev. ed. (Urbana: University of Illinois Press, 1988); and William H. Pipes, *Say Amen, Brother!: Old-Time Negro Preaching: A Study in American Frustration* (Westport, CT: Negro Universities Press, 1951).

42. Nineteenth-century Christians often referred to theologically conservative denominations as "evangelical," but historiography has tended to limit that term to Methodists, Baptists, and others who maintained that salvation required a conversion experience. As an example of the scope of "evangelical" in the antebellum period, Robert Baird's *Religion in America* identified as "unevangelical" few affiliations: Roman Catholics, Unitarians, Universalists, Christian Connexionists, Swedenborgians, Tunkers, Jews, Rappists, Shakers, Mormons, atheists, Deists, socialists, and Fourierists ([New York: Harper and Brothers, 1844], xii).

43. Gardiner Spring, *The Power of the Pulpit; or Thoughts Addressed to Christian Ministers and Those Who Hear Them,* 2nd ed. (1848; New York: M. W. Dodd, 1854), 66–67. Cf. Edwards Park, who maintained that just as installing a pastor led directly to a more orderly, prosperous parish life, so the prevalence of Christian ministers assured the security and prosperity of the nation ("Introductory Essay on the Dignity and Importance of the Preacher's Work," *The Preacher and Pastor, by Fenelon, Herbert, Baxter, Campbell,* ed. Edwards A. Park [Andover: Allen, Morrill, and Wardwell, 1845], 21).

44. Nathaniel Hawthorne, Preface, *The House of the Seven Gables* ([Columbus]: The Ohio State University Press, 1965), 1–3. But see Nina Baym, who has argued, based on her survey of more than two thousand book reviews in American periodicals, that the distinction between "romance" and "novel" meant little in America between 1840 and 1860. The novel was both a modern offshoot of the older tradition of romance and a blanket term that included

the romance as a psychological and symbolic subcategory. Reviewers often used the terms interchangeably (*Novels, Readers, and Reviewers: Responses to Fiction in Antebellum America* [Ithaca, NY: Cornell University Press, 1984], 225–35).

45. See Lawrence Buell, "The Unkillable Dream of the Great American Novel: *Moby-Dick* as Test Case," *American Literary History* 20, nos. 1–2 (2008): 132–55. Anonymous, London *Spectator* 24 (October 25, 1851): 1026–1027, repr. in *The Critical Response to Herman Melville's Moby-Dick*, ed. Kevin J. Hayes (Westport, CT.: Greenwood Press, 1994), 3, 19.

46. Northrop Frye, *Anatomy of Criticism: Four Essays* (Princeton: Princeton University Press, 1957), 313; Sheila Post-Lauria, *Correspondent Colorings: Melville in the Marketplace* (Amherst: University of Massachusetts Press, 1996), 103–22.

47. Harriet Beecher Stowe, "Preface to the European Edition," *Uncle Tom's Cabin* (Leipzig: Tauchnitz, 1852), 1:v.

48. Walter Siti, "The Novel on Trial," in *The Novel: Volume 1, History, Geography, and Culture*, ed. Franco Moretti (Princeton: Princeton University Press, 2006), 96.

49. See Jonathan Arac, *The Emergence of American Literary Narrative, 1820–1860* (Cambridge, MA: Harvard University Press, 2005).

50. Baym, *Novels, Readers, and Reviewers*, 173–95.

51. For an analysis of the many reasons U.S. churches supported slavery, see John R. McKivigan, *The War against Proslavery Religion: Abolitionism and the Northern Churches, 1830–1865* (Ithaca: Cornell University Press, 1984) and John R. McKivigan and Mitchell Snay, "Religion and the Problem of Slavery in Antebellum America," in *Religion and the Antebellum Debate over Slavery*, ed. John R. McKivigan and Mitchell Snay (Athens: University of Georgia Press, 1998), 1–32. See historian Laura Mitchell on why Northern ministers counseled obedience to civil authorities after the passage of the Fugitive Slave Law; often their sermons hinged on an interpretation of the golden rule ("love thy neighbor as thyself") that read the Southern white, not black, as the true neighbor ("'Matters of Justice between Man and Man': Northern Divines, the Bible, and the Fugitive Slave Act of 1850," *Religion and the Antebellum Debate over Slavery*, ed. John R. McKivigan and Mitchell Snay [Athens: University of Georgia Press, 1998], 147, 134–65).

52. For a panoramic view of ministers in nineteenth-century American fiction, see Douglas Walrath, who reads the progressive devaluation of fictive ministers from the 1790s to the 1920s as a reflection of the clergy's declining cultural authority and the country's growing secularism. This argument accepts too uncritically both Douglas's thesis about a ministerial loss of authority that pre-dates the Civil War and theories of secularization that overstate the cultural acceptance of scientific advances (*Displacing the Divine: The Minister in the Mirror of American Fiction* [New York: Columbia University Press], 2010).

53. Richard Chase, *The American Novel and Its Tradition* (Garden City, NY: Doubleday, 1957), 12–28; Ian Watt, *The Rise of the Novel: Studies in Defoe, Richardson, and Fielding* (Berkeley and Los Angeles: University of California Press, 1957), 12. On the intersection of literary realism and the sermon form, see Gregory Jackson's *The Word and Its Witness: The Spiritualization of American Realism* (Chicago: University of Chicago Press, 2009). Jackson shows how the postbellum "homiletic novel," by which he means Protestant fiction indebted to post-Reformation narrative strategies of inspiring conversion and spiritual transformation, contributed to a form of American literary realism that defies secularist epistemologies.

54. Raymond Chapman, *Forms of Speech in Victorian Fiction* (London: Longman, 1984), 93.

55. Frances Knight details the evolving expectations of ministers in *The Nineteenth-Century Church and English Society* (Cambridge, UK: Cambridge University Press, 1995), 106–50.

56. My work thus follows up on Lawrence Buell's reflection that the "major American renaissance authors," including Hawthorne, Melville, Dickinson, and Thoreau, saw themselves in competition with religion and that many of their works "are either sermons (like Emerson's Divinity School Address and Parker's *Discourse of the Transient and Permanent in Christianity*) or at one remove from sermons, like Emerson's *Nature* or Brownson's *New Views*." Buell notes that the influence of the sermon on the era's literary production has gone largely uninvestigated "undoubtedly because of scanty background information about the sermon form," an observation that holds true today (*Literary Transcendentalism: Style and Vision in the American Renaissance* [Ithaca: Cornell University Press, 1973], 103–4). Cf. Buell, "The Unitarian Movement and the Art of Preaching in 19th-Century America," *American Quarterly* 24, no. 2 (1972): 167.

57. Exemplary monographs in this vein include Philip Gura, *The Wisdom of Words: Language, Theology, and Literature in the New England Renaissance* (Middletown, CT: Wesleyan University Press, 1981); Jenny Franchot, *Roads to Rome: The Antebellum Protestant Encounter with Catholicism* (Berkeley: University of California Press, 1994); Amy Benson Brown, *Rewriting the Word: American Women Writers and the Bible* (Westport: Greenwood Press, 1999); John Gatta, *Making Nature Sacred: Literature, Religion, and Environment in America from the Puritans to the Present* (New York: Oxford University Press, 2004); Ilana Pardes, *Melville's Bibles* (Berkeley: University of California Press, 2008); and Katherine Clay Bassard, *Transforming Scriptures: African American Women Writers and the Bible* (Athens: University of Georgia Press, 2010).

58. Jordan Alexander Stein and Justine S. Murison's overview of the evolving methodological approaches to religion and early American literature suggests that similar tendencies have governed work on literature before 1830 ("Introduction: Religion and Method," *Early American Literature* 45, no. 1 [2010]: 9–10). Stein and Murison note how the advent of poststructuralist literary theory in the 1970s fueled the tendency in the 1980s for early Americanists to stress the determining role of language and rhetoric in colonial religious life; a distinct yet often complementary strand of scholarship, typified by the work of Sacvan Bercovitch, treated religion as myth or ideological system. Though Stein and Murison also identify scholarship analyzing religion as a form of experience, this approach seems to have had less purchase on literary studies. In the same issue, Wendy Raphael Roberts pushes back against the field's persistent deracination of the religious, calling attention to how the interconnected realms of the oral and religious shaped eighteenth-century literature, in particular poetry ("Demand My Voice: Hearing God in Eighteenth-Century American Poetry," *Early American Literature* 45, no. 1 [2010]: 119–44).

59. My point here resonates with Buell's suggestion that literary scholars stand to benefit from a closer engagement with religious studies, in particular the study of lived religion, which he sees as potentially useful to them in that, like literary studies, it "too prefers to conceive of religion as culture" and, in emphasizing the fluidity and creativity of religion, avoids the binaries of secular and sacred. Approaching religion in this light can help students of literature resist constraining "assumptions such as that a text's religious dimension must reside chiefly in some sort of thesis or idea structure and/or that religious motives are to be decoded in terms of such secular motives as political resistance or cultural survival" ("Religion on the American Mind," *American Literary History* 19, no. 1 [2007]: 32–55).

60. Stephen Railton has pointed out that the "five major works of the American Renaissance"—*Nature, Moby-Dick, Walden, Leaves of Grass,* and *The Scarlet Letter*—all relied upon the model of the Protestant sermon in that the writers were concerned with explicating a text (e.g., nature or a pond or an embroidered letter), much as a preacher would explicate the Bible.

Railton leaves this parallel behind in his readings but notes that writers who would seek to fill the role of preachers lacked institutional privilege and an authorizing scripture or theology (*Authorship and Audience: Literary Performance in the American Renaissance* [Princeton: Princeton University Press, 1991], 107–8).

61. My emphasis on the sermon's spokenness dovetails with the recent scholarly upsurge of interest in orality and aurality among scholars of American Studies. See, for instance, Peter Hoffer, *Sensory Worlds in Early America* (Baltimore: The Johns Hopkins University Press, 2003); Richard Cullen Rath, *How Early America Sounded* (Ithaca, NY: Cornell University Press, 2003); the emphasis on spoken language found throughout the essays in Greil Marcus and Werner Sollors, eds., *A New Literary History of America* (Cambridge, MA: Harvard University Press, Belknap Press, 2009); and the essays in *Sound Clash: Listening to American Studies,* ed. Kara Keeling and Josh Kun, *American Quarterly* 63, no. 3 (2011), especially Keeling and Kun's survey of recent work in this area, "Introduction: Listening to American Studies" (445–59).

62. Richard Whately, *Elements of Rhetoric: Comprising an Analysis of the Laws of Moral Evidence and of Persuasion with Rules for Argumentative Composition and Elocution,* ed. Douglas Ehninger (Carbondale: Southern Illinois University Press, 1963), 191.

63. See Sacvan Bercovitch, *The American Jeremiad* (Madison: University of Wisconsin Press, 1978).

64. Cf. Robyn Warhol-Down, who remarks that contemporary critics disdain nineteenth-century novels' "engaging" narrators because these voices are associated with women authors (*Gendered Interventions: Narrative Discourse in the Victorian Novel* [New Brunswick: Rutgers University Press, 1989], vii–viii).

65. J. Paul Hunter, *Before Novels: The Cultural Contexts of Eighteenth-Century English Fiction* (New York: Norton, 1990), 226.

66. George Lippard, *The Quaker City; or, the Monks of Monk Hall. A Romance of Philadelphia Life, Mystery, and Crime,* ed. David S. Reynolds (Amherst: University of Massachusetts Press, 1995), 135; Herman Melville, *Moby-Dick; or The Whale,* vol. 6, *The Writings of Herman Melville,* ed. Harrison Hayford, Hershel Parker, and C. Thomas Tanselle (Evanston and Chicago: Northwestern University Press and The Newberry Library, 1988), 74; William Wells Brown, *Clotel, or, The President's Daughter: A Narrative of Slave Life in the United States* (London: Partridge and Oakey, 1853), 245.

67. Robert Frost, "The Figure a Poem Makes," *The Collected Prose of Robert Frost,* ed. Mark Richardson (Cambridge, MA: Harvard University Press, Belknap Press, 2007), 132.

68. Siti, 119.

69. Danièle Hervieu-Leger, *Religion as a Chain of Memory,* trans. Simon Lee (New Brunswick: Rutgers University Press, 2000), 27.

70. On the etymologies of "religion" and "secular" and the difficulty of mapping these terms onto the modern world, see Craig Calhoun, Mark Juergensmeyer, and Jonathan VanAntwerpen, Introduction to *Rethinking Secularism,* ed. Craig Calhoun, Mark Juergensmeyer, and Jonathan VanAntwerpen (New York: Oxford University Press, 2011), 7–9.

71. Karel Dobbelaere, "The Meaning and Scope of Secularization," in *The Oxford Handbook of the Sociology of Religion,* ed. Peter B. Clarke (New York: Oxford University Press, 2009), 600.

72. Ibid., 601.

73. Pierre Bourdieu, *The Field of Cultural Production: Essays on Art and Literature* (New York: Columbia University Press, 1993), 140.

74. Although there is no sociological analysis comparable to Bourdieu's for nineteenth-century American literary production, see Lawrence Levine for a landmark study of cultural

hierarchization in the period (*Highbrow/Lowbrow: The Emergence of Cultural Hierarchy in America* [Cambridge, MA: Harvard University Press, 1988]), and Barbara Sicherman on how a "bourgeois culture of reading" helped define respectability and class boundaries in mid- to late-nineteenth-century America ("Reading and Middle-Class Identity in Victorian America: Cultural Consumption, Conspicuous and Otherwise," in *Reading Acts: U. S. Readers' Interactions with Literature, 1800–1950*, ed. Barbara Ryan and Amy M. Thomas,]Knoxville: University of Tennessee Press, 2002], 137–60).

75. On the difficulties of defining secularization and the debates over secularization theory, see R. Wallis and S. Bruce, "Secularization: The Orthodox Model," in *Religion and Modernization*, ed. Steve Bruce (Oxford: Clarendon Press, 1992), 8–30 and Philip S. Gorski and Ateş Altınordu, "After Secularization?", *Annual Review of Sociology* 34 (2008): 55–85.

76. José Casanova, "A Secular Age: Dawn or Twilight?" in *Varieties of Secularism in a Secular Age*, ed. Michael Warner, Jonathan VanAntwerpen, and Craig Calhoun (Cambridge, MA: Harvard University Press, 2010), 273.

77. See, for instance, Craig Calhoun, Mark Juergensmeyer, and Jonathan VanAntwerpen, eds., *Rethinking Secularism* (New York: Oxford University Press, 2011), especially José Casanova, "The Secular, Secularizations, Secularisms," 54–74; *Secularisms*, ed. Janet R. Jakobsen and Ann Pellegrini (Durham: Duke University Press, 2008); Michael Warner, "Secularism," in *Keywords for American Cultural Studies*, ed. Bruce Burgett and Glenn Hendler (New York: New York University Press, 2007), 209–12; and Talal Asad, *Formations of the Secular: Christianity, Islam, and Modernity* (Stanford: Stanford University Press, 2003).

78. See most notably Charles Taylor's critique of the "subtraction stories" implicit in many historical and sociological narratives, in which once religion is "subtracted" from a social formation, what is left is assumed to be natural and self-evident (*A Secular Age* [Cambridge, MA: Harvard University Press, Belknap Press, 2007], 22).

79. See Talal Asad, *Genealogies of Religion: Discipline and Reasons of Power in Christianity and Islam*, on the often unacknowledged dependence of Western rationality on antecedent religious modes of thought (Baltimore: The Johns Hopkins University Press, 1993).

Chapter 1

1. Melville, *Moby-Dick*, 40.

2. Ralph Waldo Emerson, "An Address Delivered before the Senior Class in Divinity College, Cambridge, Sunday Evening, July 15, 1838," *Emerson's Prose and Poetry: Authoritative Texts, Contexts, Criticism*, ed. Joel Porte and Saundra Morris (New York: Norton, 2001), 75; Spring, *The Power of the Pulpit*, 57.

3. Henry Ware, Jr., *The Connexion Between the Duties of the Pulpit and the Pastoral Office: An Introductory Address Delivered to the Members of the Theological School in Cambridge* (Cambridge, MA: Hilliard and Brown, 1830), 28; Edwards A. Park, "Introductory Essay," 40; George Bethune, *The Eloquence of the Pulpit, with Illustrations from St. Paul. An Oration before the Porter Rhetorical Society of the Theological Seminary at Andover, Mass. 1842* (Andover, MA: William Peirce, 1842), 6.

4. Orville Dewey, *The Pulpit, as a Field of Exertion, Talent, and Piety: A Sermon Delivered at the Installation of the Rev. Edward B. Hall, as Pastor of the First Congregational Society in Providence* (New Bedford: Benjamin Lindsey, 1832), 4.

5. Emerson turned this idea on its head when he claimed that the democratic mixing that came with church attendance was more valuable than the sermon itself: "What was once a mere circumstance, that the best and worst men in the parish, the poor and the rich, the

learned and the ignorant, young and old, should meet one day as fellows in one house, in sign of an equal right in the soul,—has come to be a paramount motive for going thither" ("An Address," 78).

6. Lawrance Thompson, *Melville's Quarrel with God* (Princeton: Princeton University Press, 1952), 163.

7. See Donald O. Scott, *From Office to Profession: The New England Ministry, 1750–1850* ([Philadelphia]: University of Pennsylvania Press, 1978). Sidney E. Mead proposed a slightly less dramatic picture of the changes in the antebellum ministry, claiming that while the minister lost his "priestly dimension," he was now conceived of as a "consecrated functionary, called of God, who directed the purposive activities of the visible church," an interpretation that emphasizes how the ministry continued to be perceived as a sacred and collective enterprise, rather than, say, an association of entrepreneurial service providers ("The Rise of the Evangelical Conception of the Ministry in America: 1607–1850," *The Ministry in Historical Perspectives*, ed. H. Richard Niebuhr and Daniel D. Williams [New York: Harper, 1956], 228). On changes in the clerical profession during this period, see also Holifield, 103–43, and on the crisis of authority among clergy in the mid-twentieth-century United States, which reflects the chronic challenges of maintaining religious leadership under voluntarism, see James Gustafson, "The Clergy in the United States," *The Professions in America*, ed. Kenneth S. Lynn and the editors of *Daedalus* (Boston: Houghton Mifflin, 1965), 70–90.

8. Unitarian minister Samuel Osgood commented wryly on the spate of literature bemoaning the problem of underpaid clerics: "No subject, except perhaps the Slave question, has been handled more frequently of late than that of parish life, especially in respect to its trials, and at least a half dozen books have been sent out within two or three years, claiming as much sympathy for the clerical martyr and his consort, as is claimed for Uncle Tom and Aunt Chloe" (*Mile Stones in Our Life-Journey* [New York: Appleton, 1855], 42).

9. See Philip Hamburger, *Separation of Church and State* (Cambridge, MA: Harvard University Press, 2002), 79–88, 111–29, 243–46. Scott describes how clergy developed a mystique of sacred difference around the pulpit in the first three decades of the nineteenth century by avoiding political preaching (18–35). See Jonathan D. Sassi on how the New England clergy between 1783 and 1833 sought to demonstrate the relevance of Christian beliefs and values to public issues (*A Republic of Righteousness: The Public Christianity of the Post-Revolutionary New England Clergy* [Oxford: Oxford University Press, 2001]). Richard J. Carwardine has shown that evangelical ministers largely abided throughout the 1830s and 1840s by the cultural mandate that clergy remain politically neutral, especially in the pulpit. However, when in the late 1840s and 1850s the political issues at the center of national debate shifted from economic ones with seemingly little religious significance to the more heated ones of "temperance, Roman Catholicism, war, the extension or restriction of slavery, and the future of the Union itself," more and more evangelical ministers preached on political issues (*Evangelicals and Politics in Antebellum America* [1993; Knoxville: University of Tennessee Press, 1997], 30).

10. Gedge, 113. On changes in ministerial preparation, see also Scott, 60–64, and Glenn T. Miller, *Piety and Intellect: The Aims and Purposes of Ante-Bellum Theological Education* (Atlanta, GA: Scholars Press, 1990). As Buell has pointed out, students at Harvard and Andover in the early nineteenth century devoted nearly all of their third year to the study of homiletics. Buell also notes the advent of university chairs of sacred rhetoric, beginning with Andover in 1809, and the fact that the men who occupied these positions (e.g., Henry Ware, Jr. at Harvard, Henry Ripley at Newton, and Ebenezer Porter, William Russell, and Edwards A. Park at Andover) often wrote on homiletics as well ("Unitarian Movement," 172).

11. Scott, 131.

12. Occasionally there were objections to the primacy of preaching in ministers' professional lives. One physician-missionary to Hawaii published a tract objecting to the weight that Protestants placed on pulpit preaching, arguing that the word "preach" was interpreted too narrowly—as delivering sermons only, rather than promulgating the gospel through various means. "The press is neglected; private personal influence is neglected; the sabbath school is neglected; familiar bible-class studies are neglected; and even social conferences for prayer and praise are frequently deserted, because, forsooth, preaching is the method of God's ordination. Immured in his silent study, occasionally the Minister appears, a visitant from another land, to perform the wondrous preaching; then for a week retires; and again appears to accomplish his pantomime of apostolic labor" (L. H. Gulick, *A Sermon on the Foolishness of Preaching* [Honolulu: Government Press, 1853], 13). Gulick added that the disproportionate value assigned to preaching ended up underrating the labors of others working in the mission field, including physicians, teachers, and all women.

13. Ebenezer Porter, *Lectures on Homiletics and Preaching, and on Public Prayer; together with Sermons and Letters* (Andover, MA: Flagg, Gould and Newman; New York: Jonathan Leavitt, 1834), 229. Buell notes the importance of preaching for Boston Unitarians ("Unitarian Movement," 171).

14. On the Unitarian dominance of antebellum literary institutions, see Buell, "The Literary Significance of the Unitarian Movement," 212–23.

15. Gedge, 112. David D. Field, *The Reciprocal Duties of Ministers and People . . .* (Middletown, CT: T. Dunning, 1817), 6, 7, 9.

16. Samuel Seabury, *The Relation of the Clergy and Laity: A Discourse Preached in St. Paul's Chapel and St. Clement's Church* (New York: Henry M. Onderdonk, 1844), 7.

17. Ibid., 23.

18. Charles Grandison Finney, *Lectures on Revivals of Religion* (Cambridge, MA: Harvard University Press, Belknap Press, 1960), 207.

19. Porter, 182.

20. Heman Humphrey, *Thirty-four Letters to a Son in the Ministry* (Amherst: J. S., & C. Adams; New York: Dayton and Newman; Boston: Crocker and Brewster, 1842), 17.

21. Bethune, 36.

22. Henry Ward Beecher, *Yale Lectures on Preaching* (New York: J. B. Ford and Company, 1872), 10.

23. John R. Knott, Jr., *The Sword of the Spirit* (Chicago: University of Chicago Press, 1980), 7–10.

24. Humphrey, 349.

25. S[idney] W[illard]?, "On the Mutual Relations, Duties, and Interests of Minister and People, No. 4." *Christian Register and Boston Observer* (Sept. 11, 1841), 145.

26. John Brazer, "On the Value of the Public Exercises of Our Religion," *The Liberal Preacher* 2 (1832): 16.

27. Ware, *Connexion*, 10, 17.

28. S[idney] W[illard]?, "On the Mutual Relations, Duties, and Interests of Minister and People, No. 4," 145.

29. Antebellum homiletic rhetoric seldom alluded to masculinity, a discourse that became more pronounced after the Civil War with the rise of "muscular Christianity," a movement that emphasized men's health and strength as integral to their Christian lives. Henry Ward Beecher's *Yale Lectures on Preaching*, for instance, is saturated with such masculinist rhetoric as, "A true minister is a man whose manhood itself is a strong and influential argument with his people" and "Manhood is the best sermon" (29–31). On the rhetoric of manhood, masculinist

character-building, and muscular Christianity in mid- to late nineteenth-century homiletic texts, see Roxanne Mountford, *The Gendered Pulpit: Preaching in American Protestant Spaces* (Carbondale: Southern Illinois University Press, 2003), 40–64.

30. Hugh Blair, *Lectures on Rhetoric and Belles Lettres,* 13th American ed. (New York: James and John Harper, 1824), 282, 286. This work went through twenty-six editions in Great Britain and thirty-seven in the United States (James L. Golden and Edward P. J. Corbett, *The Rhetoric of Blair, Campbell, and Whately, with Updated Bibliographies* [Carbondale: Southern Illinois University Press, 1990], 25).

31. Finney, 198.

32. Augustine, *On Christian Teaching,* trans. R. P. H. Green (Oxford: Oxford University Press, 1997), 118.

33. On the Romantic principles underwriting nineteenth-century American preaching, see O. C. Edwards, Jr., "The Preaching of Romanticism in America," *American Transcendental Quarterly* 14, no. 4 (2000): 297–312, as well as Edwards, *A History of Preaching,* 624–37. See also Perry Miller, *The Life of the Mind in America: From the Revolution to the Civil War* (New York: Harcourt, Brace, & World, A Harvest Book, 1965), 59–66.

34. Edwards, *A History of Preaching,* 474.

35. Emerson, "An Address," 80.

36. H. W. Beecher, 222.

37. Spillers, "Moving on Down the Line," *American Quarterly* 40, no. 1 (1988): 104.

38. Porter, 170.

39. Ibid., 89.

40. Bethune, 49.

41. David Reynolds argues in "From Doctrine to Narrative: The Rise of Pulpit Storytelling" that nineteenth-century preaching was marked by a new, anecdotal pulpit style. This claim is almost certainly true of the revival sermons of the Second Great Awakening, especially Finney, who defended his sermon style against detractors who thought it lowered the dignity of the pulpit by pointing out that "story-telling ministers" merely followed the example of Jesus, who told parables: "Tells stories!" he wrote. "Why, that is the way Jesus preached. And it is the only way to preach" (Finney, 209). However, I have seen little evidence of either anecdote or extended storytelling in the weekly and occasional sermons of white, non-Methodist, Northeastern preachers before the Civil War. Reynolds's argument appears stronger for postbellum preachers, who increasingly worked narrative into their sermons: e.g., the "story sermons" of Presbyterian DeWitt Talmage or Congregationalist Charles Sheldon's original serialization of *In His Steps* in his weekly sermons.

42. Arens, 386.

43. Analyzing the sermon themes of five ordinary ministers from various regions and denominations, Mark Y. Hanley argues that sermons in the 1840s and 1850s emphasized religious issues such as "sin, salvation, judgment, and 'separation from the world'" over cultural or material ones (*Beyond a Christian Commonwealth: The Protestant Quarrel with the American Republic, 1830–1860* [Chapel Hill: University of North Carolina Press, 1994], 125, 136–56).

44. As T. D. Bilhartz has argued, the pervasiveness of evangelical rhetoric and techniques among traditionally non-evangelical denominations reflected the new realities of voluntaristic religion. When traditional methods of recruiting church members fell short, antebellum ministers across the theologically conservative denominations turned to the evangelical rhetoric of personal accountability that had worked so well for the Methodists ("Sex and the Second Great Awakening: The Feminization of American Religion Reconsidered," *Belief and Behavior: Essays in the New Religious History,* ed. Philip R. Vandermeer and Robert P. Swierenga [New Brunswick: Rutgers University Press, 1991], 117–35).

45. Erich Auerbach, *Mimesis: The Representation of Reality in Western Literature,* trans. Willard R. Trask (Princeton: Princeton University Press, 1953), 18.

46. See Paul K. Conkin, *American Originals: Homemade Varieties of Christianity* (Chapel Hill: University of North Carolina Press, 1997), 74–75. Quoting Schleiermacher, who claimed to be "a Hernhutter [Moravian], though of a higher kind," Bernhard Lang notes that all liberal theologians, European or American, "remained Moravians of a higher kind, i.e., men and women interested not so much in Christianity as a body of doctrine but in practical spirituality that helps one to cope with life" (190). On the liberal critique of evangelical emotion in preaching and the liberals' own use of emotion, see Daniel Walker Howe, *The Unitarian Conscience: Harvard Moral Philosophy, 1805–1861* (Cambridge, MA: Harvard University Press, 1970; Middletown, CT: Wesleyan University Press, 1988), 163–65.

47. Francis Parkman, "The Object, Reasonableness, and Spirituality of the Christian Worship," *Liberal Preacher,* n.s., 6 (1843): 32.

48. George Putnam, *Spiritual Renewal the Great Work of the Christian Church and Ministry: A Sermon Delivered at the Ordination of Rev. Frederic D. Huntington, as Pastor of the Second Congregational Church, in Boston, October 19, 1842* (Boston: William Crosby & Co, 1842), 6.

49. Aaron Bancroft, "The Importance of Attending to Our Own Salvation," *Liberal Preacher* 3 (1830): 161–68.

50. Howe, 166.

51. "Practical Preaching," *Christian Register and Boston Observer* (Oct. 23, 1841): 170.

52. Conkin notes that by 1850 most antebellum Unitarians were probably Universalist in their sentiments, believing that all of humanity would eventually be saved, often after a purgatorial waiting period (105).

53. *Hints on Preaching without Reading* (Philadelphia: R. E. Peterson, 1850), 65; Spring, *The Power of the Pulpit,* 112–13.

54. Based on a random sampling of titles in Orville Roorbach's *Bibliotheca Americana,* Candy Gunther Brown has estimated that individually printed sermons accounted for less than two percent of the overall book market between 1852 and 1855, down from 2.6 percent in the previous century. Yet she also notes that this apparent decrease is complicated by the fact that sermons also circulated in denominational periodicals and literary annuals, often repackaged in new forms (*The Word in the World: Evangelical Writing, Publishing, and Reading in America, 1789–1880* [Chapel Hill: University of North Carolina Press, 2004], 50). Sermons may have made it to print more often than other public addresses: "of printed discourses the proportion of sermons to other public addresses is probably not less than a hundred to one" (Dewey, *The Pulpit,* 5).

55. Spring, *The Power of the Pulpit,* 116. This excerpt also ran in a front-page article titled "The Sermon Preached, and the Sermon Printed" in the Congregationalist *Independent* (December 7, 1848).

56. Liberal ministers disparaged the mass emotion generated when a well-spoken preacher addressed a crowd. Edward T. Channing warned Harvard seniors: "We are not to go to church that we may catch sympathy and fervor from a crowd, which we shall never experience elsewhere"—counsel that highlights the appeal of sermons as shared religious experiences (*Lectures Read to the Seniors in Harvard College* [Boston: Ticknor and Fields, 1856], 131).

57. Edwards A. Park, *The Indebtedness of the State to the Clergy: A Sermon Delivered before His Excellency George N. Briggs, Governor, His Honor John Reed, Lieutenant Governor, The Honorable Council, and the Legislature of Massachusetts, at the Annual Election, January 2, 1851* (Boston: Dutton and Wentworth, 1851), 12. See also Spring, who estimated that a rural

pastor preaching three times a week—twice on Sunday and once during the week, plus on special occasions such as weddings, funerals, baptisms, and fast days—was "distributing" the equivalent of 46,800 tracts a year, and that he did so at a much lower cost than those hypothetical tracts and with a much greater effectiveness (*The Power of the Pulpit*, 112).

58. Calvin Stowe, Sept. 1, 1854, in *Annals of the American Pulpit; or Commemorative Notices of Distinguished American Clergymen of Various Denominations, from the Early Settlement of the Country to the Close of the Year Eighteen Hundred and Fifty-Five. With Historical Introductions*, ed. William B. Sprague (New York: R. Carter, 1857), 2:479.

59. Humphrey, 109; Abraham Messler, *The Elements of Power in the Christian Ministry. A Sermon Preached in the Second Reformed Dutch Church of Coxsackie, on Occasion of the Installation of Rev. John Steele* (New Brunswick: J. Terhune & Son, 1853), 22–23. See Russel Hirst on the centrality of ministerial ethos to nineteenth-century conservative homiletics. Distinguishing between conservative and "revivalist-charismatic" homileticians, he argues that conservatives, who privileged *logos* over *pathos*, credited proper ethos primarily to learned ministers who presented Christian truth according to principles of harmony, symmetry, and balance ("*Ethos* and the Conservative Tradition in Nineteenth-Century American Protestant Homiletics," in *Ethos: New Essays in Rhetoric and Critical Theory*, ed. James S. Baumlin and Tita French Baumlin [Dallas: Southern Methodist University Press, 1994], 293–318).

60. Humphrey, 109. The maxim more traditionally ascribed to Luther is "*Bene orasse est bene studuisse*," or to have studied well is to have prayed well (Porter, 89).

61. *Views and Feelings Requisite to Success in the Gospel Ministry*, repr. from the *Quarterly Christian Spectator*, December 1833 (New Haven: Stephen Cooke, 1833), 5.

62. H. W. Beecher, 125–26.

63. Edward D. Griffin, *A Sermon on the Art of Preaching, Delivered before the Pastoral Association of Massachusetts in Boston, May 25, 1825* (Boston: T. R. Marvin, 1825), 11.

64. Henry Ware, Jr., *Hints on Extemporaneous Preaching*, 3rd ed. (1824; Boston: Hilliard, Gray, Little and Wilkins, 1831), 83; Ware, *Connexion*, 8–9.

65. Orville Dewey. *On the Preaching of Our Saviour. A a* [sic] *Sermon Delivered at the Ordination of Joseph Angier as Pastor of the First Congregational Church in New-Bedford. May 20, 1835* (New Bedford: Benjamin T. Congdon, 1835), 29, 30. Cf. Osgood praising his childhood minister: "Every thought, whether original or from books, bore the stamp of the preacher's own individuality" (25).

66. Qtd. in Robert Collyer, *Father Taylor* (Boston: American Unitarian Association, 1906), 39.

67. The extent to which preachers adopted extemporaneity deserves further investigation; see Buell, "Unitarian Movement," 179. On the debate over manuscript-based versus extemporaneous preaching in nineteenth-century England, where manuscript preaching was also on the wane, see Robert H. Ellison, *The Victorian Pulpit: Spoken and Written Sermons in Nineteenth-Century Britain* (Selinsgrove, PA: Susquehanna University Press; London: Associated University Presses, 1998), 33–42.

68. Blair, too, had strongly discouraged reading in the pulpit, on the grounds that no persuasive discourse could "have the same force when read, as when spoken" (288). He recommended that most preachers should speak from notes, except for novices who needed to learn the art of sermon construction and experienced ministers who wanted to work through a theological issue for their own edification.

69. Ralph Waldo Emerson, *Journals of Ralph Waldo Emerson, 1820–1872*, 10 vols., ed. Edward Waldo Emerson and Waldo Emerson Forbes (Boston and New York: Houghton Mifflin Company, 1912), 7:169; Ware, *Hints*, viii, 17, 24, 13, 90, 93. The similarity of Emerson's

rhetoric to Ware's is not coincidental. Emerson served as assistant pastor to Ware at Second Church in Boston in 1828 and succeeded him there in 1829. Calling attention to the neglected connection between Ware and Emerson, Tim Jensen has explored Emerson's debt in the Harvard Divinity School address to Ware's *Hints* ("'Their Own Thought in Motley': Emerson's Divinity School Address and Henry Ware Jr.'s *Hints on Extemporaneous Preaching*," *Journal of Unitarian-Universalist History* 24 [1997]: 17–30).

70. Ware, *Hints,* 24, 6.

71. Ibid., 12, 23.

72. Ibid., 4, 87, 89.

73. Ibid., 21, 22, 26.

74. See, for instance, *Views and Feelings Requisite to Success in the Gospel Ministry,* 31.

75. Finney, 211, 216, 218.

76. Humphrey, 118, 119.

77. Henry J. Ripley, *Sacred Rhetoric; Or, Composition and Delivery of Sermons. To Which are Added* Hints on Extemporaneous Preaching, *by Henry Ware, Jr. D.D.* (Boston: Gould, Kendall, and Lincoln, 1849), 180.

78. Humphrey, 124. *Hints on Preaching without Reading,* 8–9, 71. The pamphlet alludes to 2 Samuel 24:24, in which David insists on paying for the oxen he is about to sacrifice: "neither will I offer burnt offerings unto the LORD my God of that which doth cost me nothing."

79. William Russell, *Pulpit Elocution: Comprising Suggestions on the Importance of Study; Remarks on the Effect of Manner in Speaking; The Rules of Reading, Exemplified from the Scriptures, Hymns, and Sermons; Observations on the Principles of Gesture; and a Selection of Pieces for Practice in Reading and Speaking* (Andover, MA: Allen, Morrill and Wardwell, 1846), 333–50.

80. Humphrey, 13. Porter, 93.

81. "unction, n.," OED Online. December 2011. Oxford University Press. http://www.oed.com/view/Entry/211077?redirectedFrom=unction (accessed December 28, 2011).

82. H. Ripley, 128.

83. W. Russell, 50.

84. Ibid., 47. [Charles Buck and Ebenezer Henderson], "Declamation of the Pulpit," in *Fessenden & Co.'s Encyclopedia of Religious Knowledge: or Dictionary of the Bible, Theology, Religious Biography, All Religions, Ecclesiastical History, and Missions,* ed. J. Newton Brown (Brattleboro', VT: Brattleboro' Typographic Company, 1840), 447.

85. Porter, 93, 81.

86. Ibid., 157; Finney, 202.

87. S[idney] W[illard]?, "On the Mutual Relations, Duties, and Interests of Minister and People, No. 6: Mutual Duties in Regard to Public Instruction," *Christian Register and Boston Observer* (Sept. 25, 1841), 154.

88. George Campbell, *The Philosophy of Rhetoric,* ed. Lloyd F. Bitzer (Carbondale: Southern Illinois University Press, 1963), vii, liv, 26.

89. Porter, 180; Bethune, 23.

90. Bethune, 21.

91. F. W. P. Greenwood, "The Charge," in Orville Dewey, *On the Preaching of Our Saviour,* 37. The rule against making parishioners laugh may have begun to relax after mid-century. H. W. Beecher told ministers that they were not to *try* to make their listeners laugh by, for instance, telling jokes, but that if laughter occurred naturally, they should not attempt to stifle it (178–79).

92. Mark 4:9. Cf. Mark 4:23, 7:16; Matthew 11:15 and 13:9, 43; Luke 8:8, 14:35.

93. George Whitefield, "Directions How to Hear Sermons," *The Works of the Reverend George Whitefield*, 6 vols. (London: E. and C. Dilley, 1771–72), 5:421–22.

94. Humphrey, 63.

95. Whitefield, 424.

96. Robert Hall, "On Hearing the Word of God," *The Publications of the New England Tract Society* 145 (Andover, MA: Flagg and Gould, 1823), 8.

97. Luke 4:4; cf. Matthew 4:4. Finney, 241.

98. Abbott, 9. The argument that a sleepy pastor made for a sleepy congregation was the more typical formulation. See, for instance, Bethune: "It is easy to tell what kind of a speaker is in the pulpit by observing his auditory. If they sit listless, lounging unconcerned, or looking carelessly around, however good a man he may be, he is a poor preacher; but if they bend their eyes intently upon his countenance, listening *ut avis cantu aliquo*, or their cheeks be flushed, their tears starting, or their hands clenched, and there is a hush over all, so that his lowest whisper is heard in every part, he must be eloquent" (10).

99. S[idney] W[illard]?, "On the Mutual Relations, Duties, and Interests of Minister and People, No. 7: Mutual Duties in Regard to Public Worship," *Christian Register and Boston Observer* (Oct. 2, 1841), 158.

100. R. Hall, 13, 10.

101. Samuel Seabury, *On Hearing the Word; A Sermon* (New York: New-York Protestant Episcopal Tract Society, 1831), 10.

102. Porter, 36.

103. Gregory Godolphin, *The Unique, a Book of Its Own Kind: Containing a Variety of Hints, Thrown out in a Variety of Ways, for Evangelical Ministers, Churches, and Christians* (Boston: Putnam, 1844), 135–37.

104. Osgood, 174–75.

105. S[idney] W[illard]?, "On the Mutual Relations, Duties, and Interests of Minister and People, No. 6," 154.

106. Henry W. Bellows, *Re-Statements of Christian Doctrine in Twenty-Five Sermons* (New York: D. Appleton & Company, 1859), 64.

107. Emerson, "An Address," 72.

108. George W. Burnap, *Lectures on the Sphere and Duties of Woman* (Baltimore: John Murphy, 1841), 267.

Chapter 2

1. Henry David Thoreau, *Walden, Civil Disobedience, and Other Writings: Authoritative Texts, Journal, Reviews and Posthumous Assessments, Criticism*, 3rd ed., ed. William Rossi (New York: Norton, 2008), 75.

2. Terence Martin, *The Instructed Vision: Scottish Common Sense Philosophy and the Origins of American Fiction* (Bloomington: Indiana University Press, 1961), 57–103.

3. Michael Davitt Bell, *The Development of American Romance: The Sacrifice of Relation* (Chicago: University of Chicago Press, 1980), 37, 12–14.

4. Ronald J. Zboray, *A Fictive People: Antebellum Economic Development and the American Reading Public* (New York: Oxford University Press, 1993), 130–33.

5. See David Paul Nord, *Faith in Reading: Religious Publishing and the Birth of Mass Media in America* (Oxford: Oxford University Press, 2004), 115–18; C. Brown, 96–97; Paul C. Gutjahr, "No Longer Left Behind: Amazon.com, Reader-Response, and the Changing Fortunes

of the Christian Novel in America," *Book History* 5 (2002): 211–15. See also Paul Gutjahr, "Religion," *A Companion to American Fiction, 1780–1865*, ed. Shirley Samuels (Malden, MA: Blackwell, 2004), 89–90.

6. Barbara Hochman, "Readers and Reading Groups," *The Cambridge History of the American Novel*, ed. Leonard Cassuto, Clare Virginia Eby, and Benjamin Reiss (Cambridge, UK: Cambridge University Press, 2011), 600, 611n3.

7. See, for instance, the Zborays' reference to "the novel's mid-century triumph" (Ronald Zboray and Mary Saracino Zboray, "The Novel in the Antebellum Book Market," in *The Cambridge History of the American Novel*, ed. Leonard Cassuto, Clare Virginia Eby, and Benjamin Reiss [Cambridge, UK: Cambridge University Press, 2011], 79) and the excerpt from Baym titled "The Triumph of the Novel," in *The Novel: An Anthology of Criticism and Theory, 1900–2000*, ed. Dorothy J. Hale (Malden, MA: Blackwell, 2006), 779–91.

8. Baym, *Novels, Readers, and Reviewers*, 14. Cf. William Charvat, *The Origins of American Critical Thought, 1810–35* (Philadelphia: University of Pennsylvania Press, 1936), 156–63, and G. Harrison Orians, who maintains that the novel did not gain "any widespread approbation before the fourth decade of our political independence" ("Censure of Fiction in American Romances and Magazines 1789–1810, *PMLA* 52, no. 1 [1937]: 195).

9. James L. Machor, *Reading Fiction in Antebellum America: Informed Response and Reception Histories, 1820–1865* (Baltimore: The Johns Hopkins University Press, 2011), 29.

10. See James L. Machor, "Fiction and Informed Reading in Early Nineteenth-Century America," *Nineteenth-Century Literature* 47, no. 3 (1992): 328–33; cf. Machor, *Reading Fiction*, 36.

11. Ronald J. Zboray and Mary Saracino Zboray, "'Have You Read . . . ?': Real Readers and Their Responses in Antebellum Boston and Its Region," *Nineteenth-Century Literature* 52, no. 2 (1997): 148. The Zborays tend to ground reader responses in local discourses, or "interchanges about social and family relations, activities, and events" ("'Have You Read . . . ?,'" 169). James L. Machor, "Historical Hermeneutics and Antebellum Fiction: Gender, Response Theory, and Interpretive Texts," in *Readers in History: Nineteenth-Century American Literature and the Contexts of Response*, ed. James L. Machor (Baltimore: The Johns Hopkins University Press, 1993), 64. Cf. Machor, "Fiction and Informed Reading," 325. In *Reading Fiction*, Machor tones down claims for the primacy of periodical discourse, writing that it created and extended "*a* public sphere of interpretation that paralleled and helped form middle-class reading formations for the reception of fiction" (32; my emphasis).

12. Machor acknowledges this point but discounts it (e.g., "Historical Hermeneutics," 64). Baym mentions that *Godey's, Harper's*, and *The New York Ledger* all ran fiction (*Novels, Readers, and Reviewers*, 14–18) and notes that the *Ledger* was "the nation's most popular fiction weekly" (18).

13. Orians, 210.

14. On the "corporate and communal" nature of reviewing, see Machor, "Historical Hermeneutics," 64. Cf. Cheryl D. Bohde, who reads antebellum literary periodicals as a repressive institution that advanced a "monistic American ethos" by advocating utilitarianism in the arts and silencing diversity and political dissent ("'Magazines as a Powerful Element of Civilization': An Exploration of the Ideology of Literary Magazines, 1830–1850," *American Periodicals* 1, no. 1 [1991]: 34–45).

15. Lara Cohen, "Democratic Representations: Puffery and the Antebellum Print Explosion," *American Literature* 79, no. 4 (2007): 656.

16. John Austin, "United States, 1780–1850," in *The Novel: Volume 1, History, Geography, and Culture*, ed. Franco Moretti (Princeton: Princeton University Press, 2006), 455–65.

17. Zboray, *A Fictive People,* 164.

18. Zboray and Zboray, "The Novel in the Antebellum Book Market," 68.

19. Mary Kelley, *Learning To Stand and Speak: Women, Education, and Public Life in America's Republic* (Chapel Hill: University of North Carolina Press for the Omohundro Institute of Early American History and Culture, 2006), 185.

20. Ronald J. Zboray and Mary Saracino Zboray, *Everyday Ideas: Socioliterary Experience among Antebellum New Englanders* (Knoxville: University of Tennessee Press, 2006), 249.

21. Kelley, *Learning to Stand and Speak,* 184.

22. On the boom in religious fiction, see David S. Reynolds, *Faith in Fiction: The Emergence of Religious Literature in America* (Cambridge, MA: Harvard University Press, 1981); Jan Blodgett, *Protestant Evangelical Literary Culture and Contemporary Society* (Westport, CT: Greenwood Press, 1997), 11–31; and Gregory Jackson, "Religion and the Nineteenth-Century American Novel," in *The Cambridge History of the American Novel,* ed. Leonard Cassuto, Clare Virginia Eby, and Benjamin Reiss (Cambridge, UK: Cambridge University Press, 2011), 167–91.

23. Gutjahr, "Religion," 90. C. Brown, 96.

24. Nord, 117. See Buell, who notes that Unitarians were more accepting of fiction than the orthodox but still placed their "practice of fiction within rather prim boundaries" ("Literary Significance," 219).

25. Kelley also notes this discrepancy between conduct books and periodical reviewers, 182–83n40.

26. Sarah E. Newton, *Learning to Behave: A Guide to American Conduct Books Before 1900* (Westport, CT: Greenwood Press, 1994), 4.

27. See Nancy Armstrong on how eighteenth-century British conduct books shaped modern bourgeois subjectivity by addressing a broadly middle-class readership ("The Rise of the Domestic Woman," *The Ideology of Conduct: Essays on Literature and the History of Sexuality,* ed. Nancy Armstrong and Leonard Tennenhouse [New York: Methuen, 1987], 96–141).

28. Isabel Lehuu, *Carnival on the Page: Popular Print Media in Antebellum America* (Chapel Hill: University of North Carolina Press, 2000), 127.

29. The conduct books referenced in this chapter were all authored by Americans, with the exception of Arthur Freeling's *The Young Bride's Book: An Epitome of the Domestic Duties and Social Enjoyments of Woman, as Wife and Mother* (New York: Wilson and Company, 1849).

30. Machor, "Historical Hermeneutics," 65; cf. Machor, *Reading Fiction,* 32.

31. Richard Brodhead, *Cultures of Letters: Scenes of Reading and Writing in Nineteenth-Century America* (Chicago: University of Chicago Press, 1993), 47.

32. William Warner, "Licensing Pleasure: Literary History and the Novel in Early Modern Britain," in *The Columbia History of the British Novel,* ed. John Richetti (New York: Columbia University Press, 1994), 4.

33. Daniel Smith, *Lectures to Young Men on Their Dangers, Safeguards, and Responsibilities* (New York: Lane & Scott, 1852), 48–49.

34. Here I extend and revise the work of scholars who focus on how antebellum conduct books policed women's reading. See, for instance, Kelley, *Learning to Stand and Speak,* 157–59; Jane E. Rose, "Conduct Books for Women, 1830–1860: A Rationale for Women's Conduct and Domestic Role in America," in *Nineteenth-Century Women Learn to Write,* ed. Catherine Hobbs (Charlottesville: University Press of Virginia, 1995), 37–58; and Suzanne Ashworth, "Susan Warner's *The Wide, Wide World,* Conduct Literature, and Protocols of Female Reading in Mid-Nineteenth-Century America," *Legacy* 17, no. 2 (2000): 141–64. Whereas Ashworth finds conduct books discouraging novel-reading as "a precursor to nervous disorders, paranoia, a fragile constitution, and fatal diseases" (146), I discovered only light emphasis on the physical

dangers of reading fiction. For perhaps the most influential account of how conduct books inscribed normative behavior for women, see Nancy Armstrong, *Desire and Domestic Fiction: A Political History of the Novel* (New York: Oxford University Press, 1987), 59–95. David M. Stewart touches on advice writers' admonitions to men to avoid novel-reading in *Reading and Disorder in Antebellum America* (Columbus: The Ohio State University Press, 2011), 9–13.

35. Machor, *Reading Fiction*, 29; Zboray, *A Fictive People*, 164. Cf. Ronald J. Zboray, "Reading Patterns in Antebellum America: Evidence in the Charge Records of the New York Society Library," *Libraries & Culture* 26, no. 2 (1991): 306, 309. Zboray notes the gender differences in the types of novels men and women read. Men were somewhat more likely to read Cooper; women, sentimental novels such as *Fashion and Famine* and *Grantley Manor* (*A Fictive People*, 164–65). In *Everyday Ideas*, the Zborays report that the letters and diaries of New Englanders indicate few differences in the reading material of men and women, a continuity they attribute to the practice of reading aloud in mixed-gender groups (338n2).

36. S. Newton, 51–61.

37. William A. Alcott, *The Young Husband, or Duties of Man in the Marriage Relation* (Boston: George W. Light, 1839), 207.

38. George W. Burnap, *Lectures to Young Men, on the Cultivation of the Mind, the Formation of Character, and the Conduct of Life: Delivered in Masonic Hall, Baltimore* (Baltimore: John Murphy, 1840), 54.

39. William G. Eliot, Jr., *Lectures to Young Men*, 5th ed. (Boston: Crosby, Nichols, 1855), 74–75. Holifield notes that from the colonial era to the Civil War, ministers accounted for 262 of the 288 college presidents (119). Cf. the advice of James Waddel Alexander to workingmen in *The American Mechanic* (1838); he lamented that by reading novels year after year, workers lost all mental vigor, just as surely as their stomachs "would have lost all tone, if for a period they would have been fed nothing but pastries, ices, and confections" (qtd. in Zboray, *A Fictive People*, 124).

40. Jane G. Swisshelm, *Letters to Country Girls* (New York: J. C. Riker, 1853), 151–52. On Swisshelm, see Sylvia D. Hoffert, *Jane Grey Swisshelm: An Unconventional Life, 1815–1884* (Chapel Hill: University of North Carolina Press, 2004).

41. Thomas M. Clark, *Early Discipline and Culture: A Series of Lectures to Young Men and Women* (Providence, RI: George H. Whitney, 1855), 65, 68.

42. Janice Radway, "Reading Is Not Eating: Mass-Produced Literature and the Theoretical, Methodological, and Political Consequences of a Metaphor," *Book Research Quarterly* 2, no. 3 (1986): 11. See D. Stewart for a recuperation of the reading as eating metaphor, insofar as reading was linked to actual eating practices and had bodily effects (93–117).

43. Lehuu has pointed out that conduct books regularly used temperance rhetoric in their commentary on reading (137); I would add that this language appears most prominently with respect to fiction.

44. John Todd, *The Daughter at School* (Northampton: Hopkins, Bridgman, and Company, 1854), 118–19.

45. Swisshelm, 151.

46. Catharine Maria Sedgwick, *Means and Ends, or Self-Training* (Boston: Marsh, Capen, Lyon, & Webb, 1839), 246.

47. T. Clark, 65.

48. Virginia Cary, *Letters on Female Character, Addressed to a Young Lady, on the Death of Her Mother* (Richmond, VA: A. Works, 1828), 125.

49. Todd, *The Daughter at School*, 119.

50. S. H. Barnes, *A Book for the Eldest Daughter* (Boston: Massachusetts Sabbath School Society, 1849), 118, 121. Nord also cites this line, attributing it to the November 1847 issue of

the American Tract Society's newspaper, the *American Messenger* (118; 194n13); apparently Barnes either copied the sentence verbatim or was the original unnamed author of the article.

51. T. Clark, 66; Daniel Wise, *The Young Man's Counsellor; or Sketches and Illustrations of the Duties and Dangers of Young Men. Designed to be a Guide to Success in This Life, and to Happiness in the Life Which Is To Come,* 3rd ed. (Boston: C. H. Peirce and W. J. Reynolds, 1851), 214; Alcott, *The Young Husband,* 208; Daniel Wise, *The Young Lady's Counsellor; or, Outlines and Illustrations of the Sphere, the Duties and the Dangers of Young Women: Designed to be a Guide to True Happiness in This Life, and To Glory in the Life Which Is to Come,* 10th ed. (New York: Carlton & Phillips, 1852), 188.

52. Although we might speculate, as Kelley does, that it was "[f]iction's power to shape a more expansive subjectivity that gave cultural arbiters pause," it is worth stressing that the conduct book authors themselves did not grant fiction this power (*Learning to Stand and Speak,* 182). What we might see as expanded subjectivity, they regarded as useless wanderings of the imagination.

53. Margaret Coxe, *The Young Lady's Companion: In a Series of Letters* (Columbus, OH: I. N. Whiting, 1839), 69.

54. Mrs. L. G. Abell, *Woman in her Various Relations: Containing Practical Rules for American Females* (New York: R. T. Young, 1853), 274. Jennifer Brady discusses how antebellum conduct literature critiqued fiction for rousing sympathies without providing an outlet for action, thus casting all novels as having sentimental effects ("Theorizing a Reading Public: Sentimentality and Advice about Novel Reading in the Antebellum United States," *American Literature* 83, no. 4 [2011]: 720–46).

55. Zboray and Zboray, "The Novel in the Antebellum Book Market," 74.

56. T. S. Arthur, *Advice to Young Ladies on Their Duties and Conduct in Life* (Boston: Phillips & Sampson, 1848), 60.

57. T. S. Arthur, *Advice to Young Men on Their Duties and Conduct in Life* (Boston: N. C. Barton, 1848), 61.

58. T. Clark, 63; Matthew Hale Smith, *Counsels Addressed to Young Women, Young Men, Young Persons in Married Life, and Young Parents. Delivered in the Second Presbyterian Church, Washington City, on the Evenings of the Sabbaths in April, 1846* (Washington, DC: Blair and Rives, 1846), 54; John Todd, *The Moral Influences, Dangers and Duties, Connected with Great Cities* (Northampton, MA: J. H. Butler, 1841), 202.

59. D. Smith, 47.

60. Alcott, *The Young Husband,* 206.

61. Horace Mann, "A Few Thoughts for a Young Man: A Lecture, Delivered Before the Boston Mercantile Library Association, on its 29th Anniversary" (Syracuse, NY: L. W. Hall, 1850), 54–55.

62. Martin, 71–72.

63. Wise, *The Young Man's Counsellor,* 214–15. Davidson, 107.

64. Wise, *The Young Man's Counsellor,* 214.

65. See, for instance, Arthur, *Advice to Young Ladies,* 60; T. Clark, 66; Coxe, 70; Freeling, 56. See also Ashworth, who notes the prevalence in advice manuals of the ideas that novels taught women "false views of life," thus unfitting them for domestic duties (160n–161n).

66. Arthur, *Advice to Young Ladies,* 60.

67. Sarah Gould, *A Golden Legacy to Daughters, or Advice to Young Ladies* (Boston: Higgins, Bradley and Dayton, 1857), 3–4.

68. T. Clark, 67.

69. Coxe, 171–72, 70. Cf. Mrs. [Mary Martha] Sherwood, *The Lady of the Manor. Being a*

Series of Conversations on the Subject of Confirmation. Intended for the Use of the Middle and Higher Ranks of Young Females, vol. 1 (New York: E. Bliss and E. White, 1825), 266.

70. William A. Alcott, *Letters to a Sister; or Woman's Mission. To Accompany the Letters to Young Men* (Buffalo, NY: Geo. H. Derby and Co., 1850), 89.

71. Wise, *The Young Lady's Counsellor,* 188–89.

72. Lehuu, 129; [William A. Alcott], *The Young Man's Guide* (Boston: Lilly, Wait, & Co., 1833), 200. Alcott repeated this advice about novels verbatim in the 1846 edition of *The Young Man's Guide* (Boston: T. R. Marvin, 1846), 219–220.

73. D. Smith, 47.

74. Wise, *The Young Man's Counsellor,* 213. In a reversal of the slippery slope argument that bad fiction led to worse, see Thomas Augst on how the 1853 report of the New York Mercantile Library justified the heavy percentage of fiction in its collection by arguing that novels would lead to more substantive reading (*The Clerk's Tale: Young Men and Moral Life in Nineteenth-Century America* [Chicago: University of Chicago Press, 2003], 197).

75. Cary, 125.

76. T. Clark, 69.

77. Arthur, *Advice to Young Ladies,* 61–62.

78. Lehuu maintains that advice books from the 1830s to the 1850s tended to argue for moderation in reading in general (132).

79. Eliot, 73.

80. Coxe, 171.

81. T. Clark, 69.

82. Burnap, *Lectures to Young Men,* 55.

83. Barnes, 119.

84. Sedgwick, 246.

85. Cary, 126.

86. Burnap, *Lectures to Young Men,* 57, 55.

87. Todd, *The Daughter at School,* 119. Cf. Kelley, who writes that Scott was "spared the condemnation that attended the reading of fiction" (*Learning to Stand and Speak,* 181).

88. [Alcott], *The Young Man's Guide,* 200.

89. Sedgwick, 247.

90. Alcott, *The Young Husband,* 209–210.

91. Arthur, *Advice to Young Ladies,* 61.

92. Catharine E. Beecher and Harriet Beecher Stowe, *The American Woman's Home* (New York: J. B. Ford & Co., 1869), 292–94.

93. Nathaniel Hawthorne, *The Scarlet Letter,* vol. 1 of *The Centenary Edition of Nathaniel Hawthorne,* ed. William Charvat, Roy Harvey Pearce, and Claude M. Simpson (Columbus: The Ohio State University Press, 1962), 10; Susan Warner, *The Wide, Wide World* (New York: City University of New York, The Feminist Press, 1987), 564. Cf. Cathy Davidson, who calls Hawthorne's anxiety about the value of imaginative writing a "vestigial" holdover from the Puritans (*Revolution and the Word: The Rise of the Novel in America,* expanded ed. [Oxford: Oxford University Press, 2004], 5).

Chapter 3

1. Michael T. Gilmore, "The Book Marketplace I," *The Columbia History of the American Novel,* ed. Emory Elliott (New York: Columbia University Press, 1991), 54. Gilmore notes that

The Quaker City sold 60,000 copies in 1845 and 30,000 each year for the next five years. David Reynolds, *George Lippard: Prophet of Protest: Writings of an American Radical, 1822–1854* (New York: Peter Lang, 1986), 5.

2. See, for instance, David S. Reynolds's influential take on Lippard throughout *Beneath the American Renaissance: The Subversive Imagination in the Age of Emerson and Melville* (Cambridge, MA: Harvard University Press, 1988). Reynolds draws a more detailed portrait of Lippard, including his linked religious and political beliefs, in *George Lippard* (Boston: Twayne Publishers, 1982), and in his introduction to *George Lippard: Prophet of Protest,* esp. 27–29; see also his *Faith in Fiction,* 187–96. Lippard has been read most often in terms of class. See, for instance, Leslie Fiedler, who wrote that Lippard had a "kind of natural access to the erotic dreams and paranoid fantasies of the male members of the working class" (Introduction, *The Monks of Monk Hall* by George Lippard [New York: Odyssey, 1970], ix); Michael Denning, who has called Lippard "the most overtly political dime novelist of his or subsequent generations" (*Mechanic Accents: Dime Novels and Working-Class Culture in America* [London: Verso, 1987], 87); and Paul Erickson, who has explained that Lippard saw his work as a writer and editor as the moral and practical equivalent of manual labor, regarding it as "neither a 'profession' nor a 'calling' but as work" ("New Books, New Men," *Early American Studies* 1, no. 1 [2003]: 312). Against this last, I would maintain that Lippard regarded authorship as both work *and* calling.

3. Daniel Couégnas, "Forms of Popular Narrative in France and England: 1700–1900," in *The Novel, Volume I: History, Geography, and Culture,* ed. Franco Moretti (Princeton: Princeton University Press, 2006), 324.

4. Leslie A. Fiedler, *Love and Death in the American Novel* (1966; Normal, IL: Dalkey Archive Press, 1997), 246; Reynolds, *Beneath the American Renaissance,* 91. R. L. Moore similarly downplays Lippard's religious seriousness by foregrounding his economic motivation: Lippard "wished to sensationalize moral and religious instruction so that it sold a lot of books" (28). In *Faith in Fiction,* Reynolds presents religion as more important to Lippard's work: "his novels were a repository for a large variety of religious forces, satirical and affirmative, that had been gathering strength since the 1820s" (188).

5. On Lippard as a "visionary interpreter of Jesus," see Dan McKanan, *Prophetic Encounters: Religion and the American Radical Tradition* (Boston: Beacon Press, 2011), 113–14.

6. G[eorge] L[ippard], "Literature," *Quaker City,* June 2, 1849. Dwight Thomas and David K. Jackson, *The Poe Log: A Documentary Life of Edgar Allan Poe, 1809–1849* (Boston: G. K. Hall, 1987), 778. Edgar Allan Poe, "The Poetic Principle," *The Complete Works of Edgar Allan Poe,* ed. James A. Harrison (New York: AMS Press, 1965), 14: 266–92, 271. "The Poetic Principle" was first printed posthumously, in the October 1850 issue of *Sartrain's Union Magazine* (ibid., 266).

7. [George Lippard], *Quaker City,* June 2, 1849; [Lippard], "A National Literature," *Quaker City,* February 10, 1849.

8. Emilio De Grazia, *The Life and Works of George Lippard* (Ann Arbor, MI: University Microfilms, 1970), 30.

9. [John Bell Bouton], *The Life and Choice Writings of George Lippard* (New York: H. H. Randall, 1855), 10.

10. Reynolds remarks that while little is known of Lippard's childhood, "we get the general picture of a frail, feverishly imaginative boy finding refuge from misfortune in religion, in solitary walks out to the country, and in the incessant reading of the Bible, history, and fiction" (*George Lippard,* 3).

11. Roger Butterfield, "George Lippard and His Secret Brotherhood," *Pennsylvania Magazine of History and Biography* 79 (July 1955): 292.

12. Of this incident, Bouton wrote, "[W]e don't know exactly how much of the following anecdote is fact, and how much playful 'enlargement.' At any rate this is the circumstance to which Lippard used to attribute his 'backsliding' from the ministry" (*Life and Choice Writings,* 13).

13. Reflecting the paper's new breadth, Lippard changed the name to *The Home Journal and Citizen Soldier* in January 1844.

14. "The Spermaceti Papers" ran from May 31, 1843 to August 16, 1843.

15. [George Lippard], "The Spermaceti Papers," *Citizen Soldier* (July 5, 1843), 148.

16. George Lippard, "Adrian, the Neophyte," *Citizen Soldier* (July 26, 1843), 169-70; (Aug. 2, 1843), 177–78; George Lippard, *Adrian, the Neophyte* (Philadelphia: I. R. and A. H. Diller, 1843).

17. See, for instance, Lippard's story, "The Carpenter's Son," *The Nineteenth Century* 1, no. 2 (1848): 72–99; his essays in *The White Banner,* including "Brotherhood Versus Atheistic Sectarianism" (123–40); and his ritual address to new members of the Brotherhood of the Union, in which he proclaimed the coming day when "at last mankind are knit in Brotherhood,—at last God our father dwells with his children" (Brotherhood of the Union Papers, Series A, folder 4, a folio ms.,10p., Library Company). Lippard distanced himself from anti-Catholicism, arguing that Protestant "priests" were just as disruptive of domesticity and claiming that the virtues of Catholicism were lost on those who decried the Pope. They could not see the Church's "love for the beautiful in poetry, painting, and sculpture," "its reverence for woman in its almost deification of Mary the Virgin Mother," or "its thousand appeals to the senses, the heart, and the soul" ("Brotherhood," 126–27). Shelley Streeby explains that although Lippard critiqued nativism, including restrictions on immigration and naturalization, and defended Catholics in general, he remained suspicious of the Catholic priesthood as an enemy to democracy and liberty (*American Sensations: Class, Empire, and the Production of Popular Culture* [Berkeley and Los Angeles: University of California Press, 2002], 49–51).

18. George Lippard, "Jesus the Democrat," *The Home Journal and Citizen Soldier* (Jan. 31, 1844), 37–38.

19. Lippard recycled and expanded "Jesus the Democrat" as part of his 1848 story, "Jesus and the Poor." The later version depicts the preacher even more unfavorably, calling him "Rev. Dr. Five-thousand-a-year" and pricing the pews at "$800 cash, or $1000 in copper stock, at par" ("Jesus and the Poor," *The Nineteenth Century* 1, no. 1 [1848]: 74; the story also ran in the May 26, 1849, issue of the *Quaker City*). This later version is newly focused on those at the bottom of the social hierarchy. The transfigured Jesus calls "Come!" repeatedly, and while the rich do not respond, the poor, the widowed, the orphaned, "a Black Man," and a condemned felon come forward. The face of Jesus shines away their rags and suffering. See Timothy Helwig on Lippard's racial politics, which while stopping short of abolitionism, included opposition to chattel slavery and a willingness to see African Americans as fellow exploited laborers ("Denying the Wages of Whiteness: The Racial Politics of George Lippard's Working-Class Protest," *American Studies* 47, no.3/4 [2006]: 87–111).

20. See Streeby, "Haunted Houses," 451, 469n25; McKanan, 114–15; and Carsten E. Seecamp, "The Chapter of Perfection: A Neglected Influence on George Lippard," *Pennsylvania Magazine of History and Biography* 94 (1970): 192–212.

21. Scholars regularly note Lippard's friendship with Universalist minister Charles Chauncey Burr without considering the congruence between Lippard's work and Universalist theology and politics. Larzer Ziff comes closest in remarking that Lippard's belief that preachers had a duty to stand up for the poor against the rich "brought him into close alliance with

Philadelphia's maverick Universalist preachers" (*Literary Democracy: The Declaration of Cultural Independence in America* [New York: The Viking Press, 1981], 92).

22. See David Robinson, *The Unitarians and Universalists* (Westport, CT: Greenwood Press, 1985), 54–55.

23. Bruce Laurie, *Working People of Philadelphia, 1800–1850* (Philadelphia: Temple University Press, 1980), 67–83.

24. McKanan, 24. In the 1830s Kneeland would leave Universalism to lead Boston's Society of Free Enquirers and, on charges of atheism, become the defendant in what would be the last blasphemy trial in the United States. Philip S. Foner, *William Heighton: Pioneer Labor Leader of Jacksonian Philadelphia, With Selections from Heighton's Writings and Speeches* (New York: International Publishers, 1991), 22–33. See William Heighton, *An Address to the Members of Trade Societies and to the Working Classes Generally* (Philadelphia, 1827). While Foner does not specify at which Universalist church in Philadelphia Heighton spoke, McKanan writes that Heighton gave a series of addresses at First (23–24), and Laurie notes that Heighton gave one of his addresses in 1827–1828 at the Second Universalist Church (76). On Fisk, see Edward Pessen, *Most Uncommon Jacksonians: The Radical Leaders of the Early Labor Movement* (Albany: State University of New York Press, 1967), and David R. Roediger, *The Wages of Whiteness: Race and the Making of the American Working Class,* new ed. (1991; New York: Verso, 2007), 74–75. Theophilus Fisk, *Capital Against Labor: An Address Delivered at Julien Hall, Before the Mechanics of Boston, on Wednesday Evening, May 20* (Boston, 1835); Theophilus Fisk, *Labor the Only True Source of Wealth, or The Rottenness of the Paper Money Banking System Exposed . . .* (Charleston, SC, 1837). Though less overtly political than Kneeland or Fisk, First Church's next minister, Abel Thomas, who served from 1830 to 1839 and again from 1849 to 1863, would in 1839 take a pastorate in Lowell, Massachusetts, where he helped organize the literary labors of the women working in the mills. The result was the *Lowell Offering,* which he edited until 1842.

25. Laurie, 162, 165–68.

26. Ann Lee Bressler, *The Universalist Movement in America, 1770–1880* (New York: Oxford University Press, 2001), 71.

27. Publisher's Advertisement, *Washington and His Generals, or, Legends of the Revolution* (Philadelphia: G. B. Zieber, 1847), 1. Abel C. Thomas, *A Century of Universalism in Philadelphia and New-York, with Sketches of Its History in Reading, Hightstown, Brooklyn, and Elsewhere* (Philadelphia, 1872), 113. Thomas reports that after Burr stepped down, supply preachers filled the pulpit for nine months, then the church stood "silent as a tomb" for another fifteen months (ibid.).

28. Laurie, 165.

29. George Lippard, *The Quaker City; or, the Monks of Monk Hall. A Romance of Philadelphia Life, Mystery, and Crime,* ed. David S. Reynolds (Amherst: University of Massachusetts Press, 1995), 223. Subsequent references are to this edition unless otherwise noted. George Lippard, "The Gospel of the New World," *Quaker City,* October 6, 1849; the subhead indicates that it was originally given as a speech at the City Hall in Wilmington, Delaware, on September 30, 1848. George Lippard, *Memoirs of a Preacher; or, Mysteries of the Pulpit* (1849; Philadelphia: T. B. Peterson & Brothers, 1864), 58.

30. [George Lippard], "The Dream," The White Banner (1851): 125.

31. [George Lippard], "Religion," *The White Banner* (1851): 120–21.

32. [George Lippard], "Two Parties in Every Church," *The White Banner* (1851): 127.

33. Bressler details Universalist opposition to capital punishment (83–84).

34. George Lippard, "Jesus and the Poor," *The Nineteenth Century* 1, no. 1 (1848): 69.

35. George Lippard, *"The Bible." What It Is, and What It Is Not* (Canton, OH: Klippart & Webb, 1854), 4.

36. A. Thomas, 82.

37. T[heophilus] Fisk, *The Pleasures of Sin: A Discourse Delivered at the Capitol, in the City of Washington, on Sunday Morning, December 16, 1827* (Philadelphia, 1828), 7.

38. Ibid., 5.

39. Asher Moore, *Universalism, the Doctrine of the Bible* (Philadelphia: Gihon, 1847), 85.

40. Lippard, *The Quaker City*, 4.

41. Here I follow Denning, who writes that although Lippard's prose is often called pornographic, "voyeuristic" is the apter word (99).

42. See Shelley Streeby, who points out that Lippard's writing partook of the "antebellum 'culture of sentiment' that is almost exclusively, though wrongly, identified with female readers and writers" ("Opening Up the Story Paper: George Lippard and the Construction of Class," *boundary 2*, 24, no. 1 [1997]: 189). Although Mary Chapman and Glenn Hendler's groundbreaking collection, *Sentimental Men: Masculinity and the Politics of Affect in American Culture* (Berkeley: University of California Press, 1999), and subsequent work in this vein has done much to disrupt the association of sentimentalism with women, Lippard's fiction is seldom read through this framework.

43. Gedge discusses how Pyne "monstrously distorted the clergyman's masculine roles as professional, pastor, and father" (4).

44. Lippard, *The Quaker City*, 263.

45. Ibid., 202. When Devil-Bug lights the fire meant to suffocate Byrnewood Arlington, he uses fat pine and charcoal, remarking, "Cuss it how the fat pin [*sic*] blazes!" (ibid., 110). Cf. the "Housewarming" chapter of *Walden*, in which Thoreau describes how "a few pieces of fat pine were a great treasure" to his fire-building (170).

46. Although the earliest definition of "dick" as penis in the *Oxford English Dictionary* is from 1891, "ball" for testicle dates from the fourteenth century ("Dick, n.1," OED Online, December 2011, Oxford University Press, accessed February 19, 2012; "ball, n.1," OED Online, December 2011, Oxford University Press, accessed February 19, 2012).

47. Reynolds, Introduction, *George Lippard*, xxxvi.

48. George Lippard, "Key to the Quaker City: or, The Monks of Monk Hall," in George Lippard, *The Quaker City; or, The Monks of Monk-Hall: A Romance of Philadelphia Life, Mystery, and Crime* (Philadelphia: George Lippard, 1845), 4.

49. Lippard, *The Quaker City*, 263, 262, 267.

50. Ibid., 201.

51. Ibid., 268.

52. When Stephen Girard, a Philadelphia tycoon, died in 1830, he left $2 million so that Philadelphia could build a college for poor white orphan boys. Because the authorities objected to Girard's stipulation that no clergy could ever enter the college, the school remained unbuilt in 1845, fifteen years after his death. Throughout the 1840s Lippard railed against this notorious situation as a symbol of the indifference of the privileged classes to the poor; the school eventually opened in 1848.

53. Lippard, *The Quaker City*, 269.

54. Arens, 370. Here "prophetic" does not relate to predicting the future, though Lippard is also fascinated with prophesying in that sense, as evident in the astrologer's fortune-telling, the prophecy of greatness that Dora heard as a child, Lorrimer's vision of his death on the water, and Devil-Bug's elaborate vision.

55. Lippard, *The Quaker City*, 270. This is the sort of passage that prompted a burlesque of

Lippard in the *Mechanic's Advocate:* "He stood upon the field of blood! Ha! ha! Upon the field of blood stood he! [. . .] He was a perfect picture as he uplifted his right arm in the light of the big round moon—Ha! ha! Ho!! Ho!! He!!! He!!!" (April 22, 1848), 156.

56. Lippard, *The Quaker City*, 270.

57. A version of "Adonai" titled "The Entranced, or the Wanderer of Eighteen Centuries" originally ran in the *Quaker City* under the column heading "Pulpit of the Poor" on December 30, 1848; January 6, 1849; January 13, 1849; February 10, 1849; and February 17, 1849; then without this heading on April 28, 1849, and May 19, 1849. On "Adonai," see Streeby, *American Sensations,* 44–52, as well as Streeby, "Haunted Houses: George Lippard, Nathaniel Hawthorne, and Middle-Class America," *Criticism* 38, no. 3 (1996): 452–58.

58. Lippard, *The Quaker City*, 447.

59. See Max Weber, *On Charisma and Institution Building: Selected Papers,* ed. S. N. Eisenstadt (Chicago: University of Chicago Press, 1968), 18–27.

60. Lippard, *The Quaker City*, 448.

61. Ibid., 425, 422. For a more sympathetic reading of Ravoni as a critique of anti-Mormon and anti-Catholic exposé literature, see Carl Ostrowski, "Inside the Temple of Ravoni: George Lippard's Anti-Exposé," *ESQ,* 55, no. 1 (2009): 1–26.

62. Lippard, *The Quaker City*, 448.

63. Ibid., 93–94.

64. Ibid., 135.

65. Mark 3:29; cf. Matt. 12:31–32.

66. Lippard, *The Quaker City*, 383.

67. Ibid., 384. George Lippard, Address to the Brotherhood of the Union, October 4, 1852, in Manuscript Volume 1 in the Brotherhood of the Union Papers, Library Company.

68. Lippard, *The Quaker City*, 413.

69. See Luke 12:48; Lippard, *The Quaker City*, 123.

70. Harriet Jacobs, *Incidents in the Life of a Slave Girl, Written by Herself,* enlarged ed., ed. Jean Fagan Yellin (Cambridge, MA: Harvard University Press, Belknap Press, 2009), 69.

71. Lippard, *The Quaker City*, 223–24.

72. Lippard, "Key to the Quaker City," 6, 10. The review was by I. R. Diller, publisher of *The Citizen Soldier.*

73. Lippard, *The Quaker City*, 2.

74. Ibid. Cf. Matt. 7:1–2.

75. *Memoirs of a Preacher* appeared in fourteen installments (though originally slated for eight) in the *Quaker City* from December 30, 1848 to May 12, 1849. It was published in May 1849 as two books: *Memoirs of a Preacher, A Revelation of the Church and the Home* (Philadelphia: Jos. Severns, 1849) and the "sequel" (or latter half of the story), *The Man with the Mask: A Sequel to The Memoirs of a Preacher, a Revelation of the Church and the Home* (Philadelphia: Jos. Severns and Company, [1849]). It was then reprinted as *Mysteries of the Pulpit: Or, a Revelation of the Church and the Home* (Philadelphia: E. E. Barclay, 1851) and again in a single volume, which included the entire two-part story, *Memoirs of a Preacher; or, Mysteries of the Pulpit* (Philadelphia: T. B. Peterson & Brothers, 1864). Subsequent citations are to the 1864 edition, unless otherwise noted.

76. George Lippard, Prologue to "Memoirs of a Preacher: A Revelation of the Church and the Home," *Quaker City* (December 30, 1848).

77. Lippard, *Memoirs of a Preacher,* 176.

78. See Butterfield, who links Jervis and Maffitt (306), and Gedge, who explores the "dangerously intimate" relationship of clergy and women in the nineteenth century and the complex power dynamics of clerical scandals (4).

79. *The Great Divorce Case! A Full and Impartial History of the Trial of the Petition of Mrs. Sarah M. Jarvis, for a Divorce from Her Husband, the Rev. Samuel F. Jarvis, D.D. L.L.D. Before a Committee of the Legislature of the State of Connecticut* (New York, 1839), 4, 8; Gedge, 51.

80. *Report of the Trial of Mr. John N. Maffitt, Before a Council of Ministers of the Methodist Episcopal Church, Convened in Boston, December 26, 1822* (Boston: True and Greene, 1823), 6, 12, 14.

81. Ibid., 15.

82. Moses Elsemore, *An Impartial Account of the Life of the Rev. John Newland Maffitt* (New York: John F. Feeks, 1848), 6, 10.

83. On Sprague, see John M. Mulder and Isabelle Stouffer, "William Buell Sprague: Patriarch of American Collectors," *American Presbyterians* 64, no. 1 (1986): 2–17.

84. Elsemore, 21. Elsemore is ambiguous about when the first wife died; the announcement of Maffitt's second wedding was circulating in the papers at "about the same time" (ibid., 15).

85. For a thorough account of the scandal surrounding Maffitt's second marriage, see Elsemore, 14–31. On the debate over the causes of Maffitt's death, see Rufus F. Hibbard, *Startling Disclosures Concerning the Death of John N. Maffitt* (New York: M. B. Wynkoop, Book, & Job, 1856).

86. [George Lippard], "The Memoirs of a Preacher," *Quaker City,* March 10, 1849.

87. Ibid., June 2, 1849.

88. [George Lippard], "Rev. J. N. Maffitt," *Citizen Soldier* (May 31, 1843), 106.

89. Elsemore, 11; Lippard, *Memoirs of a Preacher,* 47, 49.

90. Lippard, *Memoirs of a Preacher,* 48.

91. Ibid., 25–26. On the association of sermons with the rhetoric of the sublime, see Dawn Coleman, "The Antebellum American Sermon as Lived Religion," in *A New History of the Sermon: The Nineteenth Century,* ed. Robert H. Ellison (Leiden: Brill, 2010), 532–36.

92. Lippard, *Memoirs of a Preacher,* 47, 26.

93. Ibid., 52.

94. Ibid., 58.

95. Lippard, *The Quaker City,* 263.

96. Lippard, *Memoirs of a Preacher,* 46.

97. Ibid., 59.

98. [George Lippard], "A Quire of Writing Paper, a Bottle of Ink, and a Steel Pen," *Quaker City,* January 27, 1849.

99. Ibid., 123. This chapter revises and expands an editor's column Lippard had written six years earlier for the October 4, 1843 issue of the *Citizen Soldier.*

100. George Lippard, "Valedictory of the Industrial Congress," *The Nineteenth Century* 1, no. 2 (1848): 186–89.

101. Lippard, *Memoirs of a Preacher,* 123–25.

102. Lippard, *Memoirs of a Preacher,* 125. Lippard, "Valedictory," 188.

103. Lippard, *Memoirs of a Preacher,* 124.

104. Ibid., 124–25.

105. On Methodist preachers' vivid descriptions of heaven and hell, see Coleman, "Antebellum American Sermon," 536–38.

106. George Lippard, "Twenty-Three Thoughts," *Quaker City,* May 12, 1849.

107. Joseph Jackson, "George Lippard: Misunderstood Man of Letters," *Pennsylvania Magazine of History and Biography* 59 (1935): 387.

108. Bouton, *Life and Choice Writings,* 73–74.

109. [George Lippard], "H. F.," *The White Banner* (1851): 3.

110. Ziff discusses Lippard's fascination with the Illuminati (105–7).

111. [George Lippard], "To the Men Who Work—Another Word," *Quaker City,* September 29, 1849.

112. On the links between the Brotherhood and later labor organizations, see Reynolds, *Prophet of Protest,* 38–41 and McKanan, 117.

113. See Reynolds on how *The Scarlet Letter* seems to borrow from Lippard's *The Quaker City* (*Beneath the American Renaissance,* 265–68).

Chapter 4

1. Rose Hawthorne Lathrop, *Memories of Hawthorne* (Boston: Houghton, Mifflin, 1897), 453–54.

2. Nathaniel Hawthorne, *Our Old Home: A Series of English Sketches,* vol. 5 of *The Centenary Edition of Nathaniel Hawthorne,* ed. Thomas Woodson (Columbus: The Ohio State University Press, 1970), 28.

3. Margaret B. Moore, *The Salem World of Nathaniel Hawthorne* (Columbia: University of Missouri Press, 1998), 104.

4. Charles W. Upham, "John Prince," *American Unitarian Biography: Memoirs of Individuals Who Have Been Distinguished by Their Writings, Character, and Efforts in the Cause of Liberal Christianity,* vol. 1, ed. William Ware (Boston and Cambridge: James Munroe, 1850), 101–16.

5. For more on the churchgoing habits of the Manning family and the religious milieu of Salem during Hawthorne's lifetime, see M. Moore, 102–22.

6. Hawthorne, "The Spectator," *Miscellaneous Prose and Verse,* vol. 23 of *The Centenary Edition of Nathaniel Hawthorne,* ed. Thomas Woodson, Claude M. Simpson, and L. Neal Smith (Columbus: The Ohio State University Press, 1994), 21.

7. Hawthorne, *Miscellaneous Prose,* 31.

8. Nathaniel Hawthorne to Elizabeth M. Hathorne, October 28, 1821, in *The Letters, 1813–1843,* vol. 15 of *The Centenary Edition of Nathaniel Hawthorne,* ed. Thomas Woodson, L. Neal Smith, and Norman Holmes Pearson (Columbus: The Ohio State University Press, 1984), 159.

9. Nathaniel Hawthorne to Elizabeth C. Hathorne, March 7, 1820 (*Letters, 1813–1843,* 117).

10. Nathaniel Hawthorne to Elizabeth C. Hathorne, March 13, 1821 (*Letters, 1813–1843,* 138).

11. Nathaniel Hawthorne, August 16, [1842], *The American Notebooks,* vol. 8 of *The Centenary Edition of Nathaniel Hawthorne,* ed. Claude M. Simpson (Columbus: The Ohio State University Press, 1972), 339.

12. Nathaniel Hawthorne to Sophia Peabody, March 15, 1830, and March 30, 1840 (*The Letters, 1813–1843,* 420–21, 430–31).

13. [James T. Fields], From "Our Whispering Gallery," *Atlantic Monthly* 27 (February–May 1871), in *Hawthorne in His Own Time: A Biographical Chronicle of His Life, Drawn from Recollections, Interviews, and Memoirs by Family, Friends, and Associates,* ed. Ronald A. Bosco and Jillmarie Murphy (Iowa City: University of Iowa Press, 2007), 140. Julian Hawthorne, *Hawthorne Reading: An Essay* (Cleveland, OH: The Rowfant Club, 1902), 65, 110–11.

14. Nathaniel Hawthorne, *Mosses from an Old Manse,* vol. 10 of *The Centenary Edition of Nathaniel Hawthorne,* ed. William Charvat, Roy Harvey Pearce, and Claude M. Simpson

(Columbus: The Ohio State University Press, 1974), 215. Cf. Buell, who reads the preacher along similar lines (*Literary Transcendentalism*, 102).

15. Hawthorne, *Mosses from an Old Manse,* 416. G. R. Thompson maintains that Hawthorne in "Passages" used the Story Teller's art to parody "slap-dash writers" and to comment ironically on his own attempts to create unified stories (*The Art of Authorial Presence: Hawthorne's Provincial Tales* [Durham: Duke University Press, 1993], 224–25).

16. Hawthorne, *Mosses,* 416, 420.

17. Ibid., 421.

18. Henry James, *The American* (1877; New York: Oxford University Press, 1999), 77.

19. Hawthorne, *Mosses from an Old Manse,* 4, 3, 5.

20. For a more detailed version of this argument, see Dawn Coleman, "Critiquing Perfection: Hawthorne's Revision of Salem's Unitarian Saint," *Nathaniel Hawthorne Review* 37, no. 1 (2011): 1–19. As I read it, Dimmesdale bears more similarities to Abbot than to any previously identified individual. Richard Kopley notes that scholars have found precedent for Dimmesdale in John Cotton, Michael Wigglesworth, Hawthorne's incestuous ancestor Nathaniel Manning, and Lockhart's *Adam Blair;* Kopley also shows Hawthorne's indebtedness to James Russell Lowell's poem "A Legend of Brittany" for the description of Dimmesdale's voice during the Election Sermon (*The Threads of* The Scarlet Letter: *A Study of Hawthorne's Transformative Art* [Newark: University of Delaware Press, 2003]). Dimmesdale has also been read as a satire of Charles Wentworth Upham (James R. Mellow, *Nathaniel Hawthorne in His Times* [Boston: Houghton Mifflin Company, 1980], 300–302, 307) and as a rewriting of Stephen Batchellor, a Puritan minister and would-be adulterer (Frederick Newberry, "A Red-Hot A and a Lusting Divine: Sources for *The Scarlet Letter,*" *New England Quarterly* 60, no. 2 [1987]: 256–64).

21. See Michael Colacurcio on the scholarly tendency to downplay Hawthorne's engagement with Unitarianism (*The Province of Piety: Moral History in Hawthorne's Early Tales* [Cambridge, MA: Harvard University Press, 1984], 22–23).

22. William Ellery Channing, *A Sermon, Delivered at the Ordination of the Rev. John Emery Abbot* (Salem, MA: Cushing, 1815), 14.

23. No copy of the consolation sermon survives, but see Elizabeth Palmer Peabody, *Reminiscences of Rev. Wm. Ellery Channing, D.D.* (Boston: Roberts Brothers, 1880), 19.

24. "The Phillipses and the Abbots," rept. from the *Salem Gazette; The Massachusetts Teacher* 2, no. 12 (1849): 366.

25. *A Catalogue of the Members of the North Church in Salem, with an Historical Sketch of the Church* (Salem: W. and S. B. Ives, 1827), 29, 32, 36.

26. Megan Marshall, *The Peabody Sisters: Three Women Who Ignited American Romanticism* (Boston: Houghton Mifflin Company, 2005), 79, 97.

27. Peabody, 19.

28. Howe, 17.

29. Henry Ware, Jr., *Memoir,* in John Emery Abbot, *Extracts from Sermons by the Late Rev. John Emery Abbot, of Salem, Mass. With a Memoir of His Life, by Henry Ware, Jr.,* ed. Henry Ware, Jr. (Boston: Wait, Greene, & Co., 1830), x. Hawthorne, *The Scarlet Letter,* 120.

30. Ware, *Memoir,* xi. Hawthorne, *The Scarlet Letter,* 123.

31. "Elegiac Stanzas," line 8. Hawthorne, *The Scarlet Letter,* 120.

32. Hawthorne, *The Scarlet Letter,* 142. Francis Parkman, "Review of *Eighteen Sermons and a Charge* and *Sermons by the Late Rev. John Abbot, with a Memoir of His Life,*" in *Christian Examiner and General Review* 6, no. 33, new series 3 (July 1829): 286.

33. Parkman, "Review," 283; cf. Genesis 5:24. "Elegiac Stanzas," lines 87–88.

34. Hawthorne, *The Scarlet Letter,* 249, 251.

35. Roberta Weldon also notes how the public perception that Dimmesdale's illness is connected to his saintliness mirrors conventions of nineteenth-century ministerial biography (*Hawthorne, Gender, and Death: Christianity and Its Discontents* [New York: Palgrave Macmillan, 2008], 15).

36. Ware, *Memoir,* xv. Edmund B. Willson, "Memorial Sermon," *The First Centenary of the North Church and Society in Salem, Massachusetts* (Salem: North Church and Society, 1873), 50.

37. Hawthorne, *The Scarlet Letter,* 120.

38. Parkman, "Review," 283.

39. Ware, Memoir, xxiii. Hawthorne, *The Scarlet Letter,* 66.

40. Ware, *Memoir,* x, xii.

41. Hawthorne, *The Scarlet Letter,* 120, 215.

42. "Elegiac Stanzas (On the Death of John Emery Abbot)," (Salem: n. p., 1819), lines 15, 60.

43. Ware, *Memoir,* xvi.

44. Hawthorne, *The Scarlet Letter,* 219.

45. Edward B. Hall, *Memoir of Mary L. Ware, Wife of Henry Ware, Jr.* (Boston: Crosby, Nichols, & Co., 1853), 74–76.

46. Nina Baym details Dimmesdale's divergences from Puritan theology, associating him instead with "nineteenth-century sentimental piety" ("Passion and Authority in *The Scarlet Letter,*" *The New England Quarterly* 43.2 [1970]: 212–13). See Howe for a discussion of Abbot's "religion of the heart," which, in line with the Harvard moral philosophy he had learned while reading divinity in Cambridge between 1810 and 1815, regarded devotional piety and benevolence as different manifestations of the same emotion (153–55; 309).

47. John Emery Abbot, *Sermons of the Late Rev. John Emery Abbot, of Salem, Mass. with a Memoir of His Life, by Henry Ware, Jr.,* ed. Henry Ware, Jr. (Boston: Wait, Greene, & Co., 1829), 221, 213. Hawthorne may also have known "Knowledge of One Another in a Future State" through a reprinted excerpt in Charles Fox and Samuel Osgood's *The New Hampshire Book: Being Specimens of Literature from the Granite State* (Nahsua: David Marshall; Boston: James Monroe and Company, 1842), 129–31.

48. John Emery Abbot, *A Catechism of the New Testament* (Salem, MA: T. C. Cushing, 1817).

49. Hawthorne, *The Scarlet Letter,* 203.

50. Ibid., 220.

51. Ibid., 171.

52. See Will and Mimosa Stephenson for evidence that Hawthorne read *Adam Blair* ("*Adam Blair* and *The Scarlet Letter,*" *Nathaniel Hawthorne Review* 19, no. 2 [1993]: 1–10). Henry James emphasized those qualities in Hawthorne that made him less popular than Lockhart, including his muted depiction of illicit passion (*Hawthorne: A Biography* [1879; Ithaca, NY: Cornell University Press, 1997], 90–96).

53. J. G. Lockhart, *Some Passages in the Life of Mr. Adam Blair, Minister of the Gospel at Cross-Meikle* (Edinburgh: Edinburgh University Press, 1963), 221.

54. Hawthorne, *The Scarlet Letter,* 257, 254. On the grammatical shift in Dimmesdale's confession, see Michael Gilmore, *Surface and Depth: The Quest for Legibility in American Culture* (Oxford: Oxford University Press, 2003), 84–85.

55. Hawthorne, *The Scarlet Letter,* 250.

56. Ibid., 249. Dimmesdale supposedly preaches in 1649. The election sermon preached that year, Thomas Cobbett's to mark the election of Governor John Endicott, is not extant and

was probably never printed (M. X. Lesser, "Dimmesdale's Wordless Sermon," *American Notes and Queries* 12, no. 5 [1974]: 93–94).

57. Ezra Stiles, *The United States Elevated to Glory and Honour . . . .* , 2nd ed. (Worcester, MA: Isaiah Thomas, 1785), 8–9.

58. Henry Nash Smith, *Democracy and the Novel: Popular Resistance to Classic American Writers* (New York: Oxford University Press, 1978), 29. See also Michael Davitt Bell, *Hawthorne and the Historical Romance of New England* (Princeton: Princeton University Press, 1971), 142.

59. See Coleman, "Antebellum American Sermon," 532–36.

60. Hawthorne, *The Scarlet Letter,* 243, 248. Cf. Immanuel Kant's association of the sublime with "the lofty waterfall of a might river" and "the ocean in a state of tumult" (*The Critique of Judgment,* trans. J. H. Bernard [New York: Hafner, 1951], 100).

61. Kant, 82.

62. Hawthorne, *The Scarlet Letter,* 243.

63. Ibid., 248.

64. Coleman, "Antebellum American Sermon," 529–31, 537.

65. Hawthorne, *The Scarlet Letter,* 249. Reference to Dimmesdale's Election Sermon as inspired plays with the fact that the public celebration around Election Day was an adaptation of the English festivities surrounding Whitsuntide, or Pentecost, the day commemorating the descent of the Holy Ghost upon the apostles and the gift of tongues. See Frederick Newberry, *Hawthorne's Divided Loyalties: England and America in His Works* (Cranbury, NJ: Associated University Press, 1987), 186–93.

66. See Thomas Weiskel, *The Romantic Sublime: Studies in the Structure and Psychology of Transcendence* (Baltimore: The Johns Hopkins University Press, 1976).

67. On the Election Sermon as Dimmesdale's conversion of "sexual energy into imaginative expression," see Joel Porte, *The Romance in America: Studies in Cooper, Poe, Hawthorne, Melville, and James* (Middletown: Wesleyan University Press, 1969), 108–112. In my reading, Dimmesdale's libido plays itself out in the writing of the sermon, with the sexual imagery giving way to a language of pain in the description of the sermon's delivery.

68. Griffin, *A Sermon on the Art of Preaching,* 11; Dewey, *On the Preaching of Our Saviour,* 30.

69. Hawthorne, *The Scarlet Letter,* 141.

70. Ibid., 243, 249.

71. Ibid., 249. On Dimmesdale's pain as sublimated sexual guilt, see Frederick Crews, *Sins of the Fathers: Hawthorne's Psychological Themes* (New York: Oxford University Press, 1966), 147–48.

72. Coleman, "Antebellum American Sermon," 540–41.

73. Hawthorne, *The Scarlet Letter,* 244.

74. See Jerome McGann, who points to Romantic agony as the overlooked dark side of the Romantic conception of the imagination (*The Romantic Ideology: The Critical Investigation* [Chicago: University of Chicago Press, 1983], 131). On the centrality of pain to the Romantics, see Steven Bruhm, *Gothic Bodies: The Politics of Pain in Romantic Fiction* (Philadelphia: University of Pennsylvania Press, 1994), 1–29. Hawthorne's inspiration to treat a sermon as a pained Romantic utterance may have been Charlotte Brontë's *Jane Eyre,* another novel that exploits the discrepancy between the moral rigidity of Calvinism and the human frailty of Calvinist preachers. As Jane deliberates over whether to marry St. John Rivers, she hears him preach a magnificent sermon that seems to issue from a troubled inner life: "[I]t seemed to me—I know not whether equally so to others—that the eloquence to which I had been listening had sprung from a depth where lay turbid dregs of disappointment—where moved trou-

bling impulses of insatiate yearnings and disquieting aspirations" ([1847; New York: Knopf, 1991], 2:149–50). Both novels show a minister preaching well because he harbors painful, un-Christian secrets, with his sermon a cryptic message to a romantically invested woman.

75. Spring, *The Power of Preaching*, 304.

76. Hawthorne, *The Scarlet Letter*, 142.

77. See Amory Dwight Mayo, "The Works of Nathaniel Hawthorne," *Universalist Quarterly* 8 (July 1851): 285–90, in *The Critical Response to Nathaniel Hawthorne's* The Scarlet Letter, ed. Gary Scharnhorst (Westport, CT: Greenwood, 1992), 46.

78. Hawthorne, *Our Old Home*, 29–30.

79. Hawthorne, *The Scarlet Letter*, 191, 195.

80. Ibid., 95.

81. Hawthorne, *The Letters, 1843–1853*, 322. On the novel's composition, see Mellow, 309–12.

82. Nathaniel Hawthorne, *The English Note-Books, 1853–1856* (Columbus: The Ohio State University Press, 1997), 340.

83. Hawthorne, *The Scarlet Letter*, 4.

84. Michael T. Gilmore, *American Romanticism and the Marketplace* (Chicago: University of Chicago Press, 1985), 82; cf. Gilmore, *Surface and Depth*, 86.

85. Hawthorne, *The Scarlet Letter*, 3–4.

86. [Caleb Foote], "*The Scarlet Letter*," *Salem Gazette*, March 19, 1850, in *Nathaniel Hawthorne: The Contemporary Reviews*, ed. John L. Idol, Jr. and Buford Jones (Cambridge, UK: Cambridge University Press, 1994), 119.

87. Hawthorne, *The Letters, 1843–1853*, vol. 16 of *The Centenary Edition of Nathaniel Hawthorne*, ed. Thomas Woodson, L. Neal Smith, and Norman Holmes Pearson (Columbus: The Ohio State University Press, 1985), 324–25 and 307.

88. See Baym, *Novels, Readers, and Reviewers*, 144–46.

89. [Edwin Percy Whipple], "Review of New Books," *Graham's Magazine*, 36, no. 5 (May 1850): 345–46, in Idol and Jones, 124.

90. Burke, 84. Hawthorne, *The Scarlet Letter*, 250.

91. Cf. Railton, who argues that the Puritans applaud the sermon because it tells them what they want to hear and that Dimmesdale's penchant for pleasing the crowd is Hawthorne's commentary on how authors must pander to succeed with the public (127–28). I would contend that the listeners are described as responding not to Dimmesdale's message, but to his pain-fueled eloquence.

92. On Hester as a representation of artisanal labor, see Michael Newbury, *Figuring Authorship in Antebellum America* (Stanford, CA: Stanford University Press, 1997), 45–51.

93. Herman Melville, "Hawthorne and His Mosses," *The Piazza Tales and Other Prose Pieces, 1839–1860*, vol. 14 of *The Writings of Herman Melville*, ed. Harrison Hayford, Alma A. MacDougall, and G. Thomas Tanselle (Evanston and Chicago: Northwestern University Press and The Newberry Library, 1987), 252. Anthony Trollope, "The Genius of Nathaniel Hawthorne," *North American Review* 274 (1879): 207.

94. Hawthorne, *The Scarlet Letter*, 260.

95. Ibid.

96. Sacvan Bercovitch, *The Office of the Scarlet Letter* (Baltimore: The Johns Hopkins University Press, 1991), 13.

97. [Arthur Cleveland Coxe], "The Writings of Hawthorne," *Church Review and Ecclesiastical Register* 3, no. 4 (January 1851), in Idol and Jones, 151.

98. Dorothy Hale, "Fiction as Restriction: Self-Binding in New Ethical Theories of the Novel," *Narrative* 15, no. 2 (2007): 189.

99. Gordon Hutner, *Secrets and Sympathy: Forms of Disclosure in Hawthorne's Novels* (Athens: University of Georgia Press, 1988), 58–59.

100. Hawthorne, August 30, [1842], *The American Notebooks,* 352.

101. Hawthorne, *The Scarlet Letter,* 263.

Chapter 5

1. Orville Dewey, *On Reading. A Lecture Delivered Before the Mechanics' Library Association in New York* (Cambridge, MA: Metcalf, Torry, and Ballou, 1839).

2. Hershel Parker, *Herman Melville: A Biography; Volume 1, 1819–1851* (Baltimore: The Johns Hopkins University Press, 1996), 65–67, 467–70, 549.

3. Douglas, 21.

4. See *The Works of Orville Dewey, D.D., With a Biographical Sketch* (Boston: American Unitarian Association, 1883); for Dewey's views on slavery, see "The Slavery Question" (ibid., 326–34).

5. Melville, *The Piazza Tales,* 250.

6. Dewey, *On Reading,* 9–11.

7. Melville, *Moby-Dick,* 209.

8. Herman Melville to Nathaniel Hawthorne, June [1?], 1851, in Herman Melville, *Correspondence,* ed. Lynn Horth, vol. 14 of *The Writings of Herman Melville* (Evanston and Chicago: Northwestern University Press and The Newberry Library, 1993), 191.

9. Nathalia Wright, *Melville's Use of the Bible* (1949; New York: Farrar, Straus, and Giroux, 1980), 9.

10. Isaac Riley, "Historical Discourse," *Jubilee: The Fiftieth Anniversary of the Organization of the Thirty-Fourth Street Reformed Church of New York City, December 14–21, 1873* (New York: The Consistory, 1874), 23.

11. On Allan Melvill's churchgoing, including its possible business advantages, see Emory Elliot, "'Wandering To-and-Fro': Melville and Religion," *A Historical Guide to Herman Melville,* ed. Giles Gunn (New York: Oxford University Press, 2005), 173. T. Walter Herbert, Jr. explains how Allan Melvill's Unitarian beliefs fed an unwarranted faith that his business ventures would succeed (Moby-Dick *and Calvinism: A World Dismantled* [New Brunswick, NJ: Rutgers University Press, 1977], 45–56).

12. See Riley, 19–23.

13. Herman Melville to John R. Brodhead, December 30, 1846, in Melville, *Correspondence,* 70. For an account of Melville and Brodhead's business dealings, see H. Parker, 1:481–84.

14. [George Bethune], "Jacob Brodhead, D.D.," in Sprague, *Annals,* 9:154.

15. John Gosman to William B. Sprague, January 16, 1863, in Sprague, *Annals,* 9:155.

16. "Jacob Brodhead, D.D.," in Sprague, *Annals,* 9:152–60.

17. John T. Frederick, *The Darkened Sky: Nineteenth-Century American Novelists and Religion* (Notre Dame, IN: University of Notre Dame Press, 1969), 81.

18. Edwin Tanjore Conwin, qtd. in Frederick, 81.

19. William Buell Sprague, *A Sermon Preached in the Second Presbyterian Church, Albany, Sunday Afternoon, September 1857* . . . (Albany, NY: Van Benthuysen, 1857), 23, 26.

20. Herman Melville, *Typee: A Peep at Polynesian Life,* ed. John Bryant (New York: Penguin, 1996), 6–7.

21. Ibid., 26–27.

22. Ibid., 124–26.

23. Ibid., 195–99.

24. Herman Melville, *Redburn: His First Voyage; Being the Sailor-Boy Confessions and Reminiscences of the Son-of-a-Gentleman, in the Merchant Service,* vol. 4 of *The Writings of Herman Melville,* ed. Harrison Hayford, Hershel Parker, and G. Thomas Tanselle (Evanston and Chicago: Northwestern University Press and The Newberry Library, 1969), 176.

25. See William Braswell, who discusses this moment and others in *Redburn* as examples of how Melville argued for charity by "address[ing] his Christian readers in their own terms" (*Melville's Religious Thought: An Essay in Interpretation* [New York: Pageant Books, 1959], 42–43).

26. Melville, *White-Jacket: or The World in a Man-of-War,* vol. 5 of *The Writings of Herman Melville,* ed. Harrison Hayford, Hershel Parker, and G. Thomas Tanselle (Evanston and Chicago: Northwestern University Press and The Newberry Library, 1970), 155, 156, 158.

27. Melville, *Moby-Dick,* xviii, 4, 19, 88.

28. Ibid., 74.

29. Ibid., 37, 107, 159, 274, 307, 424–25.

30. Robert Milder, *Exiled Royalties: Melville and the Life We Imagine* (New York: Oxford University Press, 2006), 93. See also Leon Chai, who discusses how Schlegelian and Kierkegaardian ironies inform "The Mast-head" (*The Romantic Foundations of the American Renaissance* [Ithaca, NY: Cornell University Press, 1987], 319–20).

31. Anne Mellor, *English Romantic Irony* (Cambridge, MA: Harvard University Press, 1980), 12, 14.

32. Milder, 93–94. Cf. John Bryant, who argues that Ishmael's frustration with the mind's inconclusive encounters with reality produces a narrative voice defined by a "genial desperation" that "captures the rhythmic pulses of aesthetic failure *and* success" (*Melville and Repose: The Rhetoric of Humor in the American Renaissance* [New York: Oxford University Press, 1993], 199).

33. Melville, *Moby-Dick,* 424, 274. Cf. Robert Alter, who notes Ishmael's penchant for "manifestly subversive, un-Christian homilies," citing by way of example the "Consider this" sermon at the end of "Brit" (*Pen of Iron: American Prose and the King James Bible* [Princeton: Princeton University Press, 2010], 55–56).

34. Melville, *Moby-Dick,* 112, 36–37.

35. Walter E. Bezanson, "*Moby-Dick*: Work of Art," in *The Critical Response to Herman Melville's Moby-Dick,* ed. Kevin J. Hayes (Westport, CT: Greenwood, 1994), 93. Though Bezanson does not mention the "proofs" section of Puritan sermons, one might take them as included under "doctrine." On "The Line" as sermon, see also Mary K. Bercaw Edwards, *Cannibal Old Me: Spoken Sources in Melville's Early Works* (Kent, OH: Kent State University Press, 2009), 181–82.

36. Melville, *Moby-Dick,* 50, 115.

37. Ibid., 335.

38. Ibid., 37, 107, 425. On the Platonism of Ishmael's meditation in the Whaleman's Chapel, see John Wenke, *Melville's Muse: Literary Creation and the Forms of Philosophical Fiction* (Kent, OH: Kent State University Press, 1995), 124–25.

39. Melville, *Moby-Dick,* 6.

40. William Braswell, "Melville's Use of Seneca," *American Literature* 12 (1940): 98.

41. Roger L'Estrange, trans. and ed., *Seneca's Morals, By Way of Abstract, To Which Is Added a Discourse Under the Title of an After-Thought* (Philadelphia: Grigg and Elliot, 1834), 93.

42. Melville, *Moby-Dick,* 107.

43. L'Estrange, ix.

44. Melville, *Moby-Dick,* 37. L'Estrange, 156–57.

45. L'Estrange, 102.

46. Melville, *Moby-Dick,* 307.

47. Hawthorne, *The House of the Seven Gables,* 2.

48. Bellows, *Re-Statements of Christian Doctrine,* 64. Cf. Michael Kearns, who writes that Ishmael seems to believe "that his task is to bring readers to the point of contemplation but not to direct them through that activity" and that he varies his rhetorical intensity to open up spaces for response ("Morality and Rhetoric in *Moby-Dick,*" in *"Ungraspable Phantom": Essays on* Moby-Dick, ed. John Bryant, Mary K. Bercaw Edwards, and Timothy Marr [Kent, OH: Kent State University Press, 2006], 154–55).

49. From 1855 to 1975, the church was called All Souls. See Hershel Parker, *Herman Melville: A Biography; Volume 2, 1851–1891* (Baltimore: The Johns Hopkins University Press, 2002), 66. Elizabeth and perhaps Herman returned to the church in 1865 when they moved back to New York from Pittsfield (ibid., 586).

50. Rath, x.

51. Melville, *The Piazza Tales,* 307.

52. Melville, *Moby-Dick,* 39–40. In outfitting the Whaleman's Chapel, Melville borrowed the marble cenotaphs from the New Bedford Seamen's Bethel, which he visited with his brother Gansevoort in 1841 shortly before setting sail on the *Acushnet.* From Taylor's church in Boston, which he may have visited in 1849, he took the idea for a raised pulpit and an oil painting of a ship in a storm with an angel overhead (H. Parker, 1:184, 614).

53. See Charles Dickens, *Great Expectations,* ed. Margaret Cardwell (1861; Oxford: Oxford University Press, Clarendon Press, 1993), 206–9.

54. Whitman, *Prose Works 1892,* 549; Ralph Waldo Emerson, *The Journals and Miscellaneous Notebooks of Ralph Waldo Emerson,* vol. 5, 1835–1838, ed. William Gilman et al. (Cambridge, MA: Harvard University Press, Belknap Press, 1965), 5.

55. H. Parker, 1:614.

56. Gilbert Haven and Thomas Russell, *Incidents and Anecdotes of Rev. Edward T. Taylor* (Boston: B. B. Russell, 1873), 18. Melville, *Moby-Dick,* 43, 45.

57. Harriet Martineau, *Retrospect of Western Travel,* 3 vols. (London: Saunders and Otley, 1838), 3:249.

58. Melville to Hawthorne, November [17?], 1851, in Melville, *Correspondence,* 212.

59. William Spanos's reading of Mapple's pulpit as a Panoptic watchtower from which the preacher surveys his working-class hearers ignores how little attention Mapple pays to the congregation once he begins to speak (*The Errant Art of* Moby-Dick: *The Canon, the Cold War, and the Struggle for American Studies* [Durham, NC: Duke University Press, 1995], 93).

60. Mark Trafton, qtd. in *Life of Father Taylor: The Sailor Preacher* (Boston: Boston Port and Seamen's Aid Society, 1904), lxxvii.

61. Emerson, *Journals and Miscellaneous Notebooks,* 5.

62. "The Sailor Preacher at Boston," *The Sailor's Magazine and Naval Journal,* rpt. from the *Western Monthly Magazine* (November 1833): 73.

63. Melville, *Moby-Dick,* 47.

64. E. Channing, 139.

65. Here I would like to correct a point in Reynolds's *Beneath the American Renaissance* that has gained currency among scholars. Reynolds has written that slangy retellings of the Jonah story made up "a whole genre of popular antebellum sermons" contributed to the *Sailor's Magazine and Naval Journal* by popular preachers from 1829 on and that these col-

loquial sermons "directly anticipated Father Mapple's salty sermon" (29). However, his main example of American folk preaching, "six separate Jonah sermons" from the 1839–40 volume of the *Sailor's Magazine,* is not from an antebellum sermon but from a reprint of the London sailor-preacher John Newton's 1806 paraphrased republishing of a 1675 booklet of sermons on the book of Jonah written by John Ryther (1634?–1681), a nonconformist minister in Wapping, England. John Newton (1725–1807), rector at St. Mary Woolnoth, London, (and author of the hymn "Amazing Grace") published his "revised and corrected" version of Ryther's *A Plat for Mariners, or, The Seaman's Preacher: Delivered in Several Sermons upon Jonah's Voyage* (London, 1675) under the title *The Seaman's Preacher, Consisting of Nine Short and Plain Discourses on Jonah's Voyage Addressed to Mariners* (Cambridge, MA: Hilliard, 1806). Leaving Ryther's language and theology largely unchanged, Newton divided the original five discourses into nine and edited them to correct typographical mistakes and omit "many repetitions and redundancies" (*The Seaman's Preacher,* vii). The *Sailor's Magazine* published Newton's redaction from November 1839 through April 1840, then from October 1840 to December 1840. The magazine did not credit Newton or alert the reader that the original sermon was from the seventeenth century. Nor do Jonah sermons seem to be a popular subgenre of folk sermon in antebellum America, at least judging from the pages of the *Sailor's Magazine.* Only three Jonah sermons appeared there between the magazine's inception in 1829 and *Moby-Dick*'s publication in 1851. Two, printed in December 1828 and December 1830, were original; the third, appearing in November 1839, is another paraphrased excerpt from Ryther, with further modernizations and abridgments. None sounds much like Mapple, though Curtis Dahl has teased out a few similarities ("Jonah Improved: Sea Sermons on Jonah," *Extracts* 19 [1974]: 6–9). The "Worship at Sea" column that Reynolds cites as the forum for Jonah sermons ran regularly only in the first year of the journal's publication, dropping off altogether after 1833.

66. These articles ran in January 1831 (142–43), February 1831 (167–68), and April 1831 (232–33). When the topic was revisited sixteen years later in "Preaching to Seamen: The Matter and Manner" in the March and April 1847 issues, preachers were still discouraged from using the "peculiar terms and phrases of seamen"; the style should instead be "plain and simple, solemn and impressive" ([April 1847]: 226).

67. *The Sailor's Magazine and Naval Journal* (March 1847): 193–95.

68. See, for instance, Giorgio Mariani, "'Chiefly Known by His Rod': The Book of Jonah, Mapple's Sermon, and Scapegoating," in *"Ungraspable Phantom": Essays on* Moby-Dick, ed. John Bryant, Mary K. Bercaw Edwards, and Timothy Marr (Kent, OH: Kent State University Press, 2006), 37–57; Christopher Sten, *The Weaver-God, He Weaves: Melville and the Poetics of the Novel* (Kent, OH: Kent State University Press, 1996), 144–48; Jay Holstein, "Melville's Inversion of Jonah in *Moby-Dick,*" *The Iliff Review* 42, no. 1 (1985): 13–20; Daniel Hoffman, "*Moby-Dick:* Jonah's Whale or Job's?," *Sewanee Review* 69 (1961): 205–224. See also Pardes on Melville's engagement with biblical scholarship on Jonah (46–72).

69. Melville, *Moby-Dick,* 414. Bryan Short, "Multitudinous, God-omnipresent, Coral Insects: Pip, Isabel, and Melville's Miltonic Sublime," *Leviathan: A Journal of Melville Studies* 4, no. 1 (2002): 7–28, an essay included in *Melville and Milton: An Edition and Analysis of Melville's Annotations on Milton,* ed. Robin Grey (Pittsburgh, PA: Duquesne University Press, 2004), 3–24. On the sublime in *Moby-Dick,* see also Nancy Fredricks, *Melville's Art of Democracy* (Athens: University of Georgia Press, 1995), 27–41.

70. Melville, *Moby-Dick,* 42.

71. Jonah 1:4; Melville, *Moby-Dick,* 45–46.

72. Melville, *Moby-Dick,* 45. Jonah 1:6.

73. Melville, *Moby-Dick,* 44, 47.

74. E. M. Forster, *Aspects of the Novel* (1927; New York: Harcourt, 1955), 139. In highlighting how Mapple's sermon departs from Christian norms, I differ from critics who have seen Mapple as articulating Protestant ideas that Melville challenges in the rest of the novel. See, for instance, L. Thompson, 162–66, and Spanos, 83–114.

75. Jonah 1:2. Melville, *Moby-Dick*, 48.

76. Melville, *Moby-Dick*, 43, 46.

77. James J. Farrell, *Inventing the American Way of Death, 1830–1920* (Philadelphia: Temple University Press, 1980), 33.

78. Melville, *Moby-Dick*, 43, 46, 44.

79. Ibid., 43–46.

80. Ibid., 45.

81. See Coleman, "Antebellum American Sermon," 532–36.

82. Melville, *Moby-Dick*, 47, 48. For the argument that Ishmael's worshipping with Queequeg is a rejection of Mapple's message, see L. Thompson, 163, and Gilmore, *Surface and Depth*, 94.

83. Short, 20.

84. A storm during a sermon was considered a great boon to a preacher. Nantucket Presbyterian minister John S. C. Abbott, who had undoubtedly preached in many a squall, wrote: "And should the wind, admonishing of the gathering storm, moan about the building, or the rain or sleet patter upon the glass, those pensive emotions are still more strongly awakened, which ever wing the soul to explore eternity" (11). Cf. Brooklyn Presbyterian minister Samuel H. Cox: "After Dr. [Joseph] Bellamy had preached once a sermon in a thunderstorm, and used the mingled electricities of the aerial and spiritual heavens, in harmonious bursts of glory around him, as he dared the infidel to contend with the Almighty, or awed the sinner to melt at his feet, while those grand tokens were gleaming and roaring all through nature as he preached, some deacon-like committee waited on him with a request that he would be sure to print it, for they never heard such a sermon in all their life as that: the Doctor replied 'Yes, if you will also print the thunder and lightning at the same time; since this it was that made it so powerful.' The occasion could never be repeated" (Samuel H. Cox to William Buell Sprague, March 29, 1859, in Sprague, *Annals*, 6:656).

85. Melville, *Moby-Dick*, 39, 48, 47.

86. The first record of Melville owning *The Scarlet Letter* is surprisingly late—July 1870 (Jay Leyda, *The Melville Log: A Documentary Life of Herman Melville, 1819–1891* [New York: Harcourt, 1951], 2:712).

87. Melville, *The Piazza Tales*, 249.

88. Richard Chase, *Herman Melville: A Critical Study* (New York: Macmillan, 1949), 91; Howard P. Vincent, *The Trying-Out of Moby-Dick*, 1949 (Kent, OH: Kent State University Press, 1980), 75.

89. Melville, *Moby-Dick*, 48.

90. Melville, *The Piazza Tales*, 249.

91. Richard H. Brodhead, *The School of Hawthorne* (New York: Oxford University Press, 1986), 24–28.

92. Melville to Hawthorne, June [1?], 1851, in Melville, *Correspondence*, 191.

93. Ibid. Cf. Carolyn L. Karcher, who in commenting on this letter to Hawthorne remarks, "Melville felt his own truth-telling mission to be akin to a clergyman's" (*Shadow Over the Promised Land: Slavery, Race, and Violence in Melville's America* [Baton Rouge: Louisiana State University Press, 1980], 78. She identifies this mission with Ishmael's warning to America to abandon slavery.

94. 1 Corinthians 9:16. Thomas McAuley, "The Faithful Preacher, and Wages of Unfaithfulness," *The American National Preacher* 12 (January 1838): 17.

95. Melville, *Moby-Dick,* 48. Wright notes that Mapple's "woes" echo Jeremiah and other biblical prophets and that the pairing of "woes" and "delights" mirrors the structure of the beatitudes in Luke (147–48).

96. Melville, *Moby-Dick,* 48.

97. Ibid.

98. Ibid., 414.

99. Ibid., 117.

100. William E. Channing, *The Works of William E. Channing, D.D.* (Boston: James Munroe, 1848), 254.

101. Herbert, Moby-Dick *and Calvinism,* 109–113; *The New-England Primer . . . ,* ed. Paul Leicester Ford (New York: Dodd, Mead, 1899), n.p. See also T. Walter Herbert, "Calvinist Earthquake: *Moby-Dick* and Religious Tradition," in *New Essays on Moby-Dick,* ed. Richard H. Brodhead (Cambridge, UK: Cambridge University Press, 1986), 109–40.

102. Henry W. Bellows, *Relation of Christianity to Human Nature . . .* (Boston: Wm. Crosby & H. P. Nichols, 1847), 16, 20–21.

103. Two other aspects of Bellows's *Relation of Christianity to Human Nature* suggest its influence on *Moby-Dick.* One, Bellows echoes yet transforms 1 Corinthians 9:27, where Paul declares that he brings his body under subjection lest "when I have preached to others, I myself should be a castaway." Anticipating Mapple, Bellows shifts the focus from temperance to defiance of public opinion: "And he who shapes his course to heaven by the way of the public good, may find that having saved others, he is himself a cast-away" (13). Bellows also describes a type of man much like Ahab, the "moral rebel" whose "native spirit of independence and personal sovereignty" lead him to deny God as the soul's ruler, to the point that he silences his conscience: "Alas! the impenitent are not self-condemned!" (14–15).

104. Melville, *The Piazza Tales,* 243.

105. See Howe, 53–64, 93–96, 166.

106. Jonah 1:3–5.

107. Melville, *Moby-Dick,* 45.

108. Ibid., 46.

109. Herbert, Moby-Dick *and Calvinism,* 112–13.

110. L'Estrange, xii; Walker Cowen, *Melville's Marginalia,* 2 vols. (New York: Garland, 1987), 2:335.

111. L'Estrange, xii; Melville, *Moby-Dick,* 46–47.

112. Melville, *Moby-Dick,* 48. On Mapple's sermon as a response to the Fugitive Slave Law, see Charles H. Foster, "Something in Emblems: A Reinterpretation of *Moby-Dick,*" *New England Quarterly* 34, no. 1 (1961): 17–20.

113. Rowland A. Sherrill, *The Prophetic Melville: Experience, Transcendence, and Tragedy* (Athens: University of Georgia Press, 1979), 139.

114. On *Moby-Dick* as Ishmael's sermon against slavery, see Karcher (62–91) and James Duban, *Melville's Major Fiction: Politics, Theology, and Imagination* (Dekalb: Northern Illinois University Press, 1983), 82–148.

115. Andrew Delbanco, *Melville: His World and Work* (New York: Knopf, 2005), 151.

116. Melville, *Moby-Dick,* 9–10. Robert K. Wallace suggests that this scene might be based on Melville having seen Frederick Douglass preach at the Zion Methodist Church on Second Street in New Bedford when Melville was in town between December 25, 1840 and January 3, 1841 (*Douglas and Melville: Anchored Together in Neighborly Style* [New Bedford, MA: Spinner, 2005], 15–21).

117. Karcher reads this scene along similar lines (77).

118. Melville, *Moby-Dick*, 9–10.

119. Ibid., 294–95. Wallace explains that Melville may have modeled Fleece's speech on an impromptu address that Thomas van Renssalaer, an African American, gave during a white riot that broke out at the May 8, 1850 meeting of the American Anti-Slavery Society at the New York Society Library, to which Melville belonged (103–5). See also Edward Stone, who reads Fleece's sermon as a pessimistic counterpoint to Mapple's theme of self-denial, inserted late in the composition of *Moby-Dick* to highlight the greed of Ahab and his crew and to foreshadow the *Pequod*'s doom ("The Other Sermon in *Moby-Dick*," *Costerus* 4 [1972]: 215–22).

120. Cf. Steven Mailloux, who discusses how Melville gravitated to a "negative political theology" skeptical of reformism grounded in "naively optimistic religious and philosophical creeds" ("Political Theology in Douglass and Melville," *Frederick Douglass and Herman Melville: Essays in Relation*, ed. Robert S. Levine and Samuel Otter [Chapel Hill: University of North Carolina Press, 2008], 171).

Chapter 6

1. [George Frederick Holmes], "Notices of New Works," *Southern Literary Messenger* 18 (1852): 631.

2. Vernon Louis Parrington, "Harriet Beecher Stowe: A Daughter of Puritanism," in *Critical Essays on Harriet Beecher Stowe*, ed. Elizabeth Ammons (Boston: G. K. Hall, 1980), 213.

3. Douglas, 245; Jane Tompkins, *Sensational Designs: The Cultural Work of American Fiction, 1790–1860* (New York: Oxford University Press, 1985), 140. Explaining how Stowe's "sermonic use of direct address" places her in a tradition of Calvinist preachers from Jonathan Edwards to Lyman Beecher, Warhol argues that just as these preachers sought to inspire faith in the truth of Christianity, so Stowe's narrator seeks to inspire faith in the truth of her story. Warhol also highlights similarities between Stowe's and Edwards's attempts to rouse emotion in audiences (105–8). Mark Vásquez contends that the power of Stowe's novel lies in its "hybrid rhetoric" of "sermonic and instructive" discourses, both of which aim for an authority built on the sympathetic response of readers (*Authority and Reform: Religious and Educational Discourses in Nineteenth-Century New England Literature* [Knoxville, TN: University of Tennessee Press, 2003], 241). In an attempt, parallel to my own, to explore how *Uncle Tom's Cabin* taps the power of Christian ritual, Michael Gilmore proposes that Stowe, who first conceived of Uncle Tom during a communion meal, wrote a book that aimed for the same spiritual presence and transformative, sanctifying result that Protestants believe they experience in the Lord's Supper ("*Uncle Tom's Cabin* and the American Renaissance: The Sacramental Aesthetic of Harriet Beecher Stowe," in *The Cambridge Companion to Harriet Beecher Stowe*, ed. Cindy Weinstein [Cambridge, UK: Cambridge University Press, 2004], 58–76).

4. Joan D. Hedrick, *Harriet Beecher Stowe: A Life* (New York: Oxford University Press, 1994), 39–41, 59.

5. Harriet Beecher to Catharine Beecher, December 11, 1829, in Catharine E. Beecher, *Educational Reminiscences and Suggestions* (New York: J. B. Ford, 1874), 68; and Harriet Beecher to Catharine Beecher, December 14, 1829 (ibid., 71).

6. Harriet Beecher to George Beecher, February 20, [1830?], in Hedrick, 64. Hedrick makes explicit the possible link between Stowe's public speaking experience at Catharine's school and the sense of vocation she announced to George (ibid.).

7. Brekus, 271.

8. Lyman Beecher to Nathan Beman, December 15, 1827, in Lyman Beecher, *Letters of the Rev. Dr. Beecher and Rev. Mr. Nettleton, on the 'New Measures' in Conducting Revivals of Religion: with a Review of a Sermon by Novanglus* (New York: Carvill, 1828), 90. Beman, pastor of the First Presbyterian Church in Troy, New York, had partnered with Finney in a revival in Troy and was a vocal proponent of Finney's controversial revival techniques.

9. L. Beecher, *Letters*, 90–91.

10. Thomas Gossett notes that Stowe did not start referring to the book as written or inspired by God until after its completion and clarifies that in her theology, the idea of God having a hand in the book did not guarantee its infallibility or her own superiority (*Uncle Tom's Cabin and American Culture* [Dallas: Southern Methodist University Press, 1985], 93–97). Mary Kelley discusses how a number of nineteenth-century women writers, including Catharine Sedgwick, Caroline Lee Hentz, and Mary Virginia Terhune, equated their fiction-writing with the ministerial vocation, claiming to be, in Kelley's phrase, "preachers of the fictional page," while many others described their writing as inspired or guided by God (*Private Woman, Public Stage: Literary Domesticity in Nineteenth-Century America* [Oxford: Oxford University Press, 1984], 294).

11. Even when touring Europe in the 1850s, Stowe did not speak before mixed audiences. However, she became the only "eminent woman author" to give platform readings in the nineteenth century when she went on reading tours in 1872 and 1873; see Martha L. Brunson, "Novelists as Platform Readers: Dickens, Clemens, and Stowe," in *Performance of Literature in Historical Perspectives,* ed. David W. Thompson (Lanham, MD: University Press of America, 1983), 669.

12. Harriet Beecher Stowe, "Antoinette Brown in Andover," *Liberator* (Feb. 2, 1855), 20. After the Civil War, Stowe increasingly endorsed the women's rights movement but only insofar as it was compatible with her belief in the primacy of women's domestic roles; see Jeanne Boydston, Mary Kelley, and Anne Margolis, *The Limits of Sisterhood: The Beecher Sisters on Women's Rights and Woman's Sphere* (Chapel Hill: University of North Carolina Press, 1988), 258.

13. Harriet Beecher Stowe, *Uncle Tom's Cabin, or Life Among the Lowly,* ed. Elizabeth Ammons (1852; New York: Norton, 1994), 34–35.

14. Claire Parfait discusses these letters to Bailey and his printed responses to them; see "The Nineteenth-Century Serial as a Collective Enterprise: Harriet Beecher Stowe's *Uncle Tom's Cabin* and Eugene Sue's *Les Mystères de Paris,*" *Proceedings of the American Antiquarian Society* 112, no. 1 (2002): 132–33.

15. Stowe, *Uncle Tom's Cabin,* 84.

16. Matthew 19:24, Matthew 16:26.

17. Stowe, *Uncle Tom's Cabin,* 114.

18. Spillers, 94.

19. Stowe, *Uncle Tom's Cabin,* 383. My argument that the narrator's sermonic voice shifts from sentimental to prophetic parallels Joshua D. Bellin's claim that the latter half of Stowe's novel deemphasizes the possibility of a human solution to the slavery problem in favor of anticipating God's final judgment ("Up to Heaven's Gate, Down in Earth's Dust: The Politics of Judgment in *Uncle Tom's Cabin,*" *American Literature* 65, no. 2 [1993]: 287).

20. Stowe, *Uncle Tom's Cabin,* 287.

21. Bellin, 288.

22. Stowe, *Uncle Tom's Cabin,* 108.

23. Ibid., 123–24. The putatively biblical quotation Stowe invokes to assure readers of God's eventual self-revelation pieces together phrases from Isaiah 26:21, Micah 1:3, and Psalms 76:8–9.

24. Stowe, *Uncle Tom's Cabin*, 385.

25. Ibid., 388.

26. Larry J. Reynolds, *European Revolutions and the American Literary Renaissance* (New Haven: Yale University Press, 1988), 53. Susan Belasco Smith discusses how the significant coverage that the European revolutions received in the *National Era* provides an important context for the novel's treatment of slave rebellion ("Serialization and the Nature of *Uncle Tom's Cabin*," in *Periodical Literature in Nineteenth-Century America*, ed. Kenneth M. Price and Susan Belasco Smith [Charlottesville: University Press of Virginia, 1995], 75–76, 79–83).

27. See Helen Petter Westra, "Confronting Antichrist: The Influence of Jonathan Edwards's Millennial Vision," in *The Stowe Debate: Rhetorical Strategies in Uncle Tom's Cabin*, ed. Mason I. Lowance Jr., Ellen E. Westbrook, and R. C. De Prospro (Amherst: University of Massachusetts Press, 1994), 141–58.

28. Stowe, *Uncle Tom's Cabin*, 388.

29. Westra, 151. James Baldwin, "Everybody's Protest Novel," in *Critical Essays on Harriet Beecher Stowe*, ed. Elizabeth Ammons (Boston: G. K. Hall, 1980), 94.

30. Stowe, *Uncle Tom's Cabin*, 388.

31. Ibid. Stowe's ending may be indebted to Jonathan Edwards's "Sinners in the Hands of an Angry God," which concludes: "The wrath of almighty God is now undoubtedly hanging over [*sic*] great part of this congregation : let everyone fly out of Sodom: 'Haste and escape for your lives, look not behind you, escape to the mountain, lest you be consumed'" (in *A Jonathan Edwards Reader*, ed. John E. Smith, Harry S. Stout, and Kenneth P. Minkema [New Haven: Yale University Press, 1995], 105). The shared phrase, "the wrath of Almighty God," comes from Revelation 19:15, a verse Edwards's sermon analyzes at length.

32. Lyman Beecher, *A Sermon Addressed to the Legislature of Connecticut, at New Haven, on the Day of the Anniversary Election, May 3d, 1826* (New Haven, 1826), 22.

33. Increase Mather, "The Day of Trouble Is Near," *Jeremiads*, vol. 20 of *A Library of American Puritan Writings: The Seventeenth Century*, ed. Sacvan Bercovitch (New York: AMS, 1984), 31.

34. Stephen A. Hirsch points out that the *Liberator* reported that Sunday schools in Peoria and Pittsburgh had adopted the novel and that *Frederick Douglass' Paper* mentioned its use in high schools ("Uncle Tomitudes: The Popular Reaction to *Uncle Tom's Cabin*," *Studies in the American Renaissance*, ed. Joel Myerson [Boston: Twayne Publishers, 1978], 304).

35. But note that Stowe publicly supported abolitionist ministers, as when she pled for the efficacy of clerical abolitionists in her letter to Frederick Douglass ("To Frederick Douglass, July 9, 1851," *The Oxford Harriet Beecher Stowe Reader*, ed. Joan D. Hedrick [New York: Oxford University Press, 1999], 60).

36. Stowe, *Uncle Tom's Cabin*, 30.

37. Ibid., 158–59.

38. Ibid., 113. Hedrick, 226. Hedrick details the Parker-Stowe controversy, explaining how Stowe invoked the ideology of "true womanhood" to engage in male clerical disputation (ibid., 225–30).

39. "Extract from the *New York Observer*," *New York Independent* (October 7, 1852): 61, quoted in Hedrick, 227.

40. Stowe, *Uncle Tom's Cabin*, 107–8.

41. Ibid., 115.

42. Ibid., 251.

43. Ellen Moers, *Literary Women* (New York: Doubleday, 1976), 193.

44. Stowe, *Uncle Tom's Cabin*, 26.

45. Ibid., 88, 358.

46. Ibid., 343, 359.

47. Ibid., 69, 100, 166. Vásquez makes a similar point regarding the novel's decentraliza-tion of power: the book "locates authority both within the domestic arena and without, both within white culture and black culture, within 'male' and 'female' realms" (248).

48. Michael Winship discusses the difficulty of determining the exact number of copies sold in the United States in the first year and substantiates the book's success in Europe ("'The Greatest Book of Its Kind': A Publishing History of 'Uncle Tom's Cabin,'" *Proceedings of the American Antiquarian Society* 109, no. 2 [1999]: 309–332). On the novel's national impact, see Gossett and Hirsch; on the international "Uncle Tom" phenomenon on stage, see Sarah Meer, *Uncle Tom Mania: Slavery, Minstrelsy, and Transatlantic Culture in the 1850s* (Athens: Univer-sity of Georgia Press, 2005).

49. Introduction to *Uncle Tom's Cabin* (London: John Cassell, 1852), xiii.

50. Douglas, 245.

51. Lyman Beecher, *Lectures on Intemperance* (London: Clarke, Beeton, and Co., [1853?], title page).

52. On Parker's centrality to mid-nineteenth-century American religion and culture, see Grodzins, ix–xiii; on Parker's antislavery preaching, David B. Chesebrough, *Theodore Parker: Orator of Superior Ideas* (Westport, CT: Greenwood, 1999), 44–54.

53. Theodore Parker, "The Chief Sins of the People," in *Sins and Safeguards of Society,* vol. 9 of *Works,* ed. Samuel B. Stewart (Boston: American Unitarian Association, 1907), 33, 36.

54. Theodore Parker to unnamed correspondent, July 15, 1857, in *Saint Bernard and Other Papers,* vol. 14 of *Works,* ed. Charles W. Wendte (Boston: American Unitarian Associa-tion, 1911), 224.

55. Parker, *Sins and Safeguards,* 48, 7.

Chapter 7

1. William Wells Brown, *Clotel, or, The President's Daughter: A Narrative of Slave Life in the United States* (London: Partridge and Oakey, 1853), 62-64. Subsequent references are to this edition unless otherwise noted.

2. See William Wells Brown, "A Lecture Delivered before the Female Anti-Slavery Soci-ety of Salem," in *William Wells Brown: A Reader,* ed. Ezra Greenspan (Athens: University of Georgia Press, 2002), 128; William Wells Brown, "A True Story," *Anti-Slavery Advocate* 3 (De-cember 1852): 23; William Wells Brown, *Clotelle: A Tale of the Southern States* (Boston: James Redpath, 1864), 8–9.

3. Brown, "A Lecture," 128.

4. Brown's relationship to religion has received little attention. On Brown as a secular writer, see, for instance, John Ernest, who writes that *Clotel* works in the "secular space be-tween" good and evil, or Russ Castronovo, who writes that Brown "argued against slavery and racial prejudice, not by appealing to religious tenets as many white abolitionists and slave nar-rators did, but by manipulating the discourses of American politics and history" (John Ernest, *Resistance and Reformation in Nineteenth-Century African-American Literature: Brown, Wil-son, Jacobs, Delany, Douglass, and Harper* [Jackson: University Press of Mississippi, 1995], 52; Russ Castronovo, *Fathering the Nation: American Genealogies of Slavery and Freedom* [Berke-ley: University of California Press, 1995], 165–66). Although Ernest has also maintained that "Brown follows Frederick Douglass in distinguishing between the 'Christianity of this land' and the 'Christianity of Christ,'" Brown seems to have had little investment in articulating

his own interpretation of Christian theology. For instance, he decried slave-traders as "the professed followers of the meek and lowly JESUS!" and as "Christians in good and regular standing in some of the churches of America!" but did not elaborate on how one might follow Jesus more faithfully. See John Ernest, "The Governing Spirit: African American Writers in the Antebellum City on a Hill," in *A Mighty Baptism: Race, Gender, and the Creation of American Protestantism*, ed. Susan Juster and Lisa MacFarlane (Ithaca: Cornell University Press, 1996), 264, William Wells Brown, "Speech delivered at the Lecture Hall, Croydon, England, September 5, 1849," in *The Works of William Wells Brown: Using His "Strong, Manly Voice*," ed. Paula Garrett and Hollis Robbins (New York: Oxford University Press, 2006), 22.

5. On Stowe's reception in Britain, see Audrey A. Fisch, *American Slaves in Victorian England: Abolitionist Politics in Popular Literature and Culture* (Cambridge, UK: Cambridge University Press, 2000), 11–51, and Meer, 131–222. See also Brown's quotation of a review of his *Three Years in Europe* included at the end of the *Narrative of the Life and Escape of William Wells Brown*, prefatory to *Clotel*: "The extraordinary excitement produced by 'Uncle Tom's Cabin' will we hope, prepare the public of Great Britain and America for this lively book of travels by a real fugitive slave" (Brown, *Clotel*, 47).

6. See William Edward Farrison, *William Wells Brown: Author and Reformer* (Chicago: University of Chicago Press, 1969), 198–202.

7. "The Abolition Movement," *Anti-Slavery Advocate* 1 (October 1852): 3.

8. "The 'Times' Reviewer Reviewed," *Anti-Slavery Advocate* 1 (October 1852): 6–7; "International Copyright," *The Anti-Slavery Advocate* 2 (November 1852): 14; "The Slaveholders' Wager," *Anti-Slavery Advocate* 2 (November 1852): 15; "'Uncle Tom on the Continent," *Anti-Slavery Advocate* 3 (December 1853): 23; Review of *The Key to Uncle Tom's Cabin*, by Harriet Beecher Stowe, *Anti-Slavery Advocate* 8 (May 1853): 63; "Mrs. Stowe in Great Britain," *Anti-Slavery Advocate* 8 (May 1853): 60; "Annual Meeting of the British and Foreign Anti-Slavery Society," *Anti-Slavery Advocate* 9 (June 1853): 68–69; and "Mrs. Stowe's Reply on the Presentation of the Address and Testimonial from Leeds," *Anti-Slavery Advocate* 13 (October 1853): 100. Cf. John Bishop Estlin's November 1853 prefatory note to the republication of his pamphlet, *A Brief Notice of American Slavery, and the Abolition Movement* (1846), in which he explained that he brought his work before the public eye again because "the extraordinary circulation of Mrs. Stowe's *Uncle Tom's Cabin*, and her invaluable *Key*, has greatly increased the demand for anti-slavery literature" (J. B. Estlin, *A Brief Notice of American Slavery, and the Abolition Movement*, 2nd ed., revised [London: Tweedie, 1853], 2).

9. "Lectures on American Slavery," *Anti-Slavery Advocate* 6 (March 1853), 45. William Wells Brown to William Lloyd Garrison, 17 May 1853, Document 53, *The Black Abolitionist Papers, Volume 1, The British Isles, 1830–1865*, ed. C. Peter Ripley (Chapel Hill: University of North Carolina Press, 1985), 344; cf. *Liberator* (June 3, 1853), 97. My thanks to Geoff Sanborn for alerting me to the fact that Frederick Douglass in the June 10, 1853 issue of *Frederick Douglass' Paper* exposed Brown as having taken this sentence from the August 13, 1852 issue of his paper, where it appeared in an advertisement for an antislavery festival held by the Rochester Ladies' Anti-Slavery Society.

10. On Brown's borrowing of motifs and scenes from Stowe, see Peter Dorsey, "De-authorizing Slavery: Realism in Stowe's *Uncle Tom's Cabin* and Brown's *Clotel*," *ESQ* 41, no. 4 (1995): 259–62.

11. Brown, *Clotel*, iv.

12. Brown, "A Lecture Delivered before the Female Anti-Slavery Society of Salem," 115.

13. Brown, *Clotel*, 244. As R. Levine notes, Brown was both a "deadly serious moralist" and "something of a confidence man and a trickster" ("Introduction: Cultural and Historical

Background," in William Wells Brown, *Clotel; or, The President's Daughter: A Narrative of Slave Life in the United States,* ed. Robert S. Levine [Boston: Bedford/St. Martin's, 2000], 4).

14. Greenspan, Introduction, *William Wells Brown: A Reader,* xx. I avoid calling Brown a plagiarist because of the ambiguity surrounding this concept in 1853, particularly given that *Clotel* borrows largely from American texts yet was first published in England long before international copyright protections. On the anachronism of calling Brown a plagiarist, see R. Levine, "Introduction," 6.

15. William L. Andrews, "The Novelization of Voice in Early African American Narrative," *PMLA* 15, no. 1 (1990): 24.

16. R. Levine, "Sources and Revisions," in William Wells Brown, *Clotel; or, The President's Daughter: A Narrative of Slave Life in the United States,* ed. Robert S. Levine (Boston: Bedford/St. Martin's, 2000), 234.

17. Henry Louis Gates, Jr., Introduction, *Three Classic African-American Novels* (New York: Random House-Vintage, 1990), xi. Cf. Blyden Jackson's comment that *Clotel* is "a somewhat frenzied scramble, from one *exemplum* in an abolitionist homily to another" (*A History of Afro-American Literature: Volume 1, The Long Beginning, 1746–1895* [Baton Rouge: Louisiana State University Press, 1989], 339).

18. Heather Russell, *Legba's Crossing: Narratology in the African Atlantic* (Athens, GA: University of Georgia Press, 2009), 13. Similarly, Dorsey notes that the "high degree of intertextuality" in *Clotel* is consistent with "an African American aesthetic in which one's tongue is often in another's mouth" (279).

19. Brown, *Clotel,* 87. Farrison points out that Brown took Peck's name from a "Rev. Mr. Peck of Rochester" whom Brown heard argue against natural rights at a New York State Liberty Party convention in Farmington, New York, in 1846 (97).

20. Brown, *Clotel,* 137.

21. Brown, "A Lecture," 112.

22. Brown, *Clotel,* 89; [William F. Hutson], "Review of Alphonse De Lamartine, *History Of The Girondists, or Personal Memoirs of the Patriots of the French Revolution, from unpublished sources* [. . .]," *Southern Presbyterian Review* 2 (1848): 401. The borrowed passage runs from "have searched in vain" through "artificial and voluntary."

23. Brown, *Clotel,* 89. While the Declaration of Independence holds that all men "are created equal and endowed by their Creator with certain *unalienable* Rights, that among these are Life, Liberty, and the pursuit of Happiness," Jefferson's draft of the Declaration read "inherent and inalienable rights," phrasing that circulated widely in the nineteenth century. The final line of Peck's speech against natural rights is a perplexing variant of the original. *Clotel* reads, "Though man has no rights, as thus considered, undoubtedly he has the power, by such arbitrary rules of right and wrong as his necessity enforces" (Brown, *Clotel,* 89). This conclusion is the compressed borrowing of a sentence that appears several lines beneath the main passage borrowed from the review of Lamartine. The original reads: "Though man has no rights, as thus considered, undoubtedly he has the *power* by mutual and common consent, to establish in society such arbitrary rules of Right and Wrong as his necessity enforces" ([Hutson], 402) The phrases "mutual and common consent, to establish in society," missing in *Clotel,* clarify the purpose of the power Peck grants. Brown may have omitted the phrase "by mutual and common consent" because it frames power as Rousseauian in a way that Chapter 6 associates with Carlton rather than Peck (Carlton's response begins, "I regret I cannot see eye to eye with you [. . .] I am a disciple of Rousseau" [Brown, *Clotel,* 89]). Or in deleting this phrase Brown may simply have overshot the mark and skipped over the syntactically necessary phrase, "to establish in society"—the transcriptional error of haplography, when the copyist's eye moves

forward too far in the text. Or Brown may have sought to undermine Peck's reasonable-sounding yet insidious monologue by concluding it with gobbledygook.

24. [James Thornwell], "The Religious Instruction of the Black Population," *Southern Presbyterian Review* 1 (December 1847): 89–120. The excerpted passage extends from "The Bible furnishes to us" to "divided we shall become easy prey." On Thornwell, see William W. Freehling, "Defective Paternalism: James Henley Thornwell's Mysterious Anti-Slavery Movement," in *The Reintegration of American History* (New York: Oxford University Press, 1994), 59–81. For the broader context of Christian proslavery arguments, see John Patrick Daly, *When Slavery Was Called Freedom: Evangelicalism, Proslavery, and the Causes of the Civil War* (Lexington: University Press of Kentucky, 2002).

25. Brown, *Clotel*, 90.

26. Ibid.

27. Frederick Douglass, *Narrative of the Life of Frederick Douglass, an American Slave. Written by Himself* (Boston: Anti-Slavery Office, 1845), 78.

28. Thomas Bacon, *Sermons Addressed to Masters and Servants . . .* , ed. William Meade (Winchester, VA: John Heiskell, 1813), 111. From "'All things whatsoever ye would that men should do to you'" to "in obedience to his commands" comes from Sermon II (ibid., 116–17); from "You are not to be eye-servants" to "and not as to men," from Sermon I (ibid., 107–8); from "Take care that you do not fret or murmur" to "exceeding great glory hereafter" from Sermon II (ibid., 131–32). Cf. Brown, *Clotel*, 93–97. Levine notes Brown's indebtedness to Bacon and reprints an excerpt from *Sermons Addressed to Masters and Servants*; see Brown, *Clotel* (2000), 111n8, 258–62, and Brown, *Clotel* (2011), 111n8, 297–300.

29. Matthew 7:12.

30. Proslavery theologians countered the argument that the Golden Rule prohibited slavery by coupling it with another verse, "Masters give unto your servants that which is just and equal" (Col. 4:1), which clarified, so the reasoning went, that ethical norms should not upend the God-ordained social hierarchy (see Freehling, 65).

31. Brown, *Clotel*, 93.

32. Bacon, *Sermons*, 111.

33. Brown, *Clotel*, 97.

34. Charles C. Jones, *A Catechism of Scripture Doctrine and Practice, for Families and Sabbath Schools Designed also for the Oral Instruction of Colored Persons*, 6th ed. (Savannah: John M. Cooper, 1837), 129–30. This is the "Rev. C. C. Jones" referred to in Chapter 13 (Brown, *Clotel*, 133). Brown was probably working from the excerpt of Jones's catechism in William I. Bowditch's *Slavery and the Constitution* ([Boston: Robert F. Wallcut, 1849], 50). As I discuss below, Brown also borrowed the narrator's discussion of marriage in Chapter 1 from Bowditch. In citing Jones, Brown left out only the Scripture references appended to each question. Snyder's catechism follows Jones's through "Q. Is it right for the servant to run away, or is it right to harbour a runaway?—A. 'No.'" For the next question and answer—"Q. If a servant runs away, what should be done with him?—A. 'He should be caught and brought back'"—Brown paraphrased Jones, leaving out the biblical precedent Jones cites for returning runaway slaves, Paul's returning Onesimus to his master. Snyder's last six questions and answers appear to be original to Brown.

35. Brown, *Clotel*, 100.

36. Ibid. Review of *Clotel, or, The President's Daughter, a Narrative of Slave Life in the United States*, by William Wells Brown, *Anti-Slavery Advocate* 16 (January 1854), 125.

37. Brown, *Clotel*, 106. John G. Palfrey, *Papers on the Slave Power, First Published in the "Boston Whig"* (Boston: Merrill, Cobb, and Co., [1846?]), 53. The last line of Snyder's speech,

"Slavery is the incubus that hangs over the Southern States," appears to be original to Brown, though the metaphor was not unique to him (Brown, *Clotel*, 106).

38. See Frank Otto Gatell, *John Gorham Palfrey and the New England Conscience* (Cambridge, MA: Harvard University Press, 1963).

39. W. E. B. Du Bois, *The Souls of Black Folk* (1903; New York: Penguin, 1996), 155.

40. Brown, *Clotel*, 99–100.

41. Ibid., 134–35.

42. See Holmes, 633. The only positive comment on black preaching in *Clotel* comes in the description of Nat Turner, identified as a "preacher amongst the negroes, and distinguished for his eloquence, respected by the whites, and loved and venerated by the negroes" (Brown, *Clotel*, 212). Here being a preacher is a sign of social status, not of piety or spiritual leadership.

43. Brown, *Clotel*, 91. George Allen, *Resistance to Slavery Every Man's Duty: A Report on American Slavery, Read to the Worcester Central Association, March 2, 1847* (Boston: Crosby and Nichols, 1847), 13. The borrowed portion of Allen's speech runs from "We must try the character of slavery" through "to unrequited toil through life?" (Brown, *Clotel*, 91-92).

44. In December 1837 and January 1838, Allen helped convene a meeting of Worcester County Congregational ministers on the question of slavery, which issued a "Declaration of Sentiments" condemning the institution and calling for slaveowners to liberate their slaves. See *Proceedings of the Convention of Ministers of Worcester County, on the Subject of Slavery; Held at Worcester, December 5 and 6, 1837, and January 16, 1838* (Worcester: Massachusetts Spy Office, 1838).

45. Allen, 13–14.

46. Brown, *Clotel*, 92. "Thou shalt love thy neighbour as thyself" appears in Leviticus 19:18, Matthew 19:19, Matthew 22:39, Mark 12:31, Luke 10:27, Romans 13:9, Galatians 5:14, and James 2:8.

47. [Thomas Shaw B. Reade], *Christian Retirement: Or Spiritual Exercises of the Heart, By a Layman,* 2nd ed. (Kirkby Lonsdale: Arthur Foster, 1827), 376.

48. Brown, *Clotel*, 92.

49. On Brown's critique of hypocritical churchgoers, see, for instance, *Narrative of William W. Brown, A Fugitive Slave, Written by Himself* (1848), in *From Fugitive Slave to Free Man: The Autobiographies of William Wells Brown*, ed. William L. Andrews (1993; Columbia: University of Missouri Press, 2003), 41; William Wells Brown, "Speech delivered at the Town Hall, Manchester, England, August 1, 1854," in *The Works of William Wells Brown: Using His "Strong, Manly Voice,"* ed. Paula Garrett and Hollis Robbins (New York: Oxford University Press, 2006), 35–36.

50. Brown, *Clotel*, 115. La Roy Sunderland, *Anti Slavery Manual, Containing a Collection of Facts and Arguments on American Slavery*, 2nd ed. (New York: S. W. Benedict, 1837), 46. Soon after helping to found the Wesleyan Methodist Church in 1842, Sunderland had a crisis of faith and became a student of mesmerism and spiritualism; see Taves, 128–48, and J. R. Jacob, "La Roy Sunderland: The Alienation of an Abolitionist," *American Studies* 6 (1972): 1–17.

51. Brown, *Clotel*, 115. For the quotation from Porteous, see, for instance, William Jay, *Miscellaneous Writings on Slavery* (Boston: John P. Jewett, 1853), 144; La Roy Sunderland, *The Testimony of God Against Slavery* [. . .], 2nd ed. (Boston: Isaac Knapp, 1836), 159; and Charles Elliott, *Sinfulness of American Slavery* [. . .], ed. B. F. Tefft, 2 vols. (Cincinnati: L. Swormstedt and J. H. Power, 1851), 179.

52. Brown, *Clotel*, 115–16. Theodore Dwight Weld, *The Bible Against Slavery. An Inquiry into the Patriarchal and Mosaic Systems on the Subject of Human Rights,* 3rd ed., *The American Anti-Slavery Examiner* 5 (New York: American Anti-Slavery Society, 1838): 11.

53. Weld, 11. Brown, *Clotel*, 116.

54. The section from Grimké runs from "When the Redeemer was about to ascend to the bosom of the Father" through "the opening of the prison doors to those who are bound" (Brown, *Clotel*, 116–17). [Sarah Grimké], *An Address to Free Colored Americans. Issued by an Anti-Slavery Convention of American Women, Held in the City of New-York, by adjournments from 9th to 12th May, 1837* (New York: William S. Dorr, 1837), 24–25. I provided knowledge of this source for the second Bedford edition of *Clotel*; see William Wells Brown, *Clotel; or, The President's Daughter: A Narrative of Slave Life in the United States,* ed. Robert S. Levine (Boston: Bedford/St. Martin's, 2011), 128n5. On the organizational circumstances surrounding the writing of the address, see Pamela R. Durson, *The Power of Woman: The Life and Writings of Sarah Moore Grimké* (Macon, GA: Mercer University Press, 2003), 100–110, and *The Public Years of Sarah and Angelina Grimké: Selected Writings, 1835–1839,* ed. Larry Ceplair (New York: Columbia University Press, 1989), 86–87.

55. On the Grimkés, see Gerda Lerner, *The Grimké Sisters from South Carolina: Pioneers for Women's Rights and Abolition,* rev. ed. (Chapel Hill: University of North Carolina Press, 2004), as well as Durson and Ceplair.

56. Brown, *Clotel*, 116.

57. Ibid., 116-17.

58. William Weston Patton, *Slavery, the Bible, Infidelity: Pro-slavery Interpretations of the Bible: Productive of Infidelity* (Hartford: W. H. Burleigh, 1846), 4–6. [Grimké], *Address*, 14, 28. Christopher Mulvey notes and reproduces the relevant portion of Patton's sermon ("Annotations to *Clotel; or the President's Daughter: A Narrative of Slave Life in the United States. (1853),*" in *Clotel: An Electronic Scholarly Edition* [University of Virginia Press, 2006], p. 118, line 19). Among the many slight changes Brown makes to the phrasing in Grimké is the truncation of her line, "When he designed to do us good, he took upon himself the form of a servant—surely we should love and honor this office," which Georgiana echoes only through "servant"; presumably Brown thought the last phrase went too far in praise of servitude. Yet Brown seems not to have been overly concerned about the possible proslavery implications of appealing to Christ as the divine servant, as Georgiana's next two lines pick up Grimké after the deleted phrase: "He took his station at the bottom of society. He voluntarily identified himself with the poor and the despised" (Brown, *Clotel*, 120; [Grimké], Address, 14).

59. Brown, *Clotel*, 121.

60. Henry Mayer, *All on Fire: William Lloyd Garrison and the Abolition of Slavery* (New York: Norton, 1998), 116. Mayer reports that the one thousand copies of the first edition of the *Address* sold out quickly and that by August 1831, three thousand copies were in circulation (ibid.).

61. Brown, *Clotel*, 186. William Lloyd Garrison, *An Address, Delivered Before the Free People of Color, in Philadelphia, New-York, and Other Cities, During the Month of June, 1831* (Boston: Stephen Foster, 1831), 5.

62. Garrison, 5–6. Brown, *Clotel*, 186.

63. In excerpting Garrison, Brown cherry-picked lines in the order they appeared in the pamphlet: from "Remember what a singular relation you sustain to society" through "your example will lose a great portion of its influence" (6–7); from "Make the Lord Jesus Christ your refuge and exemplar" through "you are that people" (7); "You had better trust in the Lord" through "whose God is the Lord" (8); "Get as much education as possible" through "never be truly free until they are intelligent" (10). The next line in *Clotel* appears to Brown's own: "In a few days you will start for the state of Ohio, where land will be purchased for some of you who have families, and where I hope you will all prosper" (186). Then Brown had Georgiana

paraphrase the anti-colonizationist sentiments that dominate the end of Garrison's *Address:* "We have been urged to send you to Liberia, but we think it wrong to send you from your native land. We did not wish to encourage the Colonization Society, for it originated in hatred of the free coloured people" (186). The next line is from Garrison: "Its pretences are false, its doctrines odious, its means contemptible" (Garrison, 22; Brown, *Clotel*, 186). Garrison's subsequent remarks appear, only slightly modified, after the deathbed speech, as the narrator reports Georgiana's remarks on colonization: "'If we are to send away the colored population because they are profligate and vicious, what sort of missionaries will they make? Why not send away the vicious among the whites, for the same reason, and the same purpose'" (Garrison, 22; Brown, *Clotel*, 187).

64. Brown, *Clotel*, 186–87.

65. On British Unitarian involvement in the American antislavery movement and on Estlin in particular, see Douglas Charles Stange, *British Unitarians against American Slavery, 1833–65* (Cranbury, NJ: Associated University Presses, 1984).

66. Brown, *Clotel*, 57.

67. Brown, *Clotel*, 57–58. Bowditch, 56–57. Cf. Samuel Osgood, *Human Life; or, Practical Ethics. Translated from the German of De Wette*, 2 vols., vol. 13 of *Specimens of Foreign Standard Literature*, ed. George Ripley (Boston: James Munroe, 1842), 168–69. That Brown dropped the first line of Bowditch's excerpt from Osgood's translation of De Wette—"Marriage is genuine only when single and permanent"—may reflect his own marital difficulties. In 1847, Brown had separated from his wife, Elizabeth Schooner Brown, who died in 1851. Brown also took from Bowditch his two examples of church statutes supporting slavery, those of the Shiloh Baptist Association and the Savannah River Association (Brown, *Clotel*, 56–57; Bowditch, 61–62). On Brown's marriage to Schooner, as well as a reading of the novel centered on its exploration of the meaning of marriage, especially between slaves, see Tess Chakkalakal, *Novel Bondage: Slavery, Marriage, and Freedom in Nineteenth-Century America* (Urbana: University of Illinois Press, 2011), 15–30.

68. Bowditch, 57.

69. Brown, *Clotel*, 58.

70. Ibid. Bowditch, 57.

71. Brown, *Clotel*, 64.

72. Ibid. Allen, 15–16.

73. Alvan Stewart, *A Legal Argument Before the Supreme Court of the State of New Jersey, at the May Term, 1845, at Trenton, for the Deliverance of Four Thousand Persons from Bondage* (New York: Finch and Weed, 1845), 9; repr. in *Abolitionists in Northern Courts: The Pamphlet Literature*, ed. Paul Finkelman (New York: Garland, 1988), 449. I provided knowledge of this source for the second Bedford edition of *Clotel*; see Brown, *Clotel* (2011), 182n7.

74. Brown, *Clotel*, 183–84.

75. Brown, *Clotel*, 185.

76. Parker Pillsbury, *The Church as It Is: or the Forlorn Hope of Slavery* (Boston: Bela Marsh, 1847), 78.

77. Brown, *Clotel*, 185. Brown copied Hughes's text from "With respect to her philosophy" through "founded in the school of Christianity," changing only the pronouns and a few punctuation marks. See Benjamin F. Hughes, *Eulogium on the Life and Character of William Wilberforce, Esq. Delivered and Published at the Request of the People of Color of the City of New York, Twenty-second of October, 1833* (New York: Office of *The Emancipator*, 1833; Philadelphia: Rhistoric Publications, 1969), 13. *Clotel* diverges from Hughes in the final clause of the paragraph. Hughes said, "His philosophy was founded in the school of Christianity, for be it

known that Wilberforce was a Christian. He was not only an exemplary and devoted member of the established church; but at the time when religion was noticed in the higher circles only to be scoffed at, he became the author of a work entitled *A Popular View of Christianity*" (ibid.). Brown modified these lines to emphasize Georgiana's liberal-mindedness: "her philosophy was founded in the school of Christianity; though a devoted member of her father's church, she was not a sectarian" (Brown, *Clotel*, 185). A similar attempt to reframe Georgiana's religiosity occurs at the end of Chapter 10. There the narrator says that Georgiana is her father's superior and teacher and describes her in secular terms: she considers "the right to enjoy perfect liberty as one of those inherent and inalienable rights which pertain to the whole human race, and of which they can never be divested, except by an act of gross injustice" (Brown, *Clotel*, 121). Brown took this passage from Samuel McDowell Moore's speech on slavery before the Virginia Convention in 1832; see Joseph C. Robert, *The Road from Monticello: A Study of the Virginia Slavery Debate of 1832* (Durham: Duke University Press, 1941), 64.

78. Brown, *Clotel*, 189. Cf. Hughes, 15. Most of the changes to Hughes are minor—for instance, changing the gender of pronouns and adding "Christian's" before "victory," perhaps to avoid the allusion in the original to the political victory of West Indian emancipation. Brown's most significant alteration comes at the end of the passage, where he changed Hughes's line, "In what light would he consider that hypocritical priesthood who give their aid to foster a popular prejudice against a portion of the community to whom they are immeasurably indebted [. . .]," to "In what light would she consider that hypocritical priesthood who gave their aid and sanction to the infamous 'Fugitive Slave Law'" (Hughes, 14; Brown, *Clotel*, 189).

79. Maxwell Whiteman, "Robert Purvis, 1810–1898: A Bibliographical Note," in Robert Purvis, *A Tribute to the Memory of Thomas Shipley, the Philanthropist* (Philadelphia: Merrihew and Gunn, 1836; Philadelphia: Rhistoric Publications, 1969), n. p. The passage borrowed from Purvis in *Clotel* runs from "If true greatness consists" through "or make him afraid" (Brown, *Clotel*, 189; Purvis, 8). Brown mangled the syntax of this passage in adapting it. Purvis wrote that, if asked for the evidence that true greatness consisted in doing good to mankind, he "would point to broken hearts made whole—to sad and dejected countenances, now beaming with contentment and joy. I would point to the mother, now offering her free born babe to heaven, and to the father, whose cup of joy seems overflowing in the presence of his family, where none can molest him or make him afraid." Substituting "Who can think of" for "I would point to," the narrator of *Clotel* says: "Who can think of the broken hearts made whole [. . .]." Without rejoicing? Without praising Georgiana? These ideas are only implicit; the narrator begins a rhetorical question but does not complete it.

80. Brown, *Clotel*, 189-90.

81. Stowe, *Uncle Tom's Cabin*, 257.

82. The borrowed passage runs from "Death is a leveller" to "no more known on earth" (Brown, *Clotel*, 187-88); James Montgomery, *Gleanings from Pious Authors: Comprising the Wheatsheaf, Fruits and Flowers, Garden, and Shrubbery . . .* , new ed. (London, 1846; Philadelphia: Henry Longstreth, 1855), 24.

83. Stowe, *Uncle Tom's Cabin*, 257.

84. Brown, *Clotel*, 188-89. J[ane] S. W[elch], "Jairus's Daughter," *New England Offering* 1 (1848): 108.

85. Brown, *Clotel*, 189.

86. Ibid., 217.

87. Abraham Lincoln, *Speeches and Writings, 1859–1865: Speeches, Letters, and Miscellaneous Writings, Presidential Messages and Proclamations* (New York: Literary Classics of the United States, 1989), 687.

88. A Member of Congress, "Slavery in the District," *New-York Evangelist* (September 8, 1842), 1; A Member of Congress, "Slavery in the District of Colombia [*sic*]," *British and Foreign Anti-Slavery Reporter* (December 28, 1842), 1.

89. Brown, *Clotel,* 245.

90. On the "Year of Jubilee," see Leviticus 25. The phrase "value *the* common salvation" comes from Jude 1:3, where it refers to the salvation of all believers in Christ. The final sentence quotes Psalms 67:6–7.

91. Brown, *Clotel,* 245.

92. Brown, *Clotel,* 80. Brown acknowledges a debt to Child in his Conclusion. R. Levine includes "The Quadroons" in the Bedford editions.

93. Brown, *Narrative of William W. Brown,* 40. Brown reported in *My Southern Home* that "Dr. John Gaines" (the name he gave his master, Dr. John Young, in this last book) would spend Sabbath mornings reading and explaining the Bible to his slaves—"often till half of the negroes present were fast asleep" (William Wells Brown, *My Southern Home: Or, The South and Its People,* in *From Fugitive Slave to Free Man,* ed. William L. Andrews [Columbia: University of Missouri Press, 2003], 120).

94. See Farrison, 88, 95–97, 128.

95. Brown to Garrison, 17 May 1853, *Black Abolitionist Papers,* 1:345. Brown wrote this remark after hearing Calvin Stowe speak, though Stowe was a professor of biblical literature and not technically a clergyman.

96. Brown, *Clotel,* 121.

Conclusion

1. Finke and Stark, 23. Catholics rose from 5 percent of the total population in 1850 to 12 percent in 1890; as a percentage of church adherents, they accounted for approximately 14 percent in 1850 and 26 percent in 1890 (ibid., 122).

2. Gedge, 47.

3. It is beyond the scope of this book to trace the rivalry between preachers and novelists through the intervening century or so, but I would venture that for much of the twentieth century the sermon continued to play an especially significant role in the African American novel. This dynamic may be due to literarily ambitious African American writers keeping one eye on the predominately white literary establishment and another on the African American community, in which preachers still held a great deal of sway. On twentieth-century African American novels and the sermon, see Dolan Hubbard, *The Sermon and the African American Literary Imagination* (Columbia: University of Missouri Press, 1994), as well as Tuire Valkeakari's *Religious Idiom and the African American Novel, 1952–1998* (Gainesville: University Press of Florida, 2007).

4. See Gary Scharnhorst, "Howells's *The Minister's Charge:* A Satire of Alger's Country-Boy Myth," *The Mark Twain Journal* 20, no. 3 (1980–1981): 16–17, and John Graham, "Struggling Upward: *The Minister's Charge* and *A Cool Million,*" *Canadian Review of American Studies* 4 (1973): 184–96.

5. I borrow the estimate of one-third from Melanie Dawson, "Searching for 'Common Ground': Class, Sympathy, and Perspective in Howells' Social Fiction," *American Literary Realism* 39, no. 3 (2007): 196.

6. In contrast with Dawson, who describes Sewell as having an "unempathetic relation-

ship" with Barker and as marked by "alarming affective inabilities" (198), I would maintain that Sewell perceives and treats Barker with sensitivity. He intuits, for instance, the young man's love troubles and finds relatively tactful ways of securing new positions for him.

7. W. D. Howells, *The Minister's Charge, or The Apprenticeship of Lemuel Barker,* ed. David J. Nordloh and David Kleinman (Bloomington: Indiana University Press, 1978), 6.

8. Ibid., 304.

9. Ibid.

10. Ibid., 30.

11. Ibid., 239.

12. Ibid., 22.

13. Dawson critiques the minister for preferring to preach to Barker rather than talk with him, "imagining that his sermons substitute for a relationship" (198), but in light of the sermons' greater efficacy and the inescapable limitations of pastoral counsel, Sewell's preference seems sensible.

14. Howells, *The Minister's Charge,* 108.

15. Ibid.

16. Ibid., 224.

17. Ibid., 22. Here I concur with John Cyril Barton's point that Miss Vane's mockery of Sewell's sermon on sincere speech begins to erode his credibility. However, the ideas presented in the sermon are not exactly "the minister's procrustean principles." Inflexible principles are endemic to the sermon form and one of its limitations, as this novel argues. See Barton, "Howells's Rhetoric of Realism: The Economy of Pain(t) and Social Complicity in *The Rise of Silas Lapham," Studies in American Fiction* 29, no. 2 (2001): 179.

18. Howells, *The Minister's Charge,* 100.

19. Ibid., 101.

20. Ibid., 341.

21. Ibid., 341–42.

22. Ibid., 342. In reading this sermon as presented in free indirect discourse, I differ from Barton, who attributes it wholly to the narrator (183). The sermonic cadences of "Complicity" (e.g., "for good or for evil, for sorrow or joy, for sickness or health") and its theological language (e.g., "The gospel—Christ—God, so far as men had imagined him") distinguish it from the narrator's own speech.

23. Howells, *The Minister's Charge,* 341.

24. Similarly, Brook Thomas remarks that the "Complicity" sermon is "an important point of view within the novel," but not the only valid one (*American Literary Realism and the Failed Promise of Contract* [Berkeley: University of California Press, 1997], 146). See, too, Barton, who argues that Sewell's final sermon cannot stand as a definitive last word and that to take it as such is to ignore both Sewell's fallibility and the dialogism of the realist novel (177–83). Barton's quarrel on this point is mainly with Wai-Chee Dimock, who takes Sewell as representative of Howells's own philosophy (see Dimock, "The Economy of Pain: Capitalism, Humanitarianism, and the Realistic Novel," in *New Essays on The Rise of Silas Lapham,* ed. Donald E. Pease [Cambridge, UK: Cambridge University Press, 1991], 67–90).

25. Dawson, 193. Here I differ from Paul Abeln, who notes only how the sermon is critiqued. He maintains that the sermon achieves only "ephemeral effects," not "moments of cultural transformation" (*William Dean Howells and the Ends of Realism* [New York: Routledge, 2005], 23–24). I would say rather that the novel withholds judgment on the sermon's long-term effects. It does not describe social reforms resulting from this sermon but does leave open the

possibility that appealing to individuals might result in a better society by presenting without irony Sewell's belief "that you can have a righteous public only by the slow process of having righteous men and women" (341).

26. Paul Petrie, *Conscience and Purpose: Fiction and Social Consciousness in Howells, Jewett, Chesnutt, and Cather* (Tuscaloosa: University of Alabama Press, 2005), 29–30.

27. Howells, *The Minister's Charge,* 179.

28. Hebrews 13:3.

29. W. D. Howells, "Novel-Writing and Novel-Reading: An Impersonal Explanation," in *Selected Literary Criticism, Volume III: 1898–1920,* ed. Ronald Gottesman, Christoph K. Lohmann, et al. (Bloomington: Indiana University Press, 1993), 228. Cf. B. Thomas, who explains that Howells's "point is that judgment will follow if the novelist is not afraid to treat all sorts of subject matter, even the repressed ones of society" (323n39). Besides noting that Thomas seems to have meant "unafraid" for "afraid," I would say that while Howells calls for novelists to bring to light society's repressed subjects, he is not threatening them with impending judgment if they fail to do so. Instead, he makes the public, not God, the judge by refiguring the day of judgment as an ongoing event resulting from the novelist's bold exposure of "hidden things."

30. Howells, *The Minister's Charge,* 344.

31. Ibid., 341.

32. Pew Forum on Religion and Public Life, "U.S. Religious Landscape Survey: Religious Affiliation: Diverse and Dynamic" (2008), 145, 154. To disaggregate these Protestants, 86 percent of those attending evangelical churches reported attending at least a few times a year, as did 76 percent of those attending mainline churches and 88 percent of those attending historically black churches. The published survey results do not indicate the percentage of the U.S. population these attendees constitute.

33. National Endowment for the Arts, "Reading on the Rise: A New Chapter in American Literacy" (2009), 3.

34. Walt Whitman, *Leaves of Grass and Selected Prose,* ed. Lawrence Buell (New York: Modern Library, 1981), 471.

WORKS CITED

Abbot, John Emery. *A Catechism of the New Testament.* Salem, MA: T. C. Cushing, 1817.

———. *Extracts from Sermons by the Late Rev. John Emery Abbot, of Salem, Mass. With a Memoir of His Life, by Henry Ware, Jr.,* ed. Henry Ware, Jr. Boston: Wait, Greene, & Co., 1830.

———. *Sermons of the Late Rev. John Emery Abbot, of Salem, Mass. with a Memoir of His Life, by Henry Ware, Jr.,* ed. Henry Ware, Jr. Boston: Wait, Greene, & Co., 1829.

Abbott, John S. C. *A Sermon on the Reciprocal Duties of Pastor and People.* Boston: Crocker and Brewster, 1841.

Abell, Mrs. L. G. *Woman in her Various Relations: Containing Practical Rules for American Females.* New York: R. T. Young, 1853.

Abeln, Paul. *William Dean Howells and the Ends of Realism.* New York: Routledge, 2005.

[Alcott, William A.]. *Letters to a Sister; or Woman's Mission. To Accompany the Letters to Young Men.* Buffalo, NY: Geo. H. Derby and Co., 1850.

———. *The Young Husband, or Duties of Man in the Marriage Relation.* Boston: George W. Light, 1839.

———. *The Young Man's Guide.* Boston: Lilly, Wait, & Co., 1833. Boston: T. R. Marvin, 1846.

Allen, George. *Resistance to Slavery Every Man's Duty: A Report on American Slavery, Read to the Worcester Central Association, March 2, 1847.* Boston: Crosby and Nichols, 1847.

Alter, Robert. *Pen of Iron: American Prose and the King James Bible.* Princeton: Princeton University Press, 2010.

Andrews, William L. "The Novelization of Voice in Early African American Narrative." *PMLA* 15, no. 1 (1990): 23–34.

Anti-Slavery Advocate, 1852–1854.

Applegate, Debby. *The Most Famous Man in America: The Biography of Henry Ward Beecher.* New York: Doubleday, 2006.

Arac, Jonathan. *The Emergence of American Literary Narrative, 1820–1860.* Cambridge, MA: Harvard University Press, 2005.

Arens, Edmund. "Religion as Ritual, Communicative, and Critical Praxis." Trans. Chad Kautzer. In *The Frankfurt School on Religion: Key Writings by the Major Thinkers*, ed. Eduardo Mendieta, 373–96. New York: Routledge, 2005.

Armstrong, Nancy. *Desire and Domestic Fiction: A Political History of the Novel*. New York: Oxford University Press, 1987.

———. "The Rise of the Domestic Woman." In *The Ideology of Conduct: Essays on Literature and the History of Sexuality*, ed. Nancy Armstrong and Leonard Tennenhouse, 96–141. New York: Methuen, 1987.

Arthur, T. S. *Advice to Young Ladies on Their Duties and Conduct in Life*. Boston: Phillips & Sampson, 1848.

———. *Advice to Young Men on Their Duties and Conduct in Life*. Boston: N. C. Barton, 1848.

Asad, Talal. *Formations of the Secular: Christianity, Islam, and Modernity*. Stanford: Stanford University Press, 2003.

———. *Genealogies of Religion: Discipline and Reasons of Power in Christianity and Islam*. Baltimore: The Johns Hopkins University Press, 1993.

Ashworth, Suzanne. "Susan Warner's *The Wide, Wide World*, Conduct Literature, and Protocols of Female Reading in Mid-Nineteenth-Century America." *Legacy* 17, no. 2 (2000): 141–64.

Auerbach, Erich. *Mimesis: The Representation of Reality in Western Literature*. Trans. Willard R. Trask. Princeton: Princeton University Press, 1953.

Augst, Thomas. *The Clerk's Tale: Young Men and Moral Life in Nineteenth-Century America*. Chicago: University of Chicago Press, 2003.

Augustine, *On Christian Teaching*. Trans. R. P. H. Green. Oxford: Oxford University Press, 1997.

Austin, John. "United States, 1780–1850." In *The Novel: Volume 1, History, Geography, and Culture*, ed. Franco Moretti, 455–65. Princeton: Princeton University Press, 2006.

Bacon, Thomas. *Sermons Addressed to Masters and Servants, and Published in the Year 1743, by the Rev. Thomas Bacon, Minister of the Protestant Episcopal Church in Maryland. Now Republished with other Tracts and Dialogues on the Same Subject, and Recommended to all Masters and Mistresses to be Used in Their Families*, ed. William Meade. Winchester, VA: John Heiskell, 1813.

Bailey, Julius H. "Masculinizing the Pulpit: The Black Preacher in the Nineteenth-Century AME Church." In *Fathers, Preachers, Rebels, Men: Black Masculinity in U.S. History and Literature, 1820–1945*, ed. Timothy R. Buckner and Peter Caster, 80–101. Columbus: The Ohio State University Press, 2011.

Baird, Robert. *Religion in America*. New York: Harper and Brothers, 1844.

Baldwin, James. "Everybody's Protest Novel." In *Critical Essays on Harriet Beecher Stowe*, ed. Elizabeth Ammons, 92–97. Boston: G. K. Hall, 1980.

Balmer, Randall. *Mine Eyes Have Seen the Glory: A Journey into the Evangelical Subculture in America*. 4th ed. New York: Oxford University Press, 2006.

Bancroft, Aaron. "The Importance of Attending to Our Own Salvation." *Liberal Preacher* 3 (1830): 161–68.

Barnes, S. H. *A Book for the Eldest Daughter*. Boston: Massachusetts Sabbath School Society, 1849.

Barton, John Cyril. "Howells's Rhetoric of Realism: The Economy of Pain(t) and Social Complicity in *The Rise of Silas Lapham*." *Studies in American Fiction* 29, no. 2 (2001): 159–87.

Bassard, Katherine Clay. *Transforming Scriptures: African American Women Writers and the Bible*. Athens: University of Georgia Press, 2010.

Baym, Nina. *Novels, Readers, and Reviewers: Responses to Fiction in Antebellum America*. Ithaca, NY: Cornell University Press, 1984.

————. "Passion and Authority in *The Scarlet Letter*." *The New England Quarterly* 43, no. 2 (1970): 209–30.

Beecher, Catharine E., and Harriet Beecher Stowe. *The American Woman's Home*. New York: J. B. Ford & Co., 1869.

————. *Educational Reminiscences and Suggestions*. New York: J. B. Ford, 1874.

Beecher, Henry Ward. *Yale Lectures on Preaching*. New York: J. B. Ford and Company, 1872.

Beecher, Lyman. *Lectures on Intemperance*. London: Clarke, Beeton, and Co., [1853?].

————. *Letters of the Rev. Dr. Beecher and Rev. Mr. Nettleton, on the 'New Measures' in Conducting Revivals of Religion: with a Review of a Sermon by Novanglus*. New York: Carvill, 1828.

————. *A Sermon Addressed to the Legislature of Connecticut, at New Haven, on the Day of the Anniversary Election, May 3d, 1826*. New Haven, 1826.

Bell, Catherine. *Ritual Theory, Ritual Practice*. New York: Oxford University Press, 1992.

Bell, Michael Davitt. *The Development of American Romance: The Sacrifice of Relation*. Chicago: University of Chicago Press, 1980.

————. *Hawthorne and the Historical Romance of New England*. Princeton: Princeton University Press, 1971.

Bellin, Joshua D. "Up to Heaven's Gate, Down in Earth's Dust: The Politics of Judgment in *Uncle Tom's Cabin*." *American Literature* 65, no. 2 (1993): 275–95.

Bellows, Henry W. *Relation of Christianity to Human Nature: A Sermon Preached at the Ordination of Mr. Frederick N. Knapp, As Colleague Pastor of the First Congregational Church in Brookline, Mass. on Wednesday, October 6, 1847*. Boston: Wm. Crosby & H. P. Nichols, 1847.

————. *Re-Statements of Christian Doctrine in Twenty-Five Sermons*. New York: D. Appleton & Company, 1859.

Bercovitch, Sacvan. *The American Jeremiad*. Madison: University of Wisconsin Press, 1978.

————. *The Office of the Scarlet Letter*. Baltimore: The Johns Hopkins University Press, 1991.

Bethune, George W. *The Eloquence of the Pulpit, with Illustrations from St. Paul. An Oration before the Porter Rhetorical Society of the Theological Seminary at Andover, Mass. 1842*. Andover, MA: William Peirce, 1842.

Bezanson, Walter E. "Moby-Dick: Work of Art." In *The Critical Response to Herman Melville's Moby-Dick*, ed. Kevin J. Hayes, 76–98. Westport, CT: Greenwood, 1994.

Bilhartz, T. D. "Sex and the Second Great Awakening: The Feminization of American Religion Reconsidered." In *Belief and Behavior: Essays in the New Religious History*, ed. Philip R. Vandermeer and Robert P. Swierenga, 117–35. New Brunswick: Rutgers University Press, 1991.

Blair, Hugh. *Lectures on Rhetoric and Belles Lettres*. 13th American ed. New York: James and John Harper, 1824.

Blodgett, Jan. *Protestant Evangelical Literary Culture and Contemporary Society*. Westport, CT: Greenwood Press, 1997.

Bohde, Cheryl D. "'Magazines as a Powerful Element of Civilization': An Exploration of the Ideology of Literary Magazines, 1830–1850." *American Periodicals* 1, no. 1 (1991): 34–45.

Bourdieu, Pierre. *The Field of Cultural Production: Essays on Art and Literature*. New York: Columbia University Press, 1993.

[Bouton, John Bell]. *The Life and Choice Writings of George Lippard*. New York: H. H. Randall, 1855.

Bowditch, William I. *Slavery and the Constitution*. Boston: Robert F. Wallcut, 1849.

Boydston, Jeanne, Mary Kelley, and Anne Margolis. *The Limits of Sisterhood: The Beecher Sisters on Women's Rights and Woman's Sphere*. Chapel Hill: University of North Carolina Press, 1988.

Brady, Jennifer. "Theorizing a Reading Public: Sentimentality and Advice about Novel Reading in the Antebellum United States." *American Literature* 83, no. 4 (2011): 720–46.

Braswell, William. *Melville's Religious Thought: An Essay in Interpretation.* New York: Pageant Books, 1959.

———. "Melville's Use of Seneca." *American Literature* 12 (1940): 98–104.

Braude, Ann. "Women's History *Is* American Religious History." In *Retelling U.S. Religious History,* ed. Thomas A. Tweed, 87–107. Berkeley: University of California Press, 1997.

Brazer, John. "On the Value of the Public Exercises of Our Religion." *The Liberal Preacher* 2 (1832): 16.

Brekus, Catherine. *Strangers and Pilgrims: Female Preaching in America, 1740–1845.* Chapel Hill: University of North Carolina Press, 1998.

Bressler, Ann Lee. *The Universalist Movement in America, 1770–1880.* New York: Oxford University Press, 2001.

Brilioth, Yngve. *A Brief History of Preaching.* Translated by Karl E. Mattson. Philadelphia: Fortress Press, 1965.

Brodhead, Richard. *Cultures of Letters: Scenes of Reading and Writing in Nineteenth-Century America.* Chicago: University of Chicago Press, 1993.

———. *The School of Hawthorne.* New York: Oxford University Press, 1986.

Brontë, Charlotte. *Jane Eyre.* 1847. New York: Knopf, 1991.

Brooks, Gennifer Benjamin. "Preaching." In *The Oxford Handbook of Methodist Studies,* ed. William J. Abraham and James E. Kirby, 361–75. Oxford: Oxford University Press, 2008.

Brotherhood of the Union Papers, Series A, folder 4, a folio ms., 10p. Library Company.

Brown, Amy Benson. *Rewriting the Word: American Women Writers and the Bible.* Westport, CT: Greenwood Press, 1999.

Brown, Candy Gunther. *The Word in the World: Evangelical Writing, Publishing, and Reading in America, 1789–1880.* Chapel Hill: University of North Carolina Press, 2004.

Brown, William Wells. *Clotel; or, The President's Daughter: A Narrative of Slave Life in the United States.* London: Partridge and Oakey, 1853.

———. *Clotel; or, The President's Daughter: A Narrative of Slave Life in the United States,* ed. Robert S. Levine. Boston: Bedford/St. Martin's, 2000.

———. *Clotel; or, The President's Daughter: A Narrative of Slave Life in the United States,* ed. Robert S. Levine. Boston: Bedford/St. Martin's, 2011.

———. *Clotelle: A Tale of the Southern States.* Boston: James Redpath, 1864.

———. *Clotelle; or The Colored Heroine, A Tale of the Southern States.* Boston: Lee and Shepard, 1867.

———. "A Lecture Delivered before the Female Anti-Slavery Society of Salem." In *William Wells Brown: A Reader,* ed. Ezra Greenspan, 107–29. Athens: University of Georgia Press, 2002.

———. *My Southern Home: or the South and Its People.* In *From Fugitive Slave to Free Man,* ed. William L. Andrews, 110–296. Columbia: University of Missouri Press, 2003.

———. *Narrative of William W. Brown, A Fugitive Slave, Written by Himself.* 1848. In *From Fugitive Slave to Free Man: The Autobiographies of William Wells Brown,* ed. William L. Andrews, 27–109. Columbia: University of Missouri Press, 2003.

———. "Speech delivered at the Lecture Hall, Croydon, England, September 5, 1849." In *The Works of William Wells Brown: Using His "Strong, Manly Voice,"* ed. Paula Garrett and Hollis Robbins, 19–23. New York: Oxford University Press, 2006.

———. "Speech delivered at the Town Hall, Manchester, England, August 1, 1854." In *The Works of William Wells Brown: Using His "Strong, Manly Voice,"* ed. Paula Garrett and Hollis Robbins, 33–39. New York: Oxford University Press, 2006.

———. "A True Story." *Anti-Slavery Advocate* 3 (December 1852): 23.

Bruhm, Steven. *Gothic Bodies: The Politics of Pain in Romantic Fiction.* Philadelphia: University of Pennsylvania Press, 1994.

Brunson, Martha L. "Novelists as Platform Readers: Dickens, Clemens, and Stowe." In *Performance of Literature in Historical Perspectives,* ed. David W. Thompson, 651–82. Lanham, MD: University Press of America, 1983.

Bryant, John. *Melville and Repose: The Rhetoric of Humor in the American Renaissance.* New York: Oxford University Press, 1993.

[Buck, Charles and Ebenezer Henderson]. "Declamation of the Pulpit." In *Fessenden & Co.'s Encyclopedia of Religious Knowledge: or Dictionary of the Bible, Theology, Religious Biography, All Religions, Ecclesiastical History, and Missions,* ed. J. Newton Brown, 447. Brattleboro', VT: Brattleboro' Typographic Company, 1840.

Buell, Lawrence. "The Literary Significance of the Unitarian Movement." *ESQ* 33, no. 4 (1987): 212–23.

———. *Literary Transcendentalism: Style and Vision in the American Renaissance.* Ithaca, NY: Cornell University Press, [1973].

———. "Religion on the American Mind." *American Literary History* 19, no. 1 (2007): 32–55.

———. "The Unitarian Movement and the Art of Preaching in 19th-Century America." *American Quarterly* 24, no. 2 (1972): 166–90.

———. "The Unkillable Dream of the Great American Novel: *Moby-Dick* as Test Case." *American Literary History* 20, nos. 1–2 (2008): 132–55.

Burnap, George W. *Lectures on the Sphere and Duties of Woman.* Baltimore: John Murphy, 1841.

———. *Lectures to Young Men, on the Cultivation of the Mind, the Formation of Character, and the Conduct of Life: Delivered in Masonic Hall, Baltimore.* Baltimore: John Murphy, 1840.

Butler, Jon. *Awash in a Sea of Faith: Christianizing the American People.* Cambridge, MA: Harvard University Press, 1990.

Butterfield, Roger. "George Lippard and His Secret Brotherhood." *Pennsylvania Magazine of History and Biography* 79 (1955): 285–309.

Calhoun, Craig, Mark Juergensmeyer, and Jonathan VanAntwerpen. Introduction. *Rethinking Secularism,* ed. Craig Calhoun, Mark Juergensmeyer, and Jonathan VanAntwerpen, 3–30. New York: Oxford University Press, 2011.

Campbell, George. *The Philosophy of Rhetoric,* ed. Lloyd F. Bitzer. Carbondale: Southern Illinois University Press, 1963.

Carwardine, Richard J. *Evangelicals and Politics in Antebellum America.* 1993. Knoxville: University of Tennessee Press, 1997.

Cary, Virginia. *Letters on Female Character, Addressed to a Young Lady, on the Death of Her Mother.* Richmond, VA: A. Works, 1828.

Casanova, José. "A Secular Age: Dawn or Twilight?" In *Varieties of Secularism in a Secular Age,* ed. Michael Warner, Jonathan VanAntwerpen, and Craig Calhoun, 265–81. Cambridge, MA: Harvard University Press, 2010.

Castronovo, Russ. *Fathering the Nation: American Genealogies of Slavery and Freedom.* Berkeley: University of California Press, 1995.

A Catalogue of the Members of the North Church in Salem, with an Historical Sketch of the Church. Salem: W. and S. B. Ives, 1827.

Ceplair, Larry, ed. *The Public Years of Sarah and Angelina Grimké: Selected Writings, 1835–1839.* New York: Columbia University Press, 1989.

Chai, Leon. *The Romantic Foundations of the American Renaissance.* Ithaca, NY: Cornell University Press, 1987.

Chakkalakal, Tess. *Novel Bondage: Slavery, Marriage, and Freedom in Nineteenth-Century America.* Urbana: University of Illinois Press, 2011.

Channing, Edward T. *Lectures Read to the Seniors in Harvard College.* Boston: Ticknor and Fields, 1856.

Channing, William Ellery. *A Sermon, Delivered at the Ordination of the Rev. John Emery Abbot.* Salem, MA: Cushing, 1815.

———. *The Works of William E. Channing, D.D.* Boston: James Munroe, 1848.

Chapman, Mary, and Glenn Hendler, eds. *Sentimental Men: Masculinity and the Politics of Affect in American Culture.* Berkeley: University of California Press, 1999.

Chapman, Raymond. *Forms of Speech in Victorian Fiction.* London: Longman, 1984.

Charvat, William. *The Origins of American Critical Thought, 1810–35.* Philadelphia: University of Pennsylvania Press, 1936.

Chase, Richard. *The American Novel and Its Tradition.* Garden City, NY: Doubleday, 1957.

———. *Herman Melville: A Critical Study.* New York: Macmillan, 1949.

Chesebrough, David B. *Theodore Parker: Orator of Superior Ideas.* Westport, CT: Greenwood, 1999.

Clark, Gregory, and S. Michael Halloran, eds. *Oratorical Culture in Nineteenth-Century America: Transformations in the Theory and Practice of Rhetoric.* Carbondale: Southern Illinois University Press, 1993.

Clark, Thomas M. *Early Discipline and Culture: A Series of Lectures to Young Men and Women.* Providence, RI: George H. Whitney, 1855.

Cohen, Lara. "Democratic Representations: Puffery and the Antebellum Print Explosion." *American Literature* 79, no. 4 (2007): 643–72.

Colacurcio, Michael. *The Province of Piety: Moral History in Hawthorne's Early Tales.* Cambridge, MA: Harvard University Press, 1984.

Coleman, Dawn. "The Antebellum American Sermon as Lived Religion." In *A New History of the Sermon: The Nineteenth Century,* ed. Robert H. Ellison, 521–54. Leiden: Brill, 2010.

———. "Critiquing Perfection: Hawthorne's Revision of Salem's Unitarian Saint." *Nathaniel Hawthorne Review* 37, no. 1 (2011): 1–19.

Collyer, Robert. *Father Taylor.* Boston: American Unitarian Association, 1906.

Conkin, Paul K. *American Originals: Homemade Varieties of Christianity.* Chapel Hill: University of North Carolina Press, 1997.

Couégnas, Daniel. "Forms of Popular Narrative in France and England: 1700–1900." In *The Novel, Volume 1: History, Geography, and Culture,* ed. Franco Moretti, 313–35. Princeton: Princeton University Press, 2006.

Cowen, Walker. *Melville's Marginalia,* 2 vols. New York: Garland, 1987.

Coxe, Margaret. *The Young Lady's Companion: In a Series of Letters.* Columbus, OH: I. N. Whiting, 1839.

Crews, Frederick. *Sins of the Fathers: Hawthorne's Psychological Themes.* New York: Oxford University Press, 1966.

Dahl, Curtis. "Jonah Improved: Sea Sermons on Jonah." *Extracts* 19 (1974): 6–9.

Daly, John Patrick. *When Slavery Was Called Freedom: Evangelicalism, Proslavery, and the Causes of the Civil War.* Lexington: University Press of Kentucky, 2002.

Davidson, Cathy. *Revolution and the Word: The Rise of the Novel in America.* Expanded ed. Oxford: Oxford University Press, 2004.

Dawson, Melanie. "Searching for 'Common Ground': Class, Sympathy, and Perspective in Howells' Social Fiction." *American Literary Realism* 39, no. 3 (2007): 189–212.

De Grazia, Emilio. *The Life and Works of George Lippard.* Ann Arbor, MI: University Microfilms, 1970.

Delbanco, Andrew. *Melville: His World and Work.* New York: Knopf, 2005.

———. *William Ellery Channing: An Essay on the Liberal Spirit in America.* Cambridge, MA: Harvard University Press, 1981.

Denning, Michael. *Mechanic Accents: Dime Novels and Working-Class Culture in America.* London: Verso, 1987.

Dewey, Orville. On the Preaching of Our Saviour. *A a* [*sic*] *Sermon Delivered at the Ordination of Joseph Angier as Pastor of the First Congregational Church in New-Bedford.* May 20, 1835. New Bedford: Benjamin T. Congdon, 1835.

———. On Reading. *A Lecture Delivered Before the Mechanics' Library Association in New York.* Cambridge, MA: Metcalf, Torry, and Ballou, 1839.

———. *The Pulpit, as a Field of Exertion, Talent, and Piety: A Sermon Delivered at the Installation of the Rev. Edward B. Hall, as Pastor of the First Congregational Society in Providence.* New Bedford: Benjamin Lindsey, 1832.

———. *The Works of Orville Dewey, D.D., With a Biographical Sketch.* Boston: American Unitarian Association, 1883.

Dickens, Charles. *Great Expectations,* ed. Margaret Cardwell. 1861. Oxford: Oxford University Press, Clarendon Press, 1993.

Dimock, Wai-Chee. "The Economy of Pain: Capitalism, Humanitarianism, and the Realistic Novel." In *New Essays on* The Rise of Silas Lapham, ed. Donald E. Pease, 67–90. Cambridge, UK: Cambridge University Press, 1991.

Dobbelaere, Karel. "The Meaning and Scope of Secularization." In *The Oxford Handbook of the Sociology of Religion,* ed. Peter B. Clarke, 599-615. New York: Oxford University Press, 2009.

Dorsey, Peter. "De-authorizing Slavery: Realism in Stowe's *Uncle Tom's Cabin* and Brown's *Clotel.*" *ESQ* 41, no. 4 (1995): 259–62.

Douglas, Ann. *The Feminization of American Culture.* New York: Farrar, Strauss, Giroux, Noonday Press, 1998.

Douglass, Frederick. *Narrative of the Life of Frederick Douglass, an American Slave. Written by Himself.* Boston: Anti-Slavery Office, 1845.

Douglass-Chinn, Richard J. *Preacher Woman Sings the Blues: The Autobiographies of Nineteenth-Century African American Evangelists.* Columbia: University of Missouri Press, 2001.

Duban, James. *Melville's Major Fiction: Politics, Theology, and Imagination.* Dekalb: Northern Illinois University Press, 1983.

Du Bois, W. E. B. *The Souls of Black Folk.* 1903; New York: Penguin, 1996.

Durkheim, Émile. *The Elementary Forms of Religious Life,* ed. Mark S. Cladis, trans. Carol Cosman. New York: Oxford University Press, 2001.

Durson, Pamela R. *The Power of Woman: The Life and Writings of Sarah Moore Grimké.* Macon, GA: Mercer University Press, 2003.

Edwards, Jonathan. *A Jonathan Edwards Reader,* ed. John E. Smith, Harry S. Stout, and Kenneth P. Minkema. New Haven: Yale University Press, 1995.

Edwards, Mary K. Bercaw. *Cannibal Old Me: Spoken Sources in Melville's Early Works.* Kent, OH: Kent State University Press, 2009.

Edwards, O. C., Jr. *A History of Preaching.* Nashville: Abingdon Press, 2004.

———. "The Preaching of Romanticism in America." *American Transcendental Quarterly* 14, no. 4 (2000): 297–312.

"Elegiac Stanzas (On the Death of John Emery Abbot)." Salem: n. p., 1819.

Eliot, William G., Jr. *Lectures to Young Men.* 5th ed. Boston: Crosby, Nichols, 1855.

Elliot, Emory. *Power and the Pulpit in Puritan New England.* Princeton: Princeton University Press, 1975.

———. "'Wandering To-and-Fro': Melville and Religion." *A Historical Guide to Herman Melville*, ed. Giles Gunn, 167–204. New York: Oxford University Press, 2005.

Elliott, Charles. *Sinfulness of American Slavery: Proved from Its Evil Sources; Its Injustice; Its Wrongs; Its Contrariety to Many Scriptural Commands, Prohibitions, and Principles, and to the Christian Spirit; and from Its Evil Effects; Together with Observations on Emancipation, and the Duties of American Citizens in Regard to Slavery*, ed. B. F. Tefft. 2 vols. Cincinnati: L. Swormstedt and J. H. Power, 1851.

Ellison, Robert, ed. *A New History of the Sermon: The Nineteenth Century*. Leiden: Brill, 2010.

———. *The Victorian Pulpit: Spoken and Written Sermons in Nineteenth-Century Britain*. Selinsgrove, PA: Susquehanna University Press. London: Associated University Presses, 1998.

Elsemore, Moses. *An Impartial Account of the Life of the Rev. John Newland Maffitt*. New York: John F. Feeks, 1848.

Emerson, Ralph Waldo. *Emerson's Prose and Poetry: Authoritative Texts, Contexts, Criticism*, ed. Joel Porte and Saundra Morris. New York: Norton, 2001.

———. *The Journals and Miscellaneous Notebooks of Ralph Waldo Emerson*. Vol. 5, 1835–38, ed. William Gilman et al. Cambridge, MA: Harvard University Press, Belknap Press, 1965.

———. *Journals of Ralph Waldo Emerson, 1820–1872*. Vol. 7, ed. Edward Waldo Emerson and Waldo Emerson Forbes. Boston and New York: Houghton Mifflin Company, 1912.

Erickson, Paul. "New Books, New Men: City-Mysteries Fiction, Authorship, and the Literary Market." *Early American Studies* 1, no. 1 (2003): 273–312.

Ernest, John. "The Governing Spirit: African American Writers in the Antebellum City on a Hill." In *A Mighty Baptism: Race, Gender, and the Creation of American Protestantism*, ed. Susan Juster and Lisa MacFarlane, 259–79. Ithaca, NY: Cornell University Press, 1996.

———. *Resistance and Reformation in Nineteenth-Century African-American Literature: Brown, Wilson, Jacobs, Delany, Douglass, and Harper*. Jackson: University Press of Mississippi, 1995.

Estlin, J[ohn] B[ishop]. *A Brief Notice of American Slavery, and the Abolition Movement*, 2nd ed., revised. London: Tweedie, 1853.

Farrell, James J. *Inventing the American Way of Death, 1830–1920*. Philadelphia: Temple University Press, 1980.

Farrison, William Edward. *William Wells Brown: Author and Reformer*. Chicago: University of Chicago Press, 1969.

Ferrell, Lori Anne and Peter E. McCullough, eds. *The English Sermon Revised: Religion, Literature, and History 1600–1750*. Manchester, UK: Manchester University Press, 2000.

Fiedler, Leslie A. Introduction. *The Monks of Monk Hall* by George Lippard, ed. Leslie A. Fiedler, vii–xxxii. New York: Odyssey, 1970.

———. *Love and Death in the American Novel*. 1966. Normal, IL: Dalkey Archive Press, 1997.

Field, David D. *The Reciprocal Duties of Ministers and People: A Sermon, Preached in the First Society of Killingworth, June 11, 1817, at the Ordination of the Rev. Hart Talcott*. Middletown, CT: T. Dunning, 1817.

[Fields, James T.]. "Our Whispering Gallery." *Atlantic Monthly* 27, Feb. to May 1871. In *Hawthorne in His Own Time: A Biographical Chronicle of His Life, Drawn from Recollections, Interviews, and Memoirs by Family, Friends, and Associates*, ed. Ronald A. Bosco and Jillmarie Murphy, 130–50. Iowa City: University of Iowa Press, 2007.

Finke, Roger and Rodney Stark. *The Churching of America, 1776–2005: Winners and Losers in Our Religious Economy*. 2nd ed. New Brunswick: Rutgers University Press, 2005.

Finney, Charles Grandison. *Lectures on Revivals of Religion*. Cambridge, MA: Belknap-Harvard University Press, 1960.

Fisch, Audrey A. *American Slaves in Victorian England: Abolitionist Politics in Popular Literature and Culture*. Cambridge, UK: Cambridge University Press, 2000.

Fisk, Theophilus. *Capital Against Labor: An Address Delivered at Julien Hall, Before the Mechanics of Boston, on Wednesday Evening, May 20.* Boston, 1835.

———. *Labor the Only True Source of Wealth, or The Rottenness of the Paper Money Banking System Exposed* [. . .]. Charleston, SC, 1837.

———. *The Pleasures of Sin: A Discourse Delivered at the Capitol, in the City of Washington, on Sunday Morning, December 16, 1827.* Philadelphia, 1828.

Fliegelman, Jay. *Declaring Independence: Jefferson, Natural Language, and the Culture of Performance.* Stanford, CA: Stanford University Press, 1993.

Foner, Philip S. *William Heighton: Pioneer Labor Leader of Jacksonian Philadelphia, With Selections from Heighton's Writings and Speeches.* New York: International Publishers, 1991.

[Foote, Caleb]. "*The Scarlet Letter.*" *Salem Gazette,* March 19, 1850. In *Nathaniel Hawthorne: The Contemporary Reviews,* ed. John L. Idol, Jr. and Buford Jones, 119. Cambridge, UK: Cambridge University Press, 1994.

Forster, E. M. *Aspects of the Novel.* 1927. New York: Harcourt, 1955.

Foster, Charles H. "Something in Emblems: A Reinterpretation of *Moby-Dick.*" *New England Quarterly* 34, no. 1 (1961): 3–35.

Fox, Charles, and Samuel Osgood. *The New Hampshire Book: Being Specimens of Literature from the Granite State.* Nashua: David Marshall; Boston: James Monroe and Company, 1842.

Franchot, Jenny. "Invisible Domain: Religion and American Literary Studies." *American Literature* 67, no. 4 (1995): 833–42.

———. *Roads to Rome: The Antebellum Protestant Encounter with Catholicism.* Berkeley: University of California Press, 1994.

Frederick, John T. *The Darkened Sky: Nineteenth-Century American Novelists and Religion.* Notre Dame, IN: University of Notre Dame Press, 1969.

Fredricks, Nancy. *Melville's Art of Democracy.* Athens: University of Georgia Press, 1995.

Freehling, William W. *The Reintegration of American History.* New York: Oxford University Press, 1994.

Freeling, Arthur. *The Young Bride's Book: An Epitome of the Domestic Duties and Social Enjoyments of Woman, as Wife and Mother.* New York: Wilson and Company, 1849.

Frost, Robert. *The Collected Prose of Robert Frost,* ed. Mark Richardson. Cambridge, MA: Harvard University Press, Belknap Press, 2007.

Frye, Northrop. *Anatomy of Criticism: Four Essays.* Princeton: Princeton University Press, 1957.

Garrison, William Lloyd. *An Address, Delivered Before the Free People of Color, in Philadelphia, New-York, and Other Cities, During the Month of June, 1831.* Boston: Stephen Foster, 1831.

Gatell, Frank Otto. *John Gorham Palfrey and the New England Conscience.* Cambridge, MA: Harvard University Press, 1963.

Gates, Henry Louis, Jr., ed. *Three Classic African-American Novels: Clotel, Iola Leroy, The Marrow of Tradition.* New York: Random House, Vintage, 1990.

Gatta, John. *Making Nature Sacred: Literature, Religion, and Environment in America from the Puritans to the Present.* New York: Oxford University Press, 2004.

Gedge, Karin E. *Without Benefit of Clergy: Women and the Pastoral Relationship in Nineteenth-Century American Culture.* New York: Oxford University Press, 2003.

Genovese, Eugene D. *Roll, Jordan, Roll: The World the Slaves Made.* New York: Random House, Vintage, 1972.

Gilmore, Michael T. *American Romanticism and the Marketplace.* Chicago: University of Chicago Press, 1985.

———. "The Book Marketplace I." *The Columbia History of the American Novel,* ed. Emory Elliott, 46–71. New York: Columbia University Press, 1991.

————. *Surface and Depth: The Quest for Legibility in American Culture.* Oxford: Oxford University Press, 2003.

————. "*Uncle Tom's Cabin* and the American Renaissance: The Sacramental Aesthetic of Harriet Beecher Stowe." In *The Cambridge Companion to Harriet Beecher Stowe,* ed. Cindy Weinstein, 58–76. Cambridge, UK: Cambridge University Press, 2004.

Godolphin, Gregory. *The Unique, a Book of Its Own Kind: Containing a Variety of Hints, Thrown out in a Variety of Ways, for Evangelical Ministers, Churches, and Christians.* Boston: Putnam, 1844.

Golden, James L., and Edward P. J. Corbett, *The Rhetoric of Blair, Campbell, and Whately, with Updated Bibliographies.* Carbondale: Southern Illinois University Press, 1990.

Goody, Jack. *The Interface Between the Written and the Oral.* Cambridge, UK: Cambridge University Press, 1987.

Gorski, Philip S., and Ateş Altınordu. "After Secularization?" *Annual Review of Sociology* 34 (2008): 55–85.

Gossett, Thomas. *Uncle Tom's Cabin and American Culture.* Dallas: Southern Methodist University Press, 1985.

Gould, Sarah. *A Golden Legacy to Daughters, or Advice to Young Ladies.* Boston: Higgins, Bradley and Dayton, 1857.

Graham, John. "Struggling Upward: *The Minister's Charge* and *A Cool Million.*" *Canadian Review of American Studies* 4 (1973): 184–96.

The Great Divorce Case! A Full and Impartial History of the Trial of the Petition of Mrs. Sarah M. Jarvis, for a Divorce from Her Husband, the Rev. Samuel F. Jarvis, D.D. L.L.D. Before a Committee of the Legislature of the State of Connecticut. New York, 1839.

Greenspan, Ezra. Introduction. *William Wells Brown: A Reader,* ed. Ezra Greenspan, ix–xxv. Athens: University of Georgia Press, 2002.

Grey, Robin, ed. *Melville and Milton: An Edition and Analysis of Melville's Annotations on Milton.* Pittsburgh, PA: Duquesne University Press, 2004.

Griffin, Edward D. *A Sermon on the Art of Preaching, Delivered before the Pastoral Association of Massachusetts in Boston, May 25, 1825.* Boston: T. R. Marvin, 1825.

[Grimké, Sarah]. *An Address to Free Colored Americans. Issued by an Anti-Slavery Convention of American Women, Held in the City of New-York, by adjournments from 9th to 12th May, 1837.* New York: William S. Dorr, 1837.

Grodzins, Dean. *American Heretic: Theodore Parker and Transcendentalism.* Chapel Hill: University of North Carolina Press, 2002.

Gulick, L. H. *A Sermon on the Foolishness of Preaching.* Honolulu: Government Press, 1853.

Gura, Philip. *The Wisdom of Words: Language, Theology, and Literature in the New England Renaissance.* Middletown, CT: Wesleyan University Press, 1981.

Gustafson, James. "The Clergy in the United States." In *The Professions in America,* ed. Kenneth S. Lynn and the editors of *Daedalus,* 70–90. Boston: Houghton Mifflin, 1965.

Gustafson, Sandra M. *Eloquence Is Power: Oratory and Performance in Early America.* Chapel Hill: University of North Carolina Press for the Omohundro Institute of Early American History and Culture, 2000.

————, and Caroline F. Sloat, eds. *Cultural Narratives: Textuality and Performance in American Culture before 1900.* Notre Dame: University of Notre Dame Press, 2010.

Gutjahr, Paul C. "No Longer Left Behind: Amazon.com, Reader-Response, and the Changing Fortunes of the Christian Novel in America." *Book History* 5 (2002): 209–36.

————. "Religion." In *A Companion to American Fiction, 1780–1865,* ed. Shirley Samuels, 87–96. Malden, MA: Blackwell, 2004.

Hale, Dorothy. "Fiction as Restriction: Self-Binding in New Ethical Theories of the Novel." *Narrative* 15, no. 2 (2007): 187–206.

———, ed. *The Novel: An Anthology of Criticism and Theory, 1900–2000.* Malden, MA: Blackwell, 2006.

Hall, David D., ed. *Lived Religion in America: Toward a History of Practice.* Princeton: Princeton University Press, 1997.

Hall, Edward B. *Memoir of Mary L. Ware, Wife of Henry Ware, Jr.* Boston: Crosby, Nichols, & Co., 1853.

Hall, Robert. "On Hearing the Word of God." *The Publications of the New England Tract Society* 145. Andover, MA: Flagg and Gould, 1823.

Hambrick-Stowe, Charles. *Charles G. Finney and the Spirit of American Evangelicalism.* Grand Rapids, MI: William B. Eerdmans, 1996.

———. *The Practice of Piety: Puritan Devotional Disciplines in Seventeenth-Century New England.* Chapel Hill: University of North Carolina Press for the Institute for Early American History and Culture, 1982.

Hamburger, Philip. *Separation of Church and State.* Cambridge, MA: Harvard University Press, 2002.

Hanley, Mark Y. *Beyond a Christian Commonwealth: The Protestant Quarrel with the American Republic, 1830–1860.* Chapel Hill: University of North Carolina Press, 1994.

Hatch, Nathan O. *The Democratization of American Christianity.* New Haven: Yale University Press, 1989.

Haven, Gilbert, and Thomas Russell. *Incidents and Anecdotes of Rev. Edward T. Taylor.* Boston: B. B. Russell, 1873.

Hawthorne, Julian. *Hawthorne Reading: An Essay.* Cleveland, OH: The Rowfant Club, 1902.

Hawthorne, Nathaniel. *The American Notebooks.* Vol. 8 of *The Centenary Edition of Nathaniel Hawthorne,* ed. Claude M. Simpson. Columbus: The Ohio State University Press, 1972.

———. *The English Note-Books, 1853–1856.* Vol. 21 of *The Centenary Edition of Nathaniel Hawthorne,* ed. Thomas Woodson and Bill Ellis. Columbus: The Ohio State University Press, 1997.

———. *The House of the Seven Gables.* Vol. 2 of *The Centenary Edition of Nathaniel Hawthorne.* Columbus: The Ohio State University Press, 1965.

———. *The Letters, 1813–1843.* Vol. 15 of *The Centenary Edition of Nathaniel Hawthorne,* ed. Thomas Woodson, L. Neal Smith, and Norman Holmes Pearson. Columbus: The Ohio State University Press, 1984.

———. *The Letters, 1843–1853.* Vol. 16 of *The Centenary Edition of Nathaniel Hawthorne,* ed. Thomas Woodson, L. Neal Smith, and Norman Holmes Pearson. Columbus: The Ohio State University Press, 1985.

———. *Miscellaneous Prose and Verse.* Vol. 23 of *The Centenary Edition of Nathaniel Hawthorne,* ed. Thomas Woodson, Claude M. Simpson, and L. Neal Smith. Columbus: The Ohio State University Press, 1994.

———. *Mosses from an Old Manse.* Vol. 10 of *The Centenary Edition of Nathaniel Hawthorne,* ed. William Charvat, Roy Harvey Pearce, and Claude M. Simpson. Columbus: The Ohio State University Press, 1974.

———. *Our Old Home: A Series of English Sketches.* Vol. 5 of *The Centenary Edition of Nathaniel Hawthorne,* ed. Thomas Woodson. Columbus: The Ohio State University Press, 1970.

———. *The Scarlet Letter.* Vol. 1 of *The Centenary Edition of Nathaniel Hawthorne,* ed. William Charvat, Roy Harvey Pearce, and Claude M. Simpson. Columbus: The Ohio State University Press, 1962.

Haywood, Chanta. *Prophesying Daughters: Black Women Preachers and the Word*. Columbia: University of Missouri Press, 2003.

Hedrick, Joan D. *Harriet Beecher Stowe: A Life*. New York: Oxford University Press, 1994.

Helwig, Timothy. "Denying the Wages of Whiteness: The Racial Politics of George Lippard's Working-Class Protest." *American Studies* 47, no. 3/4 (2006): 87–111.

Herbert, T. Walter, Jr. "Calvinist Earthquake: *Moby-Dick* and Religious Tradition." *New Essays on* Moby-Dick, ed. Richard H. Brodhead, 109–40. Cambridge, UK: Cambridge University Press, 1986.

———. Moby-Dick *and Calvinism: A World Dismantled*. New Brunswick, NJ: Rutgers University Press, 1977.

Hervieu-Leger, Danièle. *Religion as a Chain of Memory*. Trans. Simon Lee. New Brunswick, NJ: Rutgers University Press, 2000.

Hibbard, Rufus F. *Startling Disclosures Concerning the Death of John N. Maffitt*. New York: M. B. Wynkoop, Book, & Job, 1856.

Hints on Preaching without Reading. Philadelphia: R. E. Peterson, 1850.

Hirsch, Stephen A. "Uncle Tomitudes: The Popular Reaction to *Uncle Tom's Cabin*." In *Studies in the American Renaissance*, ed. Joel Myerson, 303–38. Boston: Twayne Publishers, 1978.

Hirst, Russel. "*Ethos* and the Conservative Tradition in Nineteenth-Century American Protestant Homiletics." In *Ethos: New Essays in Rhetorical and Critical Theory*, ed. James S. Baumlin and Tita French Baumlin, 293–318. Dallas: Southern Methodist University Press, 1994.

Hochman, Barbara. "Readers and Reading Groups." In *The Cambridge History of the American Novel*, ed. Leonard Cassuto, Clare Virginia Eby, and Benjamin Reiss, 600–14. Cambridge, UK: Cambridge University Press, 2011.

Hoffer, Peter. *Sensory Worlds in Early America*. Baltimore: The Johns Hopkins University Press, 2003.

Hoffert, Sylvia D. *Jane Grey Swisshelm: An Unconventional Life, 1815–1884*. Chapel Hill: University of North Carolina Press, 2004.

Hoffman, Daniel. "*Moby-Dick:* Jonah's Whale or Job's?" *Sewanee Review* 69 (1961): 205–224.

Holifield, E. Brooks. *God's Ambassadors: A History of the Christian Clergy in America*. Grand Rapids, MI: William B. Eerdmans, 2007.

[Holmes, George Frederick]. "Notices of New Works." *Southern Literary Messenger* 18 (1852): 630–38.

Holstein, Jay. "Melville's Inversion of Jonah in *Moby-Dick*." *The Iliff Review* 42, no. 1 (1985): 13–20.

Howe, Daniel Walker. *The Unitarian Conscience: Harvard Moral Philosophy, 1805–1861*. Cambridge, MA: Harvard University Press, 1970. Middletown, CT: Wesleyan University Press, 1988.

Howells, W. D. "Novel-Writing and Novel-Reading: An Impersonal Explanation." In *Selected Literary Criticism, Volume III: 1898–1920*, ed. Ronald Gottesman, Christoph K. Lohmann, et al., 215–31. Bloomington: Indiana University Press, 1993.

———. *The Minister's Charge, or The Apprenticeship of Lemuel Barker*, ed. David J. Nordloh and David Kleinman. Bloomington: Indiana University Press, 1978.

Hubbard, Dolan. *The Sermon and the African American Literary Imagination*. Columbia: University of Missouri Press, 1994.

Hughes, Benjamin F. *Eulogium on the Life and Character of William Wilberforce, Esq. Delivered and Published at the Request of the People of Color of the City of New York, Twenty-second of October, 1833*. New York: Office of *The Emancipator*, 1833. Philadelphia: Rhistoric Publications, 1969.

Humphrey, Heman. *Thirty-four Letters to a Son in the Ministry.* Amherst: J. S., & C. Adams; New York: Dayton and Newman; Boston: Crocker and Brewster, 1842.

Hunter, J. Paul. *Before Novels: The Cultural Contexts of Eighteenth-Century English Fiction.* New York: Norton, 1990.

Hutner, Gordon. *Secrets and Sympathy: Forms of Disclosure in Hawthorne's Novels.* Athens: University of Georgia Press, 1988.

[Hutson, William F.]. "Review of Alphonse De Lamartine, *History of the Girondists, or Personal Memoirs of the Patriots of the French Revolution, from unpublished sources* [. . .]." *Southern Presbyterian Review* 2 (1848): 387–413.

Jackson, Blyden. *A History of Afro-American Literature: Volume 1, The Long Beginning, 1746–1895.* Baton Rouge: Louisiana State University Press, 1989.

Jackson, Gregory. "America's First Mass Media: Preaching and the Protestant Sermon Tradition," 402–25. Malden, MA: Blackwell, 2005.

———. "Religion and the Nineteenth-Century American Novel." In *The Cambridge History of the American Novel,* ed. Leonard Cassuto, Clare Virginia Eby, and Benjamin Reiss, 167–91. Cambridge, UK: Cambridge University Press, 2011.

———. *The Word and Its Witness: The Spiritualization of American Realism.* Chicago: University of Chicago Press, 2009.

Jackson, Joseph. "George Lippard: Misunderstood Man of Letters." *Pennsylvania Magazine of History and Biography* 59 (1935): 376–91.

Jacob, J. R. "La Roy Sunderland: The Alienation of an Abolitionist." *American Studies* 6 (1972): 1–17.

Jacobs, Harriet. *Incidents in the Life of a Slave Girl, Written by Herself,* enlarged ed., ed. Jean Fagan Yellin. Cambridge, MA: Harvard University Press, Belknap Press, 2009.

Jakobsen, Janet R. and Ann Pellegrini, eds. *Secularisms.* Durham: Duke University Press, 2008.

James, Henry. *The American.* 1877. New York: Oxford University Press, 1999.

———. *Hawthorne: A Biography.* 1879. Ithaca, NY: Cornell University Press, 1997.

Jay, William. *Miscellaneous Writings on Slavery.* Boston: John P. Jewett, 1853.

Jensen, Tim. "'Their Own Thought in Motley': Emerson's Divinity School Address and Henry Ware Jr.'s *Hints on Extemporaneous Preaching.*" *Journal of Unitarian-Universalist History* 24 (1997): 17–30.

Jones, Charles C. *A Catechism of Scripture Doctrine and Practice, for Families and Sabbath Schools Designed also for the Oral Instruction of Colored Persons.* 6th ed. Savannah: John M. Cooper, 1837.

Kant, Immanuel. *The Critique of Judgment,* trans. J. H. Bernard. New York: Hafner, 1951.

Karcher, Carolyn L. *Shadow Over the Promised Land: Slavery, Race, and Violence in Melville's America.* Baton Rouge: Louisiana State University Press, 1980.

Kaufmann, Michael. "The Religious, the Secular, and Literary Studies: Rethinking the Secularization Narrative in Histories of the Profession." *New Literary History* 38, no. 4 (2007): 607–28.

Kearns, Michael. "Morality and Rhetoric in *Moby-Dick.*" *"Ungraspable Phantom": Essays on Moby-Dick,* ed. John Bryant, Mary K. Bercaw Edwards, and Timothy Marr, 147–64. Kent, OH: Kent State University Press, 2006.

Keeling, Kara and Josh Kun. "Introduction: Listening to American Studies." *American Quarterly* 63.3 (2011): 445–59.

Kelley, Mary. *Learning to Stand and Speak: Women, Education, and Public Life in America's Republic.* Chapel Hill: University of North Carolina Press for the Omohundro Institute of Early American History and Culture, 2006.

————. *Private Woman, Public Stage: Literary Domesticity in Nineteenth-Century America.* Oxford: Oxford University Press, 1984.

Kilde, Jeanne Halgren. *When Church Became Theatre: The Transformation of Evangelical Architecture and Worship in Nineteenth-Century America.* New York: Oxford University Press, 2002.

Knight, Frances. *The Nineteenth-Century Church and English Society.* Cambridge, UK: Cambridge University Press, 1995.

Knott, John R., Jr. *The Sword of the Spirit: Puritan Responses to the Bible.* Chicago: University of Chicago Press, 1980.

Kopley, Richard. *The Threads of* The Scarlet Letter: *A Study of Hawthorne's Transformative Art.* Newark: University of Delaware Press, 2003.

Lang, Bernhard. *Sacred Games: A History of Christian Worship.* New Haven: Yale University Press, 1997.

Lathrop, Rose Hawthorne. *Memories of Hawthorne.* Boston: Houghton, Mifflin, 1897.

Laurie, Bruce. *Working People of Philadelphia, 1800–1850.* Philadelphia: Temple University Press, 1980.

Lehuu, Isabel. *Carnival on the Page: Popular Print Media in Antebellum America.* Chapel Hill: University of North Carolina Press, 2000.

Lerner, Gerda. *The Grimké Sisters from South Carolina: Pioneers for Women's Rights and Abolition.* Rev. ed. Chapel Hill: University of North Carolina Press, 2004.

Lesser, M. X. "Dimmesdale's Wordless Sermon." *American Notes and Queries* 12, no. 5 (1974): 93–94.

L'Estrange, Roger, trans. and ed. *Seneca's Morals, By Way of Abstract, To Which Is Added a Discourse Under the Title of an After-Thought.* Philadelphia: Grigg and Elliot, 1834.

Levine, Lawrence W. *Highbrow/Lowbrow: The Emergence of Cultural Hierarchy in America.* Cambridge, MA: Harvard University Press, 1988.

Levine, Robert S. "Introduction: Cultural and Historical Background." In William Wells Brown, *Clotel; or, The President's Daughter: A Narrative of Slave Life in the United States,* ed. Robert S. Levine, 3–27. Boston: Bedford/St. Martin's, 2000.

————. "Sources and Revisions." In William Wells Brown, *Clotel; or, The President's Daughter: A Narrative of Slave Life in the United States,* ed. Robert S. Levine, 231–37. Boston: Bedford/St. Martin's, 2000.

Leyda, Jay. *The Melville Log: A Documentary Life of Herman Melville, 1819–1891.* 2 vols. New York: Harcourt, 1951.

Life of Father Taylor: The Sailor Preacher. Boston: Boston Port and Seamen's Aid Society, 1904.

Lincoln, Abraham. *Speeches and Writings, 1859–1865: Speeches, Letters, and Miscellaneous Writings, Presidential Messages and Proclamations,* ed. Don E. Fehrenbacher. New York: Literary Classics of the United States, 1989.

Lippard, George. Address to the Brotherhood of the Union, October 4, 1852. Manuscript Volume 1 in the Brotherhood of the Union Papers, Library Company.

————. "Adrian, the Neophyte." *Citizen Soldier* (July 26, 1843), 169–70; (August 2, 1843), 177–78.

————. *Adrian, the Neophyte.* Philadelphia: I. R. and A. H. Diller, 1843.

————. *"The Bible": What It Is, and What It Is Not.* Canton, OH: Klippart and Webb, 1854.

————. "Brotherhood Versus Atheistic Sectarianism." *The White Banner* (1851): 123–40.

————. "The Carpenter's Son." *The Nineteenth Century* 1, no. 2 (1848): 72–99.

————. "The Dream." *The White Banner* (1851): 125.

————. "Jesus the Democrat." *The Home Journal and Citizen Soldier* (Jan. 31, 1844), 37–38.

————. "Jesus and the Poor." *The Nineteenth Century* 1, no. 1 (1848): 57–81.

————. "Key to the Quaker City: or, The Monks of Monk Hall." In George Lippard, *The Quaker*

City; or, The Monks of Monk-Hall: A Romance of Philadelphia Life, Mystery, and Crime. Philadelphia: George Lippard, 1845.

——. *The Man with the Mask: A Sequel to The Memoirs of a Preacher, a Revelation of the Church and the Home.* Philadelphia: Jos. Severns and Company, [1849].

——. *Memoirs of a Preacher, A Revelation of the Church and the Home.* Philadelphia: Jos. Severns, 1849.

——. *Memoirs of a Preacher; or, Mysteries of the Pulpit.* Philadelphia: T. B. Peterson & Brothers, 1864.

——. *Mysteries of the Pulpit: Or, a Revelation of the Church and the Home.* Philadelphia: E. E. Barclay, 1851.

——. *The Quaker City; or, the Monks of Monk Hall. A Romance of Philadelphia Life, Mystery, and Crime,* ed. David S. Reynolds. Amherst: University of Massachusetts Press, 1995.

——. "Religion." *The White Banner* (1851): 120–21.

——. "Rev. J. N. Maffitt," *Citizen Soldier* (May 31, 1843), 106.

——. "The Spermaceti Papers." *Citizen Soldier* (July 5, 1843), 148.

——. "Two Parties in Every Church." *The White Banner* (1851): 127.

Lockhart, J. G. *Some Passages in the Life of Mr. Adam Blair, Minister of the Gospel at Cross-Meikle.* Edinburgh: Edinburgh University Press, 1963.

Looby, Christopher. *Voicing America: Language, Literary Form, and the Origins of the United States.* Chicago: University of Chicago Press, 1996.

Loveland, Anne C. and Otis B. Wheeler. *From Meetinghouse to Megachurch: A Material and Cultural History.* Columbia: University of Missouri Press, 2003.

Machor, James L. "Fiction and Informed Reading in Early Nineteenth-Century America." *Nineteenth-Century Literature* 47, no. 3 (1992): 320–48.

——. "Historical Hermeneutics and Antebellum Fiction: Gender, Response Theory, and Interpretive Texts." In *Readers in History: Nineteenth-Century American Literature and the Contexts of Response,* ed. James L. Machor, 54–84. Baltimore: The Johns Hopkins University Press, 1993.

——. *Reading Fiction in Antebellum America: Informed Response and Reception Histories, 1820–1865.* Baltimore: The Johns Hopkins University Press, 2011.

Maffly-Kipp, Laurie F., Leigh Schmidt, and Mark Valeri, eds. *Practicing Protestants: Histories of Christian Life in America, 1630–1965.* Baltimore: The Johns Hopkins University Press, 2006.

Mailloux, Steven. "Political Theology in Douglass and Melville." In *Frederick Douglass and Herman Melville: Essays in Relation,* ed. Robert S. Levine and Samuel Otter, 159–80. Chapel Hill: University of North Carolina Press, 2008.

Mann, Horace. "A Few Thoughts for a Young Man: A Lecture, Delivered Before the Boston Mercantile Library Association, on its 29th Anniversary." Syracuse, NY: L. W. Hall, 1850.

Marcus, Greil and Werner Sollors, eds. *A New Literary History of America.* Cambridge, MA: Harvard University Press, Belknap Press, 2009.

Mariani, Giorgio. "'Chiefly Known by His Rod': The Book of Jonah, Mapple's Sermon, and Scapegoating." In *"Ungraspable Phantom": Essays on* Moby-Dick, ed. John Bryant, Mary K. Bercaw Edwards, and Timothy Marr, 37–57. Kent, OH: Kent State University Press, 2006.

Marshall, Megan. *The Peabody Sisters: Three Women Who Ignited American Romanticism.* Boston: Houghton Mifflin Company, 2005.

Martin, Terence. *The Instructed Vision: Scottish Common Sense Philosophy and the Origins of American Fiction.* Bloomington: Indiana University Press, 1961.

Martineau, Harriet. *Retrospect of Western Travel.* 3 vols. London: Saunders and Otley, 1838.

Mather, Increase. "The Day of Trouble Is Near." *Jeremiads.* Vol. 20 of *A Library of American Puritan Writings: The Seventeenth Century,* ed. Sacvan Bercovitch. New York: AMS, 1984.

Matthiessen, F. O. *American Renaissance: Art and Expression in the Age of Emerson and Whitman*. 1941. New York: Oxford University Press, 1968.

Mayer, Henry. *All on Fire: William Lloyd Garrison and the Abolition of Slavery*. New York: Norton, 1998.

McAuley, Thomas. "The Faithful Preacher, and Wages of Unfaithfulness." *The American National Preacher* 12 (1838): 17–25.

McDannell, Colleen. *Material Christianity: Religion and Popular Culture in America*. New Haven: Yale University Press, 1995.

McGann, Jerome. *The Romantic Ideology: The Critical Investigation*. Chicago: University of Chicago Press, 1983.

McGirr, Lisa. *Suburban Warriors: The Origins of the New American Right*. Princeton: Princeton University Press, 2001.

McKanan, Dan. *Prophetic Encounters: Religion and the American Radical Tradition*. Boston: Beacon Press, 2011.

McKivigan, John R. and Mitchell Snay. *Religion and the Antebellum Debate over Slavery*. Athens: University of Georgia Press, 1998.

———. *The War against Pro-Slavery Religion: Abolitionism and the Northern Churches, 1830–1865*. Ithaca: Cornell University Press, 1984.

Mead, Sidney E. "The Rise of the Evangelical Conception of the Ministry in America: 1607–1850." In *The Ministry in Historical Perspectives,* ed. H. Richard Niebuhr and Daniel D. Williams, 207–49. New York: Harper, 1956.

Mechanic's Advocate (April 22, 1848), 156.

Meer, Sarah. *Uncle Tom Mania: Slavery, Minstrelsy, and Transatlantic Culture in the 1850s*. Athens: University of Georgia Press, 2005.

Mellor, Anne. *English Romantic Irony*. Cambridge, MA: Harvard University Press, 1980.

Mellow, James R. *Nathaniel Hawthorne in His Times*. Boston: Houghton Mifflin Company, 1980.

Melville, Herman. *Correspondence*. Vol. 14 of *The Writings of Herman Melville*, ed. Lynn Horth. Evanston and Chicago: Northwestern University Press and The Newberry Library, 1993.

———. *Moby-Dick; or The Whale*. Vol. 6 of *The Writings of Herman Melville,* ed. Harrison Hayford, Hershel Parker, and C. Thomas Tanselle. Evanston and Chicago: Northwestern University Press and The Newberry Library, 1988.

———. *The Piazza Tales and Other Prose Pieces, 1839–1860*. Vol. 14 of *The Writings of Herman Melville,* ed. Harrison Hayford, Alma A. MacDougall, and G. Thomas Tanselle. Evanston and Chicago: Northwestern University Press and The Newberry Library, 1987.

———. *Redburn: His First Voyage; Being the Sailor-Boy Confessions and Reminiscences of the Son-of-a-Gentleman, in the Merchant Service*. Vol. 4 of *The Writings of Herman Melville,* ed. Harrison Hayford, Hershel Parker, and G. Thomas Tanselle. Evanston and Chicago: Northwestern University Press and The Newberry Library, 1969.

———. *Typee: A Peep at Polynesian Life,* ed. John Bryant. New York: Penguin, 1996.

———. *White-Jacket: or The World in a Man-of-War*. Vol. 5 of *The Writings of Herman Melville,* ed. Harrison Hayford, Hershel Parker, and G. Thomas Tanselle. Evanston and Chicago: Northwestern University Press and The Newberry Library, 1970.

A Member of Congress. "Slavery in the District." *New-York Evangelist,* September 8, 1842: 1.

———. "Slavery in the District of Colombia [*sic*]." *British and Foreign Anti-Slavery Reporter,* December 28, 1842: 1.

Messler, Abraham. *The Elements of Power in the Christian Ministry. A Sermon Preached in the Second Reformed Dutch Church of Coxsackie, on Occasion of the Installation of Rev. John Steele*. New Brunswick: J. Terhune & Son, 1853.

Milder, Robert. *Exiled Royalties: Melville and the Life We Imagine.* New York: Oxford University Press, 2006.

Miller, Glenn T. *Piety and Intellect: The Aims and Purposes of Ante-Bellum Theological Education.* Atlanta, GA: Scholars Press, 1990.

Miller, Perry. *The Life of the Mind in America: From the Revolution to the Civil War.* New York: Harcourt, Brace, & World, A Harvest Book, 1965.

———. *The New England Mind: The Seventeenth Century.* Cambridge, MA: Harvard University Press, Belknap Press, 1939.

Mills, Frederick V., Sr. "Methodist Preaching, 1798–1840: Form and Function." *Methodist History* 43, no. 1 (2004): 3–16.

Mitchell, Henry H. *Black Preaching.* Philadelphia: J. B. Lippincott, 1970.

Mitchell, Laura. "'Matters of Justice between Man and Man': Northern Divines, the Bible, and the Fugitive Slave Act of 1850." *Religion and the Antebellum Debate over Slavery,* ed. John R. McKivigan and Mitchell Snay, 134–65. Athens: University of Georgia Press, 1998.

Mizruchi, Susan L. Introduction. *Religion and Cultural Studies,* ed. Susan L. Mizruchi, ix–xxv. Princeton: Princeton University Press, 2001.

Moers, Ellen. *Literary Women.* New York: Doubleday, 1976.

Montgomery, James. *Gleanings from Pious Authors: Comprising the Wheatsheaf, Fruits and Flowers, Garden, and Shrubbery . . . ,* new ed. London, 1846. Philadelphia: Henry Longstreth, 1855.

Moody, Joycelyn. *Sentimental Confessions: Spiritual Narratives of Nineteenth-Century African American Women.* Athens: University of Georgia Press, 2001.

Moore, Asher. *Universalism, the Doctrine of the Bible.* Philadelphia: Gihon, 1847.

Moore, Margaret B. *The Salem World of Nathaniel Hawthorne.* Columbia: University of Missouri Press, 1998.

Moore, R. Laurence. *Selling God: American Religion in the Marketplace of Culture.* New York: Oxford University Press, 1994.

Mott, Wesley T. *The Strains of Eloquence: Emerson and His Sermons.* University Park: Pennsylvania State University Press, 1989.

Mountford, Roxanne. *The Gendered Pulpit: Preaching in American Protestant Spaces.* Carbondale: Southern Illinois University Press, 2003.

Mulder, John M. and Isabelle Stouffer. "William Buell Sprague: Patriarch of American Collectors." *American Presbyterians* 64, no. 1 (1986): 2–17.

Mulvey, Christopher. "Annotations to *Clotel; or the President's Daughter: A Narrative of Slave Life in the United States. (1853)." Clotel: An Electronic Scholarly Edition.* University of Virginia Press, 2006.

National Endowment for the Arts. "Reading on the Rise: A New Chapter in American Literacy" (2009), 3.

The New-England Primer: A Reprint of the Earliest Known Edition, with Many Facsimiles and Reproductions, and an Historical Introduction, ed. Paul Leicester Ford. New York: Dodd, Mead, 1899.

Newberry, Frederick. *Hawthorne's Divided Loyalties: England and America in His Works.* Cranbury, NJ: Associated University Press, 1987.

———. "A Red-Hot A and a Lusting Divine: Sources for *The Scarlet Letter." New England Quarterly* 60, no. 2 (1987): 256–64.

Newbury, Michael. *Figuring Authorship in Antebellum America.* Stanford, CA: Stanford University Press, 1997.

Newman, Richard. *Freedom's Prophet: Bishop Richard Allen, the AME Church, and the Black Founding Fathers.* New York: New York University Press, 2008.

Newton, John. *The Seaman's Preacher, Consisting of Nine Short and Plain Discourses on Jonah's Voyage Addressed to Mariners.* Cambridge, MA: Hilliard, 1806.

Newton, Sarah E. *Learning to Behave: A Guide to American Conduct Books Before 1900.* Westport, CT: Greenwood Press, 1994.

Nord, David Paul. *Faith in Reading: Religious Publishing and the Birth of Mass Media in America.* New York: Oxford University Press, 2004.

Ong, Walter. *Orality and Literacy: The Technologizing of the Word.* London: Routledge, 1982.

Orians, G. Harrison. "Censure of Fiction in American Romances and Magazines 1789–1810." *PMLA* 52, no. 1 (1937): 195–214.

Osborn, Ronald E. *Folly of God: The Rise of Christian Preaching.* St. Louis, MO: Chalice Press, 1999.

Osgood, Samuel. *Human Life; or, Practical Ethics.* Translated from the German of De Wette, 2 vols. Vol. 13 of *Specimens of Foreign Standard Literature,* ed. George Ripley. Boston: James Munroe, 1842.

———. *Mile Stones in Our Life-Journey.* New York: Appleton, 1855.

Ostrowski, Carl. "Inside the Temple of Ravoni: George Lippard's Anti-Exposé." *ESQ* 55, no. 1 (2009): 1–26.

Palfrey, John G. *Papers on the Slave Power, First Published in the "Boston Whig."* Boston: Merrill, Cobb, and Co., [1846?].

Pardes, Ilana. *Melville's Bibles.* Berkeley: University of California Press, 2008.

Parfait, Claire. "The Nineteenth-Century Serial as a Collective Enterprise: Harriet Beecher Stowe's *Uncle Tom's Cabin* and Eugene Sue's *Les Mystères de Paris.*" *Proceedings of the American Antiquarian Society* 112, no. 1 (2002): 127–52.

Park, Edwards A. *The Indebtedness of the State to the Clergy: A Sermon Delivered before His Excellency George N. Briggs, Governor, His Honor John Reed, Lieutenant Governor, The Honorable Council, and the Legislature of Massachusetts, at the Annual Election, January 2, 1851.* Boston: Dutton and Wentworth, 1851.

———. "Introductory Essay on the Dignity and Importance of the Preacher's Work." In *The Preacher and Pastor, by Fenelon, Herbert, Baxter, Campbell,* ed. Edwards A. Park, 11–46. Andover: Allen, Morrill, and Wardwell.

Parker, Hershel. *Herman Melville: A Biography; Volume 1, 1819–1851.* Baltimore: The Johns Hopkins University Press, 1996.

———. *Herman Melville: A Biography; Volume 2, 1851–1891.* Baltimore: The Johns Hopkins University Press, 2002.

Parker, Theodore. *Saint Bernard and Other Papers.* Centenary ed., vol. 14, ed. Charles W. Wendte. Boston: American Unitarian Association, 1911.

———. *Sins and Safeguards of Society.* Centenary ed., vol. 9, ed. Samuel B. Stewart. Boston: American Unitarian Association, 1907.

———. *The Transient and the Permanent in Christianity.* Centenary ed., vol. 4, ed. George Willis Cooke. Boston: American Unitarian Association, 1908.

Parkman, Francis. "The Object, Reasonableness, and Spirituality of the Christian Worship." *Liberal Preacher,* n.s., 6 (1843): 32.

———. "Review of *Eighteen Sermons and a Charge* and *Sermons by the Late Rev. John Abbot, with a Memoir of His Life.*" *Christian Examiner and General Review* 6.33, new series 3 (July 1829): 273–87.

Parrington, Vernon Louis. "Harriet Beecher Stowe: A Daughter of Puritanism." In *Critical Essays on Harriet Beecher Stowe,* ed. Elizabeth Ammons, 213–18. Boston: G. K. Hall, 1980.

Patton, William Weston. *Slavery, the Bible, Infidelity: Pro-slavery Interpretations of the Bible: Productive of Infidelity.* Hartford: W. H. Burleigh, 1846.

Peabody, Elizabeth Palmer. *Reminiscences of Rev. Wm. Ellery Channing, D.D.* Boston: Roberts Brothers, 1880.

Pessen, Edward. *Most Uncommon Jacksonians: The Radical Leaders of the Early Labor Movement.* Albany: State University of New York Press, 1967.

Petrie, Paul R. *Conscience and Purpose: Fiction and Social Consciousness in Howells, Jewett, Chesnutt, and Cather.* Tuscaloosa: University of Alabama Press, 2005.

Pew Forum on Religion and Public Life. "U.S. Religious Landscape Survey: Religious Affiliation: Diverse and Dynamic," 2008.

"The Phillipses and the Abbots." Rept. from the *Salem Gazette.* *The Massachusetts Teacher* 2, no. 12 (1849): 365–66.

Pierce, Yolanda. *Hell Without Fires: Slavery, Christianity, and the Antebellum Spiritual Narrative.* Gainesville: University Press of Florida, 2005.

Pillsbury, Parker. *The Church as It Is: or the Forlorn Hope of Slavery.* Boston: Bela Marsh, 1847.

Pipes, William H. *Say Amen, Brother!: Old-Time Negro Preaching: A Study in American Frustration.* Westport, CT: Negro Universities Press, 1951.

Poe, Edgar Allan. Vol. 14 of *The Complete Works of Edgar Allan Poe,* ed. James A. Harrison. New York: AMS Press, 1965.

Porte, Joel. *The Romance in America: Studies in Cooper, Poe, Hawthorne, Melville, and James.* Middletown: Wesleyan University Press, 1969.

Portelli, Alessandro. *The Text and the Voice: Writing, Speaking, and Democracy in American Literature.* New York: Columbia University Press, 1994.

Porter, Ebenezer. *Lectures on Homiletics and Preaching, and on Public Prayer; Together with Sermons and Letters.* Andover, MA: Flagg, Gould and Newman. New York: Jonathan Leavitt, 1834.

Post-Lauria, Sheila. *Correspondent Colorings: Melville in the Marketplace.* Amherst: University of Massachusetts Press, 1996.

"Practical Preaching." *Christian Register and Boston Observer* (Oct. 23, 1841): 170.

Proceedings of the Convention of Ministers of Worcester County, on the Subject of Slavery; Held at Worcester, December 5 and 6, 1837, and January 16, 1838. Worcester: Massachusetts Spy Office, 1838.

Publisher's Advertisement. *Washington and His Generals, or, Legends of the Revolution.* Philadelphia: G. B. Zieber, 1847.

Putnam, George. *Spiritual Renewal the Great Work of the Christian Church and Ministry: A Sermon Delivered at the Ordination of Rev. Frederic D. Huntington, as Pastor of the Second Congregational Church, in Boston, October 19, 1842.* Boston: William Crosby & Co, 1842.

The Quaker City, 1848–1850. Philadelphia.

Raboteau, Albert J. *Slave Religion: The 'Invisible Institution' in the Antebellum South.* Updated ed. Oxford: Oxford University Press, 2004.

Radway, Janice. "Reading Is Not Eating: Mass-Produced Literature and the Theoretical, Methodological, and Political Consequences of a Metaphor." *Book Research Quarterly* 2, no. 3 (1986): 7–29.

Railton, Stephen. *Authorship and Audience: Literary Performance in the American Renaissance.* Princeton: Princeton University Press, 1991.

Rath, Richard Cullen. *How Early America Sounded.* Ithaca, NY: Cornell University Press, 2003.

[Reade, Thomas Shaw B.]. *Christian Retirement: Or Spiritual Exercises of the Heart, By a Layman.* 2nd ed. Kirkby Lonsdale: Arthur Foster, 1827.

Report of the Trial of Mr. John N. Maffitt, Before a Council of Ministers of the Methodist Episcopal Church, Convened in Boston, December 26, 1822. Boston: True and Greene, 1823.

Reynolds, David. *Beneath the American Renaissance: The Subversive Imagination in the Age of Emerson and Melville*. Cambridge, MA: Harvard University Press, 1988.

———. *Faith in Fiction: The Emergence of Religious Literature in America*. Cambridge, MA: Harvard University Press, 1981.

———. "From Doctrine to Narrative: The Rise of Pulpit Storytelling." *American Quarterly* 32, no. 5 (1980): 479–98.

———. *George Lippard*. Boston: Twayne Publishers, 1982.

———. *George Lippard: Prophet of Protest: Writings of an American Radical, 1822–1854*. New York: Peter Lang, 1986.

Reynolds, Larry J. *European Revolutions and the American Literary Renaissance*. New Haven: Yale University Press, 1988.

Riley, Isaac. "Historical Discourse." *Jubilee: The Fiftieth Anniversary of the Organization of the Thirty-Fourth Street Reformed Church of New York City, December 14–21, 1873*. New York: The Consistory, 1874.

Ripley, C. Peter, ed. *The Black Abolitionist Papers, Volume 1, The British Isles, 1830–1865*. Chapel Hill: University of North Carolina Press, 1985.

Ripley, Henry J. *Sacred Rhetoric; Or, Composition and Delivery of Sermons. To Which are Added Hints on Extemporaneous Preaching, by Henry Ware, Jr. D.D*. Boston: Gould, Kendall, and Lincoln, 1849.

Roberson, Susan. *Emerson in His Sermons: A Man-Made Self*. Columbia: University of Missouri Press, 1995.

Robert, Joseph C. *The Road from Monticello: A Study of the Virginia Slavery Debate of 1832*. Durham: Duke University Press, 1941.

Roberts, Wendy Raphael. "Demand My Voice: Hearing God in Eighteenth-Century American Poetry." *Early American Literature* 45, no. 1 (2010): 119–44.

Robinson, David. *The Unitarians and Universalists*. Westport, CT: Greenwood Press, 1985.

Roediger, David R. *The Wages of Whiteness: Race and the Making of the American Working Class*. Rev. ed., 1991. New York: Verso, 2007.

Rose, Jane E. "Conduct Books for Women, 1830–1860: A Rationale for Women's Conduct and Domestic Role in America." In *Nineteenth-Century Women Learn to Write*, ed. Catherine Hobbs, 37–58. Charlottesville: University Press of Virginia, 1995.

Rosenberg, Bruce. *Can These Bones Live: The Art of the American Folk Preacher*. Rev. ed. Urbana: University of Illinois Press, 1988.

Russell, William. *Pulpit Elocution: Comprising Suggestions on the Importance of Study; Remarks on the Effect of Manner in Speaking; The Rules of Reading, Exemplified from the Scriptures, Hymns, and Sermons; Observations on the Principles of Gesture; and a Selection of Pieces for Practice in Reading and Speaking*. Andover, MA: Allen, Morrill and Wardwell, 1846.

Ruttenburg, Nancy. *Democratic Voice and the Trial of American Authorship*. Stanford: Stanford University Press, 1998.

Ryther, John. *A Plat for Mariners, or, The Seaman's Preacher: Delivered in Several Sermons upon Jonah's Voyage*. London, 1675.

Saddleback Community Church website. http://saddleback.com/aboutsaddleback/history/ (accessed January 5, 2012).

"The Sailor Preacher at Boston." *The Sailor's Magazine and Naval Journal*. Reprint from the *Western Monthly Magazine* (November 1833): 73.

The Sailor's Magazine and Naval Journal, 1829–1847.

Sassi, Jonathan D. *A Republic of Righteousness: The Public Christianity of the Post-Revolutionary New England Clergy*. New York: Oxford University Press, 2001.

Scharnhorst, Gary. *The Critical Response to Nathaniel Hawthorne's* The Scarlet Letter. New York: Greenwood Press, 1992.

———. "Howells's *The Minister's Charge:* A Satire of Alger's Country-Boy Myth." *The Mark Twain Journal* 20, no. 3 (1980–1981): 16–17.

Schmidt, Leigh Eric. *Hearing Things: Religion, Illusion, and the American Enlightenment.* Cambridge, MA: Harvard University Press, 2000.

Schultz, Kevin M. and Paul Harvey. "Everywhere and Nowhere: Recent Trends in American Religious History and Historiography." *Journal of the American Academy of Religion* 78, no. 1 (2010): 129–62.

Scott, Donald O. *From Office to Profession: The New England Ministry, 1750–1850.* [Philadelphia]: University of Pennsylvania Press, 1978.

Seabury, Samuel. *On Hearing the Word; A Sermon.* New-York: New-York Protestant Episcopal Tract Society, 1831.

———. *The Relation of the Clergy and Laity: A Discourse Preached in St. Paul's Chapel and St. Clement's Church.* New York: Henry M. Onderdonk, 1844.

Sedgwick, Catharine Maria. *Means and Ends, or Self-Training.* Boston: Marsh, Capen, Lyon, & Webb, 1839.

Seecamp, Carsten E. "The Chapter of Perfection: A Neglected Influence on George Lippard." *Pennsylvania Magazine of History and Biography* 94 (1970): 192–212.

Sherrill, Rowland A. *The Prophetic Melville: Experience, Transcendence, and Tragedy.* Athens: University of Georgia Press, 1979.

Sherwood, Mrs. [Mary Martha]. *The Lady of the Manor. Being a Series of Conversations on the Subject of Confirmation. Intended for the Use of the Middle and Higher Ranks of Young Females.* New York: E. Bliss and E. White, 1825.

Short, Bryan. "Multitudinous, God-omnipresent, Coral Insects: Pip, Isabel, and Melville's Miltonic Sublime." *Leviathan: A Journal of Melville Studies* 4, no. 1 (2002): 7–28.

Sicherman, Barbara. "Reading and Middle-Class Identity in Victorian America: Cultural Consumption, Conspicuous and Otherwise." In *Reading Acts: U.S. Readers' Interactions with Literature, 1800–1950,* ed. Barbara Ryan and Amy M. Thomas, 137–60. Knoxville: University of Tennessee Press, 2002.

Siti, Walter. "The Novel on Trial." In *The Novel: Volume 1, History, Geography, and Culture,* ed. Franco Moretti, 94–121. Princeton: Princeton University Press, 2006.

Smith, Daniel. *Lectures to Young Men on Their Dangers, Safeguards, and Responsibilities.* New York: Lane & Scott, 1852.

Smith, Henry Nash. *Democracy and the Novel: Popular Resistance to Classic American Writers.* New York: Oxford University Press, 1978.

Smith, Matthew Hale. *Counsels Addressed to Young Women, Young Men, Young Persons in Married Life, and Young Parents. Delivered in the Second Presbyterian Church, Washington City, on the Evenings of the Sabbaths in April, 1846.* Washington, DC: Blair and Rives, 1846.

Smith, Susan Belasco. "Serialization and the Nature of *Uncle Tom's Cabin.*" In *Periodical Literature in Nineteenth-Century America,* ed. Kenneth M. Price and Susan Belasco Smith, 69–89. Charlottesville: University Press of Virginia, 1995.

Spanos, William. *The Errant Art of* Moby-Dick: *The Canon, the Cold War, and the Struggle for American Studies.* Durham, NC: Duke University Press, 1995.

Spillers, Hortense J. "Moving on Down the Line." *American Quarterly* 40, no. 1 (1988): 83–109.

Sprague, William Buell, ed. *Annals of the American Pulpit; or Commemorative Notices of Distinguished American Clergymen of Various Denominations, from the Early Settlement of the*

Country to the Close of the Year Eighteen Hundred and Fifty-Five. With Historical Intro-
ductions. Vols. 1–9. New York: R. Carter, 1856–1869. Rept. New York: Arno Press, 1969.

———. *A Sermon Preached in the Second Presbyterian Church, Albany, Sunday Afternoon,*
September 1857, on Occasion of the Death of the Rev. John Ludlow, D.D., Professor in the
Theological Seminary of the Reformed Dutch Church in the United States. Albany, NY: Van
Benthuysen, 1857.

Spring, Gardiner. *The Power of the Pulpit; or Thoughts Addressed to Christian Ministers and*
Those Who Hear Them. 2nd ed. 1848. New York: M. W. Dodd, 1854.

[———]. "The Sermon Preached, and the Sermon Printed." *Independent,* December 7, 1848: 1.

Stange, Douglas Charles. *British Unitarians against American Slavery, 1833–65.* Cranbury, NJ:
Associated University Presses, 1984.

Stein, Jordan Alexander and Justine S. Murison. "Introduction: Religion and Method." *Early*
American Literature 45, no. 1 (2010): 1-29.

Sten, Christopher. *The Weaver-God, He Weaves: Melville and the Poetics of the Novel.* Kent, OH:
Kent State University Press, 1996.

Stephenson, Will and Mimosa. "*Adam Blair* and *The Scarlet Letter.*" *Nathaniel Hawthorne Re-*
view 19, no. 2 (1993): 1–10.

Stewart, Alvan. *A Legal Argument Before the Supreme Court of the State of New Jersey, at the*
May Term, 1845, at Trenton, for the Deliverance of Four Thousand Persons from Bondage.
New York: Finch and Weed, 1845. In *Abolitionists in Northern Courts: The Pamphlet Lit-*
erature, ed. Paul Finkelman, 441–92. New York: Garland, 1988.

Stewart, David M. *Reading and Disorder in Antebellum America.* Columbus: The Ohio State
University Press, 2011.

Stewart-Sykes, Alistair. *From Prophecy to Preaching: A Search for the Origins of the Christian*
Homily. Leiden: Brill, 2000.

Stiles, Ezra. *The United States Elevated to Glory and Honour: A Sermon Preached* [. . .] *At The*
Anniversary Election. May 8, MDCCLXXXIII. 2nd ed. Worcester, MA: Isaiah Thomas,
1785.

Stone, Edward. "The Other Sermon in *Moby-Dick.*" *Costerus* 4 (1972): 215–22.

Stout, Harry S. *The New England Soul: Preaching and Religious Culture in Colonial New Eng-*
land. New York: Oxford University Press, 1986.

Stowe, Harriet Beecher. "Antoinette Brown in Andover." *Liberator* (Feb. 2, 1855), 20.

———. "Preface to the European Edition." *Uncle Tom's Cabin.* Leipzig: Tauchnitz, 1852.

———. "To Frederick Douglass, July 9, 1851." In *The Oxford Harriet Beecher Stowe Reader,* ed.
Joan D. Hedrick, 58–61. New York: Oxford University Press, 1999.

———. *Uncle Tom's Cabin.* London: John Cassell, 1852.

———. *Uncle Tom's Cabin, or Life Among the Lowly: Authoritative Text, Backgrounds and Con-*
texts, Criticism, ed. Elizabeth Ammons. 1852. New York: Norton, 1994.

Streeby, Shelley. *American Sensations: Class, Empire, and the Production of Popular Culture.*
Berkeley and Los Angeles: University of California Press, 2002.

———. "Haunted Houses: George Lippard, Nathaniel Hawthorne, and Middle-Class America."
Criticism 38, no. 3 (1996): 443–72.

———. "Opening Up the Story Paper: George Lippard and the Construction of Class." *bound-*
ary 2, 24, no. 1 (1997): 177–203.

Stringer, Martin D. *A Sociological History of Christian Worship.* Cambridge, UK: Cambridge
University Press, 2005.

Sunderland, La Roy. *Anti Slavery Manual, Containing a Collection of Facts and Arguments on*
American Slavery. 2nd ed. New York: S. W. Benedict, 1837.

———. *The Testimony of God Against Slavery: A Collection of Passages from the Bible Which*

Show the Sin of Holding and Treating the Human Species as Property. With Notes. To Which is Added the Testimony of the Civilized World Against Slavery. 2nd ed. Boston: Isaac Knapp, 1836.

Swisshelm, Jane G. *Letters to Country Girls.* New York: J. C. Riker, 1853.

Taves, Ann. *Fits, Trances, & Visions: Experiencing Religion and Explaining Experience from Wesley to James.* Princeton: Princeton University Press, 1999.

Thomas, Abel C. *A Century of Universalism in Philadelphia and New-York, with Sketches of Its History in Reading, Hightstown, Brooklyn, and Elsewhere.* Philadelphia, 1872.

Thomas, Brook. *American Literary Realism and the Failed Promise of Contract.* Berkeley: University of California Press, 1997.

Thomas, Dwight and David K. Jackson. *The Poe Log: A Documentary Life of Edgar Allan Poe, 1809–1849.* Boston: G. K. Hall, 1987.

Thompson, G. R. *The Art of Authorial Presence: Hawthorne's Provincial Tales.* Durham: Duke University Press, 1993.

Thompson, Lawrance. *Melville's Quarrel with God.* Princeton: Princeton University Press, 1952.

Thoreau, Henry David. *Walden, Civil Disobedience, and Other Writings: Authoritative Texts, Journal, Reviews and Posthumous Assessments, Criticism.* 3rd ed., ed. William Rossi. New York: Norton, 2008.

[Thornwell, James]. "The Religious Instruction of the Black Population." *Southern Presbyterian Review* 1 (1847): 89–120.

Tocqueville, Alexis de. *Democracy in America.* Trans. and ed. Harvey C. Mansfield and Delba Winthrop. Chicago: University of Chicago Press, 2000.

Todd, John. *The Daughter at School.* Northampton: Hopkins, Bridgman, and Company, 1854.

———. *The Moral Influences, Dangers and Duties, Connected with Great Cities.* Northampton, MA: J. H. Butler, 1841.

Tompkins, Jane. *Sensational Designs: The Cultural Work of American Fiction, 1790–1860.* New York: Oxford University Press, 1985.

Toulouse, Teresa. *The Art of Prophesying: New England Sermons and the Shaping of Belief.* Athens: University of Georgia Press, 1987.

Trollope, Anthony. "The Genius of Nathaniel Hawthorne." *North American Review* 274 (1879): 203–22.

Tucker, Karen B. Westerfield. *American Methodist Worship.* New York: Oxford University Press, 2001.

Upham, Charles W. "John Prince." In Vol. 1 of *American Unitarian Biography: Memoirs of Individuals Who Have Been Distinguished by Their Writings, Character, and Efforts in the Cause of Liberal Christianity,* ed. William Ware, 101–16. Boston and Cambridge: James Munroe and Company, 1850.

Valkeakari, Tuire. *Religious Idiom and the African American Novel, 1952–1998.* Gainesville: University Press of Florida, 2007.

Vásquez, Mark. *Authority and Reform: Religious and Educational Discourses in Nineteenth-Century New England Literature.* Knoxville: University of Tennessee Press, 2003.

Views and Feelings Requisite to Success in the Gospel Ministry. Reprinted from the *Quarterly Christian Spectator,* December 1833. New Haven: Stephen Cooke, 1833.

Vincent, Howard P. *The Trying-Out of Moby-Dick.* 1949. Kent, OH: Kent State University Press, 1980.

W[illard?], S[idney?]. "On the Mutual Relations, Duties, and Interests of Minister and People, No. 4: On the Nature of These Relations." *Christian Register and Boston Observer* (Sept. 11, 1841), 145.

————. "On the Mutual Relations, Duties, and Interests of Minister and People, No. 6: Mutual Duties in Regard to Public Instruction." *Christian Register and Boston Observer* (Sept. 25, 1841), 154.

————. "On the Mutual Relations, Duties, and Interests of Minister and People, No. 7: Mutual Duties in Regard to Public Worship," *Christian Register and Boston Observer* (Oct. 2, 1841), 158.

Wallace, Robert K. *Douglas and Melville: Anchored Together in Neighborly Style.* New Bedford, MA: Spinner, 2005.

Wallis, R. and S. Bruce. "Secularization: The Orthodox Model." In *Religion and Modernization,* ed. Steve Bruce, 8–30. Oxford: Clarendon Press, 1992.

Walrath, Douglas. *Displacing the Divine: The Minister in the Mirror of American Fiction.* New York: Columbia University Press, 2010.

Warhol, Robyn R. *Gendered Interventions: Narrative Discourse in the Victorian Novel.* New Brunswick, NJ: Rutgers University Press, 1989.

Ware, Henry, Jr. *The Connexion Between the Duties of the Pulpit and the Pastoral Office: An Introductory Address Delivered to the Members of the Theological School in Cambridge.* Cambridge, MA: Hilliard and Brown, 1830.

————. *Hints on Extemporaneous Preaching.* 3rd ed., 1824. Boston: Hilliard, Gray, Little and Wilkins, 1831.

————. "Memoir." In John Emery Abbot, *Extracts from Sermons by the Late Rev. John Emery Abbot, of Salem, Mass. With a Memoir of His Life, by Henry Ware, Jr.,* ed. Henry Ware, Jr., ix–xxx. Boston: Wait, Greene, & Co., 1830.

Warner, Michael, ed. *American Sermons: The Pilgrims to Martin Luther King Jr.* New York: Library of America, 1999.

Warner, Michael. "Secularism." In *Keywords for American Cultural Studies,* ed. Bruce Burgett and Glenn Hendler, 209–12. New York: New York University Press, 2007.

Warner, Susan. *The Wide, Wide World.* New York: City University of New York, The Feminist Press, 1987.

Warner, William. "Licensing Pleasure: Literary History and the Novel in Early Modern Britain." In *The Columbia History of the British Novel,* ed. John Richetti, 1–22. New York: Columbia University Press, 1994.

Warren, James Perrin. *Culture of Eloquence: Oratory and Reform in Antebellum America.* University Park: Pennsylvania State University Press, 1999.

Watt, Ian. *The Rise of the Novel: Studies in Defoe, Richardson, and Fielding.* Berkeley and Los Angeles: University of California Press, 1957.

Webber, F. R. *A History of Preaching in Britain and America, Including the Biographies of Many Princes of the Pulpit and the Men Who Influenced Them.* 3 vols. Milwaukee: Northwestern, 1957.

Weber, Max. *On Charisma and Institution Building: Selected Papers,* ed. S. N. Eisenstadt. Chicago: University of Chicago Press, 1968.

Weiskel, Thomas. *The Romantic Sublime: Studies in the Structure and Psychology of Transcendence.* Baltimore: The Johns Hopkins University Press, 1976.

W[elch], J[ane] S. "Jairus's Daughter." *New England Offering* 1 (1848): 108.

Weld, Theodore Dwight. *The Bible Against Slavery. An Inquiry into the Patriarchal and Mosaic Systems on the Subject of Human Rights.* 3rd ed. *The American Anti-Slavery Examiner* 5. New York: American Anti-Slavery Society, 1838.

Weldon, Roberta. *Hawthorne, Gender, and Death: Christianity and Its Discontents.* New York: Palgrave Macmillan, 2008.

Wenke, John. *Melville's Muse: Literary Creation & the Forms of Philosophical Fiction.* Kent, OH: The Kent State University Press, 1995.

Westra, Helen Petter. "Confronting Antichrist: The Influence of Jonathan Edwards's Millennial Vision." In *The Stowe Debate: Rhetorical Strategies in Uncle Tom's Cabin,* ed. Mason I. Lowance Jr., Ellen E. Westbrook, and R. C. De Prospro, 141–58. Amherst: University of Massachusetts Press, 1994.

Whately, Richard. *Elements of Rhetoric: Comprising an Analysis of the Laws of Moral Evidence and of Persuasion with Rules for Argumentative Composition and Elocution,* ed. Douglas Ehninger. Carbondale: Southern Illinois University Press, 1963.

White, Shane and Graham White. *The Sounds of Slavery: Discovering African-American History through the Sounds of Songs, Sermons, and Speech.* Boston: Beacon Press, 2005.

Whitefield, George. "Directions How To Hear Sermons." Vol. 5 of *The Works of the Reverend George Whitefield,* 418–27. London: E. and C. Dilley, 1771–72.

Whiteman, Maxwell. "Robert Purvis, 1810–1898: A Bibliographical Note." In Robert Purvis, *A Tribute to the Memory of Thomas Shipley, the Philanthropist.* Philadelphia: Merrihew and Gunn, 1836. Philadelphia: Rhistoric Publications, 1969.

Whitman, Walt. Leaves of Grass *and Selected Prose,* ed. Lawrence Buell. New York: Modern Library, 1981.

———. *Prose Works 1892,* ed. Floyd Stovall. Vol. 2 of *The Collected Writings of Walt Whitman,* ed. Gay Wilson Allen and Sculley Bradley. New York: New York University Press, 1964.

Wigger, John H. *Taking Heaven by Storm: Methodism and the Rise of Popular Christianity in America.* New York: Oxford University Press, 1998.

Willson, Edmund B. "Memorial Sermon." *The First Centenary of the North Church and Society in Salem, Massachusetts,* 9–61. Salem: North Church and Society, 1873.

Winship, Michael. "'The Greatest Book of Its Kind': A Publishing History of 'Uncle Tom's Cabin.'" *Proceedings of the American Antiquarian Society* 109, no. 2 (1999): 309–332.

Wise, Daniel. *The Young Lady's Counsellor; or, Outlines and Illustrations of the Sphere, the Duties and the Dangers of Young Women: Designed to be a Guide to True Happiness in This Life, and to Glory in the Life Which Is to Come.* 10th ed. New York: Carlton & Phillips, 1852.

———. *The Young Man's Counsellor; or Sketches and Illustrations of the Duties and Dangers of Young Men. Designed to be a Guide to Success in This Life, and to Happiness in the Life Which Is To Come.* 3rd ed. Boston: C. H. Peirce and W. J. Reynolds, 1851.

Wright, Nathalia. *Melville's Use of the Bible.* 1949. New York: Farrar, Straus, and Giroux, 1980.

Zboray, Ronald J. "Reading Patterns in Antebellum America: Evidence in the Charge Records of the New York Society Library." *Libraries & Culture* 26, no. 2 (1991): 301–33.

———. *A Fictive People: Antebellum Economic Development and the American Reading Public.* New York: Oxford University Press, 1993.

——— and Mary Saracino Zboray. *Everyday Ideas: Socioliterary Experience among Antebellum New Englanders.* Knoxville: University of Tennessee Press, 2006.

———. "'Have You Read . . . ?': Real Readers and Their Responses in Antebellum Boston and Its Region." *Nineteenth-Century Literature* 52, no. 2 (1997): 139–70.

———. "The Novel in the Antebellum Book Market." In *The Cambridge History of the American Novel,* ed. Leonard Cassuto, Clare Virginia Eby, and Benjamin Reiss, 67–87. Cambridge, UK: Cambridge University Press, 2011.

Ziff, Larzer. *Literary Democracy: The Declaration of Cultural Independence in America.* New York: Viking Press, 1981.

INDEX

LITERATURE, RELIGION, AND POSTSECULAR STUDIES
Lori Branch, Series Editor

Literature, Religion, and Postsecular Studies publishes scholarship on the influence of religion on literature and of literature on religion from the sixteenth century onward. Books in the series include studies of religious rhetoric or allegory; of the secularization of religion, ritual, and religious life; and of the emerging identity of postsecular studies and literary criticism.